The Asbury Theological Seminary Series in World Christian Revitalization Movements

In this landmark study, Oneness scholar Daniel Segraves provides a definitive examination of the life and ministry of one of the original founders of Oneness Pentecostalism in the early twentieth century, Andrew Urshan. With his spiritual pilgrimage to North America from his roots in Eastern (and Nestorian) Christology, he provides apostolic grounding for his tradition. The study reflects Urshan's frustration, and even anguish, in being unable to effect the level of ecumenical conversation between the two disparate wings of twentieth century Pentecostalism, the Trinitarian and the Oneness branches, to which he aspired. However, this careful treatment of Urshan's life and thought does much to heighten interest in advancing this ecumenical trajectory. That speaks of revitalization, the theme which drives the series in which this timely study is now located.

J. Steven O'Malley
General Editor
The Asbury Theological Seminary Studies in World Christian Revitalization

Sub-Series Foreword
Pentecostal and Charismatic Studies

Of all the renewal traditions that have engaged the theological landscape, the Pentecostal Movement has undoubtedly made the most significant impact since it emerged at the turn of the twentieth century. Starting as a revival in a small African-American congregation on Azusa Street in Los Angeles, California, in April 1906, the movement soon swept the world, establishing itself in more than forty countries in its first three years. One hundred and ten years later Pentecostalism has grown to an estimated 600 million adherents or approximately twenty-five percent of all Christendom. In the same manner that Wesleyanism burst beyond the bounds of Methodism to embrace an interdenominational holiness movement in the mid nineteenth century, Pentecostalism transcended denominational lines in the form of the Charismatic Movement during the second half of the twentieth century.

This sub-series is designed to explore the historical, theological and intercultural dimensions of these twin twentieth-century restorationists traditions from a global perspective. This volume focuses on a single man who, with a half-dozen others, shaped the theology and general direction of the most distinctive and controversial wing of early Pentecostalism, the Oneness Movement. Within its first ten year, Pentecostalism had divided into three distinctive theological traditions. It emerged as articulating a "five-fold" gospel: Jesus as Savior, Sanctifier, Baptizer in the Holy Spirit, Healer and Coming King. This expression kept intact the Wesleyan doctrine of Entire Sanctification as a work of grace in the life of the believer that occurred instantly at a time after justification. Some six years later, Pentecostal adherents coming from a Reformed or Baptist background collapsed the doctrines of justification and sanctification into one work of grace that they called "The Finished Work of Calvary." Andrew Urshan, the subject of this volume, was one of the leaders of this second group to break ranks over the understanding of the Godhead. Rejecting the Nicene Council's view of the Trinity, Oneness leaders argued that Jesus is the Name of God who has revealed Himself as Father, Son and Holy Spirit. Baptism, therefore, should follow the formula found in the book of the Acts of the Apostles. That is, converts should be baptized in the Name of Jesus, God's revealed name.

The author, Dr. Daniel Segraves who teaches at the School of Theology that bears Urshan's name, argues that of all the early Oneness Theologians, Andrew Urshan's theology was the most nuanced. An immigrant to the United States from an area that is now part of Iran, Urshan was deeply influenced by the "Church of the East" that has Nestorian roots. Urshan believed that this Eastern tradition held an understanding of the Godhead that accurately reflected the early apostolic faith which had been distorted by the Council of Nicaea. He contended that this view preserved the unity of God while recognizing His three-fold manifestation. As an evangelist, theologian and educator, Urshan ministered on three continents: Asia, Europe and North America, spreading the message of the Oneness Movement and helping to galvanize it into a strong theological tradition.

    D. William Faupel, Former Sub-Series Editor

Andrew D. Urshan

A Theological Biography

Daniel L. Segraves

*The Asbury Theological Seminary Series in
World Revitalization Movements in Pentecostal/Charismatic Studies*

EMETH PRESS
www.emethpress.com

Andrew D. Urshan: A Theological Biography

Copyright © 2017 Daniel L. Segraves
Printed in the United States of America on acid-free paper

All rights reserved. No part of this book may be reproduced, or stored in a retrieval system or transmitted in any form or by any means, electronic, mechanical, photocopying, recording, scanning or otherwise, except as permitted by the 1976 United States Copyright Act, or with the prior written permission of Emeth Press. Requests for permission should be addressed to: Emeth Press, P. O. Box 23961, Lexington, KY 40523-3961. http://www.emethpress.com

Library of Congress Cataloging-in-Publication Data

Names: Segraves, Daniel L., 1946- author.
Title: Andrew D. Urshan : a theological biography / Daniel L. Segraves.
Description: Lexington : Emeth Press, 2017. | Series: Asbury theological seminary series in world Christian revitalization movements in Pentecostal/Charismatic studies | Includes bibliographical references.
Identifiers: LCCN 2017006224 | ISBN 9781609471101 (alk. paper)
Subjects: LCSH: Oneness doctrine (Pentecostalism)--History. | Urshan, Andrew D. | Oneness Pentecostal churches--Biography.
Classification: LCC BX8763 .S44 2017 | DDC 230/.994092--dc23
LC record available at https://lccn.loc.gov/201700622 4

Permission to use the photo of Andrew D. Urshan on the front cover given by
Flower Pentecostal Heritage Center

Contents

Foreword / ix

Acknowledgments / xi

Chapter 1: Introduction / 1

Part 1: Life and History of Andrew D. Urshan

Chapter 2: Early Years in Persia / 7

Chapter 3: Early Years in the United States / 19

Chapter 4: Return to Persia / 57

Chapter 5: Return to the United States / 85

Part 2: Theology, Christology, and Soteriology of Andrew D. Urshan

Chapter 6: Theological Influences / 139

Chapter 7: The Mystery of the Godhead / 161

Chapter 8: Doctrine of Salvation / 217

Chapter 9: Responses to Theological Criticism / 229

Chapter 10: Conclusion / 237

Appendix / 245

Bibliography / 271

General Index / 301

Scripture Index / 311

Foreword

Oneness Pentecostalism was a disruptive surprise. It appeared within the nascent Assemblies of God fellowship without warning or immediate recognition. Most ingredients could be named, but never in such an arrangement. The best label they could conjure up to describe it was the rather nebulous "New Issue."

It emerged within a period of North American Protestantism which was experiencing revival, transition and controversy. Protestantism was in the process of breaking into Fundamentalist-Modernist camps. Jesus and the "name of Jesus" were emerging as an Evangelical bulwark against the "sweet and gentle human Jesus" of liberalism. Segments of the Wesleyan Holiness movement of late-19th century were incorporating the language and experience of Baptism of the Holy Spirit, paving the way for the Pentecostal Revival. For the first decade of the new century Pentecostals were Holiness in doctrine and practice. In 1910 William Durham, a powerful Pentecostal preacher from Chicago, challenged the Holiness doctrine of entire sanctification with a teaching he called the Finished Work of Calvary. This shifted the salvation narrative in a decidedly christocentric direction and promptly precipitated the first schism in the early Pentecostal movement.

Durham's unexpected death in 1912 created a leadership vacuum which by 1914 would be filled by Frank J. Ewart, Australian evangelist and close associate of Durham. That, however, would not occur before Ewart's hearing in 1913 a baptismal sermon by Robert E. McAlister, an associate and prominent Canadian evangelist. McAlister had speculated on the exegetical reason for the Apostles' baptizing in the name of the "Lord Jesus Christ" rather than with the words of Jesus, "in the name of the Father, and of the Son and of the Holy Spirit" (Matthew 28:19).

After pondering McAlister's reflection for a year, Ewart launched a new movement claiming that water baptism must be conducted in the name of Jesus Christ and supporting it with a modalistic doctrine of God. Ironically, the argument for a christocentric baptismal formula and its exegetical hermeneutic for harmonizing Jesus' commission and the Apostolic practice (see Acts 2:38) had already been published in 1913 in a thin volume by William Phillips Hall, a premillennial Evangelical layperson.[1]

By 1915 two other leaders—Garfield T. Haywood and Franklin Small—joined the movement and immediately began to contribute theologically to what eventually became known as Oneness theology. In 1916 this "New Issue" would result

---

[1]William Phillips Hall, *What Is 'The Name'? OR 'The Mystery of God' Revealed* (Greenwich, CT: Byix the Author, 1913).

in a second schism, this time in the Assemblies of God fellowship within which the New Issue was born.

It is here that the story of Andrew D. Urshan begins, and with it this volume by Daniel Segraves. Urshan was the last of the four original theological founders of the Oneness movement. He was unique in a number of ways. He was a latecomer, joining the movement only in 1919 following his expulsion from the Assemblies of God. He was, as least initially, a reluctant Oneness, having been removed against his desire. He was the only one of the four to be personally excommunicated. He was notably the most prolific writer among the four founding theologians. He was the only early Oneness leader to have been born in and formed by the Church of the East. His Christian journey in Persia and America was rich in spiritual and theological influences: Syrian Christianity, Presbyterian, Brethren, Holiness, Pentecostal and finally Oneness.

Segraves' methodological approach for examining Urshan's views as theological biography is the right one. Urshan's Oneness theology—his evolving theological views, his Eastern understanding of theology as spirituality, his effort to integrate his newfound Oneness convictions with his deeply formed Syriac Trinitarian faith—none of it can be separated from his life history. A Oneness educator and leader, Segraves intuitively understands the nuances of his tradition. In this volume, he patiently sorts through the years of Urshan's writings, identifying consistencies and changes in his thought, and meticulously collecting biographical material that helped shape Urshan's distinctive narrative.

This book is unique as the first critical examination by a Oneness scholar of the *theology* of a founding Oneness leader. It illuminates the messiness of the formative years. It exposes the losses as well as the gains. It reveals friendships, shared beliefs and practices that would be discarded. But it also traces the journey of one man—respected in his early years by all Pentecostals, and honored for his defense of the Oneness message by his new community of faith.

In this book Segraves opens a window of opportunity for Pentecostals—Oneness and Trinitarian alike—to engage their common past in the hope that there may still be something new to be retrieved. It may also provide a template for wider ecumenical conversations in which Christian belief and the status of the fellowship that is affected by it are at stake. In 1921 Andrew Urshan embarked on a near half-century theological and spiritual journey, and did so without abandoning the God of his youth. I heartily commend this volume to you.

David A. Reed
Professor Emeritus of Pastoral Theology and Research Professor
Wycliffe College, University of Toronto

Acknowledgments

Many people contributed to this work from its earliest stage as a mere idea to this completed project. I vividly remember my days as a student at Western Apostolic Bible College in Stockton, California, sitting in a chapel service under the ministry of Andrew D. Urshan. His spiritual passion made an indelible imprint on my life. Many years later, during my time as an administrator and instructor in that same Bible College, I had the privilege of working for one decade with Phillip Dugas, Urshan's step-son. He gave me two hard-bound volumes of *The Witness of God*, the monthly journal Urshan published from 1919 until his death in 1967. I was intrigued by this profound voice from the past, a voice that spoke not merely from theoretical musings but from the authenticity of a faith tried in fiery trials of impending martyrdom and outright rejection. I am grateful to Phillip for sharing with me the treasure he inherited from his step-father. Had he not done so, I don't know if the story of Andrew D. Urshan would have come to mind when the time came to finalize a dissertation research topic. He also agreed to telephone interviews which allowed me to explore some of the background stories of Urshan's life. Phillip helped to set me on the path for this research and enriched the final project by sharing with me his life experiences. This enabled me to read between the lines.

Next, I must acknowledge the intense labor of love performed by Andy (Andrew) Dugas, Phillip's son and Andrew D. Urshan's step-grandson and namesake. Andy took those two hard-bound volumes of *The Witness of God* and carefully copied each page. The highly advanced technology he used improved the physical appearance and readability. I could not have done the research necessary without those copies. Thank you, Andy.

Dennis Mostyn, Phillip Dugas' son-in-law, contributed to this project by his archival work in Chicago's public libraries. He spent a great deal of time exploring city records during the time when Urshan lived in Chicago. Among other things, he was able to identify the address of the restaurant Urshan owned and operated just before his sanctification and the location and name of the Pentecostal Church of the Nazarene where Urshan's sanctification occurred. Dennis also located and toured the home where the Urshans lived after the birth of all four children. Thank you, Dennis, for helping to bring this story to life.

Nathaniel Paul Urshan, a grandson of Andrew D. Urshan, gave me copies of letters handwritten by his grandfather. This served to confirm some information previously available only in printed form. Thank you, Nathaniel, for opening this window on the past.

Faith St. Clair, the second daughter of Urshan, agreed to telephone interviews that offered insight into the story that could be given only by a child who lived in Urshan's home from her birth. Thank you, Faith, for your willingness to participate in this research of your father's life.

Ruth Harvey, Faith's daughter, provided valuable information from her perspective as a granddaughter. I'm grateful for permission to use as a resource a graduate paper Ruth wrote on her grandfather's life.

Robin Johnston, Curator of the Center for the Study of Oneness Pentecostalism, which houses the archives held by the United Pentecostal Church International, allowed me to copy virtually all of the holdings on Andrew Urshan. This, together with the materials provided by Phillip Dugas, got me well on my way to do the necessary research. I am also indebted to Mark E. Roberts, Director of the Holy Spirit Research Center at Oral Roberts University, for providing copies of *The Witness of God* not available at the Center for the Study of Oneness Pentecostalism. The staff at the Flower Pentecostal Heritage Center at the General Council of the Assemblies of God provided still other materials by and about Urshan. Related resources were supplied by the staff at the Regent University library.

As I talked with Amos Yong, at that time Director of the Doctor of Philosophy program at Regent University School of Divinity, about a dissertation on Andrew Urshan, he was the first to suggest that it should be a theological biography. Dale Coulter, the chairperson of my dissertation committee, offered excellent and helpful counsel along the way that contributed significantly to the depth of this project. His expertise in eastern Christianity provided valuable insight on the theological background of Nestorian Christianity. David Reed, a member of my dissertation committee, helped keep the project rooted in the historical realities of early twentieth century Pentecostalism. Vinson Synan, whose rich knowledge of Pentecostal history is unsurpassed and who was also a committee member, encouraged me to write the definitive work on Urshan.

I must also express my gratitude to David K. Bernard, General Superintendent of the United Pentecostal Church International and President of Urshan Graduate School of Theology, for his encouragement on this project and for granting me the time to finish it. Without his support, I may not have been able to squeeze the time to do the research in between my teaching and administrative duties at the seminary. I also appreciate the encouragement and support offered by the rest of the faculty and staff at UGST; they lightened my load by their diligent and responsible work.

I wouldn't think of overlooking the enormous sacrifice made by my late wife, Judy, during the three years I labored on the dissertation. She gave me up for uncounted hours, setting aside projects that needed doing and time we could have spent together. Her sacrifice was made all the more significant by the fact that she was diagnosed with inflammatory breast cancer about halfway through my dissertation journey and passed away on January 16, 2011. In spite of her suffering, Judy stood by me as I pressed on with the research and writing. I loved my wife of forty-six years with all my heart, and I am deeply grateful for the blessing she was to me.

During the two years it took me to revise the dissertation into this monograph, my wife Susan encouraged me, brought refreshments to my desk, and made me feel like a hero for doing such significant work! I am profoundly thankful to God for bringing us together and for the miraculous way He did so. We are kindred spirits who love one another without reservation. Once again, God has smiled on me.

The editorial work of D. William Faupel improved the revision of the dissertation for publication in book form. I am thankful for his careful attention to detail, for suggestions on reorganizing the material, and for his patience as I labored over this project.

I am keenly aware that it is our Lord who surrounded me with the people I have mentioned here and who has directed my steps, provided the resources, and given me the strength, health, and ability to complete this work. To Him I owe all of my love and devotion.

Daniel L. Segraves

Chapter One

Introduction

Andrew David Urshan has been identified as one of the four pioneers of early twentieth century Oneness Pentecostal theology.[1] Like the other three – Frank Ewart, Garfield T. Haywood, and Franklin Small – Urshan was prepared by his social context and theological background to make a unique contribution to this segment of Pentecostalism, sometimes referred to as Pentecostalism's third stream.[2]

Frank J. Ewart, a Baptist minister from Australia who immigrated to Canada in 1903 and who was baptized with the Holy Spirit in 1908, made his way to Los Angeles, California after being dismissed from his pastorate in Canada by the Baptist organization with which he was affiliated. In 1911 Ewart became assistant pastor to William Durham in Los Angeles. Upon Durham's death in 1912, Ewart became pastor of the church.[3] While attending the 1913 "Worldwide Camp Meeting" in Arroyo Seco Park in Los Angeles, he heard Canadian evangelist R. E. McAlister point out that "the apostles invariably baptized their converts once in the name of Jesus Christ" and "that the words Father, Son, and Holy Ghost were never used in Christian baptism."[4] After studying the matter for one year, Ewart began baptizing in Jesus' name on April 15, 1914. Through the periodical *Meat in Due Season* and at least eight books, he contributed to the development and spread of Oneness Pentecostal theology.[5]

---

[1]David A. Reed, *"In Jesus' Name": The History and Beliefs of Oneness Pentecostals*, Journal of Pentecostal Theology Supplement Series, eds. John Christopher Thomas, Rickie Moore, Steven J. Land, no. 31 (Blandford Forum, Dorset, UK: Deo Publishing, 2008), 168.

[2]The identification of Oneness Pentecostalism as the "third stream" of Pentecostalism is set forth in David A. Reed, "Origins and Development of the Theology of Oneness Pentecostalism in the United States" (PhD diss., Boston University, 1978). The other two "streams" are the Wesleyan/Holiness and the Finished Work streams.

[3]J. L. Hall, "Frank J. Ewart," in *The New International Dictionary of Pentecostal and Charismatic Movements*, rev. and expanded ed., Stanley M. Burgess, ed. (Grand Rapids: Zondervan, 2002), 623-24. Hereafter, this resource will be identified as *NIDPCM*.

[4]Frank J. Ewart, *The Phenomenon of Pentecost* (Hazelwood, MO: Word Aflame Press, 1975, rev. 2000), 93-94.

[5]Ewart, *The Phenomenon of Pentecost*, 97. See also Frank J. Ewart, *The Name and the Book* (Hazelwood, MO: Word Aflame Press, 1947, reprinted 1986); Frank J. Ewart, *The Revelation of Jesus Christ* (Hazelwood, MO: Pentecostal Publishing House, n.d.); David Reed, "Aspects of the Origins of Oneness Pentecostalism," in Vinson Synan, ed., *Aspects*

G. T. Haywood was an African-American born in Greencastle, Indiana who obtained ministerial credentials in 1911 with the Pentecostal Assemblies of the World (PAW) before the rise of Oneness Pentecostalism.[6] Haywood was baptized with the Holy Spirit in 1908 and founded what is now known as Christ Temple Apostolic Faith Assembly in Indianapolis, Indiana.[7] In 1915, after hearing the "Jesus name message" from Glenn Cook, Haywood accepted Cook's message, was rebaptized in the name of Jesus, and baptized 465 members of Christ Temple.[8] A prolific author and songwriter, Haywood also contributed to the development of Oneness Pentecostal theology by means of his charts and paintings.[9]

Franklin Small, a Canadian ordained by the American Assemblies of God in 1914, became a charter member of the Pentecostal Assemblies of Canada (PAOC) in 1917. He withdrew from the PAOC in 1921 to found the Apostolic Church of Pentecost of Canada. Like Ewart and Haywood, Small contributed to the development of Oneness Pentecostal theology as a writer and publisher. In addition to writing a history of the Winnipeg Revival of 1916-26, Small wrote *Living Waters: A Sure Guide for Your Faith* and edited *Living Waters, The Apostolic Church Advocate*, and *The Beacon*.[10]

Andrew D. Urshan was, however, the most prolific writer in the nascent Oneness Pentecostal movement. Beginning as early as 1911, Urshan wrote and published his understanding of Scripture in a variety of formats, including tracts, magazines, periodicals, sound recordings and books. Beginning in 1919, Urshan published the monthly *The Witness of God*. He continued this publication until his death in 1967. In addition, he wrote articles that appeared in a variety of publications produced by others.

Of the four pioneers of Oneness Pentecostalism, Urshan is the only one whose origins are found in the eastern rather than the western world. The cultural influence of his Assyrian-Chaldean heritage in Persia, the theological influence of Syrian Christianity, and the spiritual influence of his Presbyterian home all combine with his American experiences among holiness and Pentecostal believers to shape him as one whose "focus was on theology in relation to spirituality—a theology of lived experience—and because of that, even his most abstract musings were usually grounded in concerns of existential faith."[11] To understand Urshan's dis-

---

of Pentecostal-Charismatic Origins (Plainfield, NJ: Logos International, 1975), 145-47; and Wayne Warner, "The 1913 Worldwide Camp Meeting," *Assemblies of God Heritage*, vol. 3, no. 1 (Spring 1983): 1, 4-5.

[6]C. M. Robeck, Jr., "Garfield Thomas Haywood," in *NIDPCM*, 693-94.

[7]"Church History," Christ Temple Apostolic Faith Assembly, http://www.christtempleac.org/history.php (accessed February 11, 2009).

[8]Glenn Cook was the first person to be baptized in Jesus' name by Frank Ewart. In turn, Cook baptized Ewart.

[9]See also Paul D. Dugas, comp., *The Life and Writings of Elder G. T. Haywood* (Stockton, CA: W.A.B.C. Press, 1968); G. T. Haywood, Divine Names and Titles of Jehovah (Portland, OR: Apostolic Book Publishers, n.d.); and G. T. Haywood, *The Birth of the Spirit in the Days of the Apostles* (Portland, OR: Apostolic Book Publishers, n.d.).

[10]G. W. Gohr, "Franklin Small," in *NIDPCM*, 1075.

[11]Douglas Jacobsen, *Thinking in the Spirit: Theologies of the Early Pentecostal Move-*

tinctive approach to Oneness theological claims, one must take these formative influences into account.

Andrew D. Urshan developed a comprehensive theological outlook touching on most doctrinal loci that reflected his Oneness Pentecostal convictions while continuing to acknowledge the legitimacy of the spiritual experiences of those Christians with whom he did not agree. His example provides a model for dialogue between today's Oneness and Trinitarian Pentecostals as well as between Pentecostals and non-Pentecostals.

This study proceeds in three directions. The first is the investigation of the development of Urshan's theology and Christology. Why was it important to Urshan to affirm the oneness of God, especially when he was willing to include in that affirmation terms like "tri-unity," the "three-one God," and even "trinity," with qualifications? Since he did not reject all of the traditional language of God out of hand, why was it important to him to reshape Christology? The second direction is the investigation of Urshan's soteriology. Since he insisted that water baptism in the name of the Lord Jesus Christ was the "birth" of water and that baptism with the Holy Spirit accompanied by speaking with tongues was the "birth" of the Spirit, how is it that he could nevertheless hold out the possibility that those who had not had these experiences would not be "lost"? Finally, in view of his acceptance of the Finished Work doctrine, why did Urshan continue to describe his salvation as three sequential experiences of conversion, sanctification, and Holy Spirit baptism?

The most helpful way to comprehend the overlapping social contexts of Urshan's life and theology is a biographical approach. We will seek to remember that Urshan was influenced by tradition and other people, to eschew any idea of cultur- al or chronological imperialism, and to keep in mind the interrelationships of ideas that swirled about both within and without early 20th century Pentecostalism.[12]

---

ment (Bloomington and Indianapolis: Indiana University Press, 2003), 197.

[12] James E. Bradley and Richard A. Muller, *Church History: An Introduction to Research, Reference Works, and Methods* (Grand Rapids: Wm. B. Eerdmans, 1995), 30-31.

Part 1: Life and History of Andrew D. Urshan

Chapter Two

Early Years in Persia

Introduction

This chapter will explore the religious and political climate in Persia during the time leading up to and including Urshan's birth and early life. These were the influences that shaped Urshan's faith and socialization prior to his immigration to the United States of America. The trajectory of Urshan's life during this time included his experiences as a favored son, a youthful rebel, a student who was converted while attending the American Presbyterian School, and a teacher in the Presbyterian school in his home village.

When Urshan left Persia to fulfill his dream of traveling to America, it was not to turn his back on his religious and cultural heritage. The Syriac Christianity of the Nestorian Church[1] was formative for him, as was the influence of his father's Presbyterian Christianity and the American Presbyterian School Urshan attended as a youth.

---

[1]The term "Nestorian Church" was not used until the 13th century to designate the "The Church of the East" (Stanley M. Burgess, *The Holy Spirit: Eastern Christian Traditions* [Peabody, MA: Hendrickson Publishers, 1989], 87. This ancient oriental church now prefers to be known as the "Holy Apostolic and Catholic Assyrian Church of the East" and has rejected the label "Nestorian" as inappropriate and misleading. This is due to the fact that the link between Nestorius and the church is tenuous. Nestorius was not the founder of the church. Though Nestorius is respected by the Church of the East, Theodore of Mopsuestia (d. 428) is the Greek theologian whose Christological language and biblical exegesis most influenced the Church of the East. Theodore was an older contemporary of Nestorius. When Mar Dinkha was consecrated as the catholicos (patriarch) of the Assyrian Church of the East in 1976, he rejected the label "Nestorian" as unjustified and misleading, pointing out that Nestorius was a Greek. In the 14th century, Abdiso, the metropolitan of Soba (Nisibis) and the canonist of the Church of the East, said, "As for the Orientals [i.e., the Church of the East], since they never changed their faith, but kept it as they had received it from the Apostles, they were called 'Nestorians' quite unjustly, for Nestorius was not their patriarch, nor did they know his language" (S. P. Brock, "The 'Nestorian' Church: A Lamentable Misnomer," *Bulletin of the John Rylands University Library of Manchester* 78, no. 3:35; see also Christoph Baumer, *The Church of the East: An Illustrated History of Assyrian Christianity* [London: I. B. Tauris, 2006], 7-8). But for our purposes, since the Church of the East was formerly so widely known as the Nestorian Church, and since the American Board of Foreign Missions and Urshan so designated it, we will continue to identify it as the Nestorian Church as well as the Church of the East, the Assyrian Church

Life in Persia

Life in Persia in the late nineteenth century was a study in contrasts for an ancient nation. It sought to retain its rich cultural and religious heritage while it struggled to respond to the beckoning call of modernity. Unable to cross the threshold from the ancient to the modern alone, Persia found itself caught in a vise formed by the conflicting foreign policy between Russia and Great Britain. The British concern was linked to Persia's proximity to India, where the British program of colonization called for geographical safeguards. The Russian concern stemmed from their common border with Persia.[2]

On the political front, little had changed in Iran[3] since the eleventh century. Political power flowed from regional tribal and military leaders rather than from a strong central government. By the end of the nineteenth century, semi-autonomous nomadic tribes made up one fourth of the population. During the Qajar Dynasty, which spanned 1795-1925, nearly all of the central and regional governmental offices were bought. The exception was in Azerbaijan, where the governor-generalship was given by the Qajars to the Crown Prince.

Landholders were persons of status and power. Few people owned land. The majority of the population was made up of sharecroppers who paid rent to the landowning gentry.

The chief function of the governmental bureaucracy was to collect taxes and customs. Taxes were used to support the government bureaucracy, especially the Shah and his entourage, rather than financing roads, schools, hospitals, courts, and military protection.[4]

On November 20, 1835, the American Board of Commissioners for Foreign Missions established a beachhead in Urumia, located in northwest Persia in the region of Azerbaijan near Lake Urmia.[5] The Rev. and Mrs. Justin Perkins, accompanied by Dr. and Mrs. Asahel Grant, were sent to revitalize the ancient Nestorian Church. Dr. Grant served as Rev. Perkins' medical assistant.[6]

---

of the East, and the Holy Apostolic and Catholic Assyrian Church of the East. We do not intend by this to disregard the legitimate concerns of the church as to its name.

[2]William Bayne Fisher, *The Cambridge History of Iran: From Nadir Shah to the Islamic Republic*, vol. 7, ed. P. Avery, G. R. G. Hambly, and C. Melville (Cambridge: Cambridge University Press, 1991), 179-80.

[3]Since 1935 Persia has been known as Iran.

[4]Fisher, *Cambridge History*, 174-177. Things gradually began to change when Nasir al-Din Shah represented the Qajar Dynasty. Reigning from 1848-1896, the Shah sought to modernize Persia through science, technology, and education. This effort was stimulated by three tours of Europe which he made in 1873, 1878, and 1889. Iran Chamber Society, History of Iran, "Qajar Dynasty," http://www.iranchamber.com/ history/qajar/qajar.php (accessed June 12, 2009). See also Fisher, *Cambridge History*, 189-193.

[5]*The Columbia Encyclopedia,* 6th ed. (New York: Columbia University Press, 2007), s.v. "Urmia." A variety of spellings can be found for this city, lake, and region: Urmia, Urmiah, Urumia, Ooroomiah, Urumiyeh, etc.

[6]John Elder, *History of the Iran Mission* (N.P.), 7; *A Century of Mission Work in Iran (Persia) 1834-1934* (Beirut, Lebanon, Syria: The American Press, 1936), 1-2.

Initially, the Nestorian Church had enjoyed an enormously successful history of missionary expansion extending its influence over the entire eastern world from Seleucia-Ctesiphon[7] to Japan and Indonesia. However, beginning in the 1360's it had been devastated by repeated massacres culminating in wholesale destruction by the Muslim Tamerlane who swept across the Christian Middle East: capturing cities, exterminating any who resisted, and erecting giant pyramids built of the skulls of his victims of any age and gender. Tamerlane wreaked havoc not only in the Middle East but also in Asia, where he targeted non-Muslims. Christian remnants left behind by Tamerlane were destroyed by his grandson, Ulugh Beg. As a result, the Nestorian, Jacobite, and other Christian churches hardly survived even in name.[8] The Nestorians who did survive lost their churches and monasteries and fled for refuge to the remote mountains of Kurdistan in northern Iraq and to Hakkari in southeastern Turkey.[9] Thus the Church of the East, whose geographical expanse had once far surpassed that of the Roman Catholic Church and whose membership is estimated to number as many as ten million Christians, was crushed.[10]

George David Malech, who had been a professor of oriental languages and literature at the Presbyterian Mission College in Urmia, the school attended by Urshan, described the condition of the Syrian church upon the arrival of the missionaries as "that of a beautiful flower garden which had been destroyed and laid waste by the enemy; its beauty had disappeared, its flowers faded."[11] In spite of the economic privation and educational disadvantages, there was a spark of spiritual life remaining.

> The Syrian church was poor, as the people could not support it and the ministers lacked learning, but the spirit of life was kept up. The Syrians were a praying people, they had faith and hope, the religion of their fathers was a costly treasure, they went to church twice daily all the year around, and among them there were no infidels, no one that denied God and His presence.[12]

---

[7] Seleucia and Ctesiphon sat on the western and eastern banks of the Tigris River in ancient Mesopotamia.

[8] Philip Jenkins, *The Lost History of Christianity: The Thousand-Year Golden Age of the Church in the Middle East, Africa, and Asia—and How It Died* (New York: HarperOne, 2008), 137-38.

[9] Christoph Baumer, *The Church of the East: An Illustrated History of Assyrian Christianity* (London: I. B. Tauris, 2006), vii, 5.

[10] "The Church of the East was systematically decimated. Towards the end of the fourteenth century it collapsed and disappeared from the region around Baghdad, after it had been extinguished from China, Mongolia, Central Asia and Iran (except for the region around Urmiah). . . . The Church survived only in inaccessible Kurdistan, in Iranian Azerbaijan, in Armenia and in Kerala, which escaped Tamerlane's orgy of destruction for reasons of climate and geography. In the fifteenth century the established organization of the Church collapsed . . ." (Baumer, *The Church of the East,* 233 [See also p. 4 and Jenkins, *The Lost History of Christianity,* 100]).

[11] George David Malech, *History of the Syrian Nation and the Old Evangelical-Apostolic Church of the East* (Minneapolis, MN: 1910), 327.

[12] Malech, *History of the Syrian Nation,* 330.

When the American missionaries first arrived in the region of Azerbaijan, they were welcomed by the leaders of the suffering Nestorian Church. Due to their continuing maltreatment by the Kurds, the Nestorians hoped for political aid from Europe or Russia, but when E. Smith and H. G. O. Dwight arrived in 1830 representing the American Board of Commissioners for Foreign Missions, they submitted a report that resulted in the arrival of Justin Perkins in Urmia in 1834. His orders indicated that he was not there to convert but to seek renewal in the Nestorian Church.

> A primary object which you will have in view, will be to convince the people, that you come among them with no design to take away their religious privileges, not to subject them to any foreign ecclesiastical power. The only acknowledged head of the Church is Jesus Christ, and your only acknowledged standard in ecclesiastical matters is the New Testament. The Syrian Church acknowledges the same head and also the same standard, though it may be, with some additions. You will have, therefore, a broad common ground. But your main objective will be, to enable the Nestorian Church, through the grace of God, to exert a commanding influence in the spiritual regeneration of Asia.[13]

From the first, education was an essential component of the Presbyterian Mission to Persia. When Rev. Perkins arrived in Urmia, scarcely twenty of the men in the Nestorian Church could read so as to be functionally literate. The Patriarch's sister was the only woman who could read at all.[14] There were no printed books; their spoken language had never been reduced to writing. The few Bible manuscripts were in ancient Syriac, a language unknown to the Nestorians.[15]

The first step in Perkins' work was to reduce the spoken modern Syriac to writing and to translate the Scriptures into that language. Then the Nestorian priests and bishops could be taught to read, expound, and live the Scriptures. A literature could be developed for the church and the people could be taught to use that literature.[16]

In preparation for his work, Perkins spent his first year in Persia studying Syriac. Before the year was up he was already working on reducing the language to writing. On January 18, 1836, he opened a school in a room he had prepared in the basement of his house. Seven boys from Urmia enrolled. On the second day the number of students was seventeen. Then many from the surrounding villages, including three Nestorian deacons and a bishop, began to attend. At the end of three months, thirty Nestorians were studying at the school. The curriculum included reading, writing, arithmetic, Scripture in ancient Syriac, and English for the older students. By 1839-40 enrollment reached fifty-five students.[17]

In May, 1846, the school moved to Mount Seir, located six miles west of Urmia where it had a fine view of Lake Urmia. At this time the school accepted boarding students only. In 1865 the school reported ninety-nine graduates in the

---

[13]Baumer, *The Church of the East*, 254.
[14]Malech, *History of the Syrian Nation*, 329.
[15]*A Century of Mission Work*, 74.
[16]*A Century of Mission Work*, 74.
[17]*A Century of Mission Work*, 75-76.

school's history, ninety-two of whom were received into the communion of the Nestorian Church. During its first thirty-four years of operation the school graduated 122 students, eighty of whom entered full time Christian service.[18]

When the mission in Urmia first opened, it was considered a disgrace for a girl to study. Although a few girls ignored this cultural prohibition and studied at the school for boys, Mrs. Judith Grant opened a school for girls on March 12, 1838. Four Nestorian girls were the first to respond. By 1868, eighty girls had graduated.[19]

Andrew Bar David Urshan was born on May 17, 1884 in the village of Abajalu, located thirteen miles north of Urmia, Persia, to David Bar-Urshan, a Presbyterian minister,[20] and his wife, Nassimo.[21] Abajalu was one of 300 villages in the Urmia region, 115 of which were Assyrian. Abajalu was one of these Assyrian villages.[22] Andrew was christened and named before a congregation of relatives, friends, and neighbors.[23]

On December 27, 1870, the mission originally sponsored by the American Board of Foreign Missions was transferred to the Presbyterian Board of Foreign Missions. With this transfer came a change in focus: what at first had been the "Mission to Nestorians" became the "Mission to Persia." The change of focus had dramatic implications.

The patriarch and bishops of the Nestorian Church had at first welcomed the work of the mission but came to oppose it due to a political dimension of Dr. Asahel Grant's work. Grant had become friends with Nurallah, a chieftain subordinate to the Kurdish leader Badr Khan. However, in 1843 he refused to intervene to avoid a Kurdish invasion of the Nestorian region, professing neutrality. The Kurds massacred and mutilated fifteen to twenty thousand women and men, sending to Badr Khan the sliced off ears of their dead victims. Many young women leapt from bridges into deep chasms to avoid being sold into slavery or given to Muslim chieftains. The Kurds also stole all of the Nestorians' herds, razed their churches, destroyed their libraries, and destroyed their villages by fire. To prevent the Nestorians from returning to their homeland, the Kurds also cut down their fruit trees and destroyed their irrigation canals. Prior to this tragedy, hundreds of Nestorians had pled with Grant to speak to Nurallah on their behalf. But Grant

---

[18] *A Century of Mission Work*, 76.

[19] *A Century of Mission Work*, 76-78.

[20] Urshan does not discuss the circumstances by which his father became a Presbyterian minister. But in a report of his mission work, J. H. Shedd described spiritual renewal which had occurred in several villages in Northwest Persia, including Abajaloo, which was Urshan's home. See *The Church at Home and Abroad*, vol. 10 (Philadelphia, PA: Presbyterian Board of Publication and Sabbath-School Work, 1891), 65.

[21] Urshan also identifies Urmia, Persia as Rizayh, Iran, more commonly spelled 'Rezaiyeh.' (See Urshan, *Life Story*, 17 and *The Columbia Encyclopedia*, 6th ed., s.v. "Urmia.")

[22] Arianne Ishaya, "From Contributions to Diaspora: Assyrians in the History of Urmia, Iran," *Journal of Assyrian Academic Studies* 16, no. 1 (2002). http://www.jaas.org/toc/v16012002toc.htm (accessed December 1, 2010).

[23] Urshan, "Second Chapter—Story of My Life: The Early Life of Andrew, the Assyro-Chaldean Boy," *The Witness of God* 3, no. 34 (October 1922): 7.

was indifferent to the military preparations he saw being made in two Kurdish camps. He concerned himself only with getting an assurance that a schoolhouse he had built would be spared. As a result, the relationship between the Nestorian clergy and the missionaries deteriorated. Abandoning their original mission to bring renewal to the Nestorian Church, the missionaries began to attack the liturgical customs of the church by distributing anti-Nestorian tracts. Perkins, who had been so friendly with the Nestorians upon his arrival, said, "I do not know what more artful contrivance Satan could have invented, to substitute in the place of the pure religion of the gospel, than he has furnished with the fasts of these oriental churches."[24] As a result, the Nestorian patriarch ordered the closure of the American school in Urmia, and most of the Presbyterians left the city.

When the missionaries returned to Urumia in 1870, it would be with a change of focus. Commending the work of Rev. Perkins, who had died on December 31, 1869, the American Board of Foreign Missions declared:

> Among the Nestorians there are now few who have failed to hear the Gospel message; and the mission feels that the time has come to follow up with more earnestness the effort to evangelize other races in that region. In view of this direction of labor, the Mission will no longer be called the Mission to Nestorians but the Mission to Persia.[25]

Many would leave the Nestorian Church. Included were a former patriarch's brother, three bishops, seventy priests, and many deacons. All together, the new congregations averaged about 3,000 in attendance by 1871.

The missionaries began an aggressive campaign for conversion, leading to the establishment of the Assyrian Protestant Church.[26] Thus, when the Presbyterian mission gathered in Urumia in 1884, the year of Urshan's birth, to celebrate the fiftieth year of missions work, it was a grand occasion. Dr. Wright of the Tabriz mission and the honored American guest who was the editor of an American missionary magazine were met about twelve miles from the city by missionaries and Persian brethren to enjoy a picnic on the banks of the Nazlu River. As they journeyed on toward Urumia, they were met and welcomed repeatedly by different groups of missionaries and national believers. Pastors, teachers, elders, and deacons gathered from the plains, valleys, and mountains to welcome their guests. The governor of Urumia sent the chief of police and a squad of soldiers to welcome them on his behalf. The mission had established a successful high school and college in the city, and the students stood in line to join in the greetings. A

---

[24] Baumer, *The Church of the East*, 256.

[25] Elder, *History of the Iran Mission*, 23.

[26] Baumer, *The Church of the East*, 255-56. This account of the animosity between the Nestorian Church and the Presbyterian missionaries is not found in *A Century of Mission Work* or *History of the Iran Mission*. The collapse of the relationship between the Nestorians and the Presbyterian missionaries can be seen in a letter written by one of the missionaries in 1871: "The old church is a fossil. It is the grave of piety and Christian effort. Hence for our Christians to live at all they have been compelled to leave it. In part they have been driven out, in part they have left it, and now the separation is complete" (Elder, *History of the Iran Mission*, 22).

festive parade was formed of prancing horses and the multi-colored costumes of the Nestorians, Armenians, Persians, and Americans.[27]

In 1878 the Presbyterian Mission in Urumia purchased a fifteen acre garden two miles west of the city where the school for boys, which had been discontinued in 1875, was reorganized under the name of "College."[28] The full name was American Presbyterian Training College. At this boarding school under the principalship of Rev. J. H. Shedd, the curriculum came to include academic, industrial, theological and medical departments. Frederick G. Coan, who was later placed in charge of the college and the village schools, described the college curriculum.

> The college course, owing to very different circumstances and needs, cannot be compared to our college curriculum at home. The languages were continued; a short course was given in geology; French and Arabic were added to the languages; bookkeeping, commercial arithmetic, ethics, and chemistry with a few other subjects, were taught. We also had a theological and medical course for those who wished to become preachers, teachers or doctors.[29]

During the first half of its thirty-five years of history before the World War I, the college issued academic diplomas to 110 graduates, forty-four of whom later completed the theological course and twelve the medical course. From 1896 onward no records exist for the school. Apparently Urshan enrolled at the beginning of 1900.[30] It was a common practice during these years for groups of the boys to make evangelistic excursions on Sundays to both Assyrian and Muslim villages.[31]

Birth and Early Life

Urshan's father was an affiliated pastor of the Assyrian Protestant Church. Although none of Urshan's writings detail the process by which his father became associated with the Presbyterian mission, the following facts are known about his family background. First, Urshan takes care to point out that he himself is an Assyrian-Chaldean who speaks the Syriac language. Second, he speaks sympathetically of the Nestorians and their doctrines.[32] Third, we know that the Assyrians were historically members of the Nestorian Church.[33] Fourth, Urshan's home, the Assyrian village of Abajalu, was only thirteen miles from Urumia, the center

---

[27]Elder, *History of the Iran Mission*, 42. See also *Historical Sketches of the Missions Under the Care of the Board of Foreign Missions of the Presbyterian Church*, 3rd ed. rev. (Philadelphia: Woman's Foreign Missionary Society of the Presbyterian Church, 1891), 225-26.

[28]Although the school was known as a "college," it was not of college rank. See Mary Lewis Shedd, *The Measure of a Man: The Life of William Ambrose Shedd, missionary to Persia* by Mary Lewis Shedd (New York: George H. Doran Company, 1922), 36.

[29]Frederick G. Coan, *Yesterdays in Persia and Kurdistan* (Claremont, CA: Saunders Studio Press, 1939), 228.

[30]See Urshan, *The Life Story*, 5th ed., 21-23.

[31]*A Century of Mission Work in Iran (Persia) 1834—1934* (Beirut, Lebanon, Syria: American Press, 1936), 94.

[32]Urshan, *The Life Story*, 5th ed., 9-16.

[33]*A Century of Mission Work*, 1-2.

of the Presbyterian renewal whose influence had virtually saturated western Azerbaijan through village churches and schools. We know that Andrew was called home while in his first year of high school to teach in the village school associated with the Presbyterian Church in Abajalu.[34]

From the information available to us, we can safely assume that Urshan's family had been members of the Nestorian Church who responded to the Presbyterian mission for renewal and who subsequently found themselves part of the vibrant new evangelical church that sprang from the Urumia mission. When Urshan first arrived in America he intentionally attended a Presbyterian church.[35] His autobiography makes it clear, however, that he continued to value his family's cultural and religious heritage in the Nestorian Church.

The first chapter of the final edition of Urshan's autobiography, published seven months before his death, sets forth his understanding of his racial and religious heritage. He identifies himself as a member of the Assyrian-Chaldean race, the offspring of Noah.[36] Urshan says that "Chaldeans, Assyrians, Syrians and Armenians are almost one and the same people."[37] During the first year of Andrew's life, he suffered with weakness and sickness to such an extent that his mother twice turned him to the east to die, according to the custom of the Chaldean Christians.[38] But after reaching the age of four years, Andrew gained health and vigor. As he grew, he enjoyed running races, wrestling, fishing, swimming, and playing ball games.[39] His interest in games was so keen that he refused to eat with his family. Instead, he would sneak into the house, fill his pockets with bread, cheese, sandwiches, and dried raisins, running back out to play.[40] He also refused to help his mother care for his younger brother, Timothy. Instead, he would pinch the baby until he cried, and then tell his mother, "You see! He does not want to come to me."[41] Urshan described himself as a self-willed, headstrong, and disobedient boy whose mischievous pranks caused trouble for his parents.[42]

Youthful Rebellion

By the time he reached thirteen, Urshan's parents found themselves unable to correct his behavior. By fifteen, Urshan was gambling and stealing money from his mother. He used this stolen money to cover his gambling losses, refusing to confess when his mother discharged their maid for the theft. Urshan's parents decided that the discipline of work might check his tendency to evil, so they found a

---

[34] Urshan, *The Life Story*, 5th ed., 31-33.

[35] Urshan, *The Life Story*, 5th ed., 54-56.

[36] Urshan, *The Life Story*, 5th ed., 9.

[37] Urshan, *The Life Story*, 5th ed., 9.

[38] In the first edition his autobiography, Urshan says that the turn in his health came after his third year (Urshan, *The Story of My Life*, 1st ed., 11-12).

[39] Urshan, *The Story of My Life*, 1st ed., 12.

[40] Urshan, *The Life Story*, 5th ed., 19. In the first through the third editions of his life story, Urshan compared this behavior to that of a thief.

[41] Urshan, *The Life Story*, 5th ed., 12.

[42] Urshan, *The Story of My Life*, 1st ed., 13.

place for him in the city of Urmia in a tailor shop owned by a relative. His experiences there had the opposite effect. His behavior grew worse under the unwholesome influence of the tailor's employees and apprentices. He began drinking, hoping to find an occasion to become drunk. But before he could do this, Urshan was struck with a high fever and an acute attack of measles requiring him to be sent home. After his recovery, Urshan's father insisted that he be sent back to the tailor shop. His mother prayed this would not happen. Word subsequently arrived from the owner of the shop that his services were no longer needed.[43]

Conversion

While Attending American Presbyterian School. When they realized the tailor shop was not an option for their son, Urshan's parents sent him to the Presbyterian college which was about eighteen miles from his home. The school offered public and high school courses. Here, Urshan found himself in an environment radically different from the tailor shop. About 200 boys and men studied at the school under the disciplined administration of American missionaries. During a prayer meeting one March night in 1900, two months after his ar-rival, Urshan's life was transformed. He described it this way: "God met me . . . convicted me of sin and regenerated my soul, transforming my character . . . . Praise God for His grace, which, in the golden stage of my life, caught me in the Gospel net, and made of me a happy young servant of the Lord!"[44] Urshan's conversion came as the students sang, "Oh happy day that fixed my choice." He writes:

> . . . the Spirit of God seized me with great conviction and caused me to stop and think and ask myself the question, "Am I really happy because Jesus has washed all my sins away?" I was reproved and had to confess myself an unconscious hypocrite. That broke my heart, and I instantly burst into tears as my sins were pictured before my eyes. Then I cried to God for forgiveness and deliverance in Jesus' blessed Name, and the Lord heard my cry! I began to put my trust in the following promises: "Whosoever shall call on the name of the Lord shall be saved," and "Believe on the Lord Jesus Christ and thou shalt be saved," etc. The Spirit witnessed with my spirit that I had truly been blessed and the branch of the Divine tree in the bitter water of my life was planted afresh.[45]

---

[43]Urshan, *The Life Story,* 5th ed., 20-21.
[44]Urshan, *The Life Story,* 5th ed., 23.
[45]Urshan, *The Life Story,* 5th ed., 27. Here is a theologically significant revision from the first edition of Urshan's autobiography. The phrase "I had truly been blessed and the branch of the Divine tree in the bitter water of my life was planted afresh" replaces the first edition phrase "I had been born again and had been made a new creature in Christ Jesus" (Urshan, *The Story of My Life,* 1st ed., 30).

Further, Urshan described himself as "truly a happy blood-washed, newly conceived child of the King!"[46] He continued, "The memory of it is burning yet like a blaze of glory to God my Father, my Elder Brother, and my Comforter!"[47]

The change in Urshan's life was so sudden and dramatic that it was immediately noticed by those around him. Word reached his parents and acquaintan-ces in Abajalu. When he went home for Easter vacation, he sought to confess and make restitution for his wrongs.[48]

Teaching in a Presbyterian School

The students at the American Presbyterian Training College were interested in the life and culture of the west. After Urshan had attended the school for about eighteen months, he decided to travel to America. Gaining his parents approval, he enrolled in an English class to prepare for the trip. However, within three months, he received word that the Presbyterian minister in Abajalu wanted him to teach in the village school for the winter term.[49]

---

[46]Urshan, *The Life Story*, 5th ed., 27. Two theologically significant revisions can be seen at this point. In the first edition of his autobiography, Urshan wrote that he was "a truly happy, blood bought, blood washed child of the King" (Urshan, *The Story of My Life*, 1st ed., 30). In the third edition, he wrote that he was "truly a happy blood washed servant of The King" (Urshan, *The Story of My Life*, 3rd ed., 21).

[47]Urshan, *The Life Story*, 5th ed., 27. The first edition of Urshan's autobiography reads, "It is still burning now as a clear blaze of the glory of God the Father, God the Son, and God the Holy Ghost" (Urshan, *The Story of My Life*, 1st ed., 31). It should be remembered that the first edition of Urshan's life story was published in 1917, after his return from Persia and Russia in 1916, and well after his initial insights in 1909-1910 into what would later become known as Oneness theology. By 1933, with the publication of the third edition of his life story, theologically significant revisions in his autobiography were made, but it should not be assumed that those changes reflect substantial changes in his theology. Until his death, Urshan continued to insist that he received revelatory insight on the name of Jesus and Oneness theology from the point of his baptism with the Holy Spirit. This leaves us to wonder to what extent theologically significant revisions in his life story were made due to actual changes in his understanding and to what extent they may have been made in response to developments in Oneness theology on the larger scene.

[48]Urshan, *The Life Story*, 5th ed., 27-28.

[49]In addition to the schools for men and women located in or near Urmia, the village schools were an important part of the Presbyterian mission. The first village school opened the same year as Perkins' school in Urmia. By 1839 there were twelve village schools in operation; by 1849 there were more than seventy. By 1895, six years before Urshan was asked to return to Abajalu to teach, 117 village schools were in operation with a total enrollment of 2,410. Frederick Coan, who was in charge of the college at Urmia as well as of the village schools shortly after Urshan's departure to the United States of America, described the limitations of the village schools: "The village schools for the most part were small, dark rooms that were poorly lighted and heated, where the children sat on the floor and used the palm of the hand in place of table or desk as a support for paper in writing. The entire school equipment was most primitive. The course of study comprised the three R's with the inclusion in most of the schools of reading in Turkish and Persian as well as Syriac. In addition there were small handbooks on physiology and easy science.

Urshan had not yet completed his high school courses, which was the common requirement for teachers. He had just entered high school. But the transformation in his life had been noted by the village elders, who decided that he was qualified to teach despite his youth and his educational limitations. When the current term at the American Presbyterian Training College ended in November, 1900, Urshan returned home to accept his new duties. In addition to teaching, his responsibilities included assisting the pastor and conducting Wednesday night prayer meetings in the pastor's absence.[50]

Summary

From his birth to his immigration to America, Urshan was exposed to the rich, ancient theology of the Church of the East. This exposure was tempered with the theological influence of the American Presbyterian mission, an influence so significant that it resulted in Urshan's father becoming a Presbyterian minister and Urshan's profound and enduring spiritual experience of conversion. But further theological and spiritual influences would be brought to bear on Urshan as a result of his decision to travel to America.

The catechism and Bible held an important place throughout the course of study" (Coan, *Yesterdays in Persia and Kurdistan,* 227-28).
    [50]Urshan, *The Life Story,* 5th ed., 31-32.

Chapter Three

Early Years in the United States

Introduction

Urshan grew up in a theological environment shaped by the Church of the East and tempered by the Presbyterian influence of American missionaries. Like many youth in northwest Persia, he idealized the United States of America, imagining it to be a virtual paradise of the Christian faith. This fantasy was quickly destroyed upon his arrival in New York. In addition, his theological influences began to expand. Since he was familiar with Presbyterianism, Urshan first attended a Presbyterian church in America, but his spiritual journey included Episcopal, Methodist Episcopal, Evangelical, American Brethren, Nazarene, the nascent fundamentalism of The Moody Church, and Trinitarian Pentecostalism, leading ultimately to the Oneness Pentecostal movement. Of these influences, three were most profound: (1) baptism by immersion in the American Brethren Church resulted from searching Scripture to confirm his beliefs, which would become a pattern for his entire theological journey; (2) sanctification in the Nazarene Church, making a dramatic turning point in his spiritual fervor; and (3) membership in The Moody Church permanently influenced his theology in a fundamentalist direction.

Journey to America

Before Urshan started on his journey to America, his family was visited by Rabbi Abshalim, a missionary. The visitor, a friend of Urshan's father, warned Urshan that spiritual dangers awaited him in America. With his idealistic view of American Christianity, Urshan had never considered the possibility that powerful temptations awaited him. Discouraged by this news, Urshan prayed for direction.

At that time, Urshan suffered from an eye disease. He prayed, "Oh Lord! If Thou wilt promise to keep me pure all the days of my life in that country, heal my eyes immediately and let nothing hinder me from going; but, if you foresee that I am going to fall into sin, and you will not undertake in a special manner to keep me, then either let me die, or make me blind!"¹ Although he had not yet heard of divine healing, Urshan testified that he was healed. He continued to plan for his trip, his mother providing the fare.²

On October 6, 1901, Urshan sailed from Hamburg, Germany aboard the Hamburg American Line, arriving in New York later that month.³ Urshan experienced illness from the day he left his home until his arrival in Yonkers fifty days later.⁴ He attributed this to the emotions he expeienced on the day of his departure as he knelt in a field with his parents, relatives, friends, and ministers, praying and singing together "Till we meet at Jesus' feet."⁵

For eight days, Urshan traveled with seventeen other people in an open wagon drawn sometimes by two and sometimes by four horses. The ride was hot and rough, punctuated by a full speed dash of the horses when the wagon reached an area a few miles from Mount Ararat. Haste was necessary to avoid violent attacks by the Kurds.⁶

After passing through customs at the Russian border, Urshan was taken to the first railway station he had ever seen. His train traveled for three days through the Caucasian mountains, arriving at Tiflis, Georgia.⁷ Spending two weeks at Tiflis, Urshan visited relatives and then continued his journey passing through Kiev in route to Warsaw, Poland, where he spent a night and a day.⁸

Leaving Warsaw, Urshan boarded a train for Berlin, Germany. Before arriving, the passengers were subjected to a medical examination, a steam bath, and a shower, Urshan's first. During his stay in Berlin, Urshan arranged for his steamer

---

¹Urshan, *The Life Story*, 5ᵗʰ ed., 29.

²Urshan, *The Story of My Life*, 1ˢᵗ ed., 17.

³The precise date of Urshan's departure from Persia and arrival in the United States of America is uncertain. In the first edition of his autobiography, he says that he started for America on August 22, 1901 at the age of 17 and arrived in Yonkers, New York in October 1901 (Urshan, *The Story of My Life*, 1ˢᵗ ed., 17, 19). In the third edition of his autobiography, Urshan says he entered America in October 1902 (Urshan, *The Story of My Life*, 3ʳᵈ ed., 35). The fifth edition gives no date for his departure from Persia or his arrival in America, but the 1902 date was reiterated by Urshan not long before his death ("Andrew D. Urshan," *Gospel Tidings* [January 1968]: 2. A search of www.ellisisland.org for 1901-02 reveals no records for Urshan's arrival. The U.S. Naturalization Record Indexes, 1791-1992 (Indexed in World Archives Project) lists Urshan's arrival in New York as August 15, 1902. In view of the previous evidence, this is probably an error. A passport application indicates he sailed from Hamburg, Germany about September 15, 1901. October 6, 1901 is found on an emergency passport application. The U.S. Naturalization Record gives Urshan's birth date as May 3, 1884, also an error. He was born May 17, 1884.

⁴Urshan, *The Story of My Life*, 1ˢᵗ ed., 17; Urshan, *The Story of My Life*, 3ʳᵈ ed., 34. If he left his home on August 22, 1901, this would put Urshan's arrival in Yonkers on October 11, 1901.

⁵Urshan, *The Story of My Life*, 1ˢᵗ ed., 17.

⁶Urshan, *The Story of My Life*, 3ʳᵈ ed., 27; Urshan, *The Life Story*, 5ᵗʰ ed., 33-34. This eight day trip would have spanned August 22-30, 1901.

⁷Tiflis is now known as Tbilisi. Urshan's three day trip from the Russian border to Tiflis would have occurred on August 31-September 2, 1901.

⁸Urshan, *The Life Story*, 5ᵗʰ ed., 34-36. Urshan was in Tiflis approximately from September 2 through September 16, 2001.

passage, obtained the final seals of the United States Consul on his Persian passport, and purchased clothing appropriate for his new life in America. His two traveling companions who had planned to accompany him to America, an Assyrian minister who was a friend of his father and Urshan's cousin, Samuel Babila, had changed their plans and decided to go elsewhere. Urshan was devastated. However, he decided to continue by train to Hamburg, where with his remaining Persian companions he boarded the ship that would take them on their fifteen day journey to America.[9]

The vivid description of the conditions in steerage is shocking. Urshan described life aboard ship as "hell on the waters."[10]

> The porters in the steerage section had no mercy whatsoever upon the poor sea-sick folks. They would come and pull us by our feet from the upper berths, which were about 8 [sic] feet high, and drag us down onto the filthy, vomit-filled floors. When we groaned out in pain, they would take their dirty coarse scrubbing brooms, and hit us in the face so hard that we would be knocked into the pile of dirt they had swept to-gether [sic]. They cursed us, and mocked us until we got out of the room, and went above on deck. These porters were so base, they even threw themselves upon the poor ignorant and innocent young Polish and Jewish girls, insulting and raping them cruelly, and openly before everyone! These poor creatures were so ill, and they begged to be left alone, but to no avail. The sin was so great in the bottom of that ship, that at times, I thought Almighty God would just let us all perish, because of the vice going on.[11]

Life in New York

Urshan passed through immigration at Ellis Island on or about October 11, 1901and then proceeded by train to Yonkers, New York. He could speak only a few words in the English language had only $25.00.[12] In Yonkers he lodged in a room with a few of his countrymen.[13]

Urshan described these acquaintances as "Job's comforters," discouraging him from finding work. Some of them worked in a hat factory and others in a carpet factory. Urshan had no experience in factory work, while some of the most experienced workers had recently been laid off from the hat and carpet factories in which they worked.[14] When he prayed about the situation, the Lord said to him, "Go and see the superintendent of the factory: simply appear before him, and I will make known your need to his heart, and he will take an interest in you."[15] He found the home address of Mr. Miller, the superintendent of the hat factory,[16] and

---

[9]Urshan, *The Life Story*, 5th ed., 36-42.
[10]Urshan, *The Life Story*, 5th ed., 42.
[11]Urshan, *The Life Story*, 5th ed., 41-42.
[12]Urshan, *The Life Story*, 5th ed., 45-46.
[13]Urshan, *The Story of My Life*, 1st ed., 19.
[14]Urshan, *The Life Story*, 5th ed., 46.
[15]Urshan, *The Story of My Life*, 1st ed., 20.
[16]Urshan, *The Story of My Life*, 3rd ed., 42.

waited outside for two successive mornings. On the first day, Mr. Miller looked at Urshan as he left his home, but passed by without a word. Urshan followed him to the factory, stopping outside the door of the waiting room. On the second morning, Miller again looked at Urshan and gave a faint smile. As he passed by, Miller looked back at Urshan following him and said something in English that Urshan did not understand. Urshan said, "Give me work please sir, yes," and repeated, "Yes sir, work!"[17] When they arrived at the factory, Miller again entered his office, and Urshan remained outside.

At this point, Urshan wondered if he had really received direction from God. He returned to his room, praying, "Lord, have I been deluded?" He then heard the voice of God say, "Go, once more, in the name of the triune God, who dwells in your Saviour. He loves you above the fowls and the flowers. Go the third time."[18] On the third day, Urshan again appeared before Miller's door. This time, Miller smiled pleasantly and spoke twice as Andrew followed him. Miller then arranged for Urshan to be employed at the factory he managed.[19]

Urshan worked at the hat factory for six months. During this time he was mistreated by his fellow workers, who spat tobacco juice on him, pinched and shook him, and threw bundles of coarse paper into his face, pushing him about roughly. When the foreman saw this and fired some of those involved, the discharged workers would lie in wait for Urshan and beat him on his way home. In contrast, the head foreman liked his work, raising his wages from four to fifteen dollars per week. He was also promised he would eventually be promoted to the position of foreman, which paid twenty-five dollars per week.[20]

While working at the factory, Urshan visited local churches on Sundays, including a Presbyterian and an Episcopalian church. He sought out the Presbyterian church because he had been raised in a Presbyterian minister's home and was converted in a Presbyterian school. He enjoyed the Presbyterian service but did not return because he was embarrassed by his limited English vocabulary when greeted by the pastor following the service. The next Sunday he visited an Episcopalian church. When he joined in the singing of "Onward Christian Soldiers" in the Syriac language, the leader asked Urshan to sing a verse as a solo. Just as he concluded the verse, Mr. Slocum, the foreman at the hat factory, walked into the

---

[17]Urshan, *The Story of My Life*, 1st ed., 21.

[18]Urshan, *The Story of My Life*, 1st ed., 21. At this point in the third edition of Urshan's life story as it was serialized in *The Witness of God* an interesting revision appears. The reference to the triune God is dropped, and Urshan reports, "The small voice within said, 'Go once more, in the name of God, Who dwells in your Saviour. He loves you above the fowls and the flowers, go the third time!" (Urshan, "My First Six Months in America," *The Witness of God* [April 1962]: 3). This revision also appeared in the fifth edition, p. 49.

[19]Urshan, *The Story of My Life*, 1st ed., 22. In the first, second, and third editions of his life story, Urshan refers to his friends as Persians. Beginning with the third edition as serialized in *The Witness of God,* he refers to them as Assyrians. (See Urshan, *The Story of My Life*, 1st ed., 22; Urshan, "Chapter Five—Story of My Life: My First Six Months in America," *The Witness of God* 3, no. 34 [December 1922]: 7; Urshan, "My First Six Months in America," *The Witness of God* [April 1962]: 3; Urshan, *The Life Story*, 5th ed., 50.)

[20]Urshan, *The Story of My Life*, 1st ed., 23-25.

room. Slocum was pleased to see Urshan there and introduced him to the entire congregation as one of his best workers. This encounter enhanced the foreman's friendliness toward Urshan at work, but it did not stop the abuse Andrew received from some of his co-workers.[21]

Life in Chicago

In mid-April 1902, Urshn left New York for Chicago where he planned to enroll in Rush Medical College, where his cousin was attending, to qualify for a "high profession."[22] Upon arrival, he found his cousin hospitalized and dying. His condition improved after a few days, but Urshan discovered his cousin had lost faith in God and turned to infidelity.

Since his cousin could not help him with his plans, Urshan found employment as a servant in a high class boarding house. The cook, a practicing homosexual, became enraged when Urshan resisted his advances. He threatened to kill Urshan and forced him to do all the heavy work. When the chamber maids, yard man, and sisters of the landlady saw that Andrew could be imposed upon, they forced him to do much of their work as well. He worked seventeen hours each day for the five months he was employed.

One day after work Urshan retired to his basement room to read the Syriac language journal *Zarery D-Bara* published by the American Presbyterian Mission in Urmia. His heart broke and he began to weep as he read an article about the early missionary work of his ancestors among the Chinese. He fell on his face and prayed, "Oh God, raise up men, like as of old, to magnify Thy grace in apostolic power."[23] A strong internal voice responded, "Arise, I have heard your cry and I will make you one of my servants in apostolic faith and power."[24]

In mid-September 1902 Urshan left the boarding house to work as a busboy at the Great Northern Hotel in Chicago.[25] Mr. Dean, the head waiter, paid him a higher salary for a ten hour workday than he had earned for his seventeen hour workdays.[26] After six months, Dean began to teach Andrew how to wait on tables by waiting

---

[21]Urshan, *The Life Story,* 5th ed., 54-60.

[22]Urshan, *The Story of My Life,* 1st ed., 26.

[23]Urshan, *The Story of My Life,* 1st ed., 27.

[24]Urshan, *The Story of My Life,* 1st ed., 27.

[25]Originally named the Chicago Hotel, the Great Northern Hotel stood on the Northeast corner of Dearborn Street and Jackson Boulevard. It was sixteen stories tall, with 500 rooms, eight dining rooms, a café, and six elevators. The hotel was built in 1891 at a cost of $1,150,000 and demolished in 1940. See "Great Northern Hotel," http://www.patsabin.com/illinois/GreatNorthern.htm and "From Adams Street, Looking South," http://tigger.uic.edu/depts/ahaa/imagebase/intranet/chiviews/page157.html (accessed April 13, 2009).

[26]Urshan, "Seventh Chapter—The Story of My Life: My First Few Months in Chicago," *The Witness of God* 4, no. 37 (January 1923): 5.

on Dean at his meals for one month. Andrew was then promoted to the position of room waiter, the most respectable and financially profitable waiter's position.[27]

Dean next suggested that Urshan use his two hours of daily leisure time to work in the bar selling liquor, thereby earning an extra $3.00 per day. Although his conscience troubled him, Urshan took the job to please Dean. His fortunes began to change. One day he became embroiled in a fracas caused by over-tipping by two intoxicated customers. The two left Urshan a $4.00 tip, insisting that he keep all of it. Shortly, they returned, and the one most sober proceeded in a loud and angry tone to accuse Urshan of taking advantage of his more intoxicated friend. The bartender, who had observed the entire episode, swore at the customer and slapped him hard on the face, declaring that he was a witness for Andrew's innocence. Other men intervened, separating the bartender and the customer. Someone asked how much money the customer's friend had left for a tip. The customer answered, "Two dollars and I want them back." Although Andrew believed that God told him to give back the entire $4.00, he returned only the $2.00 the angry customer demanded.

Three weeks later, Mr. Dean left his position and Urshan was fired by his replacement. Urshan could not find employment for the next two months.[28]

Urshan finally found work in mid-July 1903 at the Lakota Hotel located at the corner of 30th Street and Michigan Avenue. It was an imposing structure, standing eleven stories tall. Mr. Sharp, an Englishman and the head waiter, had seen the Shah of Iran when he visited Queen Victoria. Intrigued by Urshan's Persian heritage, Sharp hired him immediately.[29]

Despite his training at Great Northern, Urshan had to start over as a busboy because the Lakota operated on a different system. The Great Northern followed the European model. The waiter served two or three families and had to remember all of their dishes without writing them down. Meals were charged to the hotel bill and paid in advance. The Lakota operated on an American plan. Orders were written down on a notepad and paid separately from room rent. Although Urshan was inexperienced, Mr. Sharp became a father figure, speaking highly of him to the guests and requiring the other waiters to assist him until he gained the necessary

---

[27]As a busboy, Urshan earned $25.00 per month plus about $12.00 per month in tips from the waiters. As a room waiter, his salary was $40.00 per month plus about $60.00 in tips. Urshan, "Seventh Chapter—The Story of My Life: My First Few Months in Chicago," *The Witness of God* 4, no. 37 (January 1923): 6.

[28]Although Dean and Urshan were friends, Dean influenced Urshan in ways Andrew later regretted. Besides the episode in the hotel bar, it was through Dean's influence that Urshan smoked his first and only cigar, which made him terribly sick for three days. (See Urshan, "Seventh Chapter—The Story of My Life: My First Few Months in Chicago—Cont.," *The Witness of God* 4, no. 38 [February 1923]: 6-7).

[29]Urshan misspells the name of the hotel as Lacota. The Lakota was built in 1893 and demolished in 1959. (See Carl W. Condit, *The Chicago School of Architecture: A History of Commercial and Public Building in the Chicago Area, 1875-1925* (Chicago: University of Chicago Press, 1998), 157.

skills. Urshan gave Sharp a beautiful watch with silver engravings of the Shah. Within three weeks, Urshan had become a first class waiter on the American plan.

However, change was on the near horizon. Sharp lost his position when the hotel changed management. Urshan was dismissed by his new boss, but was quickly rehired when the hotel guests protested. In the meantime, he learned of an opening at the Kenwood Hotel, an establishment patronized by wealthy religious men. Waiters were not required to serve liquor with meals.[30]

In mid-January, 1904 Urshan began waiting on tables in the main dining room of the Kenwood Hotel. Within a few weeks, he was assigned to be the private waiter for the Montgomery Ward family, which included Ward, his wife, and their daughter. With more free time, Urshan enrolled at a tailoring school, an automobile school and began to visit area churches.

Andrew noticed that Mr. Ward did not attend church on Sundays with his wife and daughter. When he asked Ward the reason, he replied, "Andrew, you go in my place." So Andrew attended the prestigious Kenwood Evangelical Church on Sunday mornings, sitting between Mrs. Ward and their daughter. Although the Wards were happy with Andrew and he enjoyed working for them, his associations and environment created within him a desire to be identified with refined society. He began dressing fashionably and thinking about having a young lady friend. Things were going so well that, in his words, "[I]t made me grow cold spiritually . . . ."[31]

Urshan worked at the Kenwood Hotel nearly two years, until approximately January 1906. During this time, a minister of a neighborhood church encouraged him to dance with the young ladies at a church sponsored ball. A young dentist who belonged to another church encouraged him to attend theaters. Although he felt miserable doing so, Andrew began to visit theaters, dance halls, and ballrooms.

At this time, he renewed his fellowship with a second cousin, a preacher in the Brethren church who had come from Persia to America. His cousin asked about Andrew's spiritual condition. Urshan told him that he frequently went to music and dance halls. Since he knew his cousin's love for music, Andrew persuaded him to go with him to a dance hall to hear the orchestra. As he danced with a young lady he had just met, Andrew looked up in the balcony where his cousin sat with a sad countenance, shaking his head. After calling Andrew to him, his cousin said, "Your feet are sliding into the degradation of black sins. If you do not quit this evil dancing you will fall into immorality!"[32]

Urshan took his cousin's warning seriously. He gave up dancing and began interpreting for his cousin when he preached in Syriac. When not accompanying

---

[30]Urshan, "Seventh Chapter—The Story of My Life: My First Few Months in Chicago—Cont.," *The Witness of God* 4, no. 38 (February 1923): 7-8. The Kenwood Hotel was located at 47th Street and Kenwood Avenue in an area of Chicago inhabited by wealthy people and characterized by large, expensive homes. It was an apartment house hotel designed by Charles Sumner Frost in the classical revival style. The Kenwood district today is on the National Register and is in a Chicago Landmark District.

[31]Urshan, "Seventh Chapter—The Story of My Life: My First Few Months in Chicago—Cont.," *The Witness of God* 4, no. 38 (February 1923): 8.

[32]Urshan, "Seventh Chapter—The Story of My Life: My First Few Months in Chica-

him to the American Brethren churches, Urshan attended the Methodist Episcopal Church at 47th Street and Drexel Boulevard in Chicago. Here he testified in English for the first time at a Wednesday night prayer meeting. His testimony produced "a nice little revival" in the church. When the people saw Urshan's willingness to testify even though his English was limited, they were convicted of their reluctance to say something for the Lord. The pastor, Dr. Mitchell, asked Urshan to testify regularly during the Wednesday night meetings, and an attorney, Mr.

---

go—Cont.," *The Witness of God* 4, no. 39 (March 1923): 4. Although we cannot be certain with which branch of the Brethren church Urshan's cousin was affiliated, all branches held many common beliefs. They understood Christ's command to be baptized as requiring threefold immersion face forward, once each in the name of the Father, Son, and Holy Spirit. They practiced foot washing and communion. Brethren were pacifists, and they would not take oaths or enter into lawsuits. (See *The New Schaff-Herzog Encyclopedia of Religious Knowledge*, vol. 4, ed. Samuel Macauley Jackson [New York: Funk and Wagnalls Company, 1909], 24; Randall Balmer, *The Encyclopedia of Evangelicalism* [Waco, TX: Baylor University Press, 2004], 100; and *The Columbia Encyclopedia*, 6th ed. [New York: Columbia University Press, 2009], s.v., "Brethren.") Brethren "were popularly known as Dunkards, Dunkers, Tunkers, from the German for 'to dip,' referring to their method of baptizing" (*The Columbia Encyclopedia*, 6th ed., s.v., "Brethren"). It is possible that Urshan's cousin was associated with the Progressive Dunkers, a group that seceded from the "Old Order" Brethren due to the "rapid growth and development of the north-central division of the United States" (*The New Schaff-Herzog Encyclopedia of Religious Knowledge*, vol. 4, 26). This group, organized as the Brethren Church in June, 1883 in Dayton, Ohio, established a mission in Chicago on November 1, 1896. (See H. R. Holsinger, *Holsinger's History of the Tunkers and the Brethren Church Embracing the Church of the Brethren, the Tunkers, the Seventh-Day German Baptist Church, the German Baptist Church, the Old German Baptists, and the Brethren Church* [Oakland, CA: Pacific Press Publishing, 1901], 573-74, 622) and a mission station in Urmia, Persia – the area from whence several members of the Urshan family migrated to America – some time after 1900. The Chicago mission was first located at 384 Southwestern Avenue but by 1901 was relocated to 940 West Van Buren Street. (See Holsinger, *Tunkers*, 573.) The Brethren welcomed women preachers. Although J. D. McFaden, the secretary of the general missionary board in 1896, was given responsibility for the new mission in Chicago, Sadie A. Gibbons was "set apart" by the laying on of hands to be the assistant pastor. When McFaden's involvement with the mission ended in May, 1898, Gibbons was solely responsible until November of that year when another man, J. C. Talley, assumed responsibility. By 1901 the new church had gathered about thirty-five members, although the number baptized exceeded that. (See Holsinger, *Tunkers*, 573-74.) In doctrine the Progressive Dunkers differ from the Conservatives in but few points. They hold that the decisions of no conference are binding upon the individual conscience. Hence, in church polity the Progressives are congregational. They differ from the Conservatives in refusing to conform to "the order," i.e., the style of dress and cut of the hair and beard prescribed by the Annual Meeting. They agree with the Conservatives in holding the general Evangelical doctrines, and in laying less emphasis upon orthodox theology than upon a pious life. They also hold with the Conservatives in the doctrines (1) of the Lord's Supper consisting of foot-washing, the love-feast, or primitive agape, the communion in bread and wine, and the salutation; (2) of baptism for adults only and by trine immersion; (3) of non-resistance of evil, which includes opposition to war and avoidance of lawsuits; and (4) of opposition to the taking of any kind of oath. (See *The New Schaff-Herzog Encyclopedia of Religious Knowledge*, vol. 4, 26.)

Hutchins, asked him to speak to the Epworth League, an organization for youth in the Methodist Episcopal Church.[33]

In his association with his Brethren cousin and the Methodist Episcopal Church, Urshan was exposed to an emphasis on the Holy Spirit, sanctification, imparted rather than merely imputed righteousness, and practical holiness.[34]

Baptism in the Brethren Church

Urshan found himself in disagreement with his cousin over the mode of baptism. After an argument during which each told the other that he was in danger of being "lost," Urshan returned to his room and opened his Syriac concordance and Bible, intending to prove his cousin wrong. Because he had been instructed in Presbyterian doctrine, Urshan believed in infant baptism. His cousin insisted in baptism by immersion. To his surprise, Urshan could find nothing in the Bible to support his view on sprinkling. Instead, he became convinced that his cousin was right. Not only did he come to believe in insisting in adult believer baptism by immersion; he also was convinced that baptism was only for those who repented and believed the gospel. He felt God speaking to him, "Arise, and go at once to your cousin and confess to him your doctrinal error and your unkind answer to him, and also ask him to baptize you."

After obeying this impulse and being immersed by his cousin in one of the Brethren churches in Chicago, Urshan felt that the Lord had blessed him for his obedience. This experience convinced him of the importance of "walking in the light": "To this very day I am so glad that I did not fail God in that new light regarding the mode of water baptism and as I walked in that light as He is in the light, the blood of Jesus Christ, his Son cleansed me from my error and stubbornness of spirit."[35]

---

[33]Urshan, "Seventh Chapter—The Story of My Life: My First Few Months in Chicago—Cont.," *The Witness of God* 4, no. 39 (March 1923): 4-5.

[34]M. E. Dieter, " Methodist Churches," *Dictionary of Christianity in America*, Daniel G. Reid et al., eds. (Downers Grove, IL: InterVarsity Press, 1990), 732.

[35]Urshan, "Seventh Chapter—The Story of My Life: My First Few Months in Chicago—Cont.," *The Witness of God* 4, no. 40 (April 1923): 8. The idea of "walking in the light" was a common theme in Holiness and Pentecostal circles, emphasizing the importance of obedience to new biblical insights. Urshan explained, "By saying the new light we mean a fresh revelation of our Lord to our hearts that came to us through the illumination of the scriptures . . . by the Holy Spirit" (Urshan, "The New Light or the More Light," *The Witness of God* 1, no. 10 [September 1920]: 1). The notion of "new light" was connected with the restorationist impulse of early twentieth century Pentecostalism. This "new light" led back to the beliefs and practices of first century Christianity. See Robin M. Johnston, "Howard A. Goss: A Pentecostal Life" (PhD diss., Regent University, 2010), 40-44.

Urshan's Membership and Experiences at Moody Church

It was probably in 1907 that Urshan began attending The Moody Church in Chicago, joining shortly thereafter.[36] In 1911, he declared he had been a member of this church. Although he would separate from the church over the issue of speaking with tongues, A. C. Dixon, pastor from 1906-1911, deeply influenced Urshan. His articles on such fundamentalist themes as defense of Scripture and the doctrines of sin and salvation, higher criticism,[37] Spiritualism,[38] Russellism,[39] and Christian Science,[40] reflect Dixon's influence.[41] Shortly after joining the church,

---

[36]Before 1908 the church was known as the Chicago Avenue Church. In 1908, during Dixon's pastorate, it was formally renamed "The Moody Church." See "The Moody Church, Information. The History of the Moody Church," _http://www.moody church.org/information/history.html (accessed January 23, 2010). See Urshan, "Some of the Lord's Work In Our Midst During the Last Fifteen Months," *Pentecostal Witness of The Grace and Truth* 1, no. 1 (October 1911): 13.

[37]See, e.g., Urshan, "Denominationalism and the World-Wide Pentecostal Movement," *The Witness of God* 2, no. 18 (June 1921): 1; Urshan, *Doctrine of the Trinity and the Divinity of Jesus Christ* (Cochrane, WI: Andrew D. Urshan, 1923), front cover; Urshan, *The Almighty God in the Lord Jesus Christ*, 20, 72-73; Urshan, "Warning Against Modern Strong Delusions," *The Witness of God* (November 1931): 5-7; Urshan, *The Almighty God in the Lord Jesus Christ*, 19-20, 63; Urshan, "Christian Battlefield's [sic]: Old and New Lines," *The Witness of God* (October 1947): 5.

[38]See, e.g., Urshan, "The Pentecostal People Versus Spiritualism," *The Witness of God* 1, no. 8 (July 1920): 8. This article was reprinted in *The Witness of God* 4, no. 46 (October 1923): 6-7. See also Urshan, "Warning Against Modern Strong Delusions," *The Witness of God* (November 1931): 5-7.

[39]See, e.g., Urshan, *The Almighty God in the Lord Jesus Christ*, 19-20, 63; Urshan, "Warning Against Modern Strong Delusions," *The Witness of God* (November 1931): 5-7; Urshan, "Editorial News and Notes," *The Witness of God* 10, no. 110 (October 1929): 2.

[40]See, e.g., Urshan, *The Almighty God in the Lord Jesus Christ*, 19-20, 63; Urshan, "Warning Against Modern Strong Delusions," *The Witness of God* (November 1931): 5-7; Urshan, "Seventh Chapter—The Story of My Life: My First Few Months in Chicago—Cont.," *The Witness of God* 4, no. 41 (May 1923): 3.

[41]Dixon, a Baptist minister and a protégé of D. L. Moody, graduated from Wake Forest College in 1874 with the A.B. While serving as a pastor in North Carolina during the years of 1874 to 1879, Dixon continued his education at Southern Baptist Seminary and the University of North Carolina. In 1886 Washington and Lee University conferred upon him the D.D. For one month in 1893, he was one of many preachers associated with D. L. Moody who preached in Chicago during the Chicago World's Fair. (See Southern Baptist Historical Library and Archives, "Inventory to the Amzi Clarence Dixon Papers," AR. 111, 2-3; H. B. Hartzler, *Moody in Chicago or the World's Fair Gospel Campaign: An Account of Six Months' Evangelistic Work in the City of Chicago and Vicinity During the Time of the World's Columbian Exposition, Conducted by Dwight L. Moody and His Associates* [New York: Fleming H. Revell Company, 1894], 37, 102-03, 106, 108, 203, 236.) A leading figure in the movement that eventually became known as fundamentalism, Dixon served as pastor of The Moody Church from October 1906 until 1911, when he accepted the pastorate of Metropolitan Tabernacle in London England, where Charles Spurgeon had

been the pastor. (See George M. Marsden, *Fundamentalism and American Culture: The Shaping of Twentieth Century Evangelicalism, 1870-1925* [New York: Oxford University Press, 1980], 37; Brenda M. Meehan, "A. C. Dixon: An Early Fundamentalist," *Foundations* 10 [January 1967]: 50-63; Southern Baptist Historical Library and Archives, "Inventory," 3.) Before becoming pastor of The Moody Church, Dixon was one of a number of evangelists and Bible teachers associated with Dwight L. Moody who began to emphasize the importance of an experience with the Holy Spirit. Dixon organized a conference on the Holy Spirit that was held in Baltimore in 1890. At this conference, the speakers emphasized "the importance for present believers to receive the Holy Spirit as described in Acts 2" (Marsden, *Fundamentalism and American Culture*, 70). George C. Needham reported that "[a]t one time no less than one hundred ministers requested prayer for the fullness of the Holy Ghost" (A. C. Dixon, ed., *The Person and Ministry of the Holy Spirit* [Baltimore: Wharton, Barron, & Co., 1890], vi). In addition to this emphasis on the Holy Spirit, Dixon and other associates of Moody became allies with many "in the new independent Holiness groups that emphasized vigorous work among the poor" (Marsden, *Fundamentalism and American Culture*, 83, 246). Dixon also was in favor of the organization and promotion of political parties for social reform, although "the only social reform he advocated was Prohibition, and that through concern for individual salvation" (Mehann, "A. C. Dixon," 51; See also A. C. Dixon, *Lights and Shadows of American Life* [New York: 1898], 103). In his proclamation of the gospel at the Chicago World's Fair, where he preached five times during the day, Dixon was described as "fresh, vigorous, and strong" (Hartzler, *Moody in Chicago,* 103). In connection with his defense of the gospel against what he considered to be compromise, Dixon wrote, "Above all things I love peace, but next to peace I love a fight, and I believe the next best thing to peace is a theological fight" (*Ecumenical Missionary Conference, New York 1900,* I [New York: American Tract Society, 1900], 364). In 1908, while serving as pastor at The Moody Church, Dixon began writing a column for the Saturday edition of the *Chicago Daily News*. Upon syndication, the column was printed in some one thousand newspapers including the *Baltimore Sun* and the *Boston Daily Herald*. (See Meehan, "A. C. Dixon," 55; Gerald L. Priest, "A. C. Dixon, Chicago Liberals, and *The Fundamentals,*" *Detroit Baptist Theological Seminary Journal* 1 [Spring 1996]: 114.) Dixon's most profound influence on nascent fundamentalism may have been his involvement in the production of *The Fundamentals,* a series of twelve volumes intended "to combat the inroads of liberalism" and that "were sent free to ministers of the gospel, missionaries, Sunday school superintendents, and others engaged in aggressive Christian work throughout the English speaking world" (R. A. Torrey, ed., *The Fundamentals*, updated by Charles L. Feinberg [Grand Rapids: Kregel Publications, 1990], 9). Eventually some three million volumes were distributed. (See Marsden, *The Shaping,* 119.) During the summer of 1909, while traveling in California, Dixon met Milton and Lyman Stewart, millionaire brothers who owned the Union Oil Company and who were generous in their support of Christian ministries. (See Meehan, "A. C. Dixon," 55; Priest, "A. C. Dixon," 125-26.) Lyman had been impressed by Dixon's opposition to the liberalism of George Foster, a professor at the University of Chicago. Dixon accepted Lyman's invitation to serve as editor-in-chief for the production of the *The Fundamentals.* He edited the first six volumes, personally contributing an article titled "The Scriptures." With Louis Meyer and Reuben Torrey, Dixon arranged for written contributions by American and British authors of a conservative bent, both scholars and popular writers. (See Priest, "A. C. Dixon," 125-27; Meehan, "A. C. Dixon," 55-56; Marsden, *The Shaping,* 118-119.) The volumes, published from 1910-1915 (Torrey, *The Fundamentals,* 11), offered articles on a variety of themes: defense of Scripture, attacks on higher criticism, apologetics, the Trinity, the doctrine of sin, the doctrine

Urshan was praying one night beneath a tree on Drexel Boulevard when he was challenged by a private security guard who thought he might be planning to rob some of the mansions in the neighborhood. The guard soon realized Urshan was a Christian. He asked if he could keep some of the tracts and booklets Andrew carried with him. This episode led to Urshan's first experience with preaching on the street.

Andrew told Mr. Cummings, the head waiter at the Kenwood Hotel, about his encounter. Cummings said, "Andrew, why don't you go into the streets and hold meetings and we will all come with our wives to hear you and I will invite these rich guys to come and hear you." The other waiters insisted that they would come with their girlfriends as well. Urshan fixed the date and time he would preach on the corner of 39th Street and Drexel Boulevard. He borrowed an Islamic priest's costume belonging to his cousin, Dr. Elisha Sayad, to prepare for the event.[42]

When the appointed time arrived, Urshan boarded the street car wearing the long Islamic robe and the turban made of about five yards of white linen. With one hand, he held a large sacred Islamic hatchet over his shoulder. A kashkool[43] filled with tracts hung from his other hand.

Immediately Urshan had the attention of the people aboard the street car. Taking advantage of this, he went from person to person distributing tracts. They were eagerly received. When he reached his destination, Andrew borrowed a large soap box from a nearby store. Stepping up on it, he attracted the attention of people from every direction. As they gathered around him, he began speaking and singing in Syriac.

Soon Mr. Cummings and the waiters from the Kenwood Hotel arrived. Several automobiles filled with passengers stopped to listen. Police officers who observed this gathering made no attempt to stop his preaching. When a heckler shouted, "Hey, hey, get down and go to work, never mind preaching, I am a working man, and I work like hell for one dollar a day," Urshan answered, "I am here to tell you that you can work like heaven for $2.00 a day." After this exchange, Mr. Cummings grabbed the heckler by the arm, pushing him roughly away with the warning, "If you open your mouth again, I will punch you in the nose." Then Cummings said to the crowd, "I want you all to know this young man works for me in the Kenwood Hotel and he does not preach for money and I am proud to be here listening to him."[44]

Urshan's success in giving his Christian witness in a variety of settings – including the Epworth League, his co-workers, and on the street corner – emboldened him to take a step that caused him to lose his job at the Kenwood Hotel. A prominent Christian Scientist practitioner lived in the hotel. Andrew wrote a letter to this lady warning her that Christian Science was a delusion that she needed to

---

of salvation, personal testimony, Russellism, Mormonism, Eddyism, Modern Spiritualism, Romanism, evangelism, and missions. (See Marsden, *The Shaping,* 119-20.)

[42]Urshan, "Seventh Chapter—The Story of My Life: My First Few Months in Chicago—Cont.," *The Witness of God* 4, no. 40 (April 1923): 7-8.

[43]The kashkool is a sacred pot made of the bones of a large fish. It is like a censer with yellow chains to be held in the palms of the hands.

[44]Urshan, "Seventh Chapter—The Story of My Life: My First Few Months in Chicago—Cont.," *The Witness of God* 4, no. 41 (May 1923): 3.

forsake in order to escape eternal damnation. He thought she would appreciate his concern for her eternal welfare. Instead, she raged with fury against him and demanded that he be fired or she would not only leave the hotel but bring a lawsuit as well. Although the manager regretted dismissing Urshan, he told Mr. Cummings that it would be best for Andrew to leave the hotel for a month or two. He thought he lady would leave the hotel by that time so Urshan could return. Thus, Urshan's career as a waiter came to an end in mid-January, 1906.[45]

Finding himself unemployed again, another cousin persuaded Urshan to put their money together to open a restaurant. The cousin, a bricklayer, would continue to work his job until the business venture could support them both. Instead, after buying the fixtures needed to open the restaurant, Urshan's cousin quit his bricklaying job and began to stay all day at the restaurant. His lack of skill in the restaurant business, his inability to speak the English language, and his outward appearance discouraged American customers. The business was doomed from the start. Eventually, Urshan bought his cousin's share of the business for $500 and moved to a new location. But the situation did not improve. In an attempt to survive, Urshan borrowed money repeatedly at fifteen percent interest. He was so discouraged that he grew careless about his spiritual wellbeing. As he neglected to read the Bible, stopped going to church, and failed to pray, he drifted back into the life of dancing and theater going. In his own words, he "even began to make love with one of my very pretty waitresses, whom I thought I might marry at some future day."[46] Besides his failure in business, Urshan did not eat properly and failed to get adequate rest. He was so worried and nervous that he frequently was tempted to commit suicide. Only his fear of going to hell kept him from killing himself. It was the darkest hour of his life.[47]

Sanctification in a Holiness Church

Facing economic failure in the restaurant business, Urshan hit bottom. However, this would prove to be a major turning point in his life. From this point on he would not waver in the face of adversity. Rather, he we allow difficult circumstances to be a motivation for spiritual growth. The gateway to spiritual recovery came via a Mr. White, an alcoholic Urshan had befriended by giving him free meals.

One day, Mr. White entered the restaurant a different man. Walking like a gentleman, he sat at one of the tables covered with white cloth. He placed a napkin in his lap and ordered in a sober and dignified way. When his meal arrived, he bowed his head in silent prayer and then began to dine. Urshan was skeptical about this behavior, thinking that White was attempting to please him in order to gain favor

---

[45]Urshan, "Seventh Chapter—The Story of My Life: My First Few Months in Chicago—Cont.," *The Witness of God* 4, no. 41 (May 1923): 3.

[46]Urshan, "Eighth Chapter—The Story of My Life," *The Witness of God*, 4, no. 41 (May 1923): 4.

[47]Urshan, "Eighth Chapter—The Story of My Life," *The Witness of God*, 4, no. 41 (May 1923): 4.

and to avoid paying for a regular meal served at a table. But as Urshan looked at him, he saw a different countenance, a brightness on White's face.

Approaching his table, Urshan asked, "How are you, Mr. White?"

"Praise God! I feel fine," White answered. He then told Urshan that he had been converted by the Spirit of God in a holiness church. "As I went to the altar," he said, "the people prayed for me, with the result that not only have I been saved from sin, but God has taken away all appetite for liquor and tobacco. My heart is simply filled with the joy of the Lord!"

Urshan was happy to see what had happened to White, but it also convicted him of his own sins. He went down into the basement of his dining room, shut the door and cried out, "My God, shall drunkards and harlots enter the kingdom before us, your children?" He sensed God saying, "Ask Brother White to take you to that church where he was blessed."

Urshan's experience at the holiness church became a turning point in his life. When the minister came to the conclusion of the service, he looked at Andrew and said, "Is there any one here who is unhappy and who feels the need of the cleansing of Jesus' blood, and who wishes to know the joy of the Lord?" Something within Urshan said, "You are that man!" He wrestled within himself. On the one hand part of him wanted to stand up, confess his sins and ask for prayer. Another part of him suggested he could pray through at home. Urshan finally arose, made his confession, and went humbly to the altar.

People gathered around him, praying in loud voices while beating their fists on the floor. Urshan thought that the devil said to him, "You have fallen in with a bunch of the wildest fanatics in Chicago: be careful lest they strike your head with their fists, in which case you will be done for!" Unable to pray, Andrew lifted his head. The people seemed so strange and noisy that he wanted to escape. As he looked for a way out, he saw that he was hemmed in so closely that he could not leave.

Behind him, he saw two children about ten years old weeping and crying to God for his deliverance. He was emotionally stirred and cried out to God in Syriac. He asked God to deliver him or let him die. As he prayed, he sensed God saying, "Get up and thank and praise me that the work is done!" Without feeling any inward change, Urshan obeyed. But as he stood, lifting his hands in praise to the Lord, he felt a sensation of fire on his head that penetrated his whole being. He thought he could jump into space, he felt so light. He was rested and happy. No longer able to stand on his feet, he fell back, reclining on a chair, lost in God's glory.

Urshan understood that his old man with his lusts and desires was nailed to the cross with Jesus, that Christ had been "experimentally" made unto him – of God – wisdom, righteousness, sanctification, and redemption, and that he was complete in him.

> Blessed discovery to know that I died and was buried and am now risen in Christ, that I now walk in newness of life, and that I now abide in my risen, conquering Lord who is my All in All! At that very moment God called me to preach the Gospel of His dear son, and anointed me for the work.

A sweet sensation, a deep brokenness of heart filled my whole being; and I saw in vision a great band of my people who are unsaved and seem chained. Oh, the love that burned in my heart for them. Hurrying back to the restaurant, I told what God had done for me. They laughed me to scorn, but after a week of persuasion two of my friends were saved, and both of them are now living witnesses for Christ.[48]

He also understood that he should have recognized all this at the beginning of his Christian life.[49]

Urshan's sanctification experience occurred in July 1906. According to Phillip Dugas, Urshan's stepson, this "Church of the Holiness People"[50] was a "Nazarene church."[51] Urshan further described it as the First Pentecostal Nazarene Church in Chicago.[52] Urshan expressed shock upon seeing the humble facility: "In my mind I pictured a large church suitable to a fashionable congregation, and presided over by an intellectual minister of dignified manners. When approaching an old frame building, I was told that 'this is the church!' It seemed to me almost sacrilege to call such a large old wooden shack 'church!'"[53]

---

[48]Urshan, "Eighth Chapter—The Story of My Life," *The Witness of God* 4, no. 41 (May 1923): 4-5. In this second edition of his life story, Urshan says that two of his friends were "saved." In the third edition, this is changed to "wonderfully converted." Also, the first sentence in the block quote above is deleted in the third edition. Beginning with the third edition as serialized in *The Witness of God* and in the following editions, the entire content of the block quote is deleted.

[49]Although Urshan continued to distinguish between his conversion, sanctification, and Holy Spirit baptism throughout his life, he also affirmed the ideal that all of these experiences should occur simultaneously. See Urshan, *Supreme Need,* 15. This description of Urshan's experience paraphrases his own as found in Urshan, *The Life Story,* 5th ed., 99-101.

[50]Urshan, *The Life Story,* 5th ed., 99; A.D.U., "Important Editor's Comments," *The Witness of God* (1962): back cover.

[51]Phillip A. Dugas, telephone interview by author, February 2, 2010.

[52]W. W. Sturdivan, "Andrew D. Urshan," *Gospel Tidings* (January 1968): 2.

[53]Urshan, *The Story of My Life,* 1st ed., 36. By 1897, "the real center of the holiness movement had shifted [from Boston] west to Chicago . . . ." (Timothy L. Smith, *Called Unto Holiness: The Story of the Nazarenes: The Formative Years* (Digital edition 08/14/06, Holiness Data Ministry; Kansas City, MO: Nazarene Publishing House, 1962), 43, http://wesley.nnu.edu/wesleyctr/books/2501-2600/HDM2593.PDF (accessed February 10, 2010). "Rev. W. E. Shepard, reporting to the Nazarene Messenger [sic] on the 'Chicago Holiness Movement,' stated that revival fires were being kindled in different parts of the city. A large basement seating from four to six hundred people had been leased on the corner of Madison and Halsted streets, where a nightly mission would be conducted" (M. E. Redford, *The Rise of the Church of the Nazarene* [Digital edition 04/12/95, Holiness Data Ministry; Kansas City, MO: Beacon Hill Press of Kansas City, 1948], 20], http://wesley.nnu.edu/wesleyctr/books/0101-0200/HDM0145.PDF [accessed February 10, 2010]). The Chicago 1908 Directory lists the First Pentecostal Church of the Nazarene at 6417 Eggleston Avenue. The pastor was Rev. Clarence E. Cornell. Although this directory was published two years after Urshan's sanctification, this could have been the location. There were many holiness missions in Chicago in the earliest years of the twentieth century. (See Smith, *Called Unto Holiness,* 116.) In 1903, a worker in one of these missions "met Dr. [Phineas F.] Bresee on a trip to Los Angeles . . . and returned home determined to persuade

First Encounter with Pentecostalism

Urshan's sanctification experience created "deeper longing" for God in Christ Jesus. In his words, "I was normally sanctified to be the clean temple for God to come in and dwell within my spirit, soul and body, to live in me showing forth

---

his associates in Chicago to become Nazarenes" (Smith, *Called Unto Holiness*, 116). The September 19, 1907 issue of the *Nazarene Messenger*, under the subheading "The Church of the Nazarene in Chicago," reprinted an article from the September 8, 1904 issue of the *Christian Witness*, a periodical published by the National Holiness Association: "Some representative holiness people, some time ago, invited Rev. P. F. Bresee, General Superintendent of the Church of the Nazarene, to hold a series of meetings in this city, at his earliest convenience, having in view the organization here of a Church of the Nazarene. . . . In accord with the invitation Dr. Bresee began meetings in a large tabernacle on Lexington avenue [sic], Sabbath, August 31. . . . At the end of the first year over 300 persons had joined. . . . It is estimated that fully 3,000 persons have been at the altar of prayer seeking salvation. Most of these have prayed through. Those who have been converted and wholly sanctified at our altars have gone 'everywhere' preaching the Word" ("The Coming General Assembly," *Nazarene Messenger* 12, no. 12 (September 19, 1907): 1-2. From October 10-17, 1907, "[d]elegates of the Association of Pentecostal Churches of America and the Church of the Nazarene convened in general assembly at Chicago" for the purpose of merging. The name adopted at this merger was "The Pentecostal Church of the Nazarene" In 1919, this name was changed to "Church of the Nazarene" due to "new meanings that had become associated with the term 'Pentecostal.'" (Official site of the international Church of the Nazarene, Preserving a legacy, Historical Statement, From the 2001 Manual of the Church of the Nazarene, http://www.nazarene.org/ministries/administration/archives/history/statement/display.aspx (accessed February 10, 2010). The theology of the Church of the Nazarene at that time was set forth by Bresee. After explaining the minimum requirement of regeneration for church membership and the right to "individual liberty of Christian thought" in non-essentials, Bresee wrote: "We therefore deem belief in the following brief statements sufficient: 1st. In one God—The Father, Son and Holy Spirit. 2nd. In the Divine inspiration of the Holy Scriptures, as found in the Old and New Testaments, and that they contain all truth necessary to faith and Christian living. 3rd. That man is born with a fallen nature, and is therefore inclined to evil and that continually. 4th. That the finally impenitent are hopelessly and eternally lost. 5th. That the atonement through Christ is universal, and that whosoever repents and believes on the Lord Jesus Christ is therefore saved from the condemnation and dominion of sin. 6th. That believers are to be sanctified wholly, subsequent to justification, through faith in the Lord Jesus Christ. 7th. The Holy Spirit bears witness to justification by faith, and also to the further work of the entire sanctification of believers. 8th. In the return of our Lord, in the resurrection of the dead, and in the final judgment" (P. F. Bresee, "The Doctrines of the Church," *Nazarene Messenger* 13, no. 21 [November 19, 1908]: 5. The Articles of Faith of the Church of the Nazarene have developed substantially since this early expression. See Official site of the international Church of the Nazarene, Discover, get connected, Preamble and Articles of Faith,http://www.nazarene.org/ministries/administration/visitorcenter/articles/display.aspx [accessed February 10, 2010]). There is no indication in Urshan's writings that he continued to be associated with the Church of the Nazarene, but it is clear that he subscribed to the holiness view of sanctification. In the final version of his autobiography, Urshan discussed his sanctification experience under the subheading "The Full Restoration!" (Urshan, *The Life Story*, 5th ed., 97).

His measureless love toward my fellow men."[54] He set out to share his experience with Mr. Morrison, a cook who had worked for him. When Urshan located Morrison's boarding house, Morrison was not in. The lady who ran the boarding house invited Andrew to wait in the parlor for Morrison's return. When she left the room, Urshan began to read from a large family Bible that had been placed on the center of a table. Then he began to pray that he would have an opportunity to tell the landlady about conversion and victorious Christian living. Seeing him holding the Bible upon her return, she said, "Isn't that a wonderful book?"

Urshan answered, "Yes, indeed! This is the wonderful book of God." Then he told her of his conversion in Persia, how God had cared for him in America, and of his sanctification experience in the holiness church located near the rooming house. He also told her of his success in winning souls for Jesus and the spiritual visions he had received.

As Urshan spoke to her, he noticed the quivering of her lips. He had never seen anything like this before, so he thought she suffered from some kind of abnormality. As he looked down lest he embarrass her, Andrew was shocked to hear her say, "Brother, I am so glad to hear of what the Lord has done for you, and I believe it all, and I see that you are ready to receive the Holy Spirit." Urshan was also taken aback because he thought his testimony about his experiences would have convinced her that he was already filled with the Holy Spirit.

Then the landlady began to tell Urshan of her spiritual experiences. She had also been sanctified in the same holiness church as he. Afterwards she had received the Holy Spirit and had spoken in other tongues. Andrew had never seen or heard anyone receiving this experience, so he could not understand what she was talking about. He had been taught in the Presbyterian Church that the days of miracles were over; the Apostles had been given miraculous gifts to proclaim the Christian faith among the heathen, but those things simply did not happen anymore.[55]

Because of his respect for the kind landlady, Urshan did not argue with her. Instead, he asked, "Is that really so? And in what kind of a church did you receive such an experience, for I would like to visit that church."

Urshan had to leave before Morrison returned. As soon as the landlady shut the door behind him, he experienced an unprecedented sensation that thrilled his

---

[54]Urshan, "Eighth Chapter—Cont., The Story of My Life—Cont.," *The Witness of God* 4, no. 42 (June 1923): 5. In the third edition of his life story as serialized in *The Witness of God,* this statement is revised to read, "I was normally sanctified by God to be an holy temple for Him to indwell and show forth to my fellowmen His measureless love and grace for all that would come unto Him, even as I had" (Urshan, "Our Own Personal Experience with the Pentecostal Movement, and the Holy Spirit Baptism!", *The Witness of God* [September 1962]: 4). This revision was retained in subsequent editions.

[55]During the time that Urshan attended the American Presbyterian Training College, the school was under the theological leadership of William Ambrose Shedd, whose father, John Haskell Shedd, had died on April 12, 1895. W. A. Shedd attended Princeton Seminary from 1889 until his graduation in 1892. B. B. Warfield, whose cessationist views were influential in Presbyterianism at the time, was the professor of theology at Princeton Seminary from 1887 until 1921. See Mary Lewis Shedd, *The Measure of a Man: The Life of*

whole being. He felt as if a bucket of cold water had been thrown upon him, or that someone was digging into his flesh with needles. Tears flowed down his cheeks. He prayed, "What meaneth this; is this the thing that lady was telling me about?" Somewhat fearful, he dismissed the matter from his mind. He would, however, think on it again at a later time.[56]

Urshan noticed that the joy he had felt following his sanctification changed to what he described as "a sorrowful spiritual mood" after hearing her testimony. He experienced a spiritual dryness. He no longer felt like shouting. However, as he questioned his motives to share his experience with Morrison, and reflected on the conversation he had with the cook's landlady, he could find nothing wrong. He was tempted to fear the Pentecostal people, but at the same time he was drawn to go and see for himself if what he had heard was true.

Prepared to resist, Urshan went to prayerfully examine everything he saw and heard at the meeting. It was all new to him. First he observed the behavior of two men sitting on the platform. One, with eyes closed, continually shook his head, and his lips moved quickly. The other was speaking fluently in a foreign language interspersed with English poems. At intervals he also shook his head, his lips moving noisily as if quickly kissing someone. While the minister spoke, ladies throughout the congregation would rise, shout loudly, and shake until the combs dropped to the floor, their hair falling on their faces, backs, and shoulders. Their hands stretched heavenward as they uttered strange speech and sat down. Some ladies fell onto the floor. Others, still sitting, would shake, shout, laugh, weep, sing, and pray.

Although Urshan rather pitied these people, he could find nothing wrong with the part of the experience he could understand. The people were exalting Jesus, his blood, his name, and his love. They praised the Lord more earnestly and vehemently than any denominational or holiness preacher he had ever seen.

After two hours, the meeting closed. The landlady who told him about the meeting greeted him warmly, happy to see that he had come. As the people left, he observed that the men kissed each other goodby and the women did the same. He went to the back to the room to see if they would continue to shake as they went home, praying that he would never receive this "shaking power." However, they behaved naturally, walking straight to the street cars, not stopping to window shop or look at passers by. As they went, many said softly "Praise the Lord," "Hallelujah," or "Glory to Jeus!"[57]

William Ambrose Shedd, missionary to Persia by Mary Lewis Shedd (New York: George H. Doran Company, 1922), xv, 53, 55, 94.

[56]Urshan, "Eighth Chapter—Cont., The Story of My Life—Cont.," *The Witness of God* 4, no. 42 (June 1923): 5.

[57]The location of this Pentecostal church is not identified by Urshan, nor is the name of the pastor. Indications are, however, that it was the North Avenue Mission where William H. Durham was the pastor. First, the time frame would fit with Durham's introduction of the Pentecostal experience to Chicago. Durham had been the pastor of the North Avenue Mission, a holiness mission in Chicago, since 1901. After a period of skepticism about the claim that speaking in tongues was the initial evidence that one had been baptized with the

Urshan Ponders Pentecostalism

On the one hour ride from his first visit to a Pentecostal church to his room, Urshan was troubled by two trains of thought. One was that the Pentecostal people were deceived, having allowed the devil to cause them to shake, babble, and fall to the floor. On the other hand, he realized they couldn't be of the devil, or they would not be exalting Jesus, trusting in the blood of his atonement and his free salvation. He also recognized that the Pentecostal landlady was sweet and kind. Although he was tempted to brand Pentecostalism as of the devil, he would not form a conclusion until he had studied what the Bible had to say about shaking, tongues, and falling prostrate in the presence of God.

When he arrived at his room, Urshan prayed, "Oh, my God! we are living in the last days, in which Thou hast warned us of false Christs; and Thou knowest that I love Thee, and dare not grieve Thy Holy Spirit. Show me, I pray that [sic] Thy own Word, if what I saw tonight was the operations of Thy Holy Spirit, for Jesus' sake, Amen."[58]

He then opened the Bible at random and read the third verse of the first chapter on the page. Trembling, he touched the Bible, saying, "In the name of the Father, Son and Holy Ghost, third verse I will read."[59] His eyes fell on 1 Corinthians 12:3: "Wherefore I give you to understand, that no man speaking by the Spirit of God

---

Holy Spirit, Durham traveled to Los Angeles in 1907 and visited the Azusa Street Mission. He was baptized with the Holy Spirit and spoke with tongues on March 2, 1907. (See Vinsin Synan, *The Century of the Holy Spirit* [Nashville, Tenn.: Thomas Nelson Publishers, 2001], 63.) When he returned to Chicago, Durham "worked tirelessly at spreading the Pentecostal message" and the "meetings at the North Avenue Mission were soon crowded past capacity as people from throughout the Midwest came to receive the baptism with the Holy Spirit" (Synan, *The Century of the Holy Spirit*, 64). Vinson Synan describes Durham as the founder of "the Pentecostal movement in the Midwest" and points out that "Durham's North Avenue Mission in downtown Chicago soon became the new mecca for those seeking the Pentecostal experience" (Vinson Synan, *The Holiness-Pentecostal Tradition: Charismatic Movements in the Twentieth Century*, 2nd ed. [Grand Rapids: Wm. B. Eerdmans Publishing Co., 1997], 104; Synan, *The Holiness-Pentecostal Tradition*, 132). Urshan dated his baptism with the Holy Spirit to July 4, 1908 at 2 a.m., making it possible that his first exposure to Pentecostalism was at the church where Durham was pastor and where Durham had begun to proclaim the Pentecostal message the previous year. Urshan describes the meeting place as "a narrow long hall" (Urshan, *The Life Story*, 5th ed., 109). The North Avenue Mission was described by Edith Blumhofer as a "modest frame building" in the middle of the block. (See Edith L. Blumhofer, "William H. Durham: Years of Creativity, Years of Dissent," in James R. Goff and Grant Wacker, eds., *Portraits of a Generation: Early Pentecostal Leaders* [Fayetteville, Ark: University of Arkansas Press, 2002], 123.)

[58]Urshan, *The Life Story*, 5th ed., 111.

[59]Urshan, *The Life Story*, 5th ed., 112. It is unlikely that as he matured in the faith, Urshan advocated this method of obtaining a word from the Lord. In view of this, the author finds it surprising that this text remained unchanged throughout all the revised editions of his autobiography.

calleth Jesus accursed: and that no man can say that Jesus is the Lord, but by the Holy Ghost."

Although he had bookmarks in other chapters, there was nothing between the pages of his Bible to cause it to open at that point. However, his natural skepticism prevented him from making a final decision about Pentecostalism. Instead, he gave himself to Bible study, prayer, and fasting.[60]

Following his experience of entire sanctification, Urshan began witnessing to young Persian men with whom he was acquainted. They had been granted the use of a room on the third floor of the Young People's Building of The Moody Church for their meetings.[61] Urshan said nothing to his Persian friends about his experiences at the Pentecostal mission. Since he was not sure whether what he observed there was of God, he did not want to be responsible if his friends went to the mission and received the power he had seen there. Instead, he asked them to join him in one week of special fasting and prayer for more love, power, and wisdom from the Lord.

Urshan was still not convinced that what he had seen at the Pentecostal mission was the power of Jesus Christ. He prayed that if these things were of God, the Persian converts – his friends – would be filled with the Holy Spirit and act just as he had seen the American Pentecostals act. He also prayed that the Holy Spirit would fall first on his Persian converts, not on him. He reasoned that if he were the first to receive, it would be solely through the influence of the Pentecostal mission. His Persian converts knew nothing about Pentecostal people and their manifestations. The only thing they had ever experienced was the brief strange utterance of a street preacher, and Urshan had not emphasized this to his converts.[62] In addition to these reasons, the Persians had not been fasting and praying to receive tongues, shaking, and the other behavior Urshan had seen at the Pentecostal mission. They had been praying only for more of the love and humility of Jesus. Urshan thought there was no danger that his converts would have Pentecostal experiences because of his influence on them.

When Andrew and the young Persian men returned home after seeing the street meeting, they knelt to pray. Abraham,[63] one of the converts, prayed in agony

---

[60]In the third edition of his life story as serialized in *The Witness of God*, the account of this event is revised to delete the phrase "it was indeed an unexpected message from the page of the Holy Writ" and to replace it with "it was a positive and definite answer to my prayer, and I accepted it as, 'thus sayeth the Lord!' " (Compare Urshan, "The Story of My Life—9th Chapter—Cont.," *The Witness of God* 4, no. 43 [July 1923]: 5 with Urshan, "Something New Happens," *The Witness of God* [October 1962]: 2.) This revised reading is retained in all subsequent editions. Urshan continued, however, to acknowledge his skepticism and prayer, fasting, and Bible study as he attempted to make up his mind about the validity of Pentecostalism.

[61]Urshan, "The Story of My Life—9th Chapter—Cont.," *The Witness of God* 4, no. 43 (July 1923): 7.

[62]Urshan, *The Life Story*, 5th ed., 113-14 and Urshan, "Something New Happens," *The Witness of God* (October 1962): 2.

[63]This was apparently Abraham Mushei, one of Urshan's cousins. See Andrew D. Urshan, "Some of the Lord's Work In Our Midst During the Last Fifteen Months," *Pentecos-

before falling into a trance. Suddenly he began to speak fluently in the ancient Syriac, a language he had never learned. Urshan, who had learned the language in high school, interpreted what Abraham was saying. It was a message of comfort and of encouragement to continue to seek God's face. The words Abraham spoke included the promise that since Jesus was coming soon, God intended to fill all of them with the Holy Ghost and to use them for his glory.

When Abraham came out of his trance, Urshan asked him to explain what had happened. He answered, "Nothing, but I feel so good." Then he continued, "Did you see those two beautiful boys dressed in white with dry sticks in their hands—how they piled them together and set fire to them, causing the beautiful flames to rise? Out of the fire came that strange writing which I could read."[64]

A few days after Abraham's experience, another of the Persian youth[65] spoke with tongues, shaking and speaking in a language none of the group could understand. These events convinced Urshan that the Pentecostal movement was of God, and he began to seek for the experience as seen in the book of Acts.

Because Urshan and his Persian converts' praying and wailing unnerved the landlady at the rooming house where they stayed, she ordered them either to quit praying in this way or to leave her house. Since they didn't wish to move out, they began to pray on an unoccupied plot of ground near Chicago on the shore of Lake Michigan. Frequently they would pray until one or two o'clock in the morning, kneeling sometimes on fragments of rock and at other times in the snow. Their hair would freeze, because they would not cover their heads while praying to their Father.[66]

During these prayer meetings, Urshan had visions of Christ on the Cross, causing him to weep almost constantly for two weeks. He sensed the presence of the heavenly Father with his protecting arms in that holy place. This protection was demonstrated one night when two men came to drive the Persians away. They intended to throw stones at the young Christians, but as they attempted to pick up the stones, the strength left their hands. The fear of the Lord came upon them, convicting them of sin. They confessed their sins. On another occasion, a big, rough sea carpenter boasted that he would put an end to these prayer meetings. As he approached, he fell to the earth in deep conviction and was converted.[67]

Andrew's restaurant business continued to decline, leaving him fifteen hundred dollars in debt. He worked twelve hours a day in an attempt to pay this off.

---

tal *Witness of the Grace and Truth* 1, no. 1 (October 1911): 12.

[64]Urshan, *The Life Story,* 5th ed., 116.

[65]This was apparently Saul Baddell, another of Urshan's cousins. See Andrew D. Urshan, "Some of the Lord's Work In Our Midst During the Last Fifteen Months," *Pentecostal Witness of the Grace and Truth* 1, no. 1 (October 1911): 12.

[66]This reflects the reading in the second edition of Urshan's life story. In the copy of the third edition in my possession, Urshan wrote a revision by hand so that it reads "because we would not cover our heads in praying to our Father in Jesus the Son." In the third edition as it is serialized in *The Witness of God* and in the subsequent editions, this is further revised to read "for we would not cover our heads while praying to God."

[67]This is how the story appears in the second and following editions of Urshan's life story. But in the first edition, it is said of the first two men that "they were both convicted of sin, and saved." Of the third man, it is said that he "was saved and baptized also in the

In addition, he spent six hours a day in ministry. Although his ministry was prospering, he became sick because he was not getting enough rest. Several Christian associates became concerned about his health and urged him to go into full time ministry. Stepping out on faith, Urshan left his secular employment, having no idea how he would pay off his debts. He left the Moody Church to establish the Persian Pentecostal Mission. A few months later, within the space of three days, someone dropped several hundred and five hundred dollar bills into a free will offering box at the mission. Urshan never learned the person's identity.[68]

Separation from The Moody Church

As a member of The Moody Church, Urshan had asked for permission to have a room where he could hold meetings with his Persian converts. He was given a room on the third floor of the Young People's Building which the Persians called "The Upper Room."[69] Urshan and his converts participated in the street meetings and church activities of The Moody Church. The congregation was delighted to have the Persian Mission become a branch work. Dr. Dixon liked Andrew. Urshan considered him to be a man of God and loved him like a father. Dixon frequently warned Urshan against the "tongue folks," telling him that a great future in ministry lay before him if he would keep away from them. In that event, God would use him as he did Gypsy Smith of England.

One night, an American evangelist who was a member of The Moody Church visited the Persian meeting out of curiosity. As he entered the room, one of the Persian Christians spoke in tongues and then interpreted into Syriac. Urshan then further translated these words into English. The message disclosed the thoughts of the guest evangelist, convincing him that God was at work among the Persians. He went home with tears in his eyes.

He returned the following night more conservatively dressed. He was not wearing the two rings or the gold chain for his eye glasses that he had worn the previous night. Even though he could not understand the Persian language in which the meeting was conducted, he put his face on the floor until he was baptized with the Holy Ghost. Prostrate, he spoke with other tongues for two hours.[70]

As word of his experience spread, other members of The Moody Church attended the Persian Mission and raised several questions about the meaning of what they saw taking place. Not only did they visit the Upper Room, but also the

---

Holy Spirit." (See Urshan, *The Story of My Life,* 1st ed., 39.)

[68] Urshan, *The Story of My Life,* 1st ed., 42.

[69] Urshan, "Some of the Lord's Work In Our Midst During the Last Fifteen Years," *Pentecostal Witness of The Grace and Truth* (October 1911): 13.

[70] Urshan, *The Story of My Life,* 1st ed., 43-44; Urshan, "The Story of My Life—9th Chapter—Cont.," *The Witness of God* 4, no. 43 (July 1923): 7; Urshan, *The Story of My Life,* 3rd ed., 84; Urshan, "Something New Happens," *The Witness of God* (October 1962): 4; Urshan, *The Life Story,* 5th ed., 118-19; Urshan, "Some of the Lord's Work In Our Midst During the Last Fifteen Months," *Pentecostal Witness of The Grace and Truth* 1, no. 1 (October 1911): 13.

prayer meeting by Lake Michigan. The superintendent of the Moody Rescue Mission, Ernest Graham, visited the midnight meeting near the lake and was baptized in the Holy Ghost. This transformed the rescue mission into a Pentecostal mission, where people were saved, healed, and baptized in the Holy Spirit.[71]

As a result, Dr. Dixon preached a Sunday morning sermon denouncing the "tongue folks" as spiritualists and religious fanatics. He explained that speaking in tongues had been given to the first century apostles so that they could preach to the heathen. Once the gospel had been established, tongues ceased. He then asked everyone in the congregation to stand who believed that what he preached was Bible truth. Most of the people did.

This was a moment of crisis for Urshan. If he did not stand, he would lose the friendship of Dr. Dixon and of many genuine friends: prominent men and women who were members of The Moody Church. However, he sensed the Lord speaking to his heart: "Will you sacrifice all and follow me in this narrow way and take your stand before all the Church?"

Urshan felt worse by the fact that he was sitting on one of the front seats near the platform in an area where the most loyal church members sat. Andrew kept his seat, feeling he was the only one in the whole church to boldly and silently reject his honored pastor's teaching. However, as the congregation stood, a voice from the balcony spoke out loudly, "Dr. Dixon, this is the rottenest sermon you have ever preached." It came from a man who attended the Upper Room meetings and who had witnessed the Spirit baptism of the evangelist. Quickly, the ushers rushed him from the auditorium.

Within a few days, Mr. Hunter, one of the leading Bible teachers of Moody Bible Institute, visited Urshan. Representing the church trustees, Mr. Hunter did his best to convince Andrew that tongues were unnecessary to prove that one had been baptized in the Holy Spirit. Urshan could remain and hold his meetings in the Upper Room if he would suppress speaking in tongues.

Urshan replied that he was too insignificant to withstand God and to quench his Holy Spirit. He asked to be removed from church membership, stating that he knew God was pouring out his latter rain on all nations, sealing his chosen ones for the rapture. He would count nothing too dear to give up; he was going on.

As they parted, Hunter said, "Andrew, you will never receive tongues, because you are a sober and chosen child of God and the Lord loves you too much to let that thing happen to you." Andrew responded, "If tongues are the sign of the baptism of the Holy Ghost, as I now understand, I will speak in tongues, for I will not let God go until He gives me the apostolic Holy Spirit baptism." Disappointed and sorrowful, Hunter left.

Urshan does not give precise information in any edition of his life story about the time and place of his baptism with the Holy Spirit. Here is the account as it appears in the first edition:

> After seeking for many months the gracious Lord met me. While I was in prayer

---

[71]Urshan, *The Story of My Life,* 1st ed., 44. Notice the distinction made between being saved, healed, and baptized in the Holy Spirit.

for an American brother that he might receive his baptism, the Lord poured His power upon me: it seem to fill my very bones, shaking my body. As I looked, through faith, upon Jesus standing above my head, I said to Him, audibly: "My Lord and Saviour, I praise Thee!" The Spirit took control of my vocal organs, and spoke through me a beautiful language which I had never before heard and which caused me great joy. I became blissfully conscious of the fact that GOD had come into my heart to abide there forever.[72]

In his book, *My Study of Modern* Pentecostals, Urshan is more specific:

> ... we wish humbly to praise God before all for His blessed spiritual baptism which He graciously poured upon us about 12 years ago, at two o'clock in the morning on the 4th of July, in a lot near Lake Michigan, in Chicago, Illinois, where with about 15 other young men [we] were praying and praising God reverently, while others were silently sleeping in their beds. We therefore "speak that we do know, and testify what we have seen."[73]

For one week after his Spirit baptism he was full of joy, constantly feeling the presence of God in a tangible way. But his joy was short-lived, and in its place came a spiritual dryness so profound Andrew could not even offer a common testimony. Urshan had an idealistic view of what life would be like after he was baptized with the Holy Spirit. He thought his spiritual experiences would greatly exceed anything he had previously known. For example, he believed that after being baptized with the Spirit people would be 'slain in the spirit' when he spoke. In addition, he thought he would immediately have a great vision of Christ, the

---

[72] Urshan, *The Story of My Life,* 1st ed., 43. The second edition gives no account of this experience but does include detail on the severe trial of faith he experienced following his baptism. (See Urshan, "The Story of My Life—11th Chapter: What Happened to Me after the Baptism of the Holy Spirit," *The Witness of God* 4, no. 46 [October 1923]: 2-3.) In the copy of the third edition in my possession, Urshan wrote by hand the words "Praise Jesus, at 2:30 am I also received the precious gift." This is marked for inclusion immediately after the paragraph describing the experience of the second Persian youth who received the Holy Spirit. The third edition includes an entire chapter devoted to his trial following baptism with the Spirit. In the third edition as it is serialized in *The Witness of God* there is no account of Urshan's experience of receiving the Spirit, but there is a description of his trial. The fifth and final edition follows the example of the second through the third. Although I have not been able to locate a complete fourth edition, the pages in my possession indicate that it follows the third edition as serialized in *The Witness of God.*

[73] Andrew D. Urshan, *My Study of Modern Pentecostals* (N.p.: 1923; Portland, OR: Apostolic Book Publishers, reprinted 1981), 61. This still leaves some uncertainty as to the precise year of Urshan's spiritual baptism. *My Study of Modern Pentecostals* was originally published in 1923. His statement "about 12 years ago" would thus suggest 1911 as the date. But the actual date was earlier than this. In an account written not long before his death, Urshan said, "In 1908, as their Pastor, God graciously baptised [sic] me with the Holy Ghost and fire" (Sturdivan, *Gospel Tidings* [January 1968]: 2). On the back cover of an issue of *The Witness of God* published in the early 1960s, Urshan reported that "on July 4, 1909 at 2 a.m., The [sic] Lord Jesus baptised [sic] me with the Holy Spirit and caused me to talk in known and unknown languages for several hours, a precious gift that remains with me to this day." But in a copy in my possession, he changed this to 1908 in his own handwriting during the year before his death.

gifts of prophecy and of working miracles. This was also the expectation of those who knew him. He felt worse than he did before he was saved. He could not pray or study the Bible. His enjoyment of worship vanished. He no longer had a love for souls. Every feeling of virtue left him. His Christian experience seemed paralyzed.

In the midst of this spiritual desert, Urshan continued to conduct the meetings of the Persian Pentecostal Mission.[74] He struggled because he felt no anointing and was haunted that his spiritually barren state was the result of not heeding the warnings of his friends at The Moody Church.

For four weeks Andrew questioned the existence of God, the inspiration of the Bible, and everything related to Christianity. He felt as if a legion of devils had entered his flesh in an attempt to force him to curse God. He could no longer believe, and he could have written a strong book on infidelity. He later likened his experience to Jesus' temptation in the wilderness. As he struggled to find internal grace, he decided to use his common sense. Occasionally he heard a still, small voice telling him to keep his balance, which kept him from losing his mind.

Once during these four weeks Urshan went to a church meeting and forced himself to stand and say, "God is true. Jesus Christ is true, and the Bible is true. Amen." After saying these words, a wave of accusation swept over him saying, "You are a hypocrite and don't believe a word of it." He answered disgustedly, "I will say it anyhow!"

Urshan's common sense told him that in his earlier faith life, the Bible alone kept him from sin when he had been tempted. When he was alone in America, a stranger in a strange land, persecuted by fellow workers in the hat factory, he had been kept from suicide by reading the Bible and praying. Based on this, he said to himself, "Forever I will cling to this Bible and stand upon its precious promises, if there is nothing more now and forever." Spiritual victory followed this decision.

After he made his declaration of faith in the Bible, Urshan had a life-changing experience in a street car on his way to a church meeting. As he sat with a downcast face, a beautiful little boy looked back at him from the seat in front of Andrew. The boy had a big smile as he looked Urshan in the face. Everyone else on the street car seemed to love the little boy. Andrew, however, couldn't enjoy the boy's smile, and he wished the lady with whom the boy sat would take him away. A voice inside him said, "How do you like this little boy?" Urshan responded, "I wish I felt right so that I might give him a kiss." The voice continued, "You are just like a crying and kicking child." Something began to burn within him. He thought he would burst. He put a handkerchief to his mouth to keep quiet. He reached his destination and went into the meeting, keeping the handkerchief over his mouth so that he would not disturb the meeting. However, he could no longer contain himself. Describing this event, Urshan wrote, "[T]he glory of God burst in my very be-

---

[74]It is not clear whether Urshan's trial of faith occurred before or after the expulsion of the Persian mission from The Moody Church.

ing as rivers. It seemed my whole being was aflame, the glory of God so filled the place and I was so mightily blessed as well as those in the meeting." He continued,

"Oh, God give me another wilderness of four weeks for it pays." His love for souls returned, and it seemed the heavens rolled away, allowing Urshan to see Jesus sitting on the throne. Words failed to describe the glorious ecstasy he experienced.

Following his trial of faith, the Bible became a new book. The Scriptures were illuminated in unprecedented ways. He claimed to have the Holy Spirit based on what the Bible said, whatever he felt. He decided to cling to the Scriptures even if angels from heaven, demons from hell, or men of the earth said there was no God, no heaven, no hell, or no Bible.

When the trial was over, Urshan asked God why he had permitted him to go through this wilderness experience. The voice inside replied so that he could understand the meaning of the Scripture, "Without Me ye can do nothing" (John 15:5). Andrew sensed that God said to him, "I wanted to show you that if you did not have me, if I did not keep you, you could not pray, believe God, love sinners, or even love me, that you never should become proud when I work through you." Urshan also learned that if nothing much was accomplished in a meeting, he should not think that God had left him. The Lord said to him,

> If you have a little spark of faith and spirit of prayer with longing of worship in your heart, that is a sure sign I am with you. Never get discouraged if there is no revival, only remember that if I was not with you, you could do nothing absolutely. Simply keep on praising, praying, and trusting. Remember I once went to my own people and I could not work no miracles [sic] – so my child, remember that the little spirit of prayer, praise, and faith you would feel in you then is the sign that I have not left you.[75]

Persian Pentecostal Mission

Upon leaving The Moody Chuch in 1909, Urshan relocated the Persian Mission to a hall at 821 North Clark Street.[76] The mission became a center for salvation, healing, and Holy Spirit baptism for people from all over the United States. Persecution arose against those who worshipped at the mission. Meetings frequently continued until after midnight as seekers would tarry until they received the Holy Spirit. Others shouted praises in other tongues. Such behavior caused neighbors to complain. Many thought Urshan had brought this strange religion from Persia.

Urshan was arrested three times and was once fined twenty-five dollars. Once he was asked to close the meetings at 10 p.m. He refused, saying the meeting would continue until people stopped coming to the altar. On another occasion the mission door was forcibly opened as law enforcement officers stormed in on

---

[75]Urshan, "The Story of My Life—11th Chapter: What Happened to Me After the Baptism of the Holy Spirit," *The Witness of God* 4, no. 46 (October 1923): 2-3.

[76]See Urshan, The Life Story, 5th ed., 118-19, 130.

people tarrying for the baptism of the Holy Spirit. As they arrested fifteen seekers, a man began to speak in tongues while lying prostrate on the floor.

Those arrested, representing four nationalities, spent the night in jail. In the morning they began to testify to hundreds who were incarcerated. The jail resounded with prayer and singing. When brought before the judge, they were fined two hundred dollars for each night their meetings had been held after ten p.m.

Urshan took these events as confirmation that their work in that neighborhood was finished. He saw this coming for some time. He conducted the final service at this location on September 18, 1911.[77] He moved the mission to a beautiful church building seating about three hundred people, located next to a headquarters of the Roman Catholic Church.[78]

The opposition did not stop with the move from Clark Street. Prayers of intercession, screams of repenting sinners, and shouts of victory could be heard for a substantial distance. Urshan reported that those who came were "saved and baptized and healed."[79]

The mission sponsored four conventions in this location that were attended by people from various parts of the United States. At the second convention, more than 150 people were baptized with the Holy Spirit. In addition, a number of people were saved and many were healed.[80] The third convention lasted for forty-five days. The people met twice daily for prayer and intercession on behalf of the whole world.

During this third convention, the neighbors drew up petitions designed to expel the Persian Pentecostal Mission as a nuisance. The petitions failed. When they were unsuccessful in ridding the neighborhood of the Pentecostals by this means, they began to throw stones through the heavy plate glass windows, breaking twenty-five and sending chips of broken glass flying among the worshipers. No one was injured.

When Urshan called a fourth convention, inviting leading Spirit-filled brethren to participate, they united in blowing trumpets of praise to God. Within two weeks more than thirty people were baptized with the Holy Spirit. When the crowds became too large for the facility, Urshan moved the convention to the Stone Church, which had a large auditorium.[81] He had learned that the members of the Stone

---

[77]Urshan, "Some of the Lord's Work In Our Midst During the Last Fifteen Months," *Pentecostal Witness of The Grace and Truth* 1, no. 1 (October 1911): 14. Urshan gives the date of the last service on Clark Street only as "Monday night. Sept. 18th." But a Monday night in September fell on the 18th only in 1911 in any year close to this date. The Persian Pentecostal Mission was still on Clark Street on May 25, 1911. (See Urshan, "We Would See Jesus," *The Latter Rain Evangel* [June 1911]: 9.)

[78]In the first edition of his life story, Urshan reported that the new church facility seated four hundred and that it was next door to "the headquarters of the Roman Catholic Church" (Urshan, *The Story of My Life,* 1st ed., 49). In the third edition of Urshan's autobiography as serialized in *The Witness of God,* the seating capacity of this second facility after leaving The Moody Church is revised to three hundred (Urshan, *The Witness of God* [October 1962]: 8). This is retained in the fourth and fifth editions.

[79]Urshan, *The Story of My Life,* 1st ed., 49.

[80]Urshan, *The Story of My Life,* 1st ed., 49.

[81]The Stone Church, first located at 3665 South Indiana Avenue in Chicago, was es-

Church were praying for revival, and he thought it was the will of God for the Persian Pentecostal Mission and the Stone Church to unite for the convention. During the first two weeks of the united effort, more than seventy were baptized with the Holy Spirit, all speaking in tongues as the Spirit gave utterance.[82]

While pastoring the Persian Pentecostal Mission, Urshan came to understand that his primary calling was that of an evangelist. As he told the story, he began to recognize this through the influence of an elderly follower of John Alexander Dowie, a Sister Fox from Shelby, Michigan.[83] On a visit to Urshan's mission, she obtained Urshan's promise that he would hold an evangelistic meeting in Shelby. At the time, Andrew did not know the difference between the office of a pastor and that of an evangelist. Many told him that he was an evangelist, and he sensed that the Lord had said, "I have made thee a threshing machine to thresh my floor."

Learning what it meant to be an evangelist, Urshan came to agree that this was his primary calling. He called Mrs. Fox, telling her to rent a hall and announce his coming. Before leaving, he told the Persian converts, "You will hear one of the two things of me, it will be either a blessed revival or of me being dead in the woods there praying."[84] Urshan then left for Shelby, bringing two female assistants, one a pianist and the other an intecessor, with him.

Mrs. Fox found difficulty securing a hall for Urshan's meetings. She finally located a deep, dank basement under a laundry which had no electricity, chairs, heat, platform, windows, or back door. An unbeliever, troubled by the behavior of the religious community who were actively trying to prevent the services

---

tablished by William Hamner Piper on December 9, 1906. Piper, who had been associated with John Alexander Dowie, had severed his ties with Dowie's Christian Catholic Church. At first, the Stone Church disavowed Pentecostalism, but in less than a year, Piper renewed his commitment to the Pentecostal experience. The Stone Church became a center of Pentecostalism with an influence compared to Topeka, Kansas and Azusa Street in Los Angeles, California. Piper died on December 29, 1911, leaving his wife, Lydia, to pastor the church until 1914. Since Urshan's mission had moved after September 18, 2011 and William Piper died on December 29, 1911, it is uncertain whether Piper or his wife was pastor of the Stone Church when the church cooperated with the Persian Pentecostal Mission for its fourth convention. See E. L. Blumhofer, "Piper, William Hamner," in *NIDPCM*, 989-90; idcag.org/history.cfm; agtv.ag.org/stone-church.

[82]Urshan, *The Story of My Life*, 1st ed., 45-50; Urshan, "Tenth Chapter—Story of My Life," *The Witness of God* 4, no. 44 (August 1923): 5-6; Urshan, *The Story of My Life*, 3rd ed., 86-89; Urshan, *The Witness of God* (October 1962): 7-8; Urshan, *The Life Story*, 5th ed., 130-34; Urshan, "Some of the Lord's Work In Our Midst During the Last Fifteen Months," *Pentecostal Witness of The Grace and Truth* 1, no. 1 (October 1911): 13-14.

[83]John Alexander Dowie (1847-1907), a "forerunner of pentecostalism," proclaimed a radical form of faith healing, founded the religious community of Zion City, Illinois, and established the Christian Catholic Church. See E. L. Blumhofer, "Dowie, John Alexander," in *NIDPCM*, 586-87.

[84]Urshan, *The Story of My Life*, 3rd ed., 101.

from taking place, arranged for a stove, chopped wood, and obtained some old oil lamps. The town undertaker loaned an odd assortment of seventy-five chairs.

When Urshan saw where the meeting would take place, he was quite discouraged. Entering the basement for the first meeting, he knelt in prayer. When he arose, he saw four or five elderly, rough looking men sitting in the back row. Although he didn't feel like singing or preaching, he forced himself. Soon two or three more men entered and sat far back. Andrew tried to preach about the blood of Christ. When finished, he felt more dry and worn out than if he had walked through a desert. He felt like he never wanted to preach again, but he knew he had to do something. He spent part of that night and the next day in prayer. Urshan questioned whether God had sent him to Shelby. However, since he had told the Persian converts in Chicago that he would not return alive if he did not get victory in Shelby, he couldn't return home in defeat.

On the second night, feeling no divine assurance, Urshan went down into the basement again. This time, the previous night's crowd was joined by five or six more people. Andrew was somewhat encouraged.

On the third night, expecting further growth, Urshan was shocked to discover the number even smaller than on the first night. Although tempted not to preach to so many empty seats, Urshan remembered the words "preach the word; be instant in season, out of season."

The fourth night brought new visitors, including young girls, a couple of young men, and a few senior citizens. Mrs. Fox's elderly sister had come to seek baptism in the Holy Spirit. She came to the altar when Urshan extended the invitation. Andrew went into one corner, buried his face in his hands, silently groaning in prayer. About fifteen minutes later he heard a knocking sound behind him on the platform. To his surprise, a girl about fourteen had come to the altar and was shaking under the power of God. Then the Holy Spirit came upon Mrs. Fox's sister, who fell on her back, shaking. Urshan instantly felt like a lion roaring with shouts of praise. He then began speaking in tongues. The young lady fell on her back, stammering. Her sister, not understanding what was happening, went out of the basement screaming, "My sister is dying!" She returned, accompanied by a pharmacist, a policeman, the town president and several young men.

These newcomers gazed in surprise at the spectacle before them: Mrs. Fox's sister, the fourteen year old girl, and Andrew walking about, shouting and speaking in tongues. Smoking a big cigar, the town president said sarcastically, "See here, young man, I advise you to leave town tomorrow if you wish to be out of trouble. Why, you have hypnotized that girl and she will die under that terrible fit!" Someone tried to lift the girl up, but Urshan shouted, "Don't touch her! If you do, God will smite you dead!" Urshan's earnestness frightened them, so they left the girl alone.

Urshan explained, "This girl is under the power of God. This power will not harm her, but will make her the happiest girl in your town. I only wish you would stay and watch till she comes through speaking in new tongues. Then you will see for yourselves how she will shine with joy." They stayed and watched. Soon the girl began to speak in a language unknown to them. She laughed and smiled sweetly while speaking in tongues. Opening her eyes, she saw her sister, leaped up, ran to her, hugged and kissed her, and said, "Oh, this is wonderful. I wish you would get it, sister!" Turning to the others, she said, "Oh, I am so happy. I love Jesus, and he is coming soon."

Mrs. Fox's sister was also baptized with the Holy Spirit. Seeing the joy and love on the faces of these two who had just received the Spirit, and hearing the words of the fourteen year old girl, the onlookers said to Urshan, "Well, we will watch and see the outcome of this thing."

On the fifth night, the basement was crowded. The stairs were filled with people, and many who could not get in stood outside in the cold winter weather, waiting for news of what was going on inside. Urshan preached on the subject of holiness, telling the people that they would be lost if they did not live a holy life. He then declared that they could not live a holy life without the baptism of the Holy Ghost. The people did not want the service to come to an end. The next day local church members arranged with Mrs. Fox for Urshan to preach in the town hall so they could all attend.

Meanwhile, the local preachers, led by the Methodist pastor, met to discuss how they could stop Urshan from preaching in Shelby. They asked a photographer to tell him that his life was in danger if he didn't leave town. Assuring Andrew that he was interested in him, the photographer spoke kindly, but said, "I know that a terrible mob is being formed to beat you to death tonight, though you mean to do us good, but you cannot. And it will be very bad for you if you don't take the first train to Chicago."

Filled with joy at the way the meetings were going, Urshan was unfazed. He thanked the photographer, but said he was prepared to die for his Master. The photographer left, believing Urshan was unafraid of the whole town. However, Urshan was concerned and prayed about this development. The Lord answered his prayer in an unusual way. When he arrived at the town hall the next night he found some of the worst characters in town waiting for him. Instead of attacking him, however, they said that they had learned of the plot and had come to protect him. They volunteered to serve as ushers for the service. The meeting was held without incident. Urshan preached on the "New Birth" to a large crowd and then distributed literature. After the service, many shook his hand with tears in their eyes, saying they were glad to meet him and to hear him preach.

The local religious leaders were not finished with their efforts to stop the meetings, however. A large group of young men, led by the Methodist Sunday school superintendent, shot fire crackers and threw rotten lemons and eggs while whistling as Urshan attempted to hold a street meeting. Andrew and those listening knelt to pray. Even this did not stop the hecklers. Then some stepped forward and said, "This is real religion, and I too want to have part of its persecution." That night, one or two were filled with the Holy Spirit.

The next morning the town leaders gathered to pass a law forbidding the "Persian sect" to hold street meetings. However, Urshan baptized over twenty people in a horse trough, including some prominent members of the Methodist church, during his five week stay in Shelby. He also reported that many were saved and healed.

When the time came for Urshan to return to Chicago, he asked the new believers to come to the train station one hour early for an open air service. A sizable crowd gathered. After leading them in song, Urshan preached on the need for repentance. The same photographer who had warned Urshan earlier was present. He took a picture of the new converts and later sold it to the towns-people on a postcard.[85]

When Urshan returned to Chicago, he was convinced of his calling. He was an evangelist. In addition to acknowledging his true calling, Urshan received three "revelations" during his pastorate at the Persian Pentecostal Mission.[86] The first had to do with divine healing. Urshan became convinced that believers should expect healing as a result of the prayer of faith, without resorting to doctors and medicine.

The second revelation involved eschatology. As a Presbyterian, Urshan had been taught that Christ would return at the end of the millennium. While pastoring the mission, he came to believe that Christ would return soon and usher in the millennium.

The third revelation was that which Urshan characterized as "a crowning truth of all other portions of truth the Lord has so graciously granted" him. He referred to this as "Christ's absolute deity." He found the following words coursing through his being: "The Father, the Son, and the Holy Ghost, the Lord Jesus Christ." Although he had never heard a sermon on the names of God or any discussion on the Godhead in the ranks of Pentecostalism, nor had read church history on this subject, Urshan came to believe that the singular name into which Jesus commanded his disciples to baptize in Matthew 28:19 was "the Lord Jesus Christ." In his understanding, the words "the Lord" stand for "the Father"; the name "Jesus" stands for "the Son"; and "Christ" stands for "the Holy Spirit." He referred to this as "the Trinity in Christ." When he saw the value of baptism "invested in faith in the One Name of the triune God," Urshan came to understand John 3:1-6 as a reference to water birth as water baptism and Spirit birth as the baptism of the Holy Spirit.[87]

Without discounting Urshan's claim to "revelations," it should be noted that he read widely, keeping abreast with theological trends circulating in the holiness, Pentecostal, and fundamentalist milieu of his day. In addition, he was well versed in earlier nineteenth century writings on subjects of interest to him. For example, the articles in The Witness of God represent a variety of theological sources.

---

[85]Urshan, *The Story of My Life,* 3rd ed., 101-07.

[86]By "revelation," Urshan meant what is commonly referred to as illumination. In his words, "By the word 'revelation' . . . we mean 'the Holy Ghost' illuminating our hearts and minds to actually understand certain scriptures . . ." (Urshan, "The Story of My Life—10th Chapter—Cont.," *The Witness of God* 4, no. 45 [September 1923]: 3). We will examine these revelations more thoroughly when we explore Urshan's theology.

[87]Urshan, "The Story of My Life—10th Chapter—Cont.," *The Witness of God* 4, no. 45 (September 1923): 3-4.

These include: Charles Gallaudat Trumbull[88]; A. C. Gaebelein[89]; A. C. Dixon[90]; F. L. Chapell[91]; John Munroe Gibson[92]; Elijah Hedding[93]; W. E. Blackstone[94]; A. B. Simpson[95]; F. F. Bosworth[96]; W. H. Durham[97]; C. I. Scofield[98]; F. H. DuVernet[99]; John Roach Straton[100]; Edwin Noah Hardy[101]; William Phillips Hall[102];

---

[88] Urshan, "Concerning the Name of our Lord," *The Witness of God* 1, no. 4 (March 1920): 7. Trumbull was the editor of the *Sunday School Times*.

[89] A. C. Gaebelein, "The Comfort of Christ's Presence," *The Witness of God* 1, no. 11 (October 1920): 8. Gaebelein was a popular dispensationalist author.

[90] A. C. Dixon, "Power from on High by Prayer," *The Witness of God* 3, no. 30 (June 1922): 7. Dixon was pastor of The Moody Church during Urshan's membership and an early editor of *The Fundamentals*.

[91] F. L. Chapell, "Names of the Deity," *The Witness of God* 4, no. 38 (February 1923): 36; F. L. Chapell, "Names of the Deity," *The Witness of God* 4, no. 39 (March 1923): 6-7; F. L. Chapell, "Names of the Deity," *The Witness of God* 4, no. 40 (April 1923): 4-6; F. L. Chapell, "Names of the Deity," *The Witness of God* 4, no. 41 (May 1923): 7-8; F. L. Chapell, "Names of the Deity," *The Witness of God* 4, no. 42 (June 1923): 7-8. Chapell was an early dispensationalist author.

[92] John Munroe Gibson, "The Trinity in Christ," *The Witness of God* 4, no. 44 (August 1923): 6-7; John Munroe Gibson, "Trinity in Christ," *The Witness of God* 10, no. 108 (August 1929): 16-17. Gibson was a late nineteenth century Presbyterian minister.

[93] Elijah Hedding, "101 Years Old Discourse on the Supreme Divinity of Christ," *The Witness of God* 5, no. 50 (February 1924): 4-8; Elijah Hedding, "101 Years Old Discourse on the Supreme Divinity of Christ," *The Witness of God* 5, no. 51 (March 1924): 6-7. Hedding was an early nineteenth century bishop of the Methodist Episcopal Church.

[94] W. E. Blackstone, "The Literal Coming of the Lord from Heaven," *The Witness of God* 6, no. 64 (May 1925): 4. Blackstone was a late nineteenth and early twentieth century author who believed in the rapture of the church before the Great Tribulation and in the premillennial return of Jesus to the earth.

[95] A. B. Simpson, "The Power of Stillness," *The Witness of God* 7, no. 65 (June and July 1925): 8; A. B. Simpson, "Thankfulness for Healing," *The Witness of God* 11, no. 8 (September 1930): 11-12. A. B. Simpson was the founder of the Christian and Missionary Alliance.

[96] F. F. Bosworth, "Triumphant Faith," *The Witness of God* 7, no. 68 (October 1925): 4-5. Bosworth, who withdrew from membership in the Assemblies of God because he did not agree that baptism with the Holy Spirit is always accompanied by speaking with tongues, was a well-known healing evangelist.

[97] W. H. Durham, "Salvation in Christ for All," *The Witness of God* 8, no. 71 (January 1926): 9-10. Durham, pastor of the North Avenue Mission in Chicago, proclaimed the "Finished Work" teaching.

[98] C. I. Scofield, "The Loveliness of Christ," *The Witness of God* 10, no. 89 (November 1927): 1, 12. Scofield was the editor of the *Scofield Reference Bible*, which was used by many early twentieth century Pentecostals, both Trinitarian and Oneness. The Bible popularized dispensationalism.

[99] F. H. DuVernet, "Real Religion," *The Witness of God* (May 1928): 13. DuVernet was an archbishop in the Church of England in Canada.

[100] John Roach Straton, "Some Statements Concerning the Deity," *The Witness of God* 10, no. 96 (August 1928): 13-14. Straton was a Baptist fundamentalist.

[101] Edwin Noah Hardy, "A Remarkable Biblical Discovery," *The Witness of God* 10, no. 105 (May 1929): 6. Hardy was the secretary of the American Tract Society.

[102] William Phillips Hall, "A Remarkable Biblical Discovery on the Apostolic Christian

Mark A. Matthews[103]; Mary L. Houghton[104]; Edward J. Higgins[105]; J. C. Ryle[106]; and Bob Jones.[107]

Toward the end of his pastoral relationship with the Persian Pentecostal Mission, Urshan attended the Apostolic Faith World-Wide Camp Meeting held in Arroyo Seco, located between Los Angeles and Pasadena, California. The camp meeting ran from April 15, 1913 to the end of May. Although Urshan did not mention it in his autobiography, it was at this camp meeting where the revelation of the Divine Name was first brought to the attention of the Pentecostal Movement.[108]

Arroyo Seco Campmeeting

Urshan went to the Arroyo Seco camp meeting with the feeling that the Lord had something in store for him that would be revealed during that time. He had visited Los Angeles earlier and enjoyed renewing old acquaintances as well as meeting hundreds of new people. Thousands gathered from the United States and Canada for the camp meeting.[109]

Shortly after Urshan's arrival, the chairman and secretary of the camp meeting asked him to sit on the front row of the platform with seventy of the leading ministers of the Pentecostal movement.[110] In Urshan's words, "I almost shrank to sit on the front and wished a back seat, but the brethren insisted that I sit in the front with the foremost brethren in the

---

Baptism," *The Witness of God* 10, no. 108 (August 1929): 5-8. Hall served as the president of The American Bible League.

[103]Mark A. Matthews, "Childlessness, the Nation's Curse," *The Witness of God* 11, no. 1 (January 1930): 4-5. Matthews was a Presbyterian minister. This article was first published in the *Moody Monthly*.

[104]Mary L. Houghton, "Satan's Strategy," *The Witness of God* 11, no. 1 (January 1930): 6-7. Houghton was a graduate of Wellesley College. This article was first published in the *Moody Monthly*.

[105]Edward J. Higgins, "Jesus!" *The Witness of God* 11, no. 1 (January 1930): 8-10. Higgins was the general of the Salvation Army. This article was first published in the *War Cry*.

[106]J. C. Ryle, "Is There a Hell?" *The Witness of God* 11, no. 3 (March and April 1930): 6-7. Ryle was a prolific author and minister in the Church of England.

[107]Bob Jones, "The Modern Atheism and Our Schools," *The Witness of God* (November 1931): 3-5. Jones was the founder of Bob Jones University.

[108]Cecil M. Robeck, Jr., *The Azusa Street Mission and Revival* (Nashville, TN: Thomas Nelson, Inc., 2006), 317.

[109]Urshan put the number of attendees at 3,000. (Urshan, *The Story of My Life*, 1st ed., 53.) Local news media were more conservative, setting attendance at 2,000. (Robeck, *The Azusa Street Mission*, 317.) Maria Woodworth-Etter (1844-1924), a well known and successful Holiness preacher from the nineteenth century, was the evening evangelist for the camp meeting. From about 1885, Woodworth-Etter had emphasized faith healing and gifts of the Spirit in protracted meetings throughout the Midwest, drawing thousands. She was "probably the best-known Holiness preacher to embrace Pentecostalism" (W. E. Warner, "Woodworth-Etter, Maria Beulah," in *NIDPCM*, 1211-13.

[110]In his explanation that William J. Seymour received no special invitation to the camp meeting, nor was he seated on the platform, Robeck says, "Those leading the movement around the country and in Canada now received pride of place"(Robeck,*The Azusa Street Mission*, 318).

movement."¹¹¹ Those in charge of the camp meeting also asked Urshan to preach to the crowds under the big tents.¹¹²

It was at this camp meeting that Urshan was ordained. "I was legally ordained to be a Gospel minister all the days of my life," he wrote, "having been ordained a few years previous to this time by the Lord Himself."¹¹³ It was also at this camp meeting that Urshan sensed the Lord saying to him, "Go to Persia."¹¹⁴

Returning to Persia had been at the back of Urshan's mind when he left Chicago for the Arroyo Seco camp meeting. In an article written before he left Chicago for Arroyo Seco, he stated, "I am leaving tomorrow for Los Angeles to attend the Campmeeting there. I wish you would pray that God will send many missionaries out from that Campmeeting to all the world. I hope He will send me to Persia from there."¹¹⁵ Seeking to establish that this desire was a call from the Lord, he asked for three confirmations. The first came in the form of two dreams. Urshan experienced a dream showing the sufferings which awaited him in Persia.

> One night in a dream I saw myself in a long tunnel of miry clay. While trudging through the thick mud and wondering when I would ever reach the end, I seemed suddenly confronted with bears and wolves; and all these wild animals were running after me so that I could not see how I would escape the horrible peril without the loss of my life; but there was a hope in me, and running, I went through the wild beasts confronting me and I came out of the tunnel. I did not know just how it was that the excited animals did not catch me to destroy my life. Then I praised the

---

¹¹¹Urshan, "The Story of My Life—13th Chapter," *The Witness of God* 4, no. 48 (December 1923): 3-4.

¹¹²See Frank J. Ewart, *The Phenomenon of Pentecost*, rev. ed. (Hazelwood, MO: Word Aflame Press, 2000), 92-94.

¹¹³Urshan, *The Story of My Life*, 1st ed., 53. There is some confusion about Urshan's ordination. Arthur L. Clanton, when editor in chief of the United Pentecostal Church, Inc., said that Urshan was ordained in 1910 by William Durham. (See Arthur L. Clanton, *United We Stand*, [Hazelwood, MO: Pentecostal Publishing House, 1970], 190.) Clanton offers no documentation for this claim. Urshan's application for ordination with the Assemblies of God in 1917 mentions his ordination by "Rescue Mission Workers of America (Pentecostal)." (See Graham, *Conservative American Protestantism*, 44, n. 1.) Robin Johnston, editor in chief of the United Pentecostal Church International, Inc., points out that this ordination would be with a group in Chicago (personal telephone conversation on April 24, 2009). But as Graham says, "It is rather strange that Urshan mentions neither Durham, nor his ordination by Durham in 1910 in any of his writings" (Graham, *Conservative American Protestantism*, 44, n. 1). One would expect some mention of Urshan's ordination by Durham, a significant figure in early twentieth century North American Pentecostalism, in Urshan's autobiography. See https://ifphc.wordpress.com/ tag/andrew-d-urshan/.

¹¹⁴Urshan, *The Story of My Life, 1st ed.*, 52. In the second edition of his life story, Urshan expands on his call: "It was then and there the Lord sweetly whispered in my heart asking me to go back to Persia and begin my journey right from Los Angeles to Persia via U.S., Canada, England, Holland and Russia. . . . Go to your own people and proclaim this apostolic Gospel" (Urshan, "The Story of My Life—13th Chapter," *The Witness of God* 4, no. 48 [December 1923]: 2).

¹¹⁵Urshan, "Our Responsibilities and Privileges," *The Latter Rain Evangel* (May 1913): 5. This article is dated April 20, 1913.

Lord that He confused the beasts and graciously delivered me from the miry clay and dark tunnel and death.[116]

In a second, the Holy Spirit said, "Suppose the Persians bring crazy people to you and say, 'Since you claim to have power to cast out demons, here is your opportunity': in such a case what would you do? And if drunkards are brought into your presence and you are challenged to exorcise demon powers, what will you do?"[117]

The second confirmation came as others, knowing nothing of Urshan's call to Persia or of his dreams, came to him saying things like, "Oh, Brother Urshan. I had some fearful dreams about you; you may finish your course as a martyr. Oh! How I am burdened for you and am praying God to give you grace and strength to enable you to go through the awful things which are awaiting your path of life."[118]

The third confirmation he asked was for God to provide his traveling expenses without him asking people for money. In response, he felt the Lord request him to ask eighteen people to intercede for him in prayer day and night. During his evangelistic efforts in the United States and Canada before departing for Persia, Urshan obtained these prayer partners. He also received sufficient funds for his travels. Upon arrival, he had $500 in reserve. Andrew used this money to print more than 5,000 booklets on true Christianity and the baptism of the Holy Spirit. He distributed these free of charge.[119]

Before leaving Los Angeles, however, Urshan was invited by a Mother Norton to rest for awhile in her cottage in Long Beach, California. Mother Norton and her husband had spent their lives in home and foreign missions. When her husband became deathly ill on the grounds of the Arroyo Seco camp meeting, he asked Andrew to officiate at his funeral. Urshan had become like a son to them, so Mother Norton took comfort from his fellowship after her husband's funeral.

One day Urshan became ill suddenly as he traveled by streetcar with Mother Norton back to her home in Long Beach. By the time they reached her home, Urshan felt so weak, he went to bed immediately, unable to eat the meal Mother Norton's sister had prepared for them. He felt like he was going to die. He asked Mother Norton to pray for him. While they were on their knees in prayer, he saw in a vision a Baptist church building.

When they finished praying, Urshan described to Mrs. Norton the church he had seen in his vision and asked if there were a Baptist church like that. She told him that she had just been wishing that Andrew were not so tired so she could take him to this Baptist church which she had often attended. Andrew said, "It must be of the Lord for us to go there or else I wouldn't have the vision." Mrs. Norton responded, "But this is Thursday, and I doubt if they have any meeting there." Urshan answered, "Let us go see the building anyhow." As soon as they decided

---

[116]Urshan, *The Story of My Life,* 1st ed., 52-53.

[117]Urshan, *The Story of My Life,* 1st ed., 53.

[118]Urshan, "The Story of My Life—13th Chapter," *The Witness of God* 4, no. 48 (December 1923): 4.

[119]Urshan, "The Story of My Life—13th Chapter," *The Witness of God* 4, no. 48 (December 1923): 4.

to go, the sickness left Urshan, his appetite returned, and he enjoyed the meal that had been prepared for him.

When they arrived at the church, a business meeting was in session. An usher found two front seats for Mrs. Norton and Urshan. Mrs. Norton urged Urshan to get up, but he didn't know what to say. He prayed silently, and just before the benediction Andrew stood and said, "Chairman, I have come way from Persia to you in this meeting, to tell you of what the Lord has done to me." As the chairman looked at him in surprise and the people looked toward him, he continued,

> I am real Baptist, for a real Baptist must not only be baptized in water, but also with the Holy Spirit. The first Baptist in the history of the world was "John the Baptist," and we know not if John really was ever baptized in water himself, but we know for sure that he was filled with the Holy Ghost while in his mother's womb. . . . no one is a full pledged Baptist unless he is really filled with the Holy Ghost.[120]

Many of the people approached Andrew with tears in their eyes, to shake his hand and to ask where he preached. Mrs. Norton said, "He is here to rest and not to preach." The people insisted, however, that they wanted to hear him, so Urshan said to Mrs. Norton, "Let them come to your house tomorrow night."

The next night, twenty-nine of these people came to Mrs. Norton's house. Urshan said, "Friends, if you knew to what class of people I belong, you wouldn't have come here. I am one of those hated tongues people, and I speak with tongues myself, though I did not say so last night." The people responded, "We want to hear you and want to have the same Spirit you received, tongues or no tongues." Among those attending was the superintendent of the city rescue mission, who had physically thrown some Pentecostal people from his mission.

Urshan spoke for more than two hours to this assembly. The next day a few of them returned to tarry for the baptism of the Holy Spirit. Urshan was invited to preach in the rescue mission, where several people received the Holy Spirit with the sign of speaking in tongues. The rescue mission was fully transformed into a Pentecostal mission.[121]

Leaving Long Beach, Urshan ministered in Los Angeles, San Francisco, Oakland, Portland, Winnipeg, St. Paul, and Chicago. In Chicago, Urshan said farewell to nearly 1,000 people gathered in the Stone Church. His closest friends went with him to the Dearborn Station, where they sang and prayed together until the break of day. From Chicago Urshan took a preaching tour to Cleveland, Detroit, Philadelphia, and finally to New York City, where he boarded the Lusitania at Ellis Island for the six day voyage to Liverpool.[122]

When Urshan reached England, he was welcomed by Mrs. Margaret Cantel, whose rest house of faith and prayer was located at 73 Highbury, New Park, Lon-

---

[120]Urshan, *The Story of My Life*, 3rd ed., 114.

[121]Urshan, *The Story of My Life*, 3rd ed., 113-14. The story of Urshan's visit to Mrs. Norton's home appears for the first time in the third edition of his life story.

[122]In the third edition of his life story, Urshan dates his departure for Persia as March 14, 1914. (See Urshan, *The Story of My Life*, 3rd ed., 122.) But he dates his arrival in his home village of Abajalu, Urmia, Persia as March 1, 1914. (See Urshan, *The Story of My Life*, 3rd

don. Here he met people from the largest Pentecostal church in London. Urshan next visited South Wales, the site of the Welsh Revival that began in 1904. The Holy Spirit was poured out during Urshan's visit in South Wales, with some receiving salvation and the baptism of the Holy Spirit.[123] From there he traveled to Amsterdam, Holland where he preached at the invitation of Pastor George R. Polman. He then journeyed through Germany, Russia, and Caucasia on his way to Persia, arriving at his home of Abajaloo, Urmia on March 1, 1914.[124]

Summary

When Urshan arrived at Ellis Island in 1901 as a youth of seventeen years, he brought with him a certain theological and social naivety. Although his social naivety was severely challenged by his experiences during his passage to America, it was further eroded by his treatment as a novice worker in a New York hat factory.

Like many young men who find themselves as strangers in a strange land, Urshan drifted from his spiritual moorings in the Presbyterian Church. But a series of circumstances led him on a spiritual and theological journey that included water baptism in an American Brethren church, sanctification in a Nazarene mission, and Holy Spirit baptism after his exposure to Pentecostalism. Along the way he made the painful decision to embrace the Pentecostal perspective on speaking with tongues even though it cost him his membership in The Moody Church.

Urshan's baptism by immersion in an American Brethren church resulted from his study of Scripture in an attempt to prove his cousin wrong. When he saw no scriptural defense for his belief that baptism was accomplished by sprinkling, he was willing to admit his error and ask for baptism by his cousin. This established a trajectory that Urshan followed throughout his life: When confronted by new ideas, he studied Scripture prayerfully until he came to a conclusion, which he then followed regardless of the consequences.

His sanctification in a Nazarene church introduced Urshan to an entirely new dimension of Christianity, the experiential. Although he had experienced a profound change at his conversion at the American Presbyterian Training College in Persia, he had never previously encountered such a thorough spiritual, emotional, mental, and physical experience as at the Nazarene altar. Throughout his life from that point, Urshan's life and ministry were characterized by this kind of experience.

Although Urshan resigned from membership in The Moody Church, he continued to value the acquaintances he had made there and what he had learned there under the ministry of A. C. Dixon. He couldn't agree with Dixon's rejection of speaking with tongues, but that didn't mean he rejected all of Dixon's views.

---

ed., 116.) The same date is given for his arrival in Urshan, *The Story of My Life,* 1st ed., 54.

[123] Urshan, *The Story of My Life,* 1st ed., 54.

[124] Urshan, *The Story of My Life,* 1st ed., 52-55; Urshan, "The Story of My Life—14th Chapter," *The Witness of God* 5, no. 49 (January 1924): 4-5; Urshan, *The Story of My Life,* 3rd ed., 113-16; Urshan, "A Strange Experience in Long Beach, California," *The Witness of God* (December 1962): 2-4; Urshan, *The Life Story,* 5th ed., 152-67.

Much of Urshan's theology, especially his understanding of eschatology and his abhorrence of Spiritualism, Christian Science, Russellism, and higher criticism, reflect Dixon's ongoing influence.

While serving as pastor of the Persian Pentecostal Mission in Chicago, Urshan began to sense a desire to return to Persia in order to proclaim the Pentecostal message in his homeland. This desire was confirmed by an experience during the World-Wide Camp Meeting of 1913 at Arroyo Seco near Los Angeles. Shortly after his arrival in his home village, Urshan found himself facing not only the skepticism of the people he knew and loved, but also political upheaval that would cost the lives of thousands and propel him from Persia to Russia.

Chapter Four

Return to Persia

Introduction

Urshan's ministry in Persia saw significant spiritual success in the midst of indescribable horror. Beginning in Ada, a town near his home village of Abajalu, and continuing in Abajalu, Karajalu, Shirabad, and Geogtapa, Urshan preached the gospel, consistently seeing his hearers baptized with the Holy Spirit. But the Armenian Genocide which began while Urshan was in Geogtapa would result in the death of 1,500,000 ethnic Armenians in addition to other ethnic minorities. Several who were associated with Urshan paid the price of martyrdom for their faith.

When the violence reached the point that nearly all the Armenians fled from northwest Persia, Urshan made his way to Russia, where he ministered in Tiflis, Armavir, and Leningrad. It was in Leningrad that he first rebaptized Christians in the name of the Lord Jesus Christ. He was also rebaptized there.

Following his successful ministry in Russia, Urshan returned to the United States via Norway and England, arriving in New York on June 25, 1916.[1]

Urshan's experiences in Persia and Russia could be described as a laboratory for his faith. Here his theories were tested and new insights were gained. His commitment to Pentecostal distinctives, including distinctives of Oneness Pentecostalism, was strengthened, and his sensitivity to the leading of the Spirit was heightened.

Ministry in Persia

When Urshan arrived at his home in Persia, he faced false reports about his activities and spiritual experiences in the United States. Rumor had it that the Persian boys whom Urshan had been instrumental in converting were becoming insane. Their parents were told that these boys went about shaking their heads and would no longer work. When they did work they gave all their money to Urshan. They had also heard that their sons would lie in the snow all night near Lake Michigan, nearly becoming ill with pneumonia. Urshan's father believed these reports. He

---

[1]This date corresponds with Urshan's description of his departure from Liverpool on June 18, 1916 for a journey of seven days (in the fifth edition of his life story) and the ship's manifest signed by Urshan at Ellis Island upon his arrival.

had written Andrew to express his feelings about his son being so weak and thin that he constantly shook and was unable to work.

Another rumor had been started by a young Persian who had returned home after becoming ill in the United States. Although Andrew and his brother Timothy loved this young man, prayed for his healing, and used their own funds to help him return home,[2] he claimed that he had never been sick and that Urshan had taken him throughout America collecting money, pretending it was for this Persian youth, but kept it for himself. The boy's father, a noted Persian preacher, believed his son. Between the two of them, they had convinced almost everyone that Urshan was the worst man who had ever walked on earth.

Urshan was unable to minister for two months after his arrival because of these rumors. He was treated as if he had murdered someone. Even some of his closest friends would only peek at him from behind walls. His parents and other friends warned him to be careful about what he said and did. Once some of his friends came to his house and attempted to break Satan's power by having a meeting on a corner outside Urshan's home. At their insistence, Andrew went out, stood with them, and sang a song.

Urshan wrote to believers in the United States about his reception in Abajalu:

> We had opportunities to testify of God's grace in our past life in the U.S.A., but surprisingly I found them very careless concerning these good things. Only their great anxiety is to know if I had plenty of money and if I had brought presents from America.
>
> With sorrow I am to say that they seem to be Gospel-hardened folks and satisfied with their dead faith in Christ. Their imaginations are very strange concerning our ministry . . . . because of the abundance of their opinions they have invented some false reports among people to hinder us.[3]

During the two months that Andrew was unable to minister, he spent his time resting, praying, and writing. Opportunities for ministry began to open up, however, due to an event at a Plymouth Brethren chapel in the village of Ada.[4]

---

[2]In the first and second editions of his life story, Urshan reports that he and his brother Timothy spent $150.00 to return this young man to Persia. (See Urshan, *The Story of My Life*, 1st ed., 62; Urshan, "The Story of My Life—15th Chapter," *The Witness of God* 5, no. 51 [March 1924]: 4). In the third edition this is revised to $50. (See Urshan, *The Story of My Life*, 3rd ed., 122.) In the third edition as serialized in *The Witness of God*, it is further revised to "we spent our own money to send him back home to Persia" (Urshan, *The Witness of God* [December 1962]: 6). This reading is retained in the fifth edition.

[3]Andrew D. Urshan, "Andrew D. Urshan Arrives in Persia," *The Christian Evangel* (n.d.): 6.

[4]There are many variants between Urshan's spelling of Persian place names and the spelling in current use. This study will use the current spellings although noting Urshan's variants. The village Urshan refers to as "Adda" is currently spelled "Ada." Urshan spells with phonetic transliterations.

Ada

In the Assyrian village of Ada, located southeast of Abajalu[5] across the Nazli River, a small group of men and women were praying one evening when one of their leaders, a man named Andrew, began to shout in a way that was strange to them. His behavior disturbed the rest of the group, reminding them of what they had heard about Urshan's ministry. A local school teacher told Andrew to share his experience with Urshan, with whom he was slightly acquainted.

At about six o'clock one Sunday morning, Urshan was awakened by someone kissing him on the cheeks. Opening his eyes in surprise, he saw Andrew smiling at him.[6] Urshan asked, "What are you doing here at this time of day?"[7] Andrew answered, "Get up, I want to tell you something. We were praying last night, and the Spirit moved upon us. Such power came upon me, that I was almost beside myself. I have come to you, to ask you if this is the baptism of the Holy Ghost, as you teach."[8]

Urshan viewed this event as a miracle and as a sign from God that the spiritual drought which had prevailed in Persia for so long was at last over. He believed that this was a message from God that he was to rise up, get busy, and go forward in the name of the Lord.

Urshan's early morning visitor wanted to go immediately to a mud hut in the vineyard where they could pray together for him to be baptized with the Holy Spirit. Urshan suggested they have breakfast first, but Andrew would not hear of it. When they reached the hut, Andrew prayed fervently, but Urshan was not quite sure what to say. He did not think Andrew was ready to be baptized with the Spirit, so he just praised God. Suddenly, however, Andrew began to shake so powerfully that he nearly shook the hut. He began to speak fluently in tongues, turning to the north, south, east, and west.[9]

Jeremiah Eshoo, who lived about three miles from Abajalu, had returned to Persia after having been converted and baptized with the Spirit under Urshan's ministry in the United States. Since his return, he had been praying for God to pour out His Spirit in Persia. Urshan knew he would be glad to hear of what had happened to Andrew. They set out for Eshoo's home. Upon arrival, they found Jeremiah praying in the fields. Seeing him in the distance, Urshan raised his hands

---

[5]Abajalu is spelled by Urshan as "Abajaloo."

[6]Beginning with the first edition of his life story and continuing through the third edition, Urshan said that this occurred on June 10, 1915, Pentecost Sunday according to the Eastern Christian tradition. (See Urshan, *The Story of My Life,* 1st ed., 64; Urshan, "The Story of My Life—15th Chapter," *The Witness of God* 5, no. 51 [March 1924]: 5; Urshan, *The Story of My Life,* 3rd ed., 123.) In the later editions of his life story the precise date is no longer identified, nor is it connected with Pentecost Sunday. Instead, the time is said to be "one Sunday morning." (See Urshan, *The Witness of God* [December 1962]: 6; Urshan, *The Life Story,* 5th ed., 176.) This leaves us to wonder why the date was first identified as Pentecost Sunday.

[7]Urshan, *The Life Story,* 5th ed., 176.
[8]Urshan, *The Life Story,* 5th ed., 176-77.
[9]Urshan, *The Life Story,* 5th ed., 177.

and Jeremiah raised his in response. Then Andrew began running toward Jeremiah, speaking with tongues. When Jeremiah heard this, he fell on his knees, stretching his hands toward heaven. As far as Urshan knew, Jeremiah and Andrew were the only Spirit-filled people in Persia at that moment. Soon afterward, Jeremiah's brother, Abraham, who had once been Spirit-filled, but whose spiritual fervor had cooled, heard of Andrew's experience. When he did, his spiritual hunger was renewed and he was spiritually revived.

All four returned to Urshan's home in Abajalu. As they entered the house Urshan's father met them, asking, "Son, did Brother Andrew receive the baptism of the Holy Ghost?" Urshan's mother and brothers came into the parlor to look at Andrew, whose lips trembled and who from time to time spoke in tongues.

A wealthy man of the village who knew Andrew entered the house. He had not heard of Andrew's spiritual experience and was unprepared for what he found. Greeting the family, he recognized that something mysterious was happening. Stretching his hand toward his friend, Andrew asked, "Why will you remain in sin? When are you going to repent?" Startled and confused, the visitor left quickly. Once in the street, he told the people of the village what he had seen, heard, and felt. Although he was not converted, he warned the village elders not to speak lightly of Urshan and told them that Urshan had great power with God.[10]

Urshan had promised Andrew that if he were baptized with the Holy Spirit he would accompany him back to his village that evening. As they walked through a heavy rain, Urshan felt that God spoke to him promising spiritual rain. Urshan responded in faith. The rain stopped. The two of them entered the village of Ada in brilliant sunlight. The word of Andrew's experience had preceded them. Minutes after they entered his home, it was filled with women. Neighbors filled the yard. Looking from Urshan to Andrew, the women whispered, "That's the fellow that makes people faint. See, he has made Andrew to become like him. Why does Andrew shake? Did Urshan really give him that power that he has?" They would drop their eyes when Urshan looked at them, but when he looked away, they renewed their stares.

Sensing the excited awe of the people, Urshan asked why they had come. Before they could answer, Andrew began speaking with tongues. Taking Urshan's New Testament, he opened it at John 3. With a shining face and stammering lips, Andrew read the story of Nicodemus. He then handed the Bible back to Urshan, who began to preach about the new birth, asking, "What is the new birth? How do we know that we are born again?"[11]

Urshan spoke and sang Psalm 51 in a minor key, weeping as he sang. His listeners responded with "[t]errible screams" and "cries of conviction and confession."[12] When Urshan later recalled this event, He wrote, "I do not remember how many were under conviction, but about six got saved with a thorough and square salvation. . . . The power fell on those that were saved, and they began to shake."[13]

---

[10] Urshan, *The Life Story*, 5th ed., 178-80.
[11] Urshan, *The Story of My Life*, 1st ed., 68.
[12] Urshan, *The Life Story*, 5th ed., 182.
[13] Urshan, *The Story of My Life*, 1st ed., 69.

This Pentecostal beachhead resulted in severe persecution from "religious men" and government officials. Among other things, one of the new female converts was shot to death. The lives of all of those who embraced Urshan's message were in danger as they were threatened with death. In spite of the persecution, Urshan reported that "[a]bout fifty were saved and received the baptism of the Holy Ghost there."[14]

When political upheaval with its attendant violence reached northwest Persia shortly thereafter, Urshan understood the bloodshed in Ada as recompense for the persecution endured by the believers in that village.

> Later, when the massacres came, the town of Adda suffered frightfully. Indeed, to a greater extent than other Christian villages; the Kurds murdered their young men and insulted their young women, and destroyed their homes in a wholesale-like slaughter. "Whatsoever a man soweth, that shall he also reap." Some of the people of Adda had shed the innocent blood of that young convert, and as a result, their blood was shed, in a hundred-fold reaping![15]

Abajalu

Urshan returned to his home village after the outbreak of the Pentecostal experience in Ada. He invited the people from Ada who had been baptized with the Holy Spirit to join him. He met the new believers on the outskirts of Abajalu where they "had a glorious time shaking hands and talking in tongues."[16] Urshan then took them to his home where they sang and prayed for Abajalu, "capturing it, by faith, for God,"[17] and shared a meal prepared by Urshan's mother. Then began a meeting where the same phenomena occurred that had happened in Ada. Urshan reported:

> The wife of our Brother Abraham shook, and called on the Lord. She got saved and baptized with the Holy Ghost.... Brother Jeremiah's niece got saved and baptized also.... My brother Joseph and some other children went out to pray in the fields, and he got his baptism. Others were saved also with him.... we were there a few weeks. About thirty were saved, and about twenty-five received their baptism, one of whom was my precious mother.[18]

---

[14]Urshan, *The Story of My Life*, 1st ed., 70.

[15]Urshan, *The Life Story*, 5th ed., 184. The massacres to which Urshan referred were carried out under the authority of the Ottoman Empire during its waning days, from 1915-1923. The first incursion into northwest Persia occurred on January 8, 1915. On this day Turkish and Kurdish gangs attacked Armenian and Assyrian villages, remaining around the cities of Tabriz and Urmia until January 29. More than 18,000 Armenians, Assyrians, and Muslims fled to Caucasus from Urmia alone. Resolutions under consideration in the United States House of Representatives and Senate at the date of this writing claim that 1,500,000 Armenian men, women, and children were killed and another 500,000 survivors expelled from their homes during these days of violence.

[16]Urshan, *The Story of My Life*, 1st ed., 70.

[17]Urshan, *The Story of My Life*, 1st ed., 71.

[18]Urshan, *The Story of My Life*, 1st ed., 71. In the second edition of his life story Urshan revised the phrase "[s]he got saved and baptized with the Holy Ghost" to read "[s]he got

Karajalu

In Karajalu, where Urshan's brothers Jeremiah and Abraham lived, religious leaders threatened Urshan with death if he entered the town. After drawing a circle on the ground, Jeremiah figuratively bound his brother's opponents in it by saying, "You shall not move from here until the church of God is established in my town."[19] As Urshan approached the town, singing, "There's a Highway, Blessed Way," those who were opposed to him readied themselves with clubs for his arrival. Someone warned Urshan that he should be careful and go into a house rather than remaining in the streets. He answered, "I will die here" and continued to sing.[20]

So many of the villagers came to hear Urshan that the street was too small to accommodate the crowd. They moved to a hayfield. As the people sang and Urshan preached, his opponents stood afar off. Then "[t]he power of God fell upon Jeremiah's wife, and she got saved." Urshan reported that in the matter of three or four weeks "about forty got their baptism, and I do not know how many got saved in this third village."[21]

While Urshan was in Karajalu he learned that a mob following religious leaders sought him. Screams rang from the homes and throughout the streets. He hurried into a home of those who embraced his ministry. They locked the doors and bolted the windows. As the mob approached the house, they beat on the door. Confusion arose among them. As a result they began to curse and fight each other. Finally they scattered in several directions. Those in the house with Urshan had said, "They will have to kill us, before they touch you!" He had answered, "Don't be frightened, you will see what the Lord will do."[22]

When Urshan's life was threatened, the women who responded to his preaching often circled him on their knees and threatened to kill themselves if he were harmed. Frequently, they would also pull down their hair in an attempt to appeal to those who would harm him.[23] Urshan explained the significance of this act:

> In the eastern countries, where ancient customs are still observed, this is a sign of utter desperation . . . as their hair is kept bound together and usually covered from

---

converted and baptized with the Holy Ghost." The phrase "[a]bout thirty were saved" was revised to read "[a]bout thirty were wonderfully converted" (Urshan, "The Story of My Life—17th Chapter," *The Witness of God*, 5, no. 52 [April 1924]: 3). Further revision is seen in the third edition. The phrase "Brother Jeremiah's niece got saved and baptized also" became "Brother Jeremiah's niece got blest also." The phrase that originally read "[a]bout thirty were saved" was revised to read "[a]bout thirty were wonderfully blest" (Urshan, *The Story of My Life*, 3rd ed., 129. A fourth level of revision is seen in the third edition as serialized in *The Witness of God*. The phrase that originally read "[s]he got saved" now read "[s]he got blessed" (Urshan, "Revival at First Town 'Adda' in Iran Continues from Last Issue," *The Witness of God* [January 1963]: 2.

[19] Urshan, *The Story of My Life*, 1st ed., 71.
[20] Urshan, *The Story of My Life*, 1st ed., 71.
[21] Urshan, *The Story of My Life*, 1st ed., 72.
[22] Urshan, *The Life Story*, 5th ed., 186.
[23] Urshan, *The Story of My Life*, 1st ed., 72.

sight; so the men know when a woman exposes her hair in such a manner, it must be a matter of life and death . . . . Therefore this act always touches the heart . . . and they begin to stop their deeds.[24]

Shirabad[25]

To this point, Urshan's ministry had been received in Ada, southwest of his home village of Abajalu and across the Nazli River, in Abajalu, and in Karajalu, on the same side of the Nazli and much closer to Abajalu but still southwest. Now, his ministry would move to the village of Shirabad, almost directly north of Abajalu.[26]

The wife of Abraham, Urshan's brother, had been baptized with the Holy Spirit. Under her influence, the daughter of a Protestant minister in Shirabad was also baptized with the Spirit. This woman was a school teacher, making it possible for Urshan to hold meetings primarily for young women and to start a school for young girls. In connection with this, "God saved and baptized about twenty-five young girls and two young men."[27]

Threatened with Prison

Urshan's ministry created such a stir that some priests of the Greek Catholic Church presented a petition to the government requesting that he be sent back to America. Urshan and three of those who followed his ministry were called before the governor, who sentenced them to prison. The Muslim chief of police treated Urshan and those with him with kindness, serving them tea in "a beautiful parlor among his guests." In their discussion of Urshan's situation, the Muslims said to one another, "Do you know why this minister Urshan is here? He says to the people that they should not get drunk, and that is why they imprisoned him."[28]

Patting Urshan on the shoulder, the Muslims said, "You are alright, we will treat you well."[29] The four men were kept one night. The next day a telegram arrived from the American consul asking if there were a legitimate reason to imprison Urshan. Immediately Urshan was told he was free to go, but he refused to leave unless his three friends could go with him. All four were released.

---

[24]Urshan, "Revival at first Town 'Adda' in Iran Continues from Last Issue," *The Witness of God* [January 1963]: 2.
[25]Urshan spells the name of this village "Shirrabad."
[26]Assyrian International News Agency, Assyrian Maps, "115 Assyrian Villages in Urmia, Iran," http://www.aina.org/maps/urmiamap50p.htm (accessed March 2, 2010). These were four of the 115 Assyrian villages located in the region of Urmia in northwest Persia.
[27]Urshan, *The Story of My Life,* 1st ed., 72.
[28]Urshan, *The Life Story,* 5th ed., 188.
[29]Urshan, *The Life Story,* 5th ed., 188.

A Vision of War

Before he went to his next arena of ministry, the village of Geogtapa,[30] "[t]he Lord clearly showed [Urshan] that a horrible judgment, something like a massacre,"[31] would come upon Persia. He spoke publically about "the coming judgment." The Russian authorities were told that he was prophesying that they would be defeated by the Germans and Turks, implying that he was a German spy.[32] In addition, he predicted that many Persians would be killed. His warnings were ignored by most of the leaders. Since Urshan was a citizen of the United States of America, he considered returning to America to escape death. Dr. William Shedd, an American Presbyterian missionary who helped the American consul in Tabriz, signed Urshan's passport to enable him to obtain passage to the Russian frontier.[33] But as Urshan walked away, he heard a "still small voice" warning him of the dangers of being a "hireling." Shocked at this "loving rebuke," Urshan prayed, "Oh Lord, I am not the hireling, I haven't come here preaching for gain; I am not leading other men's sheep. I will not run away, but will stay with the sheep Thou hast been pleased to give me, and if need be, die with them!"[34] After this prayer, Urshan informed Dr. Shedd of his decision.

Geogtapa

Shortly after making this decision, Urshan sensed the Lord directing him to Geogtapa, a village five miles from Urmia and the farthest point yet from his home village of Abajalu. Two rivers, the Nazli and the Shahr, had to be crossed to reach Geogtapa which lay to the southwest of Abajalu.[35]

Expecting to be martyred, Urshan journeyed to Geotapa finding that his "heart was filled with joy in anticipation of the great crisis [he] was about to face."[36]

Upon arriving, Urshan preached "Christ, the Saviour, Healer, Baptizer and Coming King."[37] He reported, "Over thirty got saved, and six baptized in one night."[38] He continued, "During those four months He gave us about 170 converts, and filled them with the Holy Ghost and power. A great many more were

---

[30]Urshan spelled "Geogtapa" as "Gogtopa."
[31]Urshan, *The Life Story*, 5th ed., 189.
[32]Urshan, *The Life Story*, 5th ed., 189.
[33]Urshan, *The Life Story*, 5th ed., 189-90. Shedd's account of the devastation resulting from the invasion of northwest Persia by Turks and Kurds is included in James Bryce, *The Treatment of Armenians in the Ottoman Empire* (London: Hodder and Stoughton, 1916), 100-104.
[34]Urshan, *The Life Story*, 5th ed., 190.
[35]During the persecution, Geogtapa was plundered and burned. Because of Dr. H. P. Packard's effort, 2,000 people were saved. Dr. Packard, head of the American hospital in Urmia, pleaded with the Kurdish invaders. They allowed these people to flee. Two Syrian doctors, who also urged that these people's lives be spared, later died of typhoid fever. Paul Shimmon, "The Plight of Assyria," a letter to the editor of *The New York Times* (September 18, 1916). http://www.atour.com/~history/ny-times/20001126g.html (accessed March 2, 2010).
[36]Urshan, *The Story of My Life*, 1st ed., 75.
[37]Urshan, *The Story of MyLife*, 1st ed., 75.
[38]Urshan, *The Story of My Life*, 1st ed., 75.

converted in secret, but we only heard about them later."[39] Describing various ideas people in Geogtapa had about the source of his power – magical power, a chemical on his handkerchief which caused people to faint, hypnosis, a revolver, and supernatural power – Urshan concluded, "I cannot tell exactly how many got saved, but I believe that there were over two hundred, many of whom got their baptism."[40] Urshan ends his accout of his ministry in Geogtapa with these words, "And then the massacres cames."

The Massacres

The violence that erupted in the Ottoman Empire in 1915 and continued until 1918, followed by a brief break and resumed from 1920 to 1923, is commonly referred to as the Armenian Genocide.[41] Although 1915 is usually given as the date for the start of the atrocities, "localized massacres of Armenians had begun in autumn 1914 in the Ottoman areas bordering Persian and Russian lands."[42] Even this was not the beginning of the slaughter of Armenians. Three thousand were massacred in 1894 and 80,000 the following year.[43] All told, it is estimated that between one million and 1,500,000 Armenians died by the time the violence ended.[44]

---

[39]Urshan, *The Story of My Life,* 1st ed., 75.

[40]Urshan, *The Story of My Life,* 1st ed., 77. When Urshan visited this village forty-nine years later, he found the work intact. Writing in the *Witness of God* in January, 1963, he stated: "That blessed work is in progess to this day." This would place his ministry in this town toward the end of 1914, perhaps as late as December, for the first invasion of Urmia occurred on January 8, 1915.

[41]ANI, "Frequently Asked Questions about the Armenian Genocide," http://www.armenian-genocide.org/genocidefaq.html (accessed March 3, 2010).

[42]Donald Bloxham, "Rethinking the Armenian Genocide: Ninety Years Ago This Summer Saw the Start of the Armenian Genocide in Turkey. In His Account of the Complex Historical Background to These Events Donald Bloxham Focuses on the Issue of Great Power Involvement," *History Today,* June 2005, http://www.questia.com/PM.qst?a=o&d=5009587189.

[43]Ibid.

[44]Ibid. See also Vahakn N. Dadrian, *The History of the Armenian Genocide: Ethnic Conflict from the Balkans to Anatolia to the Caucasus* (Providence, RI: Berghahn Books, 1997); Franklin H. Littell, "Halting a Succession of Evil," *Journal of Ecumenical Studies* 34, no. 2 (1997); Sara Cohan, "A Brief History of the Armenian Genocide," *Social Education* 69, no. 6 (2005); Heather Rae, *State Identities and the Homogenisation of Peoples* (New York: Cambridge University Press, 2002); Taner Akcam, *A Shameful Act: The Armenian Genocide and the Question of Turkish Responsibility* (New York: Metropolitan Books, 2007. Despite the continued official denial of the Armenian Genocide by the government of Turkey, this event is documented by an abundance of written records and the oral testimony of many observers and survivors. A search for the phrase "Armenian Genocide" at Questia, an online research library offering the full text of books and journal articles from over three hundred publishers, returns 224 books and seventy-eight journal articles that address the genocide. This is in addition to more than 100 newspaper articles.

Various theories are offered as the reason for this "shameful act,"[45] and it is outside the scope of this study to thoroughly explore them. It should be noted, however, that the slaughter was not limited to Armenians; it included Nestorians, Jacobites, Syrian Catholics, and Chaldeans.[46]

Although the Armenian Genocide is a matter of historical record, the government of Turkey denies that it ever happened.[47]

> Despite the affirmation of the Armenian genocide by the overwhelming majority of historians, academic institutions on Holocaust and Genocide Studies, and governments around the world, the Turkish government still actively denies the Armenian genocide. Among a series of actions enacted to counter Armenian genocide recognition and education, the government even passed a law in 2004 known as Article 305 which makes it a criminal offense, punishable by up to 10 years in prison, to discuss the Armenian genocide.[48]

It is documented that as the Armenians were driven from their homes their properties were confiscated by the government, which also forbade the seizure of any Armenian properties by citizens. This does not mean, of course, that this prohibition was always obeyed.

---

[45] This phrase borrows the title of Taner Akcam's *A Shameful Act: The Armenian Genocide and the Question of Turkish Responsibility.*

[46] Margaret Lavinia Anderson, "Nation-Making Amnesia," *Commonweal* 134, no. 4 (February 23, 2007): 22-25. The Armenian Genocide remains a raw spot in the history of World War I. For pictorial evidence by American diplomat Leslie Davis beginning in 1915, see Leslie A. Davis, ed., *The Slaughterhouse Province: An American Diplomat's Report on the Armenian Genocide, 1915-1917* (New York: Aristide D. Caratzas, 1990). The testimonies of one hundred eyewitnesses may be read in Donald E. Miller and Lorna Touryan, *Survivors: An Oral History of the Armenian Genocide* (Berkeley: University of California Press, 1993). Standard works from the Armenian perspective include Richard G. Hovannisian, ed., *The Armenian Genocide in Perspective* (Oxford: Transaction Books, 1986) and Christopher Walker, *Armenia: The Survival of a Nation*, rev. 2nd ed. (New York: St. Martin's Press, 1990). Rejection of the claim of genocide may be seen in Stanford Shaw and Ezel Kural Shaw, *History of the Ottoman Empire and Modern Turkey*, vol. 2 (Cambridge: Cambridge University Press, 1977) and Esat Uras, *The Armenians in History and the Armenian Question* (Istanbul: Documentary Publications, 1988).

[47] Several web sites have been developed to document and preserve information about the Armenian Genocide: The Genocide Education Project, http://www.ge-nocideeducation.org (accessed November 23, 2010); The Choices Program, History and Current Issues for the Classroom, http://www.choices.edu (accessed November 23, 2010); Armenian Genocide, Resource Library for Teachers, http://www.teach-genocide.org (accessed November 23, 2010); Facing History and Ourselves, Helping classrooms and communities worldwide link the past to moral choices today, http://www.facinghistory.org (accessed November 23, 2010); The Legacy Project, http://www.legacy-project.org (accessed November 23, 2010); Armenian National Institute, Dedicated to the study, research, and affirmation of the Armenian Genocide, http://www.armenian-genocide.org (accessed November 23, 2010); The Armenian Geno-cide, history does not fade away, http://www.theforgotten.org (accessed November 23, 2010).

[48] Sara Cohan, "A Brief History of the Armenian Genocide," *Social Education* 69, no. 6 (2005), http://www.questia.com/PM.qst?a=o&d=5011757237.

The implementation of the policy of genocide began in January 1915 with the disarming of Armenians in the Turkish army, who were then put into labour battalions until they were taken out in groups of eighty to one hundred and executed. This was followed on the night of 23-24 April 1915 with the arrest of hundreds of intellectuals and leaders of the Armenian community in Constantinople. They were deported to Anatolia where they were put to death. Before the deportations took place all able-bodied men in towns and villages were rounded up. They were ordered to assemble at the local government building and then marched to the outskirts of the town or village and executed. . . . They were shot, hacked to death, and in some cases taken out to sea and drowned. . . . Throughout the whole process Armenian property was seized by the government.

. . . Women, children and older men were deported from their homes and driven into the desert . . . . They were subjected to rape and murder along the way, with many young girls and young women being carried off and never seen again. The Armenians were attacked by members of the army, the Special Organisation, bands of Kurds and in some cases the local Muslim population. Many died along the way from starvation, exposure or mistreatment, and many, particularly women, threw themselves and their children into the Euphrates as the only way to avoid further suffering. . . . Between March and August 1916, orders came from Constantinople to liquidate the last survivors remaining in the camps along the railway and the banks of the Euphrates.[49]

Urshan found himself in northeast Persia in the earliest days of World War I and during the beginning of the attempt by the waning Ottoman Empire to purge Armenians from its borders.[50] That Urshan's life was truly in danger is a certainty; he was physically located in one of the centers of carnage, he identified himself as an Assyrian-Chaldean, and he was a Christian who valued his Nestorian heritage.

In general, Urshan's discussion of the causes of the genocide is in keeping with more extended and scholarly treatments noted above. He sees the contributing factors as political, economic, and religious.[51] Although he makes no attempt to justify the violence, Urshan notes that even though the Turks came to the conclusion "that all their Christian subjects were nothing more than traitors" and "encouraged their absolute annihilation," "the Turks, and the Persian government, cannot be judged too severely, for God alone knows what the so-called Christian governments would have done to the Turks, if they were their subjects, and during a gigantic struggle, like the first World War, they should have been proven traitors."[52]

In his treatment of the economic causes (Urshan uses the term "commercial cause"[53]), Urshan compares the alleged industriousness and prosperity of the Armenians, Assyrians, and Syrians to that of the Jews in Russia, Poland, and the Balkan states, and writes,

---

[49]Heather Rae, *State Identities and the Homogenisation of Peoples* (New York: Cambridge University Press, 2002), 161, http://www.questia.com/PM.qst?a=o&d= 105181035.
[50]Urshan, *The Life Story*, 5th ed., 197.
[51]Urshan, *The Life Story*, 5th ed., 196-97.
[52]Urshan, *The Life Story*, 5th ed., 196.
[53]Urshan, *The Life Story*, 5th ed., 196.

The Near East Christians, being connected with America and Europe, religiously, and in commerce, brought lots of money into Turkey, Persia, and Mesopotamia. That . . . made them live far above the common peasant Muslims. Their Muslim neighbors, therefore, were just waiting for an opportunity to plunder and ransack the Christian villages, and seize their beautiful girls, and house-goods.[54]

As it relates to the religious causes of the Armenian Genocide, Urshan stated,

We were informed in Persia, that it was the scheme of the Central Powers[55] to urge and agitate the Turks to declare "JEHAD" or Muslim's the Holy War. They had imagined that by this scheme, they would cripple England, Russia, and France; raising revolutions in their Mohammedan countries, against them, and they had hoped also to win Persia, Turkestan, Afghanistan, Buchara and Arabia, all Mohammedan nations, to their side, through this Religious War.

. . . the Mohammedan peasants, and warriors, were instructed by their "Moolas" (priests), that the more Christians they slaughtered, the more excellent sacrifices they would make to Allah (The Almighty); so the poor fanatics were aflame to joyfully torture and slay their Christian neighbors, without pity, in order to please God.[56]

According to Arian Ishaya,

In November of 1914 Turkey declared "Jihad" (holy war) at the same time that it formed an alliance with Germany. The German authorities had instigated the call to Jihad in order to mobilize all Muslims, irrespective of denominational differences into action against the "Christian" allies. In doing so they were aware that it would put the civilian Christian population at risk . . . .[57]

Further, Ishaya asserts,

Although Persia declared its neutrality during WWI, nevertheless the call for Jihad instigated the local Muslim population to take advantage of the chaotic wartime conditions and even up their scores with the local Christians. Thus . . . the Christian communities in Persia came under attack from three fronts: the Ottoman Turks, the Kurds, and the local Muslims.[58]

---

[54]Urshan, *The Life Story,* 5th ed., 196.

[55]During World War I the term "Central Powers" referred to an alliance between Germany, Austria-Hungary, the Ottoman Empire and other allied nations that opposed the Allied (or "Entente") powers.

[56]Urshan, *The Life Story,* 5th ed., 197.

[57]Arian Ishaya, "A Commentary on Professor Zirinsky's Article American Presbyterian Missionaries at Urmia During the Great War," *Journal of Assyrian Academic Studies* 12, no. 1: 30. Ishaya references the work of Gabriele Yonan, "a German scholar who . . . speaks the eastern dialect of the Syriac language [and] has devoted over 30 years to the study of the history of Christianity and the present situation of the Assyrian people in their homeland. Her [research addresses] German involvement in the Assyrian Holocaust, and the impact German state policies had on the crushing of the Christian presence due to the Turkish-German alliance in the years of World War I" (Majidi Ann Warda, TAAS – Chairperson of the Publication Committee, Symposium Syriacum VIII & The Assyrian Genocide Seminar, Posted: Wednesday, July 19, 2000 10:07 am CST, http://www.atour.com/education/20000719a.html [accessed March 6, 2010]).

[58]Arian Ishaya, "A Commentary on Professor Zirinsky's Article American Presbyte-

Further confirmation of the declaration of jihad and the involvement of the non-military citizenry in the atrocities is included in Rae's comments:

> ... The CUP[59] incited the population by emphasising the religious differences between Muslim and Armenian subjects which ... retained a high level of salience in the Ottoman Empire. The genocide was declared a *jihad*, a holy war against the infidels, which was a deliberate means of inflaming religious feeling and part of a propaganda campaign which ensured the participation of many ordinary Turks in the deportations and massacres of the Armenians.[60]

Thus, Urshan's description of the religious dimension of the genocide is quite accurate. Jihad had been declared, validating the slaughter of Christians. Determined to keep their faith in the face of what seemed to be certain death, Urshan and seventy-five believers in Geogtapa were prepared to embrace martyrdom. Urshan declared, "We could truly say that we loved the Name of Our Lord to such an extent, that we did not mind being trampled under the feet of the horses of those wild murderers, and even being thrust through with their bayonets, while standing and calling on the Name of the Lord."[61]

On February 24, 1915, news reached Geogtapa that the Russian army – the stabilizing force in the region – had fled, leaving the Kurds and Turks free to attack. The word on the street was that the Muslim neighbors of the Christians in the area were preparing to plunder and kill the Christians. W. A. Shedd wrote a letter to The Honorable J. L. Caldwell, the American Minister stationed in Teheran, dated June 23, 1915.

> The Russian army left Urumia on January 2nd .... The Turkish troops arrived on January 4th .... During this period the loss of life in the Christian population here [in the city of Urmia] has been about 1,000 persons killed and about 4,000 persons who have died of disease.... we have records of about 3,600 burials in the city of Urumia and at our college compound.... The total Christian population here on January 1st ... was some 5,600 families living in the city and villages of the plain and 800 to 1,000 families, who fled here from the mountains .... the number of souls was 32,000 to 33,000. When the Russians left there was a large exodus of Christians and the number remaining here was probably about 25,000, so that the loss of life in less than five months was about 20% of the total number. Of the 6,500 families, certainly not over a thousand families escaped without being totally robbed of all their possessions and many of these were partially robbed.... Not a thousand houses are left with doors and windows and half or more of them have had the roof timbers removed.... The property loss to the Christian population is

---

rian Missionaries at Urmia During the Great War," 31.

[59]The acronym CUP stands for the Committee of Union and Progress which "came to power in the Ottoman Empire in the revolution of 1908 [and] was animated by a chauvinist strand of Turkish nationalism, and was intent on building a rationalised and homogeneous Turkish national state. Accordingly, minority groups, of whom the Armenians were the largest and most vulnerable, were to be removed from Turkey" (Rae, *State Identities and the Homogenisation of Peoples*, 124, http://www.questia.com/-PM.qst?a=o&d=105180998.

[60]Rae, *State Identities and the Homogenisation of Peoples*, 157-58, http://www.questia.com/PM.qst?a=o&d=105181031.

[61]Urshan, *The Life Story*, 5th ed., 202.

estimated variously, the lowest estimate being at $2,500,000 while others estimate it at ten times that amount. . . . over one hundred Christian girls and women became Muslim during this period, in the large majority of cases because of fear and violence. Hundreds of women and girls were violated.

. . . the agents of destruction were Kurds, Persian villagers and Turks.

. . . When the Russians left, Kurds were ready to enter from three directions and fighting had already begun. Immediately the Kurds pressed in and simultaneously the Muslim villagers began to plunder and kill. . . . Of the 750 persons killed during this week I should say that the majority were killed by Kurds, while the larger part of the property loss was due to Muslim villagers, who were also guilty of the majority of crimes against women. . . . It was made more dangerous to Christians by the cry of Jihad (or holy war), which was deliberately made use of by responsible Turkish officials.

. . . Murders were frequent and it was very difficult to get protection for Christians outside our premises even within the city walls, while movement about the country was impossible. . . . During the last days of February two massacres were perpetrated by the Turks.[62]

When Urshan heard the news of the departure of the Russian army and the impending attack by the Kurds, Turks, and Muslim villagers, he informed those who had responded to his ministry in Geogtapa. They prayed, sang "Under the Blood," and prepared themselves for martyrdom.[63]

Before leaving, the Russian army had left some ammunition behind. Five hundred young Assyrians used the ammunition in an attempt to hold off the invaders by firing on them from the bell tower of the local cathedral. They were able to hold out for only a few hours before the Kurds and Turks gained entrance to the village. The streets filled with the sounds of the firing of rifles and machine guns, mixed with the screams of the people.

In the midst of this havoc, Urshan heard a knock on the gate of the house where several of the believers were praying. Although they were frightened, Urshan looked through the key-hole, seeing a young believer standing outside. Rushed inside, she said, with tears, "Oh! Brother Andrew, come, come!"[64] When asked where, she named a street several blocks away. The girl would not tell Urshan why he should go with her, but continued to beg him to come.

Bullets flew in every direction as Urshan accompanied the girl. Upon reaching the house, he discovered several people stretched out unconscious on the floor in a large room. Others were weeping and wailing over what was about to befall them. The girl led Urshan to a corner of the room. Several troubled people were

---

[62]Letter from W. A. Shedd to The Honorable J. L. Caldwell, American Minister, Teheran, June 23, 1915, Gomidas Institute Armenian Genocide Documentation Project, http://www.gomidas.org/gida/index_and_%20documents/867.4016_index_and_documents/docs/4016.270.pdf (accessed March 6, 2010).

[63]Urshan, *The Life Story*, 5th ed., 204.

[64]Urshan, *The Life Story*, 5th ed., 205.

watching another young lady shaking and prophesying under the power of God as she was baptized with the Holy Spirit. Urshan interpreted this as a sign that God would protect the believers. He rushed back to the house from whence he had come, passing safely again through a hail of bullets.

As the believers were praising God for Urshan's report, they heard the soldiers outside. Finding the streets deserted and the doors locked, the invaders smashed doors as those hiding inside screamed with fear.[65]

Urshan realized he was responsible for the safety of those who trusted him and who said, "If you run away, we will run away with you. If not, we will stay here and die with you, and God will take us to heaven because we died with you."[66] He made the decision to go and to take with him all who wished to accompany him to the city of Urmia. Two of the men, Elisha and Samuel, refused to leave, saying, "We will not go. We will stay in this house. The Lord will protect us, and if we cannot preach to the Kurds, why then we will die for Him."[67]

With about seventy-five people, Urshan left Geogtapa. They had gone only a short distance when they were surrounded by men with machine guns and spears. Urshan called on the name of the Lord. He felt God direct him to run in front of the people with him with his hands lifted, saying, "Jesus! Jesus!"[68] As he did this, the armed men, on horseback, rode up to him. Urshan fell on his knees but was commanded to arise. The men demanded the people's overcoats and Urshan's and Timothy's watches. Then they told the group that they would be safe if they went in another direction.

Expecting to be martyred, Urshan was "a little disappointed, having missed the privilege of dying for [his] precious Lord and Saviour."[69]

As Urshan and those with him hurried in the direction that had been pointed out to them, they saw people being slaughtered by Muslim neighbors. One of those involved in the slaughter rushed toward Urshan's group, eyes blood red. Urshan greeted him loudly in the Turkish language, "God's mercy be with you!" The Holy Spirit then led Urshan to confess to this man the sins of the nation of Persia. After Urshan assured this man that he and those with him were genuine Christians, the man seemed deeply moved, almost as if he would weep. He said, "Young man, I am going to deliver you. I will give my life to take you safely to the American quarters."[70]

This man, who at first had seemed to be a violent threat, now informed Urshan that the American flag was flying over the American Presbyterian Mission Compound in Urmia. He said, "I could take thousands of dollars from these Christians.

---

[65]Urshan, *The Life Story*, 5th ed., 206.
[66]Urshan, "The Story of My Life—21st Chapter," *The Witness of God* 6, no. 56 (August 1924): 3.
[67]Urshan, *The Life Story*, 5th ed., 207.
[68]Urshan, *The Life Story*, 5th ed., 207.
[69]Urshan, *The Life Story*, 5th ed., 208.
[70]Urshan, *The Life Story*, 5th ed., 208.

Their houses are left, and I could rob them. But I do not want anything. I cannot take you to safety by the regular road. It is filled with thieves, but follow me."[71]

The women with Urshan were afraid this man was deceiving them and that he planned to take them to some isolated place to kill them. Urshan told the man their fears, but he swore by Mohammed that he would die before he would let anyone touch them. "Let us trust God," Urshan said to the people. "He will cause this man to take us to a place of safety."[72]

Two other Muslims joined them. On their way toward the city of Urmia, a band of young Turks saw Urshan's group, not noticing that it was led by a Muslim. As the Turks ran to capture the believers, the Muslim men cried out, "Stop! These Christians are our God-given prey!"[73] The Turks then bestowed blessings on the heads of the Muslims, thinking they were highly favored of God to have captured them for slaughter.

Before reaching Urmia, Urshan's entourage passed through hails of bullets, seeing horrifying sights. Urshan described it thus:

> . . . We saw terrible sights all around us. People were being killed and stripped naked. Dead bodies lay everywhere, and wild dogs were eating their faces. Young girls were being taken away from their parents, and young wives from their husbands. But not one of the young women with us was touched. We were about seventy-five souls wonderfully kept and delivered from death by the Lord Jesus in Whom we trusted.[74]

After climbing walls, wading rocky streams, crossing vineyards, and trudging over hills and through valleys, Urshan's group reached the city of Urmia. He was surprised to see an American flag flying near the gate of the city, but soon discovered that it was carried by Dr. Packard, who rode by on horseback, shouting "fear not" in response to Urshan's call as he passed by.[75]

Urshan and his group had to pass through thousands of Muslims gathered around the walls of Urmia waiting to capture and kidnap Christians. When the Muslims saw them, they rushed up shaking their hands and telling them not to fear. This reversal of expectation caused them to weep for joy. The Muslims, thinking they were frightened, arranged for several men to accompany the group to the gates of the Presbyterian mission. As they walked for two miles through the streets filled with "mad mobs of the anti-Christians," those who saw them wept as they passed, shouting, "God keep you."[76] They had traveled through carnage and the threat of death with no harm done to them.

---

[71]Urshan, *The Life Story*, 5th ed., 208-09.
[72]Urshan, *The Life Story*, 5th ed., 209.
[73]Urshan, *The Life Story*, 5th ed., 209.
[74]Urshan, *The Life Story*, 5th ed., 209.
[75]Paul Shimmon, "The Plight of Assyria," a letter to the editor of *The New York Times* (September 18, 1916). http://www.atour.com/~history/ny-times/20001126g.html (accessed March 2, 2010). Urshan discovered later that Dr. Packard was on his way to Geogtapa, where he was able to save about 2,000 people before they were slaughtered by the Kurds.
[76]Urshan, *The Life Story*, 5th ed., 211.

Martyrs

Not all who responded to Urshan's ministry escaped death. A seventeen year old Greek Catholic girl, Sophia, attended one of Urshan's street meetings[77] and was saved.[78] The following Sunday as she sat with her family at dinner, "the power of God fell upon her" and she began shaking and saying, "Glory to Jesus!" Then she began to speak in a language she had never learned.[79]

Sophia's parents knew she had attended Urshan's meetings, and although he had never noticed her or spoken with her, they were convinced he had hypnotized their daughter. They sent for the Greek Catholic priest, who threw water upon her in an attempt to rebuke the devil. Sophia, however, continued to praise the Lord and told the priest of his need to get right with God and to pray for himself rather than for her.

Sophia faced persecution within her home. Her parents did not want her to attend Urshan's meetings or even leave the house. When she had opportunity, however, she would go out in the streets and speak to women, and the Lord would reveal to her the secrets of their hearts. They were seized with conviction, confessed their sins and repented.

Some of the young girls who had responded to the gospel were accustomed to singing in groups as they went through the streets in the evening. They would then go into the fields, where they would kneel and pray. One Sunday evening as they returned from the fields, singing, Sophia was among them. As they neared the outskirts of town, a boy eight years of age was hiding behind a house, holding a rifle. As the girls came near, the boy shouted to Sophia, "Shut your mouth! I'm going to shoot you!"[80] He then fired several shots into Sophia's abdomen.

Sophia survived for about one week. Many, including unbelievers, visited her during this time. Some "were brought to Jesus through her testimonies." Sophia's mother wanted to have the boy's parents arrested and the boy put to death, but Sophia pleaded, "Mother, forgive him. He didn't know what he was doing. The older folks taught him to shoot me, and they did not know what they were doing. Jesus was killed by those who did not know or understand Him, too."

As Sophia's death neared, Urshan was five miles away in prayer with his brother Josephaus, cousin Jonathan, and another young man in his home village of Abajalu. Urshan saw a vision of heaven open and the angels descending. The Spirit said, "Sophia is dying, and the angels of God are taking her." Deeply moved, he wept with joy. Then he had another vision. He saw a great black cloud over the town where Sophia lived. He began to lament in tongues for the sins of that town and of all Persia as he sensed their impending judgment.

---

[77]Urshan does not identify the village where Sophia lived, but as will be seen in the following story of martyrdom, it was apparently Ada, the home of Urshan's first convert, Andrew.
[78]Urshan, *The Life Story,* 5th ed., 213.
[79]Urshan, *The Life Story,* 5th ed., 213.
[80]Urshan, *The Life Story,* 5th ed., 214. All direct quotes in this episode are from the same source.

The three young men with Urshan fell prostrate on their faces as they cried to God for mercy and surrendered their lives to the Lord. His brother and cousin were still trusting Jesus when they died in 1918.

Rather than prosecuting those involved in Sophia's murder, the government officials imprisoned Andrew, Urshan's first convert in Ada. This course of action was justified on the basis that had Andrew not conducted religious meetings in the town, Sophia would not have been murdered. Andrew was found guity and sentenced to prison. During his incarceration, God told him that a terrible massacre would come upon Persia "because of their unrighteousness."

When Andrew was released from prison, he immediately began to warn the people of Ada of what lay ahead. He said, "I am going away; after two weeks, you will never see me any more." Those who heard this asked, "Why, Brother Andrew, are you going to meet Jesus?" They could not understand why they were not ready to meet Jesus if Andrew was ready. He explained that he did not know that lay ahead for him, but that God had showed him that he would be going somewhere after two weeks and that the people of Ada would never see him again until they met in heaven. Two weeks later the massacre occurred.

When the Russian army left northwest Persia, the Turkish army entered Ada with the cry of Jihad, slaughtering those who professed to be Christians. Although 30,000 people escaped, fleeing to a refuge in Urmia under the flag of the United States, some of those who had responded to Urshan's ministry, including Andrew, did not. When Andrew learned that many in Ada were without comfort and food, he told his wife and children, "I am going back to be with the people who are left there. I will preach to them, pray for them, and comfort them. If necessary, I will die with them."

Although his family pleaded with him to stay, he returned, leaving them in the home of a Muslim friend. He did what he could, but the Kurds and Turks swarmed the village, murdering young men and raping young girls and women. Finding Andrew in the midst of the people, they stripped him and asked about his faith. He joyously confessed his faith in God. For some reason, they did not kill Andrew and another Christian man at that time. They escaped and went into hiding by covering themselves with tree leaves. They were in prayer when they were discovered and executed by two Kurds.

Jeremiah Eshoo, whom Urshan had first met in Chicago, was also martyred. When Urshan met him, Jeremiah resisted the gospel, calling Urshan a fraud who was filled with the devil. But when he visited one of Urshan's meetings intending to create a disturbance, he was convicted of his sins. Later that night he dreamed of coming judgment. Waking up, "he was soundly converted, baptized with the Holy Ghost, shaking so violently under the power of God that the room . . . also shook."

Returning to Persia during the genocide, many people placed their confidence in Eshoo for deliverance from the impending violence. Some said, "Jeremiah, your God will deliver us. We will not run away, we will stay with you."

Eshoo led the people to a nearby Islamic village where they had Muslim friends. They hid Eshoo in a barn, concealed in hay. However, other villagers brought two Kurds, who broke the door open, seizing Jeremiah and slapping him on the face. They demanded, "Are you the head of these people? Will you accept Islam and work for our prophet? Are you going to keep these people to follow you?"

Eshoo kept silence, and the Kurds took him away amidst the screams of his wife and children. When they had taken him from his family, the Kurds said, "Now, give us the golden money you have in your pocket." Eshoo took his New Testament from his pocket. In anger, the Kurds asked, "Do you mean that you are not going to be a Muslim?" He lifted his Testament, saying, "Christ Jesus is my Lord and King." At that, some of the Kurds pointed their guns at him, asking, "Are you going to be a Muslim?" When he did not answer, they shot him.

One of the women believers came, putting Eshoo's New Testament under his head. There he died, another Persian martyr.

When Urshan escaped from Geogtapa with seventy-five Christian believers, eighteen or nineteen men, including Elisha and Samuel, remained behind with their families. They were all in one home. The Kurds entered the village the same evening Urshan had left. They broke down their door, struck a match, and found the people on their knees in prayer.

The Kurds said, "Oh, what a sacrifice for Allah! Now we will slay everyone of them!"[81] Samuel rose, fell at the feet of the Kurds, and cried out, "Oh! Kill us, but don't touch these women and children!"

"Why didn't you run away?" the Kurds asked.

"We believed God that He would put His mercy in you, so you wouldn't kill us. We thought also we would stay here to tell you something of our faith," answered Samuel.

At this, one of the Kurds left the house, but another said, "Let us massacre every one of them."

Samuel responded, "Will you let me say a few things before you kill us? I will sing you a song." With tears in his eyes, he began to sing a song titled "Repent, Repent, and Turn to God." One of the Kurds asked, "What is your name?" He answered, "Samuel, servant of God."

Looking around the room, the Kurds said, "Well, Samuel, we will divide what is in your house, half for us, and half for you. But these beautiful rugs and beds we will take."

Then, looking at the women, huddled and trembling in fear, the leader of the Kurds said, "Now tell these women to make us some tea." Samuel asked the leader if the women and children could go downstairs. The Kurd agreed, and Elisha and Samuel began to prepare tea for the Kurds, who asked many questions about the Russians.

As it grew late in the evening, Samuel went to see how the women and children were. The were frightened and sure that the Kurds would kill them as they slept. Samuel related this to the Kurds, who said, "Go tell them nobody will touch them. For the sake of the Holy Book in your hand, you will be spared." Samuel was holding a New Testament.

---

[81]Urshan, *The Life Story*, 5th ed., 220. All of the direct quotes in this episode of Urshan's life are taken from this source.

"We see you are all honest people," the Kurds said, "and you did not run away and trusted in Allah. We will not harm you."

As the night passed the Kurds slept, but the Christians could not.

The next morning the women told Samuel to ask permission for them to leave. The Kurdish leader granted his permission, but he told Samuel that he feared they would be killed on the way to the city of Urmia.

Deciding to take the chance, all of the believers in the house passed through one town after another where the people had been massacred. Kurds remained in these town, and as the Christians passed through the Kurds would start toward them, then turn back.

They had almost reached Urmia when a man suddenly approached them, shooting Elisha in the chest. Although he survived until he could be brought under the American flag, Elisha died the next morning. His fellow believers gathered around him, singing praises to God.

In addition to those who were killed for their faith in Jesus, Urshan classified as martyrs his mother and Kate Eshoo, who died of typhus contracted while caring for the sick. Following the massacres there was a complete lack of sanitary conditions for survivors, and many died of typhus. William Shedd reported that no less than 4,000 died of disease in Urmia during the time of the Turkish occupation.[82] Kate Eshoo, a member of the Presbyterian Church, was the wife of a medical doctor trained in Canada. She had at first opposed Urshan and tried to break up his meetings. But after speaking with him privately, "she was wonderfully converted [and] filled with the Holy Ghost."[83] Several other teachers, who came with her, also accepted the Pentecostal message.

Urshan himself contracted typhus while ministering to those afflicted with the disease. He came down with typhus while praying for his neice. The girl instantly recovered, but Urshan suffered severely. His fever was extremely high, he lost all of his hair, his skin peeled as if burned, his fingernails fell off, and he lost almost all of his sight and hearing. For thirty-six days he was bedfast.[84]

During his sickness, Urshan believed that his spirit left his body, at which time he found himself in Hades. This experience completely changed his ideas about death and the hereafter. He wrote, "I believe God allowed me to go there to realize how very precious life is in this land of living and how supremely valuable the souls of men are, so that we should try by all God's grace to save them before they die."[85]

---

[82]Shedd, "1915: Urmia : Statement By The Rev. William A. Shedd, D.D., of The American (Presbyterian) Mission Station at Urmia ; Communicated by The Board of Foreign Missions of The Presbyterian Church in The U.S.A.," http://www.atour.com/~history/1900/20000718a.html (accessed March 8, 2010).

[83]Urshan, *The Life Story*, 5th ed., 224.

[84]Urshan, *The Story of My Life*, 1st ed., 98; Urshan, "The Story of My Life—24th Chapter," *The Witness of God* 6, no. 60 [December 1924]: 2-3; Urshan, *The Life Story*, 5th ed., 225-27.

[85]Urshan, *The Life Story*, 5th ed., 226.

As Urshan lay on his bed, he suddenly heard "a mighty volume of prayers like some glorious ray of purest light from Heaven [piercing his] consciousness."[86] The prayers were in the English language and seemed to be coming from the next room. His mother, who sat at his side, could not hear them. But from that moment, Urshan began to recover. Later, he learned that believers in England and America were praying for him.

There were many attempts on Urshan's life in Persia; he expected to die on five occasions. Even before the massacre, mobs attempted to kill him, but the power of God would come upon him, and he would sing. Seeing he had no fear of death, none would touch him. A servant who had been commanded to kill Urshan angered his master when he could not do it. On one occasion a hired killer was promised a large sum of money to take Urshan's life. An unbeliever, knowing this man was a traitor, reported the plan to the authorities. The assassin was arrested and later shot with the same weapon he had planned to use to take Urshan's life.[87]

Ministry in Russia

After more than four months of suffering, a consequence of the invasion of northwest Persia by Turkish and Kurdish forces, the Russian army returned to Urmia.[88] The invaders were forced to retreat beyond the Persian borders. Urshan once again began to conduct street meetings. He found, however, that the professing Christians were bent on revenge against Muslims.

Urshan tried to convince his hearers not to seek revenge, with little success. Some women heeded his words and were saved, but tensions increased.[89] The Urmia city council ordered him to stop preaching; two days later, the Russian army departed once again.

The tables turned; the Muslims had promised that this time they would burn all Christians at the stake. Nearly all the Christians, including some of the American missionaries, fled for refuge to cities near the Russian border.

Tiflis

Urshan managed to travel to Tabriz, a city northeast of Urmia and closer to the Russian border. After he had been there a short time financial help arrived from

---

[86] Urshan, *The Life Story*, 5th ed., 226.

[87] Urshan, *The Life Story*, 5th ed., 227-28.

[88] Urshan, *The Life Story*, 5th ed., 229. An account of the comings and goings of the Russians, Turks, and Kurds may be seen in Bryce, *The Treatment of Armenians in the Ottoman Empire*, 48, 51, 56, 76, 113, 150, 157, 182, 187, 584. A chronology can be found at "Chronology of the Armenian Genocide – 1915 (January - March)," http://www.armenian-genocide.org/1915-1.html (accessed November 22, 2010); "Chronology of the Armenian Genocide – 1915 (April - June)" http://www.armenian-genocide.org/1915-2.html (accessed November 22, 2010); "Chronology of the Armenian Genocide – 1915 (July - September)" http://www.armenian-genocide.org/1915-3.html (accessed November 22, 2010); "Chronology of the Armenian Genocide – 1915 (October - December)," http://www.armenian-genocide.org/1915-4.html (accessed November 22, 2010).

[89] Urshan, *The Life Story*, 5th ed., 231.

believers in the United States.⁹⁰ Urshan was able to use these funds to travel into Russia, where he found some Persians who had responded to his ministry. Some of these he located in Tiflis.⁹¹ While ministering to these Persians, Urshan met some Russian Baptists and began to proclaim the Pentecostal message to them.

Urshan's message was met with some opposition. However, even though Russian law forbade foreigners from holding religious services, the city sent the chief of police to keep order. When Urshan left Tiflis, a group of Russian people had embraced Pentecostalism.

Armavir

From Tiflis, Urshan traveled approximately 300 miles to Armavir, Russia, where a substantial number of Armenians and Assyrians lived. Although they had heard false reports about him, he stayed a month, ministering to those who had fled from Persia. Some of the "worst characters" were converted. Later, Jacob, one of Urshan's converts, became pastor of a large assembly in the city.⁹²

While Urshan was ministering in Armavir, many refugees returned to Persia. Two men associated with Urshan in Russia joined his brother, Timothy, to minister to these refugees. Urshan provided financial support.

Urshan's passport, citizenship papers and other personal identification had been confiscated during the genocide. The United States consul informed him that he must return to the United States to renew his naturalization papers. He was given a temporary passport, good for only a few weeks, to journey through Russia, to England, and from there, back to America.⁹³

Leningrad

When he arrived in Leningrad,⁹⁴ the leader of a Free Protestant Mission who had heard of Urshan's ministry in Tiflis met Urshan and asked him to say a few words about his mission. Urshan accepted the invitation, telling the people what God had done for him in Persia. When they asked him to preach again, Urshan began, as Philip in Samaria, to preach "the kingdom of God, and the name of the Lord Jesus Christ." The attendance, which was at first about twenty-five people, increased to 200. Since the hall could seat only 150, several stood for four hours. More than "one hundred Christian backsliders came back to God. About fifty got genuinely converted, of whom thirty-five received the baptism of the Holy Ghost."⁹⁵

These people wanted Urshan to baptize them, although the water was icy. On one occasion, he was in the water for more than two hours baptizing the converts.

---

⁹⁰In the first edition of is autobiography, Urshan identified those who helped him as "the saints in the United States through the kind care of Brother Fraser and the Stone Church of Chicago" (Urshan, *The Story of My Life*, 1ˢᵗ ed., 102).

⁹¹The former Tiflis is now known as Tbilsi, located in Georgia.

⁹²Urshan, *The Life Story*, 5ᵗʰ ed., 232.

⁹³Urshan, *The Life Story*, 5ᵗʰ ed., 232-33.

⁹⁴At that time Leningrad was known as Petrograd. It is now known as Saint Petersburg.

⁹⁵Urshan, *The Life Story*, 5ᵗʰ ed., 233.

As the Spirit of the Lord fell upon them in the water, they shook, praised God, and were baptized with the Holy Spirit.

Some Protestant ministers objected to Urshan's message and attempted to close the meetings. The government sent detectives to investigate. Instead of closing the meetings as ordered, they reported that the "American evangelist is here, doing great good in our country."[96]

Division over the Formula for Baptism

While Urshan was ministering in Leningrad, he learned that the American Pentecostal Movement was dividing over the formula for water baptism. He writes,

> We had heard of a division among God's Pentecostal people in America over the use of different formulas in baptizing converts, and since we loved all these people, we did not want to take a definite step with – or against – either side. We desired to come first to the United States and investigate thoroughly before coming to any conclusion, praying for God's definite leading in the matter. But God's way is not man's. If we love the Lord, His people, and His Word, we need have no fear of being led wrongly.[97]

As Urshan reflected on this matter, he prayed what he called a "peculiar prayer":

> Oh Lord, if Thou art going to make me baptize converts in this meeting, and if Thou will have me to baptize them in the Name of the Lord Jesus, as in the Book of Acts, please cause the first one who may ask me to baptize him, or her, to ask me to be baptized according to the Book of Acts. Make that candidate show me the verse and the chapter, referring to the water baptism.[98]

Urshan had first baptized new converts in the name of the Lord Jesus Christ in 1910 in Chicago. He had, however, been opposed to rebaptizing those already baptized in the name of the Father, Son, and Holy Ghost.[99]

None of the believers in Russia were aware of this disagreement. One evening during a testimony meeting:

> ... the power of God was falling. Suddenly from the congregation a big man arose to his feet, rushed down the aisle with his Bible in his hand, and came forward towards me. He had been converted a few nights previous to this.... The tears were streaming down his cheeks, and he had a Bible, with his finger holding open one of the pages. He cried out, "Oh! Brother Urshan, the Lord Jesus told me last night to ask you to baptize me, just like this text." You may imagine my surprise when I took his Bible (he would not remove his finger from the verse) and looked where he was pointing. It was this verse, "For as yet he was fallen upon none of them: only they were baptized in the name of the Lord Jesus" (Acts 8:16).[100]

---

[96]Urshan, *The Life Story*, 5th ed., 234.
[97]Urshan, *The Life Story*, 5th ed., 234.
[98]Urshan, *The Life Story*, 5th ed., 234.
[99]Urshan, *The Life Story*, 5th ed., 237.
[100]Urshan, *The Life Story*, 5th ed., 235.

Saying nothing about the relationship between this event and his prayer, Urshan announced that he would soon conduct a baptismal service. He asked the people to pray and to locate a place where he could baptize this man and others who desired to be baptized.

A few days later, Urshan was asked to baptize eleven people in woods several miles from the city. In snow two feet deep, they found a frozen stream. Reaching the place, the men shoveled away the snow and broke a large hole in the ice. Urshan went into the stream wearing only ordinary trousers and shoes, trusting God to protect him; knowing he was doing the will of God baptizing these converts "into the name of the Lord Jesus, according to Acts 2:38."[101]

A young woman, an unbeliever, had followed them to "watch the fun." However, when the first person, also a young lady, stepped into the water, the power of God fell on her, causing the unbelieving girl to believe also. She fell on her knees in the deep snow, then rose and came running into the stream for baptism.

As a result of this baptismal service, many others repented and desired baptism in the name of Jesus. Some ninety people would be baptized at this second service. In preparation for this service, Urshan preached Isaiah 9:6.[102] He emphasized "the Sonship of Jesus, and the Divine Fatherhood in Him, our Mighty God and **The Everlasting Father**."[103]

Urshan explained why the apostles baptized in the name of the Lord Jesus. He did not anticipate that any of his hearers would ask to be rebaptized. As noted earlier, he objected to rebaptism, having come to the conclusion in 1910 "to baptize the new converts in Jesus' name, but never those who had already been baptized."[104] His resolve was challenged.

> In spite of my personal feelings on the subject, I was almost begged to baptize some who had already been baptized in water, not repeating on them [Matthew] 28:19. They already had been baptized in the Spirit. I did my best to discourage it, telling the folks it was not necessary at all, and that it would bring trouble and division among them. I went so far as to tell them of the havoc this very thing had created in America, and plainly stated that I would not rebaptize them. Then I asked them all to kneel down in the snow with me, and pray this imagination out of their minds. I prayed harder than them all, against rebaptism, and branded it to be a trick of the enemy to destroy our good revival. I thought surely, after such praying,

---

[101] Urshan, *The Life Story,* 5th ed., 236.

[102] "For unto us a child is born, unto us a son is given: and the government shall be upon his shoulder: and his name shall be called Wonderful, Counseller, The mighty God, The everlasting Father, The Prince of Peace" (Isaiah 9:6). This was the first time Urshan had ever preached on this particular text. However, the verse was at this same time being used by fundamentalists as a prophecy of the deity of Christ. Arno C. Gaebelein used the text as an indication of the uniting of deity and humanity in the Messiah (Arno C. Gaebelein, "Fulfilled Prophecy a Potent Argument," *The Fundamentals,* R. A. Torrey, ed. (Grand Rapids: Kregel Publications, 1990), 207. Urshan read fundamentalist literature and was no doubt aware of the use of Isaiah 9:6. Later, in *The Witness of God,* he printed many articles written by fundamentalist authors.

[103] Urshan, *The Life Story,* 5th ed., 237. Emphasis in the original.

[104] Urshan, *The Life Story,* 5th ed., 237.

they would all be convinced, and give up the idea of rebaptism. But alas! As soon as we stood up, with beaming faces, they looked on me, and said, "Now, Brother Urshan, we are ready to be baptized." I could not understand why they wanted to be rebaptized, when it was so cold, and there was so much ice, and it would endanger their health. To tell the truth, I was sorry for preaching that message. But what else could I do? There I was, once again, captured by God's mysterious leadings and by the united desire of these obedient souls.[105]

Finally Urshan said, "Now, since you say you see Jesus' name so much greater and more glorious and filled with all the fullness of the Godhead and his name being that one name of the Father, Son, and Holy Ghost, you may go ahead and baptize one another. I have decided to go first to America and study the matter more fully before I will baptize anyone who has already been immersed."[106]

But nothing changed the minds of the people. They answered, "God has used you to open our eyes on the deity of Christ. We plainly see that Jesus is our all in all, and His name is the name of the Father and the Holy Spirit. Your preaching has made us see our need of being rebaptized now, here, and by you."[107]

Urshan Baptized in the Name of the Lord Jesus Christ

Urshan himself had not been baptized in the name of Jesus. He had been sprinkled as a child in the Presbyterian Church in Persia, and he had been immersed in the Brethren Church in Chicago. Apparently he mentioned this, for they continued, "Oh, Brother Urshan, be baptized now, and baptize us also."[108]

Urshan asked them to kneel for prayer, hoping to discourage them. They complied but could not pray. They arose shortly thereafter, praising God for their "new light and inspiration." This time he did all the praying, asking for God to lead him.

Urshan later wrote that God spoke to him then, saying, "Are you willing to let your American friends go for my name's sake? Will you fail me and despise my name given under heaven whereby men must be saved? Arise and be baptized in the true apostolic manner." As the Lord was speaking to him, the Holy Spirit shook Urshan's head until he thought it would come off his body. Submitting, he said, "Yes, Lord, I count the cost, and I will choose the narrow way." Arising, he said to the people, "I will be baptized in Jesus' name, too."[109]

The people shouted, "Glory to God!" About fifty more said, "We will be rebaptized, too!" An elderly Russian man named Antonov,[110] who had been filled with the Spirit, baptized Urshan in the name of the Lord Jesus Christ. Then over the course of two hours in the icy water, Urshan rebaptized about seventy-five. Included among those were Nikolai P. Smorodin and his wife Maria. Later the congregation

---

[105]Urshan, *The Life Story,* 5th ed., 237-38.
[106]Urshan, *The Life Story,* 5th ed., 238.
[107]Urshan, *The Life Story,* 5th ed., 238.
[108]Urshan, *The Life Story,* 5th ed., 238.
[109]Urshan, *The Life Story,* 5th ed., 238.
[110]*The Chronicle* (Amherst: [MA?], The American Church of Christians in the Spirit of the Apostles, 1997), 9.

elected Nikolai as their pastor who then was anointed to this office by Urshan.[111] Smorodin would become an influential leader of the apostolic movement in Russia.

Urshan ministered in Leningrad for two months before leaving for America. When he came, he needed an interpreter, but was able to preach in Russian by the time he departed. He left a thriving church of 200, with 3/4ths of the congregation baptized in the Holy Spirit and the rest seeking this experience.[112] By 1920 the work had grown to 80 congregations.[113]

From Russia to America

Urshan remained in Leningrad until the time he had left on his temporary passport nearly expired. He traveled to Oslo, Norway, where he met Thomas B. Barrett, leader of the Pentecostal Movement in Norway. After preaching several times in Barrett's church, he sailed for Newcastle, England and proceeded to London.

In London, Urshan was reunited with people he knew and loved. He ministered in Royal Albert Hall with A. A. Boddy, Cecil H. Polhill, and other English Pentecostal leaders. Authur Booth-Clibborn, son-in-law of Salvation Army's founder William Booth, invited Urshan to accompany him to South Wales, where "the saving, healing and baptizing power of the Holy Ghost accompanied us in Jesus' mighty name."[114]

The Pentecostals in Great Britain warned Urshan about the "New Issue People" in America, admonishing him to keep away from them and to continue his ministry among the Trinitarians. They also urged him to send a letter to those on both sides of the issue declaring his neutrality. He complied, explaining his neutrality with regard to the doctrines of baptism and the deity of Christ.

On June 18, 1916, Urshan boarded the steamship St. Paul at Liverpool for his passage to New York. In contrast for his first journey by ship to New York, he had a safe and pleasant trip, arriving at his destination in seven days.[115]

Summary

Urshan's ministry in the Urmia district of northeast Persia and in Russia proved his mettle as a Spirit-filled Christian determined to live his life for the glory of God. Facing virtually every conceivable obstacle to ministry – personal rejection, death threats, genocide, the martyrdom of those he loved, and deadly disease – Urshan pressed on with deep, unswerving faith in God.

---

[111]*The Chronicle*, 14.

[112]Urshan, *The Story of My Life*, 1st ed., 104.

[113]Roman Lunkin, "Traditional Pentecostals in Russia," *East-West Church and Ministry Report* 12, no. 3 (Summer 2004), http://www.eastwestreport.org/articles/ ew12302.html (accessed March 10, 2010).

[114]Urshan, *The Story of My Life*, 1st ed., 106.

[115]Urshan, *The Life Story*, 5th ed., 250-51. In the first edition of his life story, Urshan says the trip took eight days (Urshan, *The Story of My Life*, 1st ed., 106.

When confronted with doctrinal challenge as it relates to the formula for water baptism, Urshan loathed the idea of rejecting those with whom he differed. Instead, he was willing to embrace diversity, if it were possible. He did not rely on his personal instinct alone. Instead, he prayed fervently for God's direction, willingly following when it ran counter to his preconceived notions.

Urshan was twenty-nine years old when he arrived in his home village of Abajalu. He spent slightly more than two years in Persia and Russia. In face of incredible opposition, he established works that endure to the present. In turn, these faith communities have reached beyond the places of their origin to impact many people in other nations of the world.[116]

---

[116] A full description of the development of the Pentecostal work in Russia can be found in *The Chronicle,* an official publication of the church that sprang from Urshan's ministry in Russia. It traces the trajectory of the progress of the church founded under his ministry in today's Saint Petersburg. See *The Chronicle* (Amherst, [MA?]: The American Church in the Spirit of the Apostles, 1997). This organization is also known as the Evangelical Church in the Spirit of the Apostles as it relates to its work in Russia. See Talmadge L. French, *Early Interracial Oneness Pentecostalism* (Eugene, OR: Pickwick Publications, 2014), 181, n. 46.

Chapter Five

Return to the United States

Introduction

When Urshan returned to the United States from his missionary journey to Persia and Russia, he expected warm greetings from all Pentecostals, regardless of where they stood on the debate that centered on the formula for water baptism and the related issue concerning the biblical testimony to the oneness of God. Despite the reports he had received while in the Middle East and Europe, he was surprised to discover the sharp division which had developed between Pentecostals in North America over these issues.

He desired to transcend the debate and to work toward the healing of the wound in the Pentecostal body. Therefore, he fellowshipped with and preached for those on both sides. For the next few years, he enjoyed a broad and successful ministry in Canada and the United States.

Earlier in his Christian walk he had vowed that he would never marry in order to focus exclusively on the ministry to which he was called. However, during this period he fell in love and married Mildred H. Hammergren, believing he had received divine permission.[1] The marriage produced two daughters and two sons, but it ended in divorce after eighteen years. The failure of Urshan's marriage temporarily terminated his itinerant ministry. This ministry included a remarkable seven-month campaign in Los Angeles in 1918, where he cooperated with other ministers affiliated with the Assemblies of God that resulted in 500 being baptized with the Holy Spirit.

It was during this Los Angeles meeting that Urshan was required by the leaders of the Assemblies of God to declare himself plainly on the matter of the "New Issue," the formula for baptism and the nature of the Godhead. Urshan's "Confession of Faith" was published in various Pentecostal periodicals.

Urshan's itinerant ministry continued among Oneness Pentecostals. But after his divorce, he could no longer engage in an evangelistic ministry. He moved to New York City where he accepted the pastorate of a church and raised his children. In 1948 he announced his return to the evangelistic field and, in 1950, remarried. Shortly thereafter, his youngest son passed away. The last years of his life were marked by active ministry as an evangelist.

---

[1]Andrew and Mildred were married on August 9, 1917 in St. Paul, Minnesota.

When Urshan died in 1967, he was on the evangelistic field. Although pastoring on four occasions, he considered himself an evangelist. In addition, he was also an author, publisher, and theologian whose influence on Pentecostalism at large, and especially on Oneness Pentecostalism, continues to this day.

Urshan did not set out to be a Oneness pioneer. Rather, he sought to embrace and proclaim fully the experiences and doctrines of the first century church as he understood them. He realized, however, that everyone did not share his views. However, he was willing to fellowship those with whom he disagreed. He was willing even to use the vocabulary of those with whom he disagreed, so long as he could shape that vocabulary to fit his understanding.[2] In short, Urshan's status as a Oneness pioneer was thrust upon him by the unwillingness of those with whom he disagreed to recognize the validity of his views.

Ministry in the United States and Canada

Urshan had written to some of his friends in New York to tell them the time of his arrival, but no one met him at the dock. It was a Sunday morning. He hurried to Glad Tidings Mission, a stopping off point for missionaries, where he expected to be welcomed with open arms.[3]

The pastor, Robert Brown, was not in the morning service. Urshan was both hurt and surprised that Robert's wife, Marie, who had founded the church, did not invite him to join her on the platform or even acknowledge his presence. Urshan sat on the back row.

By the end of the service, the people realized Urshan was in their midst. They exclaimed, "Why, it's Brother Urshan! When did you arrive? Why didn't you come up on the platform?"[4] Several gathered around him, inquiring if he would be preaching at the evening service.

At that time, Marie approached him with a faint smile. Apologizing, she said that Robert had ordered her not to call Urshan to the platform until he had been able to speak with Urshan personally to find out where he stood doctrinally. She told Urshan that the people were demanding that she let Urshan preach in the evening service. She asked him, however, to speak only about his experiences in Persia and not on any other subject.

Robert returned while they were still in conversation. Although he was overjoyed to see Urshan and apologized for what he had said to his wife about him, he anxiously asked if Urshan had embraced the "New Issue." Urshan assured Brown

---

[2]See, e.g., Andrew D. Urshan, *Doctrine of Trinity and the Divinity of Jesus Christ* (Cochrane, WI: Andrew D. Urshan, 1923), 4.

[3]The history of Glad Tidings Tabernacle, as it is now known, refers to the church as Glad Tidings Hall during the time Urshan would have visited there. See E. L. Blumhofer, "Glad Tidings Tabernacle," in *NIDPCM,* 669 and Glad Tidings Tabernacle, http://www.gladtidingsnyc.com/ (accessed March 12, 2010). See Pentecostal Pioneers, Heaven Sent Revival, "Robert A. Brown," http://www.pentecostalpioneers.org/ RobertABrown.html (accessed March 12, 2010).

[4]Urshan, *The Life Story,* 5th ed., 253.

that he did not return to the United States to preach the doctrines which were so widely discussed and that he had not taken sides on this issue. Instead, he said he intended to preach on the subjects that were needed at that time. Urshan explained to Brown that he had been baptized in Jesus' name in Russia "and had received the revelation on the Deity of Jesus Christ."[5] Brown was satisfied with Urshan's explanation and invited him to preach at Glad Tidings for at least three days. Urshan accepted this invitation.

He then continued to Chicago. He was disappointed to discover that "God's people had grown worldly, indifferent, and prejudiced, allowing the root of bitterness to spring up in their hearts, to stifle the love of Christ towards one another."[6] He became so distraught over this that he suffered a "nervous break-down." Despite this, he testified that God "healed and comforted" him; otherwise, he thought he would have died.

After his recovery, Urshan was invited to minister "for both sides,"[7] beginning at Calvary Temple in Winnipeg, Canada, where A. H. Argue was the founding pastor. Urshan wrote, "I can never thank God sufficiently for granting me the privilege of co-operation with beloved Brother A. H. Argue of Winnipeg, Man., in revival campaigns."[8] Argue was a "pioneering figure in the Pentecostal Assemblies of Canada"; Calvary Temple "was for decades one of Canada's largest pentecostal [sic] churches."[9]

On his way to Winnipeg, Urshan preached twice at the Midway Pentecostal Mission in St. Paul, Minnesota, where H. Scott was the pastor. This proved to be a momentus moment, for it was at this meeting he met Mildred Harriet Hammergren, the woman who would become his first wife.[10] Mildred's father, David I. Hammergren, also became a significant person in Urshan's life. Hammergren, a three-term assemblyman in Wisconsin and a member of the Minnesota legislature from 1905 to 1907, earned his living by publishing a newspaper in Cochran, Wisconsin. After Urshan's marriage to his daughter, he published many of Urshan's works.[11]

When Urshan reached Winnipeg, "God graciously worked to turn His children's hearts toward one another. He caused them to lay aside their issues and begin to recognize one another as the Spirit-born family of God; brothers and sisters in Christ Jesus, and they were aflame again with a new zeal for lost souls."[12] The

---

[5]Urshan, *The Life Story,* 5th ed., 254.

[6]Urshan, *The Life Story,* 5th ed., 254.

[7]The phrase "for both sides" means that Urshan was invited to minister both by Trinitarian Pentecostals and Oneness Pentecostals.

[8]Urshan, *The Story of My Life,* 1st ed., 107. One of the occasions when Argue and Urshan ministered together would have been a few months before his marriage to Mildred Hammergren. A report of this meeting notes that special "speakers were Rev. A. H. Argue and the noted Persian evangelist, Andrew Urshan. A great revival broke out, stirring many of the surrounding churches" (http://www.bethel.ca/our-church/our-history/).

[9]E. A. Wilson, "Andrew Harvey Argue," NIDPCM, 331.

[10]Urshan, "The Story of My Life—27th Chapter," *The Witness of God* 6, no. 63 (April 1925):3.

[11]"Wisconsin Assemblyman, D. I. Hammergren, Dies," *Chicago Tribune,* August 14, 1944.

[12]Urshan, *The Life Story,* 5th ed., 254.

news of this revival spread, resulting in many invitations for Urshan to minister "near and far."

One of the places where Urshan ministered during this time was at the General Council of the Assemblies of God in St. Louis, Missouri on October 1-7, 1916. He came as an honored guest less than four months after his return from Russia and preached the first evening service on October 1, 1916.[13]

> The evening message was delivered by Brother Andrew D. Urshan, our Pentecostal Persian brother, lately returned from Persia and Russia. His theme was "Jesus, the all-sufficient One." How our hearts burned within us as he spake. At the close, the altar was filled with seekers after God and the power of God was mightily present.[14]

Stanley H. Frodsham gave a similar report:

> Some most excellent Revival Services were held at the evening sessions.... Bro. Andrew Urshan of Chicago ... and others, gave us stirring Gospel messages at these, and at the close of nearly every meeting a number of seekers would be seen at the altar.[15]

Although he was not ordained by the Assemblies of God until 1917, his name was on a "temporary list" of those who did not hold credentials and "yet who were granted privileges of the floor." Robert Brown of Glad Tidings in NY asked Urshan to "make a public and frank statement of denial" which satisfied the council.[16] Thus, Urshan was present and actively participating in the council meeting when about one-fourth of the Oneness brethren withdrew due to the passage of the new articles of faith. The number of ordained ministers in the Assemblies of God decreased from 585 to 429 after the council.[17]

Marriage

When Andrew and Mildred first met, she was only sixteen years old. He was attracted to her demure manner. When they married, Mildred was seventeen; Andrew was thirty-three. Mildred was "a sheltered American girl who had not ventured far from her hometown. Andrew was a cosmopolitan Middle-Eastern man ... with an established ministry that already spanned three continents."[18] They were "worlds apart in life experience and certain aspects of their worldview, but their longing to serve together in the Lord's work was a significant unifying factor."[19]

---

[13] Minutes of the General Council of the Assemblies of God, St. Louis, MO, Oct. 1-7, 1916.

[14] Minutes of the General Council, 4.

[15] Stanley H. Frodsham, "Notes from an eyewitness at the general council," *Pentecostal Evangel* (Oct. 21, 1916): 5.

[16] E. N. Bell, "The Urshan Trouble," *The Christian Evangel*, nos. 288-89 (May 17, 1919): 6. See Talmadge L. French, *Our God Is One: The Story of the Oneness Pentecostals* (Indianapolis, IN: Voice & Vision, 1999), 75-76.

[17] J. L. Hall, "United Pentecostal Church, International," in *NIDPCM*, 1162.

[18] Ruth Harvey, "Andrew D. Urshan: A Living Legacy of Faith," 9, a paper submitted to Professor Robin Johnston in partial fulfillment of the requirements for Modern Pentecostal Movements, Urshan Graduate School of Theology, February 13, 2015.

[19] Harvey, "Andrew D. Urshan," 9.

Before meeting Mildred Hammergren, Urshan had always said he would not marry.[20] Even after his marriage, he continued to understand I Corinthians 7 to mean that "a single life for God . . . is best, for truly to be right and to do right with your wife and children you must sincerely love them, serve them, and please them as much as possible. That . . . divides our affections and makes us to be taken up with the natural, a great deal."[21]

Urshan believed there were three levels of God's will: good, better, and best. Under this rubric, it was "good" to marry, "better" to marry and raise a family, and "best" not to marry, thus avoiding "much suffering in the flesh," if a person were "called" to do so.[22]

Before deciding to marry, Urshan "put a fleece out,"[23] praying until he had the assurance of God's "permissive will." Andrew and Mildred became engaged in January 1917 and were married seven months later. The account of their marriage was carried in *The Weekly Evangel,* the official publication of the Assemblies of God.

BRO. URSHAN MARRIED.

A very precious wedding service took place at St. Paul, Minn. on August 9th, 1917, at the home of the bride's parents, 899 Case street, when Evangelist Andrew D. Urshan of Persia was united in marriage to Miss Mildred H. Hammergren.

Pastor Harvey McAllister, of Midway Tabernacle, where Miss Hammergren attended, performed the ceremony in the presence of intimate friends, among whom were Mr. and Mrs. J. Nader of Chicago, who represented the Persian mission there, and Bro. H. O. Scott of Los Angeles.

Our Lord, who attended the marriage in Cana of Galilee, and adorned it by His presence, was again present on this occasion. Although absent in body, yet manifestly present in Spirit; inasmuch as His power filled the room, thus witnessing His smile of approval on the scene.

It surely was a typical Pentecostal wedding! The songs of Zion, prayers and praises

---

[20] Although Urshan does say that before he met Mildred Hammergren he "had always said, 'NO!' when confronted with the marriage question" (Urshan, *The Life Story,* 5th ed., 255), he also wrote in the first edition of his life story that "while in Persia, the Lord showed me that I would be married to an American girl. While ministering in St. Paul, God brought to me her who, later, became my wife, just as He brought Eve to Adam. He thought it was not good for Adam to be alone, and Adam saw God present to him Eve whom he gladly accepted for his helpmeet. God was indeed good in giving to me Mildred Hammergren of St. Paul, Minn., for my wife. For all His good gifts I praise Him. She was wonderfully saved and baptized in the Holy Ghost four years ago. She is now with me prayerfully preparing for our future missionary trips if Jesus tarries and permits us to go to Russia and Persia. Already God has used her among our Persian people in Chicago who esteem her very highly in the Lord" (Urshan, *The Story of My Life,* 1st ed., 107).
[21] Urshan, *The Life Story,* 5th ed., 255-56.
[22] Urshan, *The Life Story,* 5th ed., 256.
[23] To "put out a fleece" is a reference to Gideon's efforts to determine the will of God by means of a test (Judges 6:37-40).

ascended, in such a way that one and all felt that it was good for us to be there.

Bro. and Sister Urshan are invited, by Winnipeg friends, to spend this month in Minaki, Ontario, Canada, which invitation has been accepted by them. Their address for two weeks will be: Grand View Camp, Minaki, Ontario, Canada.[24]

If the Lord tarries, Bro. and Sister Urshan will leave this coming spring, D. V., with a band of co-workers and missionaries, for Europe, Russia and Persia. His marriage is a preparation for that much desired missionary trip.

Let us all pray for Bro. Urshan and his dear wife with more fervency than ever before—that God may bless richly their new step in life to the glory and honor of His name, and that this union may result in a more fruitful ministry for our brother than ever in the past.—Mrs. Harvey McAlister.[25]

Urshan reproduced this account of the wedding in *The Witness of God*, but deleted the reference to the planned trip to Europe, Russia, and Persia. This did not take place until after his marriage to Mildred ended.[26]

Enroute to Minaki, Urshan preached twice at Calvary Temple in Winnipeg. Members of the church donated funds for the Urshans' use during their two-week honeymoon. Following their honeymoon, the Urshans traveled through St. Paul, Minnesota to Chicago, where Urshan had a preaching engagement.

After their arrival in Chicago, Urshan was called to Montreal, Quebec to help the pastor there "clear up some matters." Urshan had ministered in Montreal a few months before his marriage. He responded to this call immediately, leaving Mildred in Chicago during the three weeks he was gone.[27] Upon his return, the Urshans stayed for a few days in Chicago before departing for revivals in California. Enroute they traveled through St. Paul, Minnesota, Winnipeg, Canada, and Portland, Oregon, before arriving in San Francisco, where Urshan conducted a two week meeting at Glad Tidings Temple, pastored by Robert Craig.[28] Because of its success, the meeting was extended an extra week. Some thirty people were baptized with the Holy Spirit.[29]

---

[24]The honeymoon venue turned out to be a lakefront cottege owned by a Mr. and Mrs. Andrews. See Urshan, *The Life Story*, 5th ed., 257.

[25]Mrs. Harvey McAlister, "Bro. Urshan Married," *The Weekly Evangel* (August 25, 1917): 13.

[26]Urshan, "The Story of My Life—27th Chapter," *The Witness of God* 6, no. 63 (April 1925):3.

[27]Urshan, "The Story of My Life—27th Chapter," *The Witness of God* 6, no. 23 (April 1925): 3; Urshan, *The Life Story*, 5th ed., 257. Apparently the pastor was Charles Edward Baker, founder of the Pentecostal Assemblies of Canada work in Quebec. See https://paoc.org/family/story/archives/archives-news/item-acquired-secretary-style-desk-belonging-to-charles-baker, http://www.bethel.ca/our-church/our-history/ and *Minutes of the General Council of the Assemblies of God*, St. Louis, MO, October 1-7, 1916.

[28]GTSF History, http://gtsf.org/history-of-glad-tidings-church-san-francisco/(accessed March 13, 2010).

[29]In the second edition of his life story Urshan reported that this meeting in San Francisco lasted one month with "eighty souls [being] filled with God" (Urshan, "The Story of

From San Francisco the Urshans proceeded to Los Angeles, where he ministered for six months. The congregation grew from seventy to 3,000 for the Sunday services.

Ministry in Los Angeles

The fruit of his Los Angles mission confirmed Urshan's conviction that he had responded to a call that came to him while he was in Persia facing martyrdom during the Armenian genocide. Despite confronting almost certain death, he had experienced a strong conviction that God still had a major work from him to accomplish. For some reason he could not explain, Los Angeles was impressed upon his mind as the location. Taking the matter to prayer, he believed he heard God's answer in these words: "Because I have a ministry for you yet, and no weapon formed against thee shall prosper."[30]

Upon his return to America, Urshan had many invitations to minister in Los Angeles "from both New and Old Issue people there," but he was not moved by God to accept them. However, when he received a call from two small independent missions under the pastoral care of W. M. Collins and A. G. Osterberg, who had agreed to merge "for a special Soul-saving campaign" and to send for Urshan to take charge, he took it as "God's hand." Deferring a decision to accept an invitation to hold a meeting in Oakland, he traveled to Los Angeles to determine if God's time had come to fulfill the call he had first heard in Persia. Later, the Los Angeles group decribed this tentative decision.

> About three months ago Brothers W. M. Collins and A. G. Osterberg united their assemblies for the purpose of a Revival Campaign in Los Angeles. After a correspondence of these two brethren and A. D. Urshan, the "Persian Evangelist," extending over a period of nearly a year, Brother Urshan finally consented to come to Los Angeles for a few days to try out the situation whether or not this was God's appointed time for a great Revival in this "Jerusalem of America." His purposes were, should the test prove that this was not God's time for Los Angeles, to return to Oakland, where his services for a great Union Revival were urgently solicited.
>
> From the very first, however, it was plainly manifest to all that this was the time and place for the Unique Ministry of this faithful Evangelist and prophet of the Lord.[31]

My Life—28th Chapter," *The Witness of God* 6, no. 64 [May 1925]: 2).

[30] Urshan, "The Story of My Life—28th Chapter," *The Witness of God* 6, no. 64 (May 1925):2.

[31] W. M. Collins and A. G. Osterberg, "Committee Report of the Revival in Los Angeles," *Glad Tidings* 1, no. 5:2. Collins had been a Baptist pastor, and Osterberg, an Azusa Street pioneer who had been born of Baptist Swedish immigrants in 1885, became pastor of the "Full Gospel Assembly" on the corner of Sixty-eighth and Denver in Los Angeles at the age of twenty-four. The mission had been built by Osterberg and his father and brother, all carpenters by trade." See Grant Wacker, *Heaven Below: Early Pentecostals and American Culture* (Cambridge: Harvard University Press, 2001), 144, 213, 316, n. 13.

When Urshan arrived in Los Angeles to investigate the possibility of accepting the invitation of Collins and Osterberg,

> he recommended to the committee that all points of Doctrine that were not essential to salvation or to Godliness of life, but had a tendency to disturb the unity of the saints, be put aside, and only those truths that led to salvation of souls, to the deepening of Christian experience and the unity of the body of Christ be emphasized. The committee heartily accepted this and . . . loyally stood by him as he . . . faithfully pursued this course.
>
> The result has been that many of the breaches [were] healed, and the Lord's faithful people [were] made to see the folly of fighting over doctrinal points concerning the "mystery of the God-head."
>
> As to Water Baptism, to satisfy the conscience of every candid believer, and to constitute a broad ground as a basis of fellowship without controversy, [the committee] agreed to accept the one given by Matthew and the one as given in Luke. That this was pleasing to God was signally manifest by the Spirit of God brooding over the Baptismal waters, giving in some instances a double Baptism the same evening. The one in Water being followed by the Baptism in the Holy Spirit.
>
> The formula used is as follows: Upon a profession of your faith, "To the glory of God the Father, the Son, and the Holy Ghost, I baptise you in the name of the Lord Jesus Christ. Amen." This formula was submitted to an assembly numbering several hundred, and with an exception of less than ten people it was enthusiastically approved.[32]

Collins and Osterberg continued:

> It is our conviction that the Ministers who unduly and persistently emphasize points of Doctrine, belonging either to the "Old" or the "New" issue, as they are termed, and who endeavor to gather a congregation around some Doctrinal issue other than to Jesus Christ, the Lord, betray another Spirit than that which characterizes a true Shepherd over the flock of God.[33]

On Sunday, January 5, 1918, a series of revival meetings began that lasted until Sunday, August 11, 1918.[34] The meetings began in a hall known as the "People's Auditorium," where Maria Woodworth-Etter had held meetings the previous winter. The hall held 800 people.[35] Within two weeks it was too small to accommodate the crowds. They moved to the Ice Palace, seating 1,500.[36] They soon

---

[32] W. M. Collins and A. G. Osterberg, "Committee Report of the Revival in Los Angeles," *Glad Tidings* 1, no. 5: 2-3.

[33] W. M. Collins and A. G. Osterberg, "Committee Report of the Revival in Los Angeles," *Glad Tidings* 1, no. 5:3.

[34] Urshan's last participation in this event was on Sunday, July 21, 1918. See Urshan, "Our Farewell Meeting in Los Angeles," *The Witness of God* (May 1963): 7.

[35] Urshan reported the hall would seat "over 600 people" (Urshan, "The Story of My Life—28th Chapter," *The Witness of God* 6, no. 64 [May 1925]: 2).

[36] Urshan's account was that the Ice Palace or "Ice Skating Rink" would seat 1,200 (Urshan, "The Story of My Life—28th Chapter," *The Witness of God* 6, no. 64 [May 1925]: 2).

needed even larger quarters, so they rented the "Temple Baptist Auditorium,"[37] also known as the "Temple Auditorium" and "Clune's Theater,"[38] paying $50 for the use of the 3,000 seat auditorium for two hours each Sunday afternoon.[39]

In the midst of this seven month long meeting, those involved in its leadership decided to hold a "world wide camp-meeting" beginning June 1, 1918 and extending for at least two months. The front cover of Glad Tidings advertised "The Unsectarian Old-Time Gospel World Wide Camp-Meeting at Los Angeles, California. Beginning June 1, 1918, and lasting two months or longer."[40] Although the Urshan's first child, Grace Susannah, was born on Saturday, May 25, 1918, one week before the campmeeting began on June 1,[41] Urshan consented to remain in the city for the long expected 'World-Wide Camp Meeting'."[42]

During the course of the Los Angeles revival, Urshan wrote three books, all published by the Assemblies of God Gospel Publishing House. These included his autobiography, *The Story of My Life*, a collection of sermons preached before the Los Angeles revival, *Timely Messages of Warning*, and a collection of sermons preached during the revival, *Timely Messages of Comfort*.[43] The titles of the eight messages preached during the Los Angeles revival provides insight on Urshan's ministry:

---

[37]The Temple Baptist Auditorium was the home of the Temple Baptist Church in Los Angeles which had started on July 17, 1903 with 258 members, more than 100 of whom were from the First Baptist Church whose pastor, Joseph Smale, was active in the early twentieth century Pentecostal movement. The first pastor of the Temple Baptist Church was Robert J. Burdette, a popular speaker and humorist. Within six years the church had grown to nearly 1,000 members, necessitating the construction of a new church facility with the largest auditorium in the city of Los Angeles. The Temple Baptist congregation used the auditorium twice each Sunday morning, and it was rented out at other times. For information about Burdette's pastorate and a picture of the auditorium, see Clara Bradley Burdette, ed., *Robert J. Burdette: His Message* (Chicago: The John C. Winston Co., 1922), 254-68.

[38]The Temple Baptist Auditorium was also known as "Clune's Theater" because it was for a period of time leased by William "Billy" Clune for use as a movie theater, even while it was in use for church events. A detailed description, including a statement of seating capacity at 2,700, can be found at Cinema Treasures, "Clunes Auditorium," http://cinematreasures.org/theater/13960/ (accessed March 15, 2010).

[39]Urshan, "The Story of My Life—28th Chapter," *The Witness of God* 6, no. 64 (May 1925): 2; see also "The Present Blessed Revival in Los Angeles California," *Glad Tidings* 1, no. 5: 1-2.

[40]*Glad Tidings* 1, no. 5:1. The front cover of *Glad Tidings* advertised "The Unsectarian Old-Time Gospel World Wide Camp-Meeting at Los Angeles, Cal. Beginning June 1, 1918, and lasting two months or longer."

[41]Urshan, *The Life Story*, 5th ed., 258.

[42]*Glad Tidings* 1, no. 5:2.

[43]See inside back cover of Andrew D. Urshan, *The Story of My Life* (St. Louis: The Gospel Publishing House, n.d.) and *Glad Tidings* 1, no. 5: 12.

Sermon Title	Date preached
The Great Purpose of Redemption and the True Worship with It's Blessed Benefits	February 17, 1918
Knowing God in All Our Ways and Honoring Him in Our Hearts	February 24, 1918
First Persian Christian Martyr	February 25, 1918
What Happens after the Baptism of the Holy Ghost	No date given
Perfect Liberty in God through Jesus Christ	No date given
The Gracious Dealings of God Misunderstood	No date given
Compassion of Jesus: Are the Days of Miracles Passed?	No date given
Continual Prayer is Continual Victory	No date given[1]

Additional insight into these meetings is seen in the reports from *The Weekly Evangel*, also published by the Assemblies of God. The February 2, 1918 issue, published approximately one month after the meetings began, carried Urshan's article entitled "The Fullness of God." Urshan argued that those filled with God's fullness will love one another and will not be judgmental, bitter, proud, or envious. He notes, "We meet . . . strife and trouble creators everywhere."[44] But at the Los Angeles meetings, "The Lord is graciously working . . . uniting His people by fashioning their hearts alike, and He is rooting and grounding them in His great love."[45]

The March 2, 1918 issue carried a second article, "The Confession of Our Faults." He wrote, "The Lord graciously gave us a message this afternoon at the Revival Campaign in Los Angeles on CONFESSION."[46] He discussed the need to confess one's sins not only to God, but also to one another. Understood in the context of division caused by the "New Issue," Urshan's words are potent: "It is a sad fact that many Pentecostal ministers are busy preaching and fighting over theological doctrines and are neglecting such messages as this."[47]

---

[44]Andrew D. Urshan, "The Fulness [sic] of God," *The Weekly Evangel*, no. 225 (February 2, 1918): 3.

[45]Andrew D. Urshan, "The Fulness [sic] of God," *The Weekly Evangel*, no. 225 (February 2, 1918): 3.

[46]Andrew D. Urshan, "The Confession of Our Faults," *The Weekly Evangel*, no. 229 (March 2, 1918): 4.

[47]Andrew D. Urshan, "The Confession of Our Faults," *The Weekly Evangel*, no. 229 (March 2, 1918): 4.

C.W. Doney's article titled, "Evangelist A. D. Urshan's Addresses," appeared in the April 20, 1918 issue. Doney described three messages given by Urshan on his experiences during the massacres in Persia.

Finally, at the conclusion of the revival, Collins and Osterberg published a summary report in *Glad Tidings*:

> On sending forth this report of the blessed work accomplished during the present revival we desire to express our profound gratitude to God the Father of our Lord Jesus Christ and to bear witness that His blessings have attended us and have rested upon our efforts here in Los Angeles even beyond our most sanguine expectations.
>
> Inquiries are coming to us from all parts of the country regarding the revival meetings which began here on the 5th of last January, 1918.
>
> Furthermore, the eyes of the Saints from all quarters of the earth are turned towards Los Angeles with a particular interest and a special degree of solicitude, because it was here that this Latter Rain outpouring of the Holy Spirit spread forth in 1906, and from here the Message sounded forth to the uttermost parts of the earth.
>
> To answer these inquiries and also to a small measure satisfy the desire of the Saints at large to know of the work here we feel that we have God's approval in giving forth these facts.
>
> While we shall speak somewhat of things in general, we feel constrained to confine our remarks very largely to conditions immediately preceding and leading up to and including the Evangelistic Campaign beginning as above stated on January 5th, 1918, conducted by Andrew D. Urshan, the Persian-American Evangelist and his co-workers which extended to August 11th, making a period of exactly seven months and one week.
>
> While Los Angeles was one of the starting points of the Latter Rain Baptism in the Holy Spirit which fell April 12th, 1906, and produced a world-wide revival unsurpassed in the annals of history and which is destined to go on until Jesus comes, it is also proved to be a hotbed of heresy where false doctrines have been incubated and propagated to such an extent that not only the "Unity of the Faith" was rendered impossible, but the "Unity of the Spirit" itself was greatly marred—hundreds of the Lord's Baptized Saints were heartbroken and distressed over these conditions. They were crying "Lord revive Thy work;" "Lord send the old-time power."
>
> And just as in answer to the cries of His ancient people He sent and delivered them, so He came to our rescue. More than expected.
>
> Five Hundred Have Received the Baptism
>
> of the Holy Spirit with speaking in other tongues as the initial evidence, perhaps twice that many have been quickened into a renewed experience and a closer walk with God, while hundreds have been saved and healed.
>
> Over twelve thousand dollars have been contributed to the work during this time,

more than five thousand of which has gone to the foreign fields to support missionaries.

We believe it will be helpful to pastors and their assemblies everywhere to give some of the main causes which in our opinion have contributed to the success of the meetings.

We would place first among these purity of motive; we believe that from the leading evangelists down to the most hidden Saints engaged in these meetings there was absolute purity of motive—that the desire expressed day and night in intercessory prayer was that God would come forth and manifest His power among His people—that the object of that desire was to glorify the name of Jesus Christ, to unify His body, to purify each member thereof and to save the unsaved.

This desire, we repeat, found its expression in a spirit of prevailing prayer.

Next in importance has been the faithful ministry of the Word by Bro. Urshan and his helpers, among whom we would mention Bro. A. H. Argue, of Winnipeg, who was with us the first three months. Bro. Ed Butler, also of Winnipeg, who had been with us from the beginning; Sisters Peden and Andrews, of Canada, who have been with us much of the time; Bro. Roberts, of Indianapolis, and Bro. A. G. Garr, of Dallas, Texas all of whom have rendered efficient service. In July, Brother Lindblad, of Portland, Oregon, came with us, and finally B. S. Moore and his wife, of Japan, came, all of whom God seemed to send to us at the right time with a ministry to fit the occasion. Beside these were a number of local brothers and sisters, whose names are in the "Book of Life," who have been of very great help in many ways, particularly in praying for the sick.

But the ministry of Brother Urshan requires more than a passing notice, without in any sense depreciating the ministry of those mentioned and of some not mentioned, it is but justice to say that Andrew D. Urshan is a

"Unique Man with a Unique Ministry"

His ministry finds its source, its center, its all in Jesus Christ the Son of God. Reaching back unto the fathomless mystery of Eternity "to the time where all the universe slept in the mind of God as yet unborn; when the unnavigated ether was yet unfanned by the wing of a single Angel; where space was shoreless; when universal silence reigned and not a voice or whisper shocked the solemnity of that silence; where there was no being, and no motion, no time, and naught but God Himself, alone in His eternity; when without the song of an angel, without the attendance of even the cherubim; long ere the living creatures were born or wheels of the Chariots of Jehovah were fashioned, even there in the beginning was the Logos" and this Logos, was and is the Son—which was "Made flesh and Tabernacled among us." And that in Him, through His incarnation—His Ministry, His death, and Resurrection and Assention [sic]—His Mediation at God's right hand and His return in glory, God was ordained and provided a redemption that meets every need of the human life for Spirit, Soul and Body from the lowest depths into which sin has plunged us to the sublime heights of the glory of God in Christ His glorified

Son. He preaches this gospel with a fervency of Spirit that makes the people feel and believe that he feels and believes what he preaches. This is the message of hope. And as hope begets hope the people catch his spirit and without much effort at Unity and as noiselessly (except for the mighty volume of praise and prayer) as the Tabernacle of old went up without the sound of a hammer, the Saints are drawn to Christ and in the silence of adoration as well as the mighty outbursts of devotion you feel you can hear one united voice saying, "We are satisfied with the fatness of thy house."[48]

Despite the spiritual success of these meetings and the glowing reports of those who attended, theological trouble was brewing. Many of the ministers who participated with Urshan in the Los Angeles campaign were, like Urshan, affiliated with the Assemblies of God. Several accused him of teaching the "New Issue Doctrine." Urshan wrote,

> We felt jealousy creeping in some of the ministering brethren who were welcomed upon our large platform, but our sincere love for them would not let us believe it . . . . Nevertheless, as God continued working more and more, these very preachers were hunting to find some reason to down us. Soon they thought I was teaching the so-called New Issue Doctrine because I was exalting fervently the Name of Jesus, and the State chairman of the general Council [of the Assemblies of God] called a State conference for the purpose of condemning me on the ground of Doctrine; but they were shamefully disappointed for they could not find a cause. They however ceased not their ungodly efforts, but they wrote to the officials of the Council that I . . . appeared to be one with the General Council's Teachings, and yet I seemed to encourage the New Issue people's teaching. They urged and insisted that I must take a clear and cut stand either with the Council or with the New Issue people so-called.
>
> We were very much grieved over such ultimatum and saw at once that we were forced to do something that if we were left free we would not have done, because we loved God's baptized people without respect of persons and their particular differences in some of their doctrines. We had a special evangelistic ministry that could have benefited both schools and we therefore wished to remain neutral, but they would not have it this way.[49]

Forced to take a stand, he wrote his "Confession of Faith" in early April 1918. In the final edition of his autobiography he explained his decision:

> It was during this Revival . . . that we were forced by our leading Trinitarian brethren to take our stand – either with them, or with the Oneness Saints – whom they called the "New Issue" People. We had done our best to remain neutral and continue our ministry to both sides . . . . However, these Trinitarian brothers became determined to interfere with our progress under God's leadership. We prayed much about the matter and were led, per their demand, to print our confession of faith concerning the Dispensational Name of God which is The Lord Jesus Christ – be-

---

[48]W. M. Collins and [A]. G. Osterburg, "Committee Report of the Los Angeles Revival," *Glad Tidings* 1, no. 5 [September 1918], reprinted in Urshan, *The Life Story*, 5th ed., 264-268.

[49]Urshan, "The Story of My Life—28th Chapter," *The Witness of God* 6, no. 64 (May 1925): 3.

ing the Proper and timely Name of the Father, the Son, and the Holy Ghost, for this Dispensation of Grace.[50]

The Assemblies of God leadership promptly printed his confession in *The Weekly Evangel:*

"So then faith comes by hearing, and hearing by the word of God." Romans 10:17.

It has been reported lately from this city something that may create a wrong impression that I am supporting the advocators of the "New Issue" so-called in our great blessed revival meetings in this city. This is absolutely not so, but rather contrary. I personally believe and stand on the blessed written word of God concerning the great mystery of godliness, not on the conclusions of men, nor in their words of strife concerning God-head teaching, therefore I prayerfully and humbly confess that I believe in one **God, the Father, the Son and the Holy Ghost.** Matthew 28:19.

I believe in Jesus Christ, the Son of the Father, who is the true God and the eternal life. 1 John 5:20. 2 John 5.

I believe that there are three that bear record in heaven the Father, the Word **(Jesus Christ)** and the Holy Ghost and these three are one. 1 John 5:7.

I believe in the Spirit by which we are all baptized into one body, whether we be Jews or Gentiles, whether bond or free and have been all made to drink in one Spirit; yea one Lord, one faith, one baptism, one God and Father of all, who is above all, and in you all. 1 Cor. 12:13, and Eph. 4:5-6.

I believe this adorable Three-One God can be only approached and seen in and through the person or face of Jesus Christ, the son. 1 Timothy 6:16. Matthew 11:27. John 1:18. John 14:7-11. "For in Him dwelleth all the fullness of the God-head bodily." Col. 2:9.

I believe in one most glorious eternal incomprehensible and mysterious Being of God; and that Jesus Christ the Son, is the only true and full express image of His glorious and bright Being. Heb. 1:3. Col. 1:15-19.

I believe also and practice the emphatic and definite commandment of God through the lips of the great apostle to the Gentiles who said, "and whatsoever ye do in **word or deed**, do all in the name of the Lord Jesus, giving thanks to God and the **Father** by Him" Col. 3:17.

Now, "The grace of the Lord Jesus Christ and the Love of God, and the communion of the Holy Ghost be with you all. Amen." 2 Cor. 13:14.

Brethren, "We having the same spirit of faith, according as it is written, I believe, and therefore I have spoken; we also believe and therefore speak! 2 Cor. 4:13.

Dear saints pray for us.

---

[50]Urshan, *The Life Story*, 5th ed., 258.

Your brother, sincerely, believes in the truth and the whole truth, as it is in Christ Jesus.

ANDREW D. URSHAN

"The Old Time Gospel Revival Campaign," Los Angeles, Cal., 1041 South Broadway[51]

---

[51]Andrew D. Urshan, "Confession of Faith," The Weekly Evangel" no. 236-237 (April 20, 1918): 13. Emphasis in original. This "Confession of Faith" appeared also in *Glad Tidings* and *The Latter Rain Evangel* with some variations. In *Glad Tidings*, the first two sentences after the quotation of Romans 10:17 as they appear in *The Weekly Evangel* are replaced with the following: "For fear that a false impression may arise concerning my faith in the God-head doctrine, from a report that has recently been circulated in this city, I therefore desire to confess my faith in God as follows . . ." (Andrew D. Urshan, "Confession of Faith Concerning the God-Head," *Glad Tidings* 1, no. 5:6). Where the confession as printed in *The Weekly Evangel* reads, "I believe in one **God, the Father, the Son and the Holy Ghost**," the confession as printed in *Glad Tidings* reads, "I believe in One triune God, whose name is THE FATHER, THE SON AND THE HOLY GHOST" (Urshan, "Confession of Faith," *Glad Tidings* 1, no. 5:6). There are other variants that are apparently merely typographical errors or differences in typographical emphases. The differences between the confession as it appeared in *The Weekly Evangel* and *The Latter Rain Evangel* are minor and may be limited to typographical or stylistic issues. A variant that may have theological significance is that where *The Weekly Evangel* reads, "I believe in one most glorious eternal incomprehensible and mysterious Being of God," *The Latter Rain Evangel* reads, "I believe in the one most glorious, eternal, incomprehensible and mysterious invisible Being of God" (Andrew D. Urshan, "Confession of Faith," *The Latter Rain Evangel* 10, no. 8 (May 1918): 15). It should be pointed out, however, that where *The Weekly Evangel* reads, "and that Jesus Christ the Son, is the only true and full express image of His glorious and bright Being," *Glad Tidings* reads, "and that Jesus Christ, the Son, is the only true and full express image of His glorious and bright invincible being." It is possible that the "invisible" of *The Latter Rain Evangel* in the previous part of the paragraph became the "invincible" of *Glad Tidings* in the latter part of the paragraph or vice versa.

Regardless of other variants with possible theological significance, the one variant that seems unquestionably significant is *The Weekly Evangel* reading, "I believe in one God, the Father, the Son and the Holy Ghost" in comparison with the *Glad Tidings* reading, "I believe in One triune God, whose name is THE FATHER, THE SON AND THE HOLY GHOST." This variant begs the question as to which version of the confession is original or if Urshan revised the confession for one of the publications. On the other hand, it is possible that the editor of one, two, or all of the publications revised the confession.

The substantial agreement between *The Weekly Evangel* and *The Latter Rain Evangel* suggests the reading in these two publications as the original. The word "triune" in the *Glad Tidings* version is not unlike Urshan, however, for he used this word freely in his various writings. But the phrase "whose name is THE FATHER, THE SON AND THE HOLY GHOST" in the *Glad Tidings* version sounds unlike Urshan, who wrote that shortly after his baptism with the Holy Spirit the words "Father, Son, and Holy Ghost" coursed through his being together with "Lord Jesus Christ," from which he deduced that the name of the Father was "Lord," the name of the Son "Jesus," and the name of the Holy Ghost "Christ" (Urshan, *The Life Story*, 5th ed., 137-40). This was foundational for Urshan's theology of name, so it seems unlikely that he would have written the phrase found in the *Glad Tidings*.

Despite the controversy coming to a head in April, Urshan continued to participate in the Los Angeles meeting until Sunday, July 21, 1918. About 500 had been baptized with the Holy Spirit since the beginning of the revival.[52]

During the Los Angeles meeting, Urshan was in good standing with the Assemblies of God. According to E. N. Bell, the editor of *The Christian Evangel*, the official organ of the General Council of the Assemblies of God, Urshan had satisfied the General Council during a meeting at St. Louis:

> Bro. Urshan came on the platform and made such a statement of denial as satisfied the Council . . . and so he went out with credentials and approval from the General Council. On the ground that he did not hold these errors the Evangel allowed him to report regularly in its columns his Persian work, which resulted in hundreds and hundreds of dollars being sent to Bro. Urshan.[53]

But in retrospect, Bell believed "the whole General Council was deceived by Bro. Urshan into believing he did not have these errors in his heart, whereas now his own circulars admit he has had these things in his heart for about four years and that it was not then God's time to announce them."[54] Further, Bell claimed that "Bro. Urshan has been playing 'possum, keeping quiet on these things, concealing what he now admits was IN HIS HEART FOR YEARS."[55]

The emphasis on "mystery" in Urshan's confession is consistent with his treatment of the Godhead elsewhere. (See, e.g., Urshan, "First Chapter—Story of My Life: The Assyro-Chaldean's Race, And the Life Story of Andrew David Urshan, the Assyro-Chaldean," *The Witness of God* 3, no. 34 [October 1922]: 2-4; Urshan, "Open Letter," 4; Urshan, *The Almighty God*, 77). The concept of mystery within the Godhead was eventually eliminated or at least minimized in mainstream Oneness theology. (See Urshan, *The Life Story*, 5th ed., 14-16; David K. Bernard, *The Oneness of God* [Hazelwood, MO: Word Aflame Press, 1983], 65, 289, 295; David S. Norris, *I Am: A Oneness Pentecostal Theology* [Hazelwood, MO: WAP Academic, 2009], 57-59.)

[52]Urshan, "Our Farewell Meeting in Los Angeles," *The Witness of God* (May 1963): 7; Urshan, *The Life Story*, 5th ed., 266.

[53]E. N. Bell, "The Urshan Trouble," *The Christian Evangel*, nos. 288-89 (May 17, 1919): 6.

[54]E. N. Bell, "The Urshan Trouble," 6.

[55]E. N. Bell, "The Urshan Trouble," 6. Emphasis in original. Bell's comments are particularly interesting in light of the fact that only three years earlier he himself was charged with holding the "New Issue" doctrine. While it is true that Urshan used "New Issue" language in expressing his view of the Godhead, in his "Confession of Faith," he used it in such a way that was fully consistent with his explanation to Robert Brown at Glad Tidings in New York upon his return from his mission to Persia in 1915. He also expressed his confession in such a way that some Trinitarians could affirm had it not been written at the height of the controversy. In terms of motive, the reader must decide whether to accept Urshan's explanation that he kept neutral on the issue in an attempt to heal the division, or Bell's implication that he remained silent for four year in order to receive financial support from the Assemblies of God.

Separation from the Assemblies of God

Following the Los Angeles revival, Urshan did not accept any invitations for three months, resting and waiting for further direction from God. Specifically, he was seeking to discern whether the Lord was calling him to return to Russia.[56] During this time he believed that he received "greater revelation" and "scriptural illumination" on the deity of Christ. He wrote to the General Council of the Assemblies of God about his belief that the one name of the Father, Son, and Holy Ghost was "nothing more than Jesus Christ our Lord in whose Name we are to be baptized and hide for eternal safety."[57] In view of this, Urshan asked whether the officials of the Assemblies of God wished for him to remain in that organization.[58] They answered that they could not allow his teaching, so Urshan withdrew. He then wrote seven "open letters" to a significant number of Pentecostals, explaining his teaching.[59] At least 500 people embraced Urshan's teaching on the deity of Christ and were baptized according to Urshan's understanding of Acts 2:38 in response to his letters. Hundreds of people who had hesitated to fully embrace the Oneness Pentecostal perspective on the Godhead were "strengthened." Many, who had been preaching this doctrine in the face of persecution, "rejoiced over the good news that Brother Urshan now preaches **'Jesus Only'** truth."[60]

From Urshan's perspective, he was falsely accused:

> Since we have come forth publicly speaking that which God wants us . . . and have taken a stand for the name of the Lord Jesus Christ, the General Council [of the Assemblies of God], which is a Pentecostal people's organization, are trying to close doors of their assemblies and to prejudice the hearts of all the people of God against this glorious message of the Church of Philadelphia (which is the message of God entrusted to his faithful remnant in these last days) by accusing us through their magazines of wrong doing, seeking to stain our God-given character. Thank God, judgment has already begun at the house of God.[61]

Urshan did not explain what he meant by "judgment [having] already begun at the house of God," but he did discuss some of the problems he thought existed in the Assemblies of God under this heading: "The Invisible Forces or the Demo-

---

[56]Urshan, "The Story of My Life—28th Chapter," *The Witness of God* 6, no. 64 (May 1925): 3.

[57]Urshan, "The Story of My Life—28th Chapter," *The Witness of God* 6, no. 64 (May 1925): 3.

[58]E. N. Bell commented on Urshan's request: "Brother Urshan has offered to turn in his credentials held from the General Council, if they cannot endorse his teaching, and I am sure they cannot endorse it" (E. N. Bell, "Andrew Urshan's New Stand," *The Christian Evangel*, nos. 284-285 [April 19, 1919]: 9).

[59]The content of these seven "open letters" was subsequently published in two books by Andrew D. Urshan: *Why I was Baptized in the Name of the Lord Jesus Christ in Russia* (Chicago, IL: n.d.) and *The Almighty God in the Lord Jesus Christ* (Los Angeles: 1919).

[60]Urshan, "The Story of My Life—28th Chapter," *The Witness of God* 6, no. 64 (May 1925): 4. Emphasis in original.

[61]Andrew D. Urshan, *The Almighty God in the Lord Jesus Christ* (Los Angeles: 1919), 71.

niac Anti-Christ Armies Affecting the Pentecostal Movement."[62] He claimed that many Pentecostals had "gone into what is called 'Russellism,'"[63] due to the failure to "preach the deity of our Lord and Saviour." He also accused the Assemblies of God of legalism:

> (fundamentals) which have been formulated and confirmed by a vote set forth in print, just like all other denominations, and no one can join that organization now if he does not keep within the borders of their set doctrines. If one should go ahead of their creed, as he is led by the Holy Spirit he is cast out and pronounced dangerous.[64]

Further, he labeled the Assemblies of God as worldly, with extremes of "fanaticism" and "formality and dryness." This "worldliness" included "worldly dressing, worldly conversation, and worldly pride." It was his opinion that "ambition and formality" were working to cause the Pentecostals "to fight one another."

In Urshan's view, those who preferred the words of Jesus in Matthew 28:19 over the Book of Acts and the letters to the churches were guilty of "higher criticism."[65]

Urshan saw God at work in the "heavy, hot irons of persecution" he faced. This persecution would remove "every bit of worldly spirit and all the higher or lower criticism of His Holy Word." When this was accomplished, God would "have a people that will hear and do every command up to the last letter."[66]

The perspective of those in the Assemblies of God was, of course, quite different. "The Urshan Trouble," an article by E. N. Bell, appeared in the May 17, 1919 issue of *The Christian Evangel*. The article consisted largely of letters from people who disagreed with Urshan interspersed with Bell's comments. Bell wrote that Urshan "declares the name of the Father and of the Son and of the Holy Ghost is Jesus Christ, straight New Issue teaching."[67] He claimed that "letters of regret of Bro. Urshan's error and telling of disasters following are reaching us constantly" and urged his readers "to pray that God will reclaim our brother from his errors in teaching and errors in methods."[68]

---

[62]Urshan, *The Almighty God in the Lord Jesus Christ*, 72-73.

[63]By Russellism, Urshan did not mean that these people were Jehovah's Witnesses. Rather, he meant they were teaching that those who where not saved ceased to exist at the time of their death rather than their souls being sent to hell. This was a central teaching of the Jevhovah's Witnesses founder, Charles Taze Russell. It also, interestingly enough, was a doctrine held by Charles Parham.

[64]Urshan, *The Almighty God in the Lord Jesus Christ*, 73.

[65]Urshan, *The Almighty God in the Lord Jesus Christ*, 73.

[66]Urshan, *The Almighty God in the Lord Jesus Christ*, 73.

[67]E. N. Bell, "The Urshan Trouble," *The Christian Evangel*, nos. 288-289 (May 17, 1919): 6.

[68]Bell's reference to "disasters" apparently reflects the idea that "many who were clear and free from" Urshan's teaching "have simply plunged into it, not knowing what they were doing and NOW ARE IN DARKNESS AND TROUBLE" (Bell, "The Urshan Trouble," 6, emphasis in original).

In response to a letter that asked why Urshan did not "let our new converts alone and go and make converts himself out of sinners instead of catching our innocent lambs with his new doctrines," Bell wrote,

> This is another sad and regrettable feature about this doctrinal New Issue. Instead of seeking to make a conquest of the world to bring sinners to bow at the feet of our mighty Lord and Saviour Jesus Christ, it seeks to make a conquest of the saints, to make a conquest of the church, of those already saved and filled with the Holy Ghost, of those who already own Jesus as Lord and King. . . . Why does this issue seek to catch the saints? Could it be that a baptized saint of God is selfish enough to desire to reap the fruit of other men's labors rather than to seek fresh jewels to lay at the Master's feet and receive the approval of his Lord? . . . What causes men to act on these low standards? . . . Let us pray that God will make these dear brethren ashamed to seek to conquer the saints and assemblies. . . . If a man has the real spirit of an apostle for God, he will also scorn low methods and will seek to bring the lost of the world to the feet of his Lord.[69]

In response to a preacher who was involved in the Los Angeles meetings of 1918, Bell wrote, "God pity these dear saints now in DARKNESS AND TROUBLE on account of turning from the truth into error." Again, Bell said that Urshan's "new error" was that he taught that "Jesus Christ is the name of the Father and the Holy Ghost, thus doing away with the distinct personality of the Father and of the distinct personality of the Holy Ghost and making Jesus the only personality in the Godhead."[70]

Bell then refers to Urshan's explanation to Robert Brown when Urshan attended Glad Tidings Hall in New York upon his return from Persia, and to the views he expressed at the General Council of the Assemblies of God.

> Several years ago when Bro. Urshan came back from Persia and Russia he had a talk with Robert A. Brown in which Bro. Brown gathered from Bro. Urshan that he then believed the very errors which he is now teaching. Later at the St. Louis General Council meeting, Bro. Brown requested that as Bro. Urshan had credentials from the Council he should make a public and frank statement to the Council as to these views. This the Council requested Bro. Urshan to do. Bro. Urshan came on the platform and made such a statement of denial as satisfied the Council, including Bro. Brown; and so he went out with credentials and approval from the General Council. On the ground that he did not hold these errors the Evangel allowed him to report regularly in its columns his Persian work, which resulted in hundreds and hundreds of dollars being sent to Bro. Urshan.[71]

Then Bell proceeded to say that "the whole General Council was deceived by Bro. Urshan into believing he did not have these errors in his heart." Bell would not say that "Bro. Urshan did this PURPOSELY to DECEIVE and use our

---

[69]E. N. Bell, "The Urshan Trouble," *The Christian Evangel*, nos. 288-289 (May 17, 1919): 6.

[70]E. N. Bell, "The Urshan Trouble," *The Christian Evangel*, nos. 288-289 (May 17, 1919): 6.

[71]E. N. Bell, "The Urshan Trouble," *The Christian Evangel*, nos. 288-289 (May 17, 1919): 6.

people." Instead, he wrote, "I leave what led him to do this with him and God to judge and settle."

> We do not judge Bro. Urshan. We pray for him and leave him with God now that he has given up his credentials and left us. But we do . . . declare that we cannot, according to the light God now gives us, approve either, of his present teaching or of the methods which have really deceived both us and some of our people.[72]

Bell next alludes to a private meeting he had with Urshan in an attempt to convince him to "stand for the truth." Instead, according to Bell, Urshan's response "was to rush publicly into print and try to spread his errors all over the country."[73]

In the same issue of *The Christian Evangel*, Bell's regular column "Questions and Answers" included three questions related to the "New Issue."

Bell's charges against Urshan in *The Christian Evangel* article entitled "The Urshan Trouble" contain several inconsistencies when compared to Urshan's explanations. He claimed that Urshan declared that "the name of the Father and of the Son and of the Holy Ghost is Jesus Christ." However, Urshan stated that as he reflected on Matthew 28:19 in conjunction with Luke 24:44-48 and Acts 2:38, he came to believe that the "one proper name of God" for the gospel dispensation was "the Lord Jesus Christ." This may seem to be precisely what Bell claimed or to be only a subtle difference, but Urshan was precise about the importance of the full identity indicated by "the Lord Jesus Christ."

> I understood . . . that my Heavenly Father's adorable Name was "JESUS," the Saviour; "CHRIST," the embodiment of the Holy Spirit; and "THE LORD," the eternal God, the Possessor of Heaven and Earth—in short—
>
> "The Lord" . . . stands for "The Father."
>
> "Jesus" . . . stands for "The Son."
>
> "Christ" . . . stands for "The Holy Spirit."[74]

Bell understood Urshan to say that the name of the Father was "Jesus Christ," the name of the Son was "Jesus Christ," and the name of the Holy Spirit was "Jesus Christ." This was not Urshan's view.[75] It was important for Urshan to preserve "Lord Jesus Christ" as the name of the Father, Son, and Holy Spirit. He had held this view since 1910.[76]

Before 1921, Urshan used terms indicating that although he was convinced that the fullness of the Godhead dwelt in Jesus, he recognized a threeness in God.

---

[72] E. N. Bell, "The Urshan Trouble," *The Christian Evangel*, nos. 288-289 (May 17, 1919): 7.

[73] E. N. Bell, "The Urshan Trouble," *The Christian Evangel*, nos. 288-289 (May 17, 1919): 7. According to Bell, some of those who had sent money to Urshan for mission work now wanted him to return it so they could send it to other missionaries.

[74] Urshan, *The Life Story*, 5th ed., 140.

[75] It is not my purpose at this point to critique Urshan's view, only to report it.

[76] Urshan, *The Life Story*, 5th ed., 140.

He attempted to capture this by a variety of terms like "triune," "tri-one,"[77] and the "three-one" God. In *The Almighty God in the Lord Jesus Christ* Urshan used the term "three-one God" at least nineteen times in addition to the word "triune" and "three-in-one God." He stated,

> I personally cannot refrain from believing that there is a plurality in God's mysterious Being, and that this plurality is shown as a three-ness, not three separate, distinct Beings or Persons of God, but a mysterious, inexplicable, incomprehensible three-ness, as it is expressed by the Apostle in I Jno. 5:7 and Mat. 28:19, and that the triune office of this one God is shown in I Cor. 12, —not three offices of three Gods but one office of one God with three branches (I Cor. 12:4-6). Again, in Eph. 4:4-6, we find this three-one God, who is called "One Spirit," "One Lord," "One God (the Deity) and Father of all, who is above all, and through all, and in you all."[78]

In further contrast to the implication of Bell's claim that Urshan identified the name of the Father as "Jesus Christ," Urshan offered this explanation of John 14:9:

> This means that the Father is to be seen **only in Jesus**, that He reveals Himself to men **only in and through the Son** . . . . Jesus explained it Himself in the next verse, saying, "I am in the Father, and the Father in Me." He did not say, "I am the Father." There is a world of difference between saying He was in the Father and the claim that He is the Father.[79]

In Urshan's view, the identification of Jesus as "Father" will not occur during this era; it awaits eternity.

> [W]hy do the Apostles never call Him the Father in all their epistles? It is because the message of the Gospel is to believe on the Son of God; for the Son of God came in the flesh, to save us and reconcile us and to bring us to a place where we shall be able, sometime in the coming age, to see this deep truth. . . . I, for one, am not led to preach Jesus Christ my Heavenly Father now . . . but I truly believe that, when we shall see our Saviour face to face and see the fullness of the Deity in Him and through Him shining forth with eternal glory, we shall not shrink then from calling Him "our Father" as well as "Lord God Almighty" in the ages to come. In the meantime . . . let us preach the Gospel that the Apostles preached, and also believe all such Scriptures making Jesus Christ even our **divine Father,** and worship His Father and our Heavenly Father in Him, putting away theological controversy on

---

[77] Urshan typically spelled this as "Trione" (Urshan, *The Life Story,* 5th ed., 140). I have hyphenated this to "tri-one" for the sake of readability and to emphasize that this is not a misspelling.

[78] Urshan, *The Almighty God in the Lord Jesus Christ,* 77. Within the next two years after the publication of *The Almighty God in the Lord Jesus Christ* Urshan apparently became aware of the lack of early textual support for I John 5:7. In 1921 he wrote, "It is an evident fact that the Scriptures no where indicate the word 'Three' in connection with the Godhead, except in one place (1 John 5:7) which is no Scripture but was simply inserted into the Scriptures by Constantine during the third century, and you will not find it in any original writings at all" (A. D. Urshan, "Scriptural Facts Concerning the Godhead Question," *The Witness of God* 2, no. 19 [July 1921]: 5).

[79] Urshan, *The Almighty God in the Lord Jesus Christ,* 79. Urshan was at this point quoting an answer from an unidentified issue of *The Christian Evangel.*

the Godhead, using only the terms that the Apostles used concerning the Deity. I have no doubt that, in doing so, we shall please God, the Father, the Son, and the Holy Ghost, and that He will bless us all in and through Jesus Christ, our All.[80]

Bell seems to have reduced Urshan's views down to such simplistic terms – essentially saying that Urshan believed that Jesus Christ was the Father, the Son, and the Holy Spirit – as to misrepresent the depth and richness of Urshan's theology.[81] Bell's characterization of Urshan's views in "The Urshan Trouble" is made even more puzzling upon examination of Bell's earlier article titled "Andrew Urshan's New Stand," wherein Bell declares that he objects "to this modern invention . . . that the Name of the Lord Jesus Christ is the name of the Father, the Son, and the Holy Ghost."[82] Here, Bell acknowledges Urshan's notion that "Lord Jesus Christ," not just "Jesus Christ," represents the Father, the Son, and the Holy Ghost. He further acknowledges Urshan's assertion that "the name of the Father . . . is JEHOVAH, the LORD" as well as that "JESUS is the name of God the Son" and that "CHRIST stands for the fullness and name of the Holy Ghost."[83] In other words, Urshan's harmonization of Matthew 28:19 and the accounts of baptism in Acts (Acts 2:38; 8:12; 10:48; 19:5) retained the "threeness" of Matthew 28:19 while appropriating the "oneness" of Acts. This explanation of Urshan's view does not survive into Bell's article "The Urshan Trouble."

A second question that arises from Bell's "The Urshan Trouble" when his characterization of Urshan's beliefs is compared with Urshan's explanations elsewhere concerns Urshan's contact with Robert A. Brown upon Urshan's return to New York in 1916. According to Urshan's account, Robert Brown was not in attendance at the Sunday morning service he attended at Glad Tidings Mission on June 25, 1916. Robert's wife, Marie, did not acknowledge Urshan's presence during the service, because she had been told by her husband not to call Urshan up on the platform until Robert had an opportunity to interview Urshan in order to determine his doctrinal stance on the "New Issue."[84]

Robert returned home, apparently that afternoon, and asked Urshan if he were "New Issue." Urshan recounted their meeting:

> After assuring him that we did not return to this country to preach the doctrines over which there seemed to be much discussion, nor had we taken sides with either faction, but that we would preach the things God's people needed then, I explained that I had been baptized in Russia in Jesus' Name and had received the revelation on the Deity of Jesus Christ, however. He was satisfied with our stand and he earnestly urged us to give them special meetings, at least for three days. This we did, and God approved of it by pouring out His Spirit upon us all.[85]

---

[80]Urshan, *The Almighty God in the Lord Jesus Christ*, 95.

[81]This will be discussed more thoroughly in chapter 7.

[82]E. N. Bell, "Andrew Urshan's New Stand," *The Christian Evangel*, nos. 284-285 (April 19, 1919): 9.

[83]E. N. Bell, "Andrew Urshan's New Stand," *The Christian Evangel*, 284-285 (April 19, 1919): 9.

[84]Urshan, *The Life Story*, 5th ed., 253-54.

[85]Urshan, *The Life Story*, 5th ed., 254.

Urshan's account indicates that Brown was satisfied with his explanation sufficiently to invite him to preach at Glad Tidings Mission. Bell's account of this event is difficult to reconcile with Urshan's.

> Several years ago when Bro. Urshan came back from Persia and Russia he had a talk with Robert A. Brown in which Bro. Brown gathered from Bro. Urshan that he then believed the very errors which he is now teaching. Later at the St. Louis General Council meeting, Bro. Brown requested that as Bro. Urshan had credentials from the Council he should make a public and frank statement to the Council as to these views. This the Council requested Bro. Urshan to do. Bro. Urshan came on the platform and made such a statement of denial as satisfied the Council, including Bro Brown.[86]

If Brown "gathered from Bro. Urshan that he then believed the very errors" which Bell claimed he was "now teaching," how was it that Brown was "satisfied with [Urshan's] stand" – including Urshan's explanation of his baptism in Jesus' Name and the "revelation" he had received "on the Deity of Christ" – to the point that he urged Urshan to preach at Glad Tidings Mission for three services? Bell's description of this event implies that Brown was not satisfied with Urshan's explanation and makes no mention of Urshan's ministry at Glad Tidings Mission. Instead, Brown is cast in the role of one who questioned how Urshan's theology could permit him to hold credentials with the Assemblies of God.

In May 1963, at the age of 79 and four years before his death, Urshan wrote concerning the Los Angeles revival:

> [W]e were forced to stop our ministry to all the Pentecostal faiths, blessing them, encouraging them to love one another, to have fellowship and worship together in such soul-saving campaigns, overlooking their difference on some Bible subjects.
>
> If that had not happened we would have been still preaching to thousands of different groups of the Pentecostals together to this very day.[87]

Ministry of Evangelism

Following Urshan's resignation from the Assemblies of God, he not only experienced continued criticism from his former Trinitarian friends but also from some of those who had embraced the "New Issue." He antizipated that "the old issue people" would publish articles declaring that he had "gone into error" and claim that he "had some carnal intentions for gain." However, Urshan was surprised when some of the "New Issue" ministers "began to throw slurs at [him] in their writings and their personal conversations."[88] These ministers, whom Urshan thought would "rejoice over [his] new step" and "encourage [him] . . . with a word

---

[86]E. N. Bell, "The Urshan Trouble," *The Christian Evangel*, nos. 288-289 (May 17, 1919): 6.

[87]Urshan, "The Final and the Conclusion," *The Witness of God* (May 1963): 7.

[88]Urshan, "The Story of My Life—29th Chapter," *The Witness of God* 7, no. 65 (June and July 1925): 2.

of congratulation," instead "denounced" him for compromise. They claimed that he "knew the truth long before [he] fully preached it." Further, they said that Urshan stood with the Trinitarian Pentecostals "for the sake of some personal gain" and "long enough to do a great deal of harm to the truth." Among these critics were "supposed pioneers" of the "New Issue" message.[89]

On the other hand, many "New Issue" ministers did rejoice over Urshan's "new and firm stand for One God in Christ. New opportunities began to open to Urshan.

However, Urshan did not accept any invitation for the first three months following his departure from Los Angeles. Instead, he rented a Los Angeles theater for the first month as a place to preach "God in Christ." A few people followed him in this move, including three ladies who were leaders of a Los Angeles ministry known as the "House of Light," that operated House of Light School for the Catholic Hispanic children. He baptized these women into the name of Jesus Christ. A fourth woman friend of theirs was healed "from a chronic disease" while in the waters of baptism.[90]

At one meeting two women, unsympathetic with Urshan's views, attended the service. As the service progressed, one of them began to speak in tongues. The other gave an "interpretation," declaring Urshan to be "of the devil," and condemned his message. Then they left. Shortly thereafter, the woman who had spoken in tongues came back, screaming. Her friend had stepped in front of a street car and was killed.[91]

The women associated with the House of Light invited the Urshans to stay in their home, and the Urshans began English-speaking meetings in the school. At first they experienced little success, but after three months a man from Michigan was baptized with the Holy Spirit. Some twenty-five Hispanics were baptized in the Spirit shortly thereafter.

Before leaving Los Angeles, Urshan preached for two weeks at the Pentecostal Assembly Tabernacle, pastored by Frank J. Ewart and located at 3906 East

---

[89]Urshan, "Then Story of My Life—29th Chapter," *The Witness of God* 7, no. 65 (June and July 1925): 2. Urshan did not identify these "supposed pioneers."

[90]Urshan, "The Story of My Life—29th Chapter," *The Witness of God* 7, no. 65 (June and July 1925): 2.

[91]This episode in Urshan's life was related to me by Phillip A. Dugas, Urshan's stepson, in a telephone conversation on March 26, 2010. This would have happened after July 21, 1918, the day Urshan left the revival. Although it may be impossible to verify this event, it is interesting that the July 23, 1918 issue of the *Los Angeles Times* carries the following article under the title "Killed by Street Car": "Mrs. Francis Holland, 62 years old of No. 1480 West Temple street, was fatally injured yesterday when she was struck by an Angeleno Heights car at Patton and Bellevue streets. According to Motorman Will Donovan Mrs. Holland stumbled directly in front of the car and before he could throw on the emergency brakes she was beneath the wheels. She was taken to the Receiving Hospital, dying three hours later without regaining consciousness." Dugas is of the opinion that Urshan may have begun his meetings in the theatre immediately after his final service with the Los Angeles campaign and that, as the custom then was, the services would have been held nightly. If so, and if this newspaper account describes the story Urshan related orally, this event could have occurred on the first night of Urshan's meetings after concluding his association with the Los Angeles campaign.

First Street in Los Angeles. But before leaving the city Urshan had his first invitation outside Los Angeles. Daniel Charles Owen Opperman asked him to conduct a three week Bible Conference in Eureka Springs, Arkansas in the summer of 1919.[92] Ewart, an Australian and former Baptist pastor, immigrated to Canada in 1903 and was baptized with the Holy Spirit in 1908. After assisting William Durham in his pastorate in Los Angeles in 1911, Ewart became the pastor upon Durham's death in 1912. Ewart heard R. E. McAlister speak about baptism in Jesus' name during the Worldwide Camp Meeting of 1913 at Arroyo Seco, just outside Los Angeles. Ewart invited McAlister to his home for further discussion and worked closely with him for months, including a period of time when McAlister assisted Ewart in his pastorate.[93] On April 15, 1914, Ewart baptized Glenn A. Cook in Jesus' name during a tent meeting in Los Angeles, and Ewart was in turn baptized by Cook. Ewart published the periodical *Meat in Due Season* and wrote at least eight books.[94] Urshan's meeting with Ewart was successful, producing an invitation to return for a revival campaign of at least one month.[95]

Urshan ministered at the Spring Bible Conference in Eureka Springs in 1919.[96] One hundred people attended this meeting. Several became missionar-

---

[92]Urshan describes this as "a three-week's Spring Bible Conference" (Urshan, "The Story of My Life—29th Chapter," *The Witness of God* 7, no. 65 (June and July 1925): 2. But the first indication of this in Opperman's *The Blessed Truth* announces a camp meeting in Eureka Springs scheduled for September 4-14, 1919. This announcement does not mention Urshan, but a following issue of *The Blessed Truth* identifies Urshan as the camp evangelist. See Daniel C.O. Opperman, "Camp Meeting," *The Blessed Truth* 4, no. 11 (June 1, 1919): 7 and D.C.O.O., "Mighty Revival in Eureka Springs, Ark. Campmeeting a Glorious Success. Evangelist Urshan Used of God," *The Blessed Truth* 4, no. 18 (October 1, 1919): 1.

[93]Frank J. Ewart, *The Phenomenon of Pentecost* (Hazelwood, MO: Word Aflame Press, 2000), 94-95.

[94]J. L. Hall, "Frank Ewart," NIDPCM, 623-24.

[95]Urshan, "Coming Revival Campaign at Los Angeles," *The Witness of God* 1, no. 2 (January 1920): 5. It is interesting that in his book *The Phenomenon of Pentecost*, Ewart does not list Urshan among the "Early Pentecostal Leaders" like J. W. Welch, Howard A. Goss, Glenn A. Cook, William H. Durham, Alfred G. Garr, George B. Studd, G. T. Haywood, L. C. Hall, W. E. Kidson, Raymond G. Hoekstra, W. T. Witherspoon, A. D. Van Hoose, and Harry I. Morse. He does acknowledge Urshan in another chapter with these words: "One of those who accepted the message and was mightily used of the Lord in its propagation was the missionary evangelist Andrew D. Urshan. When he returned from Persia and saw the disunited condition of the Pentecostal movement, he felt very sad. He decided to use his influence to bring the two factions back into unity. However, after much fruitless effort and months of hard work, he came out and confessed his belief in the new message in its entirety. Throughout the years he has stood unequivocally for the absolute deity of Jesus and baptism in His name" (Ewart, *The Phenomenon of Pentecost,* 108).

[96]Urshan, "The Story of My Life—29th Chapter," *The Witness of God* 7, no. 65 (June and July 1925): 2. Opperman (1872-1926), the editor of the monthly *Blessed Truth,* was a Pentecostal evangelist and educator who had studied at Mount Morris College, a Brethren school located in Mount Morris, Illinois (I. N. H. Beahm and S. N. McCann, *Two Centuries of the Church of the Brethren* [Elgin, IL: Brethren Publishing House, 1908]; http://www.archive.org/stream/cu31924006259257/ cu31924006259257_djvu.txt), at Manches-

ies. While in Eureka Springs, Urshan wrote the treatise "The Seven Fold Deity of Jesus Christ," which was published as a special sixteen page edition of the May-June 1920 *The Witness of God*.[97]

Urshan began publication of *The Witness of God*, a monthly paper, with the December 1919 edition. Before leaving Arkansas, he announced that he planned to conduct a month-long meeting at the "Old Knox Church" in Winnipeg, Manitoba, pastored by Franklin Small, beginning November 7, 1919.[98]

Urshan traveled to Winnipeg via a circular route. He first returned to Los Angeles to conduct a two week meeting for Frank Ewart. He then went to St. Louis, where he held a meeting with Evangelist Whitney.[99] Opperman wrote, "Bro. Urshan returned to Los Angeles to conduct a revival with Bro. F. J. Ewart through October [1919] . . . ."[100] Urshan then went to St. Louis, Missouri where he held a meeting with "Evangelist Whitney."[101]

---

ter College, founded by the United Brethren Church in North Manchester, Indiana (Manchester College, "Manchester College History," http://www.manchester.edu/Common/AboutManchester/History.htm [accessed March 27, 2010]) and at Moody Bible Institute in Chicago (E. L. Blumhofer, "Daniel Charles Owen Opperman," NIDPCM, 946). A former director of education at Zion City, Opperman had met Charles Parham in 1906 and was baptized with the Holy Spirit on January 13, 1908, the same year that Urshan experienced his Spirit baptism. One of the founding members of the Assemblies of God, along with E. N. Bell, Howard Goss, Archibald P. Collins, and Mack M. Pinson (E. L. Blumhofer and C. R. Armstrong, "Assemblies of God," NIDPCM, 333), Opperman "withdrew in 1916 to become chairman of a fledgling Oneness association, the General Assembly of Apostolic Assemblies [GAAA], with headquarters in Eureka Springs, AR" (Blumhofer, "Daniel Charles Owen Opperman," NIDPCM, 947). The meeting that resulted in the formation of this new association convened in Eureka Springs on December 28, 1916. The first business session was conducted on January 2, 1917 at 2:30 p.m. with a second business meeting the next day. Opperman was elected as chairman, David Lee Floyd as secretary, and Howard A. Goss as treasurer. The ministerial list included 154 names. Many of these ministers, like Urshan, had previously been affiliated with the Assemblies of God, and "[t]hey would have been content to have remained in the Assemblies of God had this privilege not been denied them" (Clanton, *United We Stand*, 23-24).

[97]Urshan, "The Story of My Life—29th Chapter," *The Witness of God* 7, no. 65 (June and July 1925): 2.

[98]Urshan, "Rightly Spending Christmas," *The Witness of God* 1, no. 1 (December 1919): 4; Urshan, "The Story of My Life—29th Chapter," *The Witness of God* 7, no. 65 (June and July 1925): 3.

[99]See A.D.U., "Coming Revival Campaign at Los Angeles, Beginning February 8th, D.V.," *The Witness of God* 1, no. 2 (January 1920): 5. This article refers to a previous meeting in LA with Ewart that lasted two weeks, which must have been the meeting to which Opperman referred.

[100]D.C.O.O., "Mighty Revival in Eureka Springs, Ark. Campmeeting a Glorious Success. Evangelist Urshan Used of God," *The Blessed Truth* 4, no. 18 (October 1, 1919): 1.

[101]Opperman wrote, "Bro. Urshan . . . expects to come to St. Louis for a meeting in November, assisted by Evangelist Whitney" (D.C.O.O., "Mighty Revival in Eureka Springs, Ark. Campmeeting a Glorious Success. Evangelist Urshan Used of God," *The Blessed Truth* 4, no. 18 [October 1, 1919]: 1. I have been unable to further identify "Evangelist Whitney."

In addition to these meetings in 1919, Urshan spent some time writing, for he announced that his "new book," *The Almighty God in Christ*, was "ready and for sale now."[102] The book was first advertised in the September 1, 1919 issue of *The Blessed Truth*.[103] This suggests that he finalized the manuscript for publication while holding the Ewart meeting. He began publishing *The Witness of God* in December, 1919. By this time Urshan had moved his family to St. Paul, Minesota.[104]

When Urshan finally arrived in Winnipeg, his meetings with Franklin Small turned out to last three weeks. Sixty people were baptized in Jesus' name and filled with the Holy Spirit.[105] He then conducted a series of short term meetings within the radius of Winnipeg – St. Paul before returning to California. He spent three weeks, January 11-February 1, 1920 preaching revivals in Lodi and Oakland, California before continuing to Los Angeles where he was invited a third time by Frank Ewart, this time staying for one month.

Upon completion of this meeting on March 7, 1920,[106] Urshan committed the House of Light congregation to Ewart's care.[107]

He then returned to Eureka Springs, Arkansas for another conference, this one scheduled to begin on Thursday, March 25, 1920, which also lasted one month.[108]

More than 150 people attended the 1920 meeting in Eureka Springs.[109] During this conference Urshan was invited by Harvey Shearer to conduct a camp meeting in Texas and by Robert La Fleur to conduct a camp meeting in Louisiana. Andrew Baker also invited him to conduct a month-long campaign at the Pentecostal Tabernacle in Portland, Oregon to begin on June 30, 1920.[110]

---

[102]Urshan, "Concerning Our Books," *The Witness of God* 1, no.1 (December 1919): 8.

[103]"The Almighty God in the Lord Jesus Christ." *The Blessed Truth* 4, no. 18 (October 1, 1919): 4. The publication information indicates it was published in 1919 while the Urshans lived at 1121 S. Mott St. in Los Angeles.

[104]The first issue of the paper states that it was published at 837 DeSoto Street, St. Paul, Minnesota.

[105]Urshan, "The Story of My Life—29th Chapter," *The Witness of God* 7, no. 65 (June and July 1925): 3.

[106]A.D.U., "Coming Revival Campaign at Los Angeles, Beginning February 8th, D.V.," *The Witness of God* 1, no. 2 (January 1920): 5.

[107]Urshan, "The Story of My Life—29th Chapter," *The Witness of God* 7, no. 65 (June and July 1925): 3.

[108]Daniel C. Opperman, "One Month Bible Study at Eureka Springs," *The Witness of God* 1, no. 4 (March 1920): 10; D.C.O.O., "Mighty Revival in Eureka Springs, Ark. Campmeeting a Glorious Success. Evangelist Urshan Used of God," *The Blessed Truth* 4, no. 18 (October 1, 1919): 1; D.C.O.O., "Special Bible School in Eureka Springs, Ark.," *The Blessed Truth* 4, no. 22 (December 1, 1919): 2. Since the General Assembly of Apostolic Assemblies endured only one year (Clanton, *United We Stand*, 26), the organization was no longer active by the time Urshan arrived for his second meeting.

[109]Urshan, "Prayers for Coming Campaigns," *The Witness of God* 1, no. 5 (April 1920): 7. When he recalled this event later, Urshan put the number of attendees at "nearly one hundred" (Urshan, "The Story of My Life—29th Chapter," *The Witness of God* 7, no. 65 (June and July 1925): 2.

[110]Urshan, "Prayers for Coming Campaigns," *The Witness of God* 1, no. 5 (April 1920): 7.

Urshan ministered at the fifth annual convention of the Midway Pentecostal Tabernacle in St. Paul, Minnesota, from October 8-24, 1920.[111] Following this meeting, he was invited to become "temporary pastor," a role he served until March 1921.[112] While pastoring he continued his evangelistic work, ministering to other congregations.[113] Perhaps the most notable of these was a return visit to Winnipeg for a fifteen day revival in December, 1920.[114] Urshan considered the October, 1920 convention in St. Paul to be so successful that he held another on January 21-30, 1921.[115] Urshan found this dual role to be unsatisfactory. After pastoring the church in St. Paul for six months, he wrote,

> We feel led to report that the time has arrived for us to launch out again and give our whole time for Evangelistic Campaigns in the name of the Lord. We have many reasons for this move. First, because we have on hand a good many pressing invitations from U.S. and Canada. Second, because we feel Bro. & Sister Sweaze are able to occupy the pulpit of the Midway Pentecostal Tabernacle where we have been successfully laboring during last six months. Third, because we feel keenly this is God's will for us.[116]

The month following his resignation, from April 26 to May 1, 1921, Urshan conducted a revival in Little Rock, Arkansas where W. C. Stallones was the pastor.[117] From there he traveled to Picton, Ontario, Canada to preach for Howard Goss for two weeks, beginning on May 15.[118] Then for the months of June and July, he resided in Montreal, Quebec, where he "opened a campaign for Jesus," holding three services on Sundays and one service every night of the week.[119] The revival resulted in the formation of a new church which he would later return to as pastor.[120]

Urshan was the featured speaker for a camp meeting held at Lansdowne, Ontario on September 2-11, 1921.[121] He then traveled to Toronto for a meeting spon-

---

[111] Andrew D. Urshan, "Important News and Information," *The Witness of God* 1, no. 10 (September 1920): 8.

[112] Urshan wrote, "We had an urgent invitation from the deacons of the Midway Tabernacle as well as from Brother and Sister Clibborn to go there and be in charge of the work as long as the Lord leads. We have submitted to the request." "Important News and Information," *The Witness of God* 1, no. 10 (September 1920): 8.

[113] While Urshan served as "temporary pastor" in St. Paul, he also ministered in other places: "Our winter is not spent in vain but in the effectual ministry, in St. Paul, Minn., Clark, S. Dak., Winnipeg, Manitoba, Zion City, IL, Albuquerque, New Mexico, and Cochrane, Wis." "The Spring Time," *The Witness of God* 2, no. 16 (April 1921): 8.

[114] A. D. Urshan, "The Winnipeg Revival a Successful Convention," *The Witness of God* 2, no. 13 (January 1921): 8).

[115] "Midwinter Pentecostal Convention!!" *The Witness of God* 2, no. 13 (January 1921): 8.

[116] A. D. Urshan, "Editorial," *The Witness of God* 2, nos. 14-15 (February and March 1921): 14.

[117] A. D. Urshan, "News of Interest," *The Witness of God* 2, no. 17 (May 1921): 8.

[118] "The Spring Time," *The Witness of God* 2, no. 16 (April 1921): 8.

[119] Andrew D. Urshan, "News of Interest," *The Witness of God* 2, no. 18 (June 1921): 8.

[120] Andrew D. Urshan, "Revival of Revolution," *The Witness of God* 4, no. 41 (May 1923): 1.

[121] A. D. Urshan, "News of Interest," *The Witness of God* 2, no. 21 (September 1921): 8.

sored by Howard Goss on October 9-23. The meeting was held in Victoria Hall,[122] an impressive structure that was opened in 1860 by the Prince of Wales.[123] He then ministered in Hamilton, Markham and Dresden, Ontario,[124] before returning to St. Paul for a meeting of the district council of the Pentecostal Assemblies of the World, held on November 12-13, 1921.[125]

On January 30, 1922, Urshan embarked on a "missionary trip" of forty days with the intention of raising funds for missionaries. He began the trip in Indianapolis, Indiana on January 30 and ended in Dayton, Ohio on March 10. He wrote,

> Our Missionary trip of 40 days proved very successful, nearly $13000.00 were pledged to be given by April 1st, of which over $1200.00 were cash offerings. . . .
>
> The largest offering was given by the 'King's Chapel' of New York City, Sister Lightford's mission which amounted to $3,145.00. The smallest offering was a cash offering of $14.00 given by five saints which worshipped in a house in Pennsylvania. . . .
>
> We gave our valuable time free and traveled 19 cities in eleven states taking only my traveling expenses which hardly amounted to $200.00.[126] My wife helped me in part of the journey paying her own expenses. . . . The officers of the P.A. of W. has [sic] also kindly rendered their faithful service free of any charge to missionaries in this matter.[127]

On April 23 – May 16, 1922, Urshan sponsored the "Chicago Bible Conference and Revival Campaign" with the intention of establishing a new church in Chicago. The main speakers besides Urshan were G. T. Haywood, D. C. O. Opperman, and Mattie Crawford.[128] Urshan declared, "We believe you can learn more of God, in this short term Bible Conference than you would in any so-called Bible Schools for the whole year."[129] The May 1922 issue of *The Witness of God* reports:

> Chicago's Spring-time Bible Conference and the Revival Campaign began promptly April 23, ended May 16. . . . We regretted to see the terrible and undue

---

[122]"Convention, Toronto, Canada," *The Blessed Truth* 6 no. 10 (October 1, 1921): 1.

[123]The Concert Hall at Victoria Hall, http://www.concerthallatvictoriahall.com/ index_1.htm (accessed April 5, 2010).

[124]"News of Interest," *The Witness of God* 3, no. 25 (January 1922): 8.

[125]Following his departure from the Assemblies of God, Urshan affiliated with the Pentecostal Assemblies of the World. D. I. Hammergren, "To Ministers, Assemblies and Saints of the Northwest," *The Witness of God* 2, no. 23 (November 1921): 8.

[126]In the April, 1922 issue of *The Witness of God*, Urshan wrote, "We reported in our last issue of this paper that all traveling expenses hardly amounted to $200.00. But when we looked the record over we found that we had spent only $137.59. It would have been impossible to travel through eleven States in nineteen cities with that little expenditure if it were not for our economical traveling" (A. D. Urshan, "A Word About Our Recent Trip in Behalf of Our Dear Missionaries," *The Witness of God* 3, no. 28 [April 1922]: 6).

[127]A. D. Urshan, "News of Interest," *The Witness of God* 3, no. 27 (March 1922): 8.

[128]"Go! Go! Go! Go! To Chica—Go Bible Conference and Revival Campaign," *The Witness of God* 3, no. 27 (March 1922): 7-8.

[129][Urshan?], "The Last Announcement and Invitation to the Chicago Spring-time Bible Conference and the Apostolic [sic]-Brand Revival Campaign," The *Witness of God* 3, no. 28 (April 1922): 1.

prejudice that kept away our beloved Trinitarian Pentecostal brethren, and they missed the feast. But the good Lord sent us from two to three hundred church members every day representing foreigners of Chicago, who so gladly receive the Word, and a number of them were baptized into the Name of the Father, of the Son and of the Holy Spirit which is THE LORD JESUS CHRIST. Over two hundred marched on the high platform and were prayed for by Sister Crawford, being anointed with oil in the Name of the Lord. Two that were blind received their sight; a number of deaf had their hearing restored; others were delivered from rheumatism; one was wonderfully delivered from Locomoterataxi[130] and was genuinely converted; one paralyzed woman was partially restored and is improving daily; and many others were delivered from internal, long-standing, chronic diseases . . . .The afternoon meetings of the Conference were entirely given in charge of Bro. G. T. Haywood who day after day, unfolded the 'Mystery of Ages', from the [p]ages of the Holy Writ and his scientifically designed bible charts. We had delegates from almost every state in the Union and two from Canada; in all, about one hundred ministering brethren and saints. . . . The outcome of the campaign is a new God-given assembly for the Lord Jesus . . . .[131]

The Urshans vacationed in Cochrane, Wisconsin, the home of D. I. Hammergren, Mildred Urshan's father, in the summer of 1922.[132] Hammergren pastored the local Oneness Pentecostal Church.[133]

Urshan sponsored the "Second International Bible Conference" in Chicago on September 14-October 1, 1922, which featured a one week appearance of Mattie Crawford.[134] This was followed by a revival on October 24 – November 14, 1922 when L. C. Hall and C. L. Cross were the featured speakers.[135]

Beginning November 10, 1922, Urshan joined sixty ministers from several southern states to attend the Southern Pentecostal Bible Conference in Little Rock, Arkansas.[136]

Mattie Crawford returned to Chicago for a ten-day "holiday campaign" beginning on Christmas day, December 25, 1925.[137]

---

[130]Locomotor Ataxia is "syphilis of the spinal cord characterized by degeneration of sensory neurons and stabbing pains in the trunk and legs and unsteady gait and incontinence and impotence" Hpathy, Homeopathic Treatment, Cure, & Medicines, "Locomotor Ataxia,"http:// health.hpathy.com/ locomotor-ataxia-symptoms-treatment-cure.asp, (accessed April 5, 2010).

131Andrew D. Urshan, "Chicago and Mrs. Crawford's Revival Campaign," *The Witness of God* 3, no. 29 (May 1922): 7-8.

[132]Andrew D. Urshan, "News of Interest," *The Witness of God* 3, no. 30 (June 1922): 1.

[133]September 24, 2009 telephone conversation with Faith St. Clair, Andrew Urshan's daughter.

[134]Andrew D. Urshan, "Chicago's Second International Bible Conference," *The Witness of God* 3, no. 32 (August 1922): 1.

[135]Andrew D. Urshan, "Special Meetings at Chicago Continued," *The Witness of God* 3, no. 34 (October 1922): 6.

[136]"News of Interest and Current Events," *The Witness of God* 3, no. 34 (December 1922): 2.

[137]Andrew D. Urshan, "Special Holiday Campaign," *The Witness of God* 3, no. 35 (November 1922): 1.

For a period of time in 1923, Urshan pastored both in Chicago and in Montreal. He wrote, "The Lord is blessing us still with showers of the Latter Rain at the Emanuel Gospel Assembly at Montreal . . . . He is also blessing at our Assembly in Chicago . . . ."[138] During this time he sponsored a meeting on July 10 – July 1 with Abraham Silverstein, a Jew who had embraced Oneness Pentecostalism. Urshan advertised the meeting: "We wish to announce gladly that former chum of Trotsky the Premier of Soviet Russia, Mr. Abraham Silverstein of Philadelphia, Pa., will lecture on very interesting and important Bible subjects beginning D.V., on Sunday, June 10th, remaining with us for three weeks."[139]

Shortly after the conclusion of this Montreal meeting, Urshan was in Forth Smith, Arkansas on July 20-29, preaching at the Arkansas/Oklahoma camp meeting.[140] Then, on October 4-20, he spoke at a short-term Bible school and state convention in Houston, Texas.[141] After these meetings Urshan returned to Chicago to spend the winter ministering in the church he had planted there. He felt no need to return to Montreal at that time.[142]

Urshan moved the offices of *The Witness of God* from Cochrane to Chicago in January 1924.[143] In June of that year, he moved Emanuel Mission, the Chicago church he was pastoring, from 125 W. Chestnut Street to 2356 Lincoln Avenue.[144] That same month, on June 25, the Urshan's third child, Faith Edith, was born.[145]

The ninth annual "world conference" of the Pentecostal Assemblies of the World convened in Chicago on October 14-19, 1924.[146] This historic meeting led eventually to the division of "whites" and "coloreds." Urshan wrote:

> At this conference it's expected to divide the movement business matters and not **Spiritual Fellowship** into two branches, that is to say, white brethren exclusively white, and colored brethren exclusively colored branch, functioning in two different headquarters, each branch being managed by the leading men of both races. There is not a thought on the part of white brethren of separating God's church, standing for the name of Jesus, whether black or white, like some are trying to leave such an impression upon the minds of the saints—NO! a thousand times NO. . . . The P.A.W. Organization, whites and colored together has caused terrible unnecessary persecutions to the Southern white brethren and it has been the means of a set back of the Great work of the Lord in the Southern States. We therefore who love the Lord and His people, black and whites alike feel, the necessity of avoiding further setbacks to the work of the Lord in the South. We therefore are determined to sepa-

---

[138]"Lord Blessing in Montreal," *The Witness of God* 4, no. 42 (June 1923): 1.

[139]Andrew D. Urshan, "Revival of Revolution," *The Witness of God* 4, no. 41 (May 1923): 1.

[140]"A Two State Camp Meeting for Arkansas and Oklahoma, North 4th and 'O' Streets, Fort Smith, Arkansas. July 20-29, 1923," *The Blessed Truth* 8, no. 7 (July 1, 1923): 2.

[141]"Announcement!" *The Blessed Truth* 8, no. 7 (July 1, 1923): 2.

[142]Andrew D. Urshan, "The Emanuel Gospel Mission of Montreal," *The Witness of God* 4, no. 46 (October 1923): 1.

[143]"Special Notice," *The Witness of God* 5, no. 49 (January 1924): 3.

[144]*The Witness of God* 6, no. 54 (June 1924): 6.

[145]"Interesting News," *The Witness of God* 6, no. 55 (July 1924): 4.

[146]A. D. Urshan, "Interesting News," *The Witness of God* 6, no. 55 (July 1924): 4.

rate the two business functions which have been one for the last nine years—now in this convention into two separate business offices.... The P.A.W. Organization has been in terrible struggles since the beginning over this very matter of whites and colored functioning together in the legal matters. We know this is God's time for this action and He has made us to suffer wrong misrepresentations and accusations to bear them all sweetly and carry on this matter to victory in this Conference.[147]

On October 16-17 of this convention, the Apostolic Churches of Jesus Christ was formed as a "branch off" movement of the PAW.

At our last Ninth Annual Conference of the Pentecostal Assemblies of the World which was held in Chicago, our delegation from Southern States brought before the Conference some timely and very important matters pertaining to the civil laws in the South which were rather hindering the work of the Lord there from its proper and extensive progress. After hearing the sensible arguments of the brethren the ministerial staff saw the necessity of a **Branch off movement** to take away unnecessary hindrances facing many of our beloved brethren and causing a set-back of the work of the Lord at certain places in the North and in the whole South. The result was after having obtained favorable consent of the Presbytery of P.A.W. and the ministerial body in general—it was moved and resolved that some capable and trustworthy volunteer brethren to hold a separate meeting in a separate room to formulate such a forward movement. In answer to the call, Bro. H. A. Goss of Toronto, Can., Bro. William Booth Clibborn, of St. Paul, Minn., Bro. Andrew D. Urshan, of Chicago, Ill., with a number of other ministers called the meeting and opened it with prayer."[148]

H. A. Goss was chosen to serve as Chairman of the Board of Presbyters and A. D. Urshan was chosen to act as Secretary and Treasurer, as well as Foreign Missions Secretary and Treasurer, of the newly formed Apostolic Churches of Jesus Christ.[149] This group was described as **"the white ministerial branch of the P.A.W."**[150]

A Bible conference lasting ten days followed the conclusion of the PAW conference.[151]

Late in 1924, Urshan traveled to Indianapolis to preach at the Seventeenth Annual Bible Conference and Convention sponsored by G. T. Haywood. While there, he met F. F. Bosworth and was quite impressed with the man and his ministry.

We enjoyed the presence of the Lord in the meetings there and had quite liberty in preaching the word. While there we found that Brother F. F. Bosworth who is so widely known now among Christian Alliance and other denominational bodies as a mighty instrument in the hands of God to heal the sick. We attended one of his meetings and we saw the simple faith of our brother and his workers was indeed working gospel miracles and causing thousands of conversions. Brother Bosworth showed us very congenious [sic] and friendly welcome, after introducing us to

---

[147]"Editorial News of Interest," *The Witness of God* 6, no. 48 (October 1924): 1. Emphasis in original.

[148]A. D. U., "Organism and Organization," *The Witness of God* 6, no. 59 (November 1924): 1-2.

[149]"Minutes of Meeting in Chicago: October 16 and 17, 1924," *The Witness of God* 6, no. 59 (November 1924): 1.

[150]"Minutes of Meeting in Chicago: October 16 and 17, 1924," *The Witness of God* 6, no. 59 (November 1924): 8. Emphasis in original.

[151]A. D. Urshan, "Interesting News," *The Witness of God* 6, no. 55 (July 1924): 4.

his great audience of at least 12,000 people he called on us twice to lead in prayer and he then invited us to his hotel where we had a sweet short conference which encouraged our hearts and caused us to love our brother and his work there.[152]

After this encounter, Urshan advertised Bosworth's book *Christ the Healer* in various issues of *The Witness of God*.[153]

For the next several years Urshan engaged in fruitful but uneventful evangelistic ministry. His activity, though recorded in *The Witness of* God, reads more like an itinerary than it does of a detailed description of its results. December 31, 1924 – January 1, 1925 found Urhsan in Chicago for the annual Watch Night service,[154] then on January 19 – February 1, 1925 in Shreveport, Louisiana, where the local newspapers reported regularly on his sermons.[155] While in Louisiana Urshan conducted a meeting at a Methodist church in Grand Cane and spoke for four days in Oakdale where "Bro. Fuselier" was pastor and for "Sis. Shaver," the pastor in Mansfield.[156]

On February 17-27, 1925, Urshan attended the Southern Bible Conference in Jackson, Tennessee.

> Among many evangelists, pastors and teachers, Bro. Urshan, of Chicago, Bro. Booth-Clibborn, of St. Paul, Bro. McBryde, of Houston, Texas, and Bro. Goss, of Toronto, will be the chief speakers. . . . This New Movement, the offspring of the P.A.W., will arrange prayerfully all the business arrangements, that the ministers may have their credentials and annual certificates.[157]

At this meeting the name "Pentecostal Ministerial Alliance" (PMA) was chosen to replace the "Apostolic Churches of Jesus Christ." Those involved in both organizations were "Pentecostal ministers who do not desire to be bound by a creed, or any certain set of doctrines . . . ." They desired to "keep the unity of the Spirit in the bond of peace with all the Spirit filled saints of God, until we all come into the unity of the faith." L.C. Hall was chosen as the chairman of the PMA, H. A. Goss as the secretary, and A. D. Urshan as the missionary secretary and treasurer.[158]

---

[152]A.D.U., "Indianapolis Visit," *The Witness of God* 7, no. 61 (January and February 1925): 8.

[153]Bosworth was a member of the Assemblies of God from 1914. But he resigned in 1918 because he did not believe that speaking in tongues was necessarily the initial evidence that one had been baptized with the Holy Spirit. Bosworth then joined the Christian and Missionary Alliance. By the time Urshan met him, Bosworth had been ministering with remarkable results in cities in the United States and Canada. See R. M. Riss, "Fred Francis Bosworth," NIDPCM, 439-40.

[154]A.D.U., "Watch Night," *The Witness of God* 7, no. 61 (January and February 1925): 8.

[155]"Our Shreveport Visit," *The Witness of God* 7, no. 62 (March 1925): 14.

[156]*The Witness of God,* 7, no. 62 (March 1925): 14.

[157]"Third Annual Southern Bible Conference," *The Witness of God* 7, no. 61 (January and February 1925): 13.

[158]See "All About the Pentecostal Ministerial Alliance of 'The Church'," *The Witness of God* 7, no. 62 (March 1925): 13.

Urshan was in DeQuincy, Louisiana on July 2-12, 1925 to "take charge" of the camp meeting sponsored by the PMA.[159] Reported attendance was 2,000 nightly, with 3,000 on Sunday.[160] From there, he spent July 13-21, 1925 ministering in Bell, Eunice, Oakdale, and Merryville, Louisiana and in Beaumont and Port Arthur, Texas.[161] Following these meetings, Urshan went to Philadelphia, Mississippi for an engagement on August 6-20, 1925 with the church pastored by Charley Smith.[162] The next month, on September 1-10, 1925, Urshan preached for a camp meeting in Orange, Texas. According to police reports, 2,000 people attended the meeting.[163]

Urshan then continued his evangelistic tour in Indianapolis, Indiana at Oak Hill Tabernacle, pastored by T. C. Davis. The meetings began on November 1, 1925, concluding six weeks later on December 13.[164] Then, on December 19-25, Urshan preached for B. H. Hite, pastor in St. Louis, Missouri.[165] He then moved to St. Paul, Minnesota, where he participated with other preachers from December 27, 1925 – January 1, 1926 in a meeting sponsored by L. R. Ooton.[166]

During January and February 1927,[167] Urshan conducted two campaigns in Indianapolis, Indiana and Columbus, Ohio. These consisted of ten days with T. C. Davis and a Sunday afternoon with G. T. Haywood.[168] During March-June, he ministered in Columbus, Ohio where W. T. Witherspoon was pastor and in Akron, Ohio, pastored by "Bro. Norman."[169]

He then returned to Toronto, Ontario for a three-week revival on April 1-22, 1928.[170] The host pastor was Howard A. Goss of Danforth Pentecostal Tabernacle.[171] From June 10 – July 2, 1928, Urshan took a lengthy ministry trip to Yakima, Washington.

> We found the citizens of [Yakima] very congenial people and quite void of religious retaliation. They invited us to speak at their Church Men's Club luncheon in the beautiful Elks lodge cafeteria, where the Mayor and some of the Judges of the district were present with many prominent business men and women.
>
> The Lions Club of the city also gave us opportunity to address their weekly gather-

---

[159]"Oakdale, Louisiana," *The Witness of God* 7, no. 62 (March 1925): 14.

[160]A.D.U., *The Witness of God* 7, no. 66 (August 1925): 1.

[161]A.D.U., "Old-Fashioned Revival," *The Witness of God* 7, no. 66 (August 1925): 1.

[162]A.D.U., "Old-Fashioned Revival," *The Witness of God* 7, no. 66 (August 1925): 1.

[163]A.D.U., "Old-Fashioned Revival," *The Witness of God* 7, no. 66 (August 1925): 1.

[164]Pastor T. C. Davis, "Report of the Oak Hill Tabernacle, Indianapolis, Ind.," *The Witness of God* 8, no. 71 (January 1926): 11.

[165]Pastor B. H. Hite, "Report of a Real Revival in Saint Louis, MO," *The Witness of God* 8, no. 71 (January 1926): 11.

[166]L. R. Ooton, "Report of the Work at St. Paul, Minn.," *The Witness of God* 8, no. 71 (January 1926): 11. These dates are estimated.

[167]I am unable to determine Urshan's schedule for 1926.

[168]A. D. U., "Editorial," *The Witness of God* 10, no. 81 (February 1927): 13.

[169]A.D.U., "Editorial," *The Witness of God* 10, no. 81 (February 1927): 13.

[170]These dates are estimated, and I am unable to determine any further events from June 1927 to this time.

[171]Andrew D. Urshan, "Editorials," *The Witness of God* no. 94 (May 1928): 6.

ing at the Commerical Hotel luncheon, where many business men, Jews, Gentiles, Protestants and Catholics were present.

The *Yakima Daily Republic* and *Herald*, the two large daily newspapers of that community gave us several free write-ups, boosting our tent services. Mr. John Lampert, the owner of the Lampert Implement Co., of Yakima, the Methodist Church secretary, gave us a nice 100 mile round trip car ride in his new Hudson Six, showing us the valley and the mountains around it. He also motored us to the great Rimrock Dam, from which the Yakima valley is irrigated. . . .

The Emanuel Mission of Yakima, we found it to be a faithful band of one year old Jesus Only people. . . .

God blessed the earnest efforts of the saints during our 22 days stay with them. . .

Early Tuesday morning, July 3, we left Yakima for Bend Oregon with some sweet memories.[172]

From Yakima, Urshan traveled to Bend, Oregon, arriving at 9 p.m. and preaching the same night. The pastor was "Sister Marling." Urshan preached in Bend July 3-6.[173] Next, he went to Salem, Oregon July 7-10, 1928 preaching for "Bro. Bullock."[174] On July 11-14, he ministered in Aberdeen, Montesano, and McCleary, Washington.[175] Then, for seven days, on July 15-21, 1928, he preached in Seattle for "Bro. Opsand."[176]

He then returned to his home in Chicago for a period of rest before heading to Regina, Saskatchewan, Canada, where he preached on October 9-30, 1928.[177]

Urshan was back in Newark, Ohio on March 31 – April 9, 1929[178] to help conduct a meeting for James A. Frush.[179] This was followed by an engagement in St. Paul, Minnesota on April 25 – May 5, 1929 where J. A. Nelson was pastor. The church was holding its seventh annual spring convention.[180] While there, his son Andrew David Urshan, Jr. was born on April 26, 1929. Urshan reported,

> The staff of the *Witness of God* has increased. On April 26, Friday morning at 4:15 o'clock a baby boy weighing 10 pounds was born and added to us. His mother calls him Andrew David Urshan, Jr. Sister Urshan and baby were both in excellent condition and now they are by this time both looking at each other and pleasantly

---

[172] A.D.U., "Our Recent Trip to the West Coast," *The Witness of God* 10, no. 96 (August 1928): 2.

[173] "Bend Oregon," *The Witness of God* 10, no. 96 (August 1928): 3.

[174] "Our Four Days Campaign in Salem, Oregon," *The Witness of God* 10, no. 96 (August 1928): 3.

[175] "Our Visit to Seattle, Wash.," *The Witness of God* 10, no. 96 (August 1928): 3.

[176] "Our Visit to Seattle, Wash.," *The Witness of God* 10, no. 96 (August 1928): 3.

[177] "Trip to Western Canada," *The Witness of God* 10, nos. 99 and 100 (November and December 1928): 28.

[178] These dates are estimated.

[179] "Editorial News and Notes," *The Witness of God* 10, no. 104 (April 1929): 2.

[180] "Editorial News and Notes," *The Witness of God* 10, no. 104 (April 1929): 2.

smiling. . . . Our other children are: Grace Susanna 11, Nathaniel Andrew, 9, and Faith Edith 5.[181]

Urshan was once again with G. T. Haywood in Indianapolis for "an eight-day old fashioned apostolic faith campaign on May 19-26, 1929.[182] From there he traveled to Norphlet, Arkansas, where he preached on June 2-12, 1929 for Pastor Thomas Guy.[183] During this trip Urshan also ministered at Louann, Arkansas and Haynesville, Minden and Shreveport, Louisiana, and Kirbyville, Texas.[184] On June 13-23, 1929 he was in Haynesville, Louisiana preaching at a Pentecostal Ministerial Alliance camp meeting.[185] While there, Urshan accepted an invitation to conduct the PMA camp meeting in Laurel, Mississippi on August 10-25, 1929.[186]

During September 1929, Urshan responded to a call for help in St. Paul Minnesota at Midway Tabernacle, the church he had formerly pastored.

> Our recent experience at the Midway Tabernacle at St. Paul, Minn., has caused the birth of this special issue. We were called upon to at once leave Chicago for St. Paul by both Board of Trustees and the church. Not knowing what had happened there, we went and to our own sorrow, we found the assembly torn up into two factions by a self styled preacher who is only a photographer. This fellow had come in with a seemingly nice spirit, claiming his faith in Jesus Name and etc. But after getting into confidence with the assembly he suddenly had come out with his teaching of Russellism under the cloak of the Pentecostal garb. Some of the Trustees had courage enough to stop him preaching his No-Hell teaching. He being determined to carry on his propaganda had pulled out, taking out a number of the young people with him and starting a new work in opposition to the Tabernacle . . . .[187]

With the New Year, Urshan was at the Midway Gospel Tabernacle in Mishawaka, South Bend, Indiana preaching for G. B. Rowe on January 26 – February 9, 1930.[188] He moved on to Morgantown, West Virginia on March 9-19, 1930, where the pastor was H. I. Goodin.[189] Then he went to Cincinnati, Ohio to preach for F. E. Curts on March 30 – April 6, 1930.[190] During the summer of 1930, Urshan preached in Flint, Michigan, Portsmouth, Ohio, and other places.[191] In October he was back in Indianapolis, in November in Morgantown, West Virginia, and in December in New Salem, Ohio.[192]

---

[181]"Editorial News and Notes," *The Witness of God* 10, no. 105 (May 1929): 2.
[182]"Editorial News and Notes," *The Witness of God* 10, no. 104 (April 1929): 2.
[183]"Editorial News and Notes," *The Witness of God* 10, no. 104 (April 1929): 2.
[184]"Editorial News and Notes," *The Witness of God* 10, no. 108 (August 1929): 2.
[185]"Editorial News and Notes," *The Witness of God* 10, no. 104 (April 1929): 2.
[186]"Important Camp Announcement," *The Witness of God* 10, no. 106 (June and July 1929): 2.
[187]"Editorial News and Notes," *The Witness of God* 10, no. 110 (October 1929): 2.
[188]G. B. Rowe, "The Spirit Falling at the Midway Gospel Tabernacle, Mishawaka, South Bend, Ind.," *The Witness of God* 11, no. 2 (February 1930): 5.
[189]"For Your Information," *The Witness of God* 11, no. 2 (February 1930): 10.
[190]"For Your Information," *The Witness of God* 11, no. 2 (February 1930): 10.
[191]"Our Campaigns," *The Witness of God* 11, no. 9 (October 1930): 2.
[192]"Our Campaigns," *The Witness of God* 11, no. 9 (October 1930): 2.

1931 opened with Urshan in Newark, Ohio on January 8-18, 1931. On January 27-31 he spoke at a ministers' conference in Chicago, and he was back in Winnipeg on February 8-22, 1931.[193]

On March 5-19, Urshan was in Auroraville, Wisconsin and on March 24 – April 2, he was back in Chicago. At some other point in March, he ministered in Wewoka, Oklahoma. Urshan returned to St. Paul on April 24 – May 3 for the annual northwestern convention. In June he was in Rewey, Wisconsin for a ten-day campaign. On July 5 he began a "state gathering" in Nampa, Idaho.[194]

In November 1931 Urshan came to St. Louis to participate in the ill-fated attempt to merge the Pentecostal Assemblies of the World and the Apostolic Church of Jesus Christ.

> One of the grandest things that ever has happened in the Pentecostal world is the recent merger of the Pentecostal Assemblies of the World and the Apostolic Church of Jesus Christ. This timely merging took place last November in St. Louis, Mo., being advocated and carried on by most of the executive officials of both organizations. . . .
>
> This two-in-one organized effort is bringing together nearly one thousand good preachers abreast, the ministers who are not afraid to say . . . baptism into His Name remits sins and is the birth of water as our Lord taught according to John 3:1-5. . . . they have adopted a sweet name for his merger which is the Pentecostal Assemblies of Jesus Christ . . . . The people shall call us no more 'of the world,' but of Him . . . .
>
> Personally I have been a P.A. of W. minister (elder) for many years and a very close friend of the late Bishop G. T. Haywood who was indeed an apostle and therefore a real Bishop, he derived his education through much suffering, traveling and diligent study . . . . this merger has made the old P.A. of W. a greater movement with a better name and for mightier results. I have already taken my ministerial credentials with Pentecostal Assemblies of Jesus Christ . . . . this needed merger, strengthening the unity of all 'Jesus Only' or oneness preachers, irrespective of color or race.
>
> . . . Everything is fifty-fifty for Jesus with a very wise provision made for the southern brethren who join this P.A. of J.C., and it will save them from unnecessary persecution in the southern states. . . .
>
> The official organ of this great movement, "The Pentecostal Outlook."[195]

In spite of Urshan's grand expectations, this experiment was not to endure. D. A. Reed describes the causes and process that led to the reinstitution of the PAW:

> An unstable merger was accomplished in 1931 between the PAW and . . . the Apostolic Church of Jesus Christ (ACJC), forming the Pentecostal Assemblies of Jesus Christ (PAJC). Concern over the change of name, abandonment of the Episcopal

---

[193] "Our Campaigns," *The Witness of God* (January 1931): 2.
[194] "Editorial News and Notes," *The Witness of God* (June 1931): 2.
[195] Andrew D. Urshan, "The Grand and Good New Merger," *The Witness of God* (May 1932): 6-7.

polity, and lack of trust resulted in the reconstitution of the PAW, with Samuel Grimes of New York City as its presiding bishop. The interracial experiment of the PAJC collapsed in 1937, and most black members returned to the PAW.[196]

In December 1931 Urshan ministered for three weeks in Twin Falls, Idaho, as well as in Duluth, Minnesota and elsewhere. In January 1932 he wrote,

> We just reached home, having gone to Twin Falls, Idaho. We had a three week's campaign in Twin Falls where we preached to hundreds in the little Bethel Temple and to thousands through broadcasting from Station KTFI at Twin Falls.... We not only preached in Twin Falls, but in other places as well, and after staying home a few days we had to rush to Duluth, Minn., to take charge of the first Northwestern Pentecostal Young People's Convention where God blessed.[197]

During the spring of 1932, he preached in Melbourne, Florida for Pastor Raymond and Miami, Florida for Pastor Geiger. In May he was back in St. Paul, Minnesota for the "Tenth Annual Conference for the Northwestern Apostolic Faith Church. Also in May he ministered in Columbus, Ohio and elsewhere.[198]

In July 1932, Urshan traveled to Baltimore, Maryland preaching for "Bishop Turpin and his large assembly." August 7-19 found him in Hodge, Louisiana for a "state camp and convention." After the camp closed, he went to Shreveport, Louisiana for a ten-day meeting with Pastor S. E. Langford.[199] At the conclusion of his ministry in Shreveport, Urshan went to St. Louis, Missouri for the convention of the Pentecostal Assemblies of Jesus Christ, which was scheduled for August 30 – September 5 at 4017 Easton Ave. He reported that "all P.A. of W. Bishops except one are for this blessed merger with the general secretary of P.A. of W. and the most of them . . . expected to attend."[200]

During the winter of 1932 Urshan preached in River Falls, Wisconsin for Pastor Ebert and St. James, Minnesota for Pastor Marsh. With the beginning of the New Year, he ministered for Elder Karl F. Marsh in the "large assembly hall" in Columbus, Ohio.[201] Before the month of May, Urshan held two additional campaigns, one in Chicago for Pastor Holly at 3813 Indiana Ave. and the other was once again in Indianapolis for pastor T. C. Davis at Oakhill Tabernacle.[202]

---

[196] D. A. Reed, "Pentecostal Assemblies of the World," NIDPCM, 965. Reed rightly commends the Oneness tradition for its continuing effort to bring about racial unity within its ranks thoughout much of the Jim Crow era. This is especially significant in view of the fact that such efforts were abandoned in the other two wings of the Pentecostal movement by 1914 when most of the white ministers left the Church of God in Christ to form the Assemblies of God. See also Talmadge L. French, *Early Interracial Oneness Pentecostalism* (Eugene, OR: Pickwick Publications, 2014).

[197] "Editorial News and Notes," *The Witness of God* (January 1932): 2.
[198] "Our Campaigns," *The Witness of God* (May 1932): 1.
[199] "Announcing," *The Witness of God* (July 1932): 1.
[200] "The St. Louis Convention," *The Witness of God* (August 1932): 1.
[201] "Columbus for Jesus," *The Witness of God* (January 1933): 2.
[202] "Editorial News and Notes," *The Witness of God* (April 1933): 2.

In May 1933, Urshan ministered for four weeks for Pastor James Thrush at 25 N. 23rd St. in Newark, Ohio.[203] He wrote, "We have several important invitations for the month of June."[204]

In the final revision of his life story, Urshan offered a summary statement of his evangelistic ministry from 1920-1934:

During these years of evangelistic labor, the Lord added to His Oneness churches over one thousand souls from 1920-1934. Thus the Jesus' Name people everywhere were encouraged and increased in number and in strength – with the most Holy Faith of the Apostolic Doctrine and Practice. Today, you will meet folks in the United States and Canada who will testify of God's blessings granted to them during these never-to-be-forgotten campaigns, for which we freely give God all the glory.[205]

Urshan's words at this point, including the identification of 1934 as a conclusion of sorts for his evangelistic ministry, anticipates a dramatic turn in his life. Trouble was looming in his family.

Not only did Urshan conduct a busy evangelistic ministry, requiring him to be away from home for extended lengths of time. He also published monthly *The Witness of God*; Mildred edited the publication. In addition, the couple conducted a "soul-saving campaign" in Chicago and opened "a new mission for the Name of the Lord."[206] Their first child, Grace Susannah, was born on May 25, 1918 during the extended Los Angeles meeting. Nathaniel Andrew was born on August 29, 1920, Faith Edith on June 25, 1924, and Andrew David Urshan, their fourth and last child, on April 26, 1929. Urshan wrote, "From this time on, I resumed my Evangelistic Campaigns all over the United States and Canada; [sic] *leaving my family in Chicago.*"[207]

The words "leaving my family in Chicago"

would have a profound impact on the Urshan family. Just twenty-four years of age, Mildred was left to raise their children. Her brief epilogue in the third edition of Urshan's life story subtly alludes to her struggle, "Our life has been a constant one of labor, *though at times almost too heavy to bear*, yet the thought of serving others in the name of Jesus has rendered unto us courage, strength and joy, which has enabled us to proceed successfully." Referencing both their spiritual and biological children, she requests, "Won't you pray for them please and also for us who mean to follow Christ and serve His great cause till He comes.—Amen." These words, written in 1933, indicate her intention to remain faithful. Nevertheless, within two years, Mildred would make some regrettable choices.[208]

---

[203] "Our Last Campaign," *The Witness of God* (June 1933): 2.
[204] "Our Next Campaign," *The Witness of God* (May 1933): 2.
[205] Urshan, *The Life Story*, 5th ed., 260.
[206] Urshan, *The Story of My Life*, 5th ed., 259.
[207] Quoted by Harvey from Urshan, *The Story of My Life*, 5th ed., 259-260. Emphasis added.
[208] Harvey, "Andrew D. Urshan," 11.

Urshan's Marriage Fails

While Urshan traveled widely in a successful ministry across North America, things were not going well at home. Although some details are lost to history, he refers to the mid-1930s as his "fiery furnace of testing." In 1935, Mildred divorced Andrew. According to Faith Edith, Urshan's daughter, her mother was "untrue" to her father. The family lived in a beautiful home in Chicago at that time, but the children knew something was not right. Urshan wrote:

> Our move to Chicago must have angered Satan much against myself and family. He must have challenged God to let him turn loose on us, to afflict our very lives, for we did go through some awful tests, trials, temptations, afflictions, and heart-breaking sorrows. The things which happened in our family circle, we do not feel led to write about, but we can say that even in those very dark hours of unexpected and unforeseen battles with the "powers of darkness," we held on to the Holy Name of Jesus, and He (blessed be His glorious Name) hid us in that strong tower again from the wrath of our enemies.[209]

It is evident from his choice of words that Urshan found himself in solidarity with the biblical Job. He saw this event as a spiritual battle resulting from a challenge Satan made to God.

In order to devote himself to the evangelistic ministry, Urshan had turned Emmanuel Mission, the church he and Mildred began, over to the care of others. There Mildred met the young Harry Hester. Although he was ten years younger than Mildred, Harry was married. He and his wife had several small children. Hester's wife fell ill, and Mildred helped with cooking and cleaning. Hester would transport Mildred and Faith to his home in the back seat of his car. It was his practice to generously compliment Mildred. Eventually, Mildred moved to the front seat, with Faith sitting between her mother and Harry.

Faith realized something was wrong and dreamed that during a shopping trip with her mother, Mildred disappeared. In her dream, Faith tried in vain to find her mother in the store's dressing rooms until finally, she opened the door to the last room. There stood her mother, who before her eyes turned into a mannequin that fell over and shattered on the floor. Faith awakened, frightened, and ran to tell her mother the dream. Mildred promised Faith that she would never leave her. Soon, however, Mildred divorced Andrew and abandoned her four children for Hester. As she left her family, Nathaniel, now fifteen years old, ran after her, begging her not to leave.[210]

After Mildred's marriage to Hester, who had divorced his wife, he transformed into a jealous and abusive alcoholic, isolating Mildred and preventing her, as much as possible, from visiting her family or friends. For a period of thirty-five years, she rarely saw her children.

---

[209]Urshan, *The Life Story*, 5th ed., 260.

[210]This account and much of what follows detailing the events leading up to and after the divorce follows Harvey's paper and discussions and email exchanges I have had with her during January-February 2015. The accuracy of this account has been repeatedly confirmed by Faith, who was eleven years old when Mildred abandoned her children.

Eventually the Hesters moved to San Antonio, Texas, where, until her death, they lived in relative poverty in a house trailer. Mildred's death was hastened by Harry's abusive treatment of her. In a drunken rage, he knocked her backwards out the door of the trailer, breaking her pelvic bone. She never walked again.

When Mildred suffered this abuse, a neighbor contacted Grace, Nathaniel, and Faith.[211] They visited her before she died on June 16, 1971 at the age of 75. In some of her last words, "Mildred told her children that Andrew had been a wonderful godly husband."[212] During this final visit, Mildred's children ministered to her spiritual and physical needs. This helped heal the emotional wounds of abandonment and led Mildred to repentance. One last time, she spoke with tongues, finding spiritual cleansing and renewal. Grace, Nathaniel, and Faith attended Mildred's funeral, as did Beth, another of Faith's daughters.

Andrew Urshan, who died before Mildred in 1967, did not speak ill of Mildred or allow his children to do so. He often retreated to his bedroom, praying "with groaning anguish," but would come out praising God.[213] When she heard of Andrew's impending death, Mildred managed to come to his hospital bed in Bay City, Texas. She was the last person to talk with Andrew before he died. In response to her tearful plea for forgiveness, he said, "Mildred, I forgave you a long time ago."[214]

The Move to New York

Urshan did not discuss the details of the divorce in print, but he did state that his children had "been motherless since June 1935."[215] When his marriage failed, Urshan's life took an immediate and drastic turn. Whereas he had previously been busily engaged in evangelistic ministry across North America while Mildred stayed home with the children, he now found himself a single parent with four children. His new circumstances resulted in new direction for his ministry and personal life.

First, Urshan relocated from Chicago to New York.

. . . we are to move away from Chicago soon, . . . to New York City for the next two months at least. . . .

The Satisfaction Tabernacle Gospel Hall is still open for all who are near us and for those who may come to New York City for a visit, to attend our nice little meetings. . . . we are but few . . . . This little work is going on in this great city . . . .

We feel the Lord is leading us away from Chicago . . . . We feel we have done our best for that city during the last 12 years and now our work is done there.[216]

---

[211]Andy, Andrew and Mildred's fourth child, had died on July 28, 1951.
[212]Harvey, "Andrew D. Urshan," 13.
[213]Harvey, "Andrew D. Urshan," 14.
[214]Harvey, "Andrew D. Urshan," 14.
[215]"Important Editor's Comments," *The Witness of God* (1962): back cover.
[216]"Important!" *The Witness of God* (May 1935): 1. The Satisfaction Tabernacle Gos-

Although Urshan planned to be in New York for a short time, he remained there in the pastoral role until the end of 1948. Then, in the August-September 1948 issue of The Witness of God, he announced, "Your Editor, who has been pastoring his God-given little assembly here in New York City for the last 14 years, is about to launch out into the evangelistic fields for the blessed Name of Jesus."[217]

Second, Urshan's itinerant ministry came to an end with Mildred's departure.[218] It was necessary for him to care for his four children, the youngest of whom – Andrew David Urshan, Jr. – suffered with muscular dystrophy.[219] At the time of Urshan's divorce, Grace Susannah, his oldest child who was born on May 25, 1918, would have been about sixteen years old. Nathaniel Andrew, born on August 29, 1920, was about fifteen. Faith Edith, the third child, was born on June 25, 1924 and would have been about ten. The youngest, Andrew "Andy," was born on April 26, 1929 and was about five.

Grace was able to provide some help with the younger children. However, Urshan left Andy with his grandmother in Cochrane, Wisconsin. When Andy was nine years old his grandmother took him to New York to be examined by medical specialists. At that point Andy required a wheel chair. Hospitalization and physical therapy did not help him; Andy continued to grow weaker. Urshan brought his son home where Grace, Faith, and Nathaniel, along with friends, participated in his care.[220]

A New Marriage and a Renewed Evangelistic Ministry

In the fall of 1948 Urshan announced that he was reentering the evangelistic field: "Your Editor, who has been pastoring his God-given little assembly here in New York City for the last 14 years, is about to launch out into the evangelistic fields for the blessed Name of Jesus."[221] Although not stating specifics, he wrote: "We hope in God's will when this January copy reaches you, we will be in California. We are planning, God willing, to spend this and the next three months in differ-

---

pel Hall was later renamed as the Apostolic Faith Christian Church (Faith Edith Schmidt, "Loving Memorial to Andrew David Urshan," *The Witness of God* (December 1967): 7.

[217]"Editorial News," *The Witness of God* (August-September 1948): 2.

[218]From 1919 to 1933, *The Witness of God* reports regularly on Urshan's itinerant ministry. Although I have not been able to assemble a complete run of all issues of the paper from 1934-1948, when Urshan announced his departure from pastoral work and his intention to reenter the evangelist field, I do have eighteen issues from that time period. No mention is made of any ministry engagements apart from his pastoral work in New York. A telephone conversation with Phillip Dugas on April 6, 2010 confirms that Urshan was not active in itinerant ministry during his years in New York.

[219]"Andy's Obituary," *The Witness of God* (October 1951): 2.

[220]"Andy's Obituary," *The Witness of God* (October 1951): 2; "Andy's Brief Biography," *The Witness of God* (October 1951): 3.

[221]"Editorial News," *The Witness of God* (August-September 1948): 2.

ent parts of the sunny state . . . ."[222] While in California, Urshan contacted Ethel Dugas, a widow living in the state. Soon he had another announcement:

> This is our third trip to California from New York City for [the] last three years, but this time we came here to attend to a very personal matter . . . we have been praying and waiting for its development in God's will since 1933. These have been seventeen long years of untold suffering and waiting, but thanks be unto Him who knows all about our struggles and now is guiding to the day that is done.[223]

Urshan married Ethel Dugas on April 7, 1950, Ethel's fifty-second birthday. Urshan turned sixty-six on May 17. The wedding was in Indianapolis, Indiana, Nathaniel A. Urshan, Andrew's son, presiding.

Urshan first met the Dugas family in Boise, Idaho in 1937, when Ethel's husband, Fred, was still living. Urshan and Ethel were both ministers in the Pentecostal Assemblies of Jesus Christ. The Dugas family subscribed to *The Witness of God,* occasionally sending money to help support Urshan's ministry. Urshan went to Boise to dedicate the new church his brother Joseph had just built. The Dugas family drove about 300 miles from their home in Prineville, Oregon to attend the dedication. Afterward, Urshan treated the family to a meal in a local restaurant.

The Dugas family later moved to Long Beach, California, where Fred died in 1947. Ethel wrote to tell Urshan about her husband's death. Andrew quickly wrote back, expressing his concern for her family. A short time later, Urshan wrote to his friend B. M. David, pastor of a church in Twin Falls, Idaho, asking him to invite Ethel to come there for a visit. Urshan wanted the David family to get to know Ethel, so they could offer him advice about their suitability for marriage. He then wrote Ethel, asking her to make the trip and sending her a list of questions to help him decide whether they should marry. A major issue for Urshan was the need to care for his son Andy.[224]

About one year later, Urshan wrote again, asking Ethel if she thought Pastor Harvey of Long Beach would be interested in having him come for a revival. At the time, Ethel wondered why Urshan did not contact the pastor directly. However, he was extended a two-week invitation. While there, he baptized Phillip Dugas and his brother Glen in the name of the Lord Jesus Christ. He also took the Dugas fmily to eat at one of Ethel's favorite restaurants.

Before his divorce, Urshan printed an article in *The Witness of God* by B. E. Echols titled "Some Overlooked Qualifications for the Ministry." Under the subheading "No Divorced Person to Enter or Abide," Echols wrote,

> . . . Paul DEMANDED of those who were to be ordained, concerning their NUMBER OF WIVES, "A bishop (which will refer to most all of the ministry) then MUST be (blameless) the HUSBAND of ONE wife! ONE wife! ONE wife! ONE wife. Yes, ONE wife, by all means, under ALL conditions, and ALL circumstances. Paul did not allow for any EXCEPTIONS either, when it was a question of quali-

---

[222] A. D. Urshan, "Editorial News and Comments," *The Witness of God* (January 1949): 2.
[223] "Editorial Message and News," *The Witness of God* (April 1950): 12.
[224] This account of Urshan's marriage to Ethel Dugas is informed by telephone conversations with Phillip Dugas on April 7 and 20, 2010.

fication for ministry . . . . The fact that God saves people who are married to and living with their SECOND, THIRD, and FOURTH companions is NO proof that they are also qualified for the ministry. . . . I cannot find any scripture in all the Bible that will allow for or inform us to ordain ministers with more than ONE wife (or companion) living.[225]

But in the June 1948 "Special Divorce Issue" of *The Witness of God,* Urshan printed W. T. Witherspoon's article "Marriage and Divorce In and Out of the Church," which took a considerably more nuanced approach than Echols:

Then comes the question of a saint re-marrying after they have obtained a divorce on Scriptural grounds. Who is there who has any right to order a normal man or woman of youth or middle age to live their life without a companion. Some preachers lay down the rules that they themselves could not follow. When the unbelieving departs (and presumably gets a divorce), a brother or sister is not under bondage in such cases. Who then could say that a brother or sister, whose former companion was untrue and dissolved the marriage union, must remain single?[226]

In the June-July 1950 issue of *The Witness of God,* Urshan expressed the newly married couple's appreciation for the greetings they had received from their friends: "Thanks to you all who so graciously have sent us your friendly congratulations. Both of us are very grateful to God for all of you. . . . Having moved now from Atlantic to the Pacific Ocean, we had to unpack . . . . our new address [is] 412 East 21st St., Apt. F, Long Beach, California."[227]

Andy's Death

On July 28, 1951, Andy, Urshan's youngest child, died. Urshan had hoped that the climate on the West Coast would prove therapeutic to Andy, but that was not to be. He grew progressively weaker and for the final fifteen days of his life was hospitalized under an oxygen tent. Many prayed for his recovery, but Andy asked to be allowed to "go to his Lord and Master whom [he] had seen in a vision." Andy died singing, "Jesus, I love thy name."[228]

In September of 1951 the Urshans departed Long Beach for an extended trip. Most of Urshan's travels were by train; he did not drive an automobile.

With a broken heart over the death of our beloved boy, Andy . . . and with much prayers, we decided to get away from our happy home here in Long Beach, California, for a few day's trip. . . . we started for San Francisco to visit our cousins . . . . They surely did their utmost and it helped us much to take our further journey East. We then started for Indianapolis, Indiana, on September 8th, to visit Andy's grave

---

[225]B. E. Echols, "Some Overlooked Qualifications for the Ministry," *The Witness of God* (January 1931): 15.

[226]W. T. Witherspoon, "Marriage and Divorce In and Out of the Church," *The Witness of God* (June 1948): 8.

[227]A. D. Urshan, "Editorial News," *The Witness of God* (June and July 1950): 1.

[228]Arthur Witherspoon, "Andy's Obituary," *The Witness of God* (October 1951): 2; Andrew D. Urshan, "Andy's Brief Biography," *The Witness of God* (October 1951): 3; Urshan, *The Life Story,* 5th ed., 261.

and to mingle our tears with Andy's sister, Mrs. Wm. Schmidt, and his brother, Pastor Nathaniel A. Urshan, both of Indianapolis. . . . We also ministered to the large congregation of the Calvary Tabernacle there. While I preached in the tabernacle, Mrs. Urshan ministered to an interested crowd under a gospel tent of the Tabernacle a few miles away."[229]

The Urshans had planned to be away from home only a few days, but their trip extended as they received ministry invitations along the way. In October 1951 they were invited to Columbus, Ohio.

While in Indianapolis, we had a long distance telephone call from the useful young Pastor and his wife (Pastor Arthur Witherspoon) of Columbus, Ohio, to go there and give them a meeting for a couple of days. Here we had to stay eight days with God's blessing upon the Pastorate and their large congregation. . . . We left these precious people for St. Paul, Minnesota, to visit Andy's sister, Mrs. John A. Larson.[230]

The Urshans left Columbus in October to spend a few days with Andy's sister Grace Susannah, the wife of John Larson. But S. G. Norris, the pastor of Midway Pentecostal Tabernacle and founder of Apostolic Bible Institute, St. Paul, Minnesota, had other ideas.

We had planned to stay at Andy's sister's for two or three days before returning to the west, but Pastor S. G. Norris, the minister of their large Midway Pentecostal Tabernacle and Dean of the Apostolic Bible Institute, urged us to help him in their profitable and very interesting services for a few days. Here we found about one hundred Bible students . . . . The church and the school have purchased a large, beautiful, red-brick Lutheran Church in St. Paul . . . We were privileged to deliver the welcome address on Sunday, October 7, 1951.[231]

Another pastor in the area also issued an invitation: "While serving at the school, Pastor Bob Martin of Minneapolis opened his large church doors wide also for my wife and myself to minister to his congregation in our spare time."[232]

On their return home, the Urshans visited with the Davids in Twin Falls, Idaho: "Before leaving the northwest we received an urgent invitation from Bishop B. M. David to stop at Twin Falls, Idaho, for a few days' visit on our way to California. This we did and we surely enjoyed the hospitality of Bro. and Sis. David and the saints in their fine homes."[233]

---

[229]"God's Acknowledgment and Our Trip East!" *The Witness of God* (October and November 1951): 3.

[230]"God's Acknowledgment and Our Trip East!" *The Witness of God* (October and November 1951): 3, 8.

[231]"God's Acknowledgment and Our Trip East!" *The Witness of God* (October and November 1951): 8.

[232]"God's Acknowledgment and Our Trip East!" *The Witness of God* (October and November 1951): 3, 8.

[233]"God's Acknowledgment and Our Trip East!" *The Witness of God* (October and November 1951): 3, 8.

Faithful until the End

Less than a year later, Andrew embarked on another trip to the eastern part of the United States. This time Ethel stayed home in Long Beach:

> . . . you read in our last *Witness* that we were to take a trip to the Eastern states, and this your editor did in the name of the Lord.
>
> We took the Los Angeles Limited train from L.A. to Chicago. . . . When we reached Chicago we were welcomed by our Assyrian relatives and friends to be entertained by them . . . .
>
> Next day we reached Milwaukee, Wisconsin. Pastor F. J. Ellis met us to usher us to a district fellowship meeting in a town seventy miles from Milwaukee. There the Lord gave us a message that they will never forget. It was good to meet all those United Pentecostal district ministers and enjoy their happy faces and brotherly courtesy. This was on Saturday, April 26. On Sunday morning we started our two week special services in Milwaukee. . . . We thank the Lord for blessing us not only in Milwaukee, but in Oak Park, Michigan, Indianapolis, Indiana, and in Duluth, Minnesota.
>
> We shall not omit that Sister Urshan, your editor's wife, who chose to stay at home sending me to all these states, stood by us, in fastings and prayers . . . .
>
> Now . . . the two months of our trip are over and we have returned back home to enjoy the good old balmy sunny weather in Long Beach, California.[234]

During the summer and fall of 1953, Urshan evangelized in various states. He was sixty-nine years old at the time: ". . . your Editor has been traveling the last few months and evangelizing both in California and other states."[235]

In August of 1955 he attended the Western District Camp Meeting of the United Pentecostal Church in Frazier Park, California.[236] In September he was arranging a two-week revival with David Gray, pastor of Revival Tabernacle in San Diego.[237]

In 1956, Urshan turned seventy-two years but still had the energy to conduct revivals in thirteen churches.[238] For the first time, his name was included in the Ministerial Directory of the United Pentecostal Church that year.[239] Urshan himself described his journey of organizational affiliation:

---

[234]"Editorial News and Comments," *The Witness of God* (June 1952): 8.

[235]"Editorial News and Notes," *The Witness of God* (November 1953): 1.

[236]"Editorial News and Comments," *The Witness of God* (September 1955): 1.

[237]"Editorial News and Comments," *The Witness of God* (September 1955): 1.

[238]"Editor's News and Comments," *The Witness of God* (January 1957): 4.

[239]This information is provided by Robin Johnston, the editor-in-chief of the United Pentecostal Church International, Inc. Urshan was affiliated with the Pentecostal Assemblies of Jesus Christ, which merged with the Pentecostal Church, Inc. in 1945 to form the United Pentecostal Church, but he waited for about a decade before affiliating with the new organization. This is in spite of the fact that his ministry during these years was largely within the fellowship of the United Pentecostal Church.

When returning to USA [from his 1914-1916 missionary trip to Persia and Russia] I was with the Assemblies of God which was newly organized.[240] We attended both schools and services [by this he means he fellowshipped with both Trinitarian and Oneness Pentecostals] and I found a better spirit with the Jesus Name Pentecostal people. In 1918 I returned my credentials to the Assemblies of God [and] joined the Pentecostal Assemblies of the World, [of] which [the] late Bro. Haywood was executive Bishop. I kept in their fellowship until [the] United Pentecostal Church, Inc. was organized.[241] Later I took membership with this good organization until this very day, enjoying their sweet fellowship and the true doctrine of the Apostles of the Lord Jesus Christ.[242]

During the summer months of 1957 Urshan was the Bible teacher for the Illinois District Camp Meeting of the United Pentecostal Church. He was teamed with J. T. Pugh:

> The month of July found us busy at the Illinois District United Pentecostal Church Camp Meeting at Murphysboro, Illinois. . . .
>
> We were asked to give the Bible Lessons each afternoon of the camp meeting and our congregation numbered from 100-300 each day and at the evening services there were from 700 to 900 people who came to hear Pastor and Evangelist J. T. Pugh of Port Arthur, Texas.[243]

In August of 1957 he once again enjoyed the camp meeting of the Western District of the United Pentecostal Church.[244]

In the spring of 1958 Urshan ministered in the states of Washington, Oregon, and California. He was now seventy-four years of age.

> We enjoyed . . . Puyallup, Washington; Albany, Oregon; Springfield, Oregon; Salem, Oregon; and Portland, Oregon . . . .
>
> . . . we preached the gospel and the deeper things of God. . . .

---

[240]Urshan was ordained with the Assemblies of God on September 13, 1917 even though he did not fully endorse the statement of fundamental truths of the organization. He wrote, "I do not object [to] the formula which is written in Acts 2:38, not as the New Issue folks explain it but simply because it is [the] written word of God" (Stephen Ray Graham, "Conservative American Protestantism and the Origins of Pentecostalism: A Case Study of Andrew D. Urshan" [MA thesis, Wheaton College, 1982], 47).

[241]The Pentecostal Assemblies of Jesus Christ resulted from a short-lived merger of the Pentecostal Assemblies of the World with the Apostolic Churches of Jesus Christ. See Andrew D. Urshan, "The Grand and Good New Merger," *The Witness of God* (May 1932): 6-7; A. D. Urshan, "Interesting News," *The Witness of God* 6, no. 55 (July 1924): 4; "Editorial News of Interest," *The Witness of God* 6, no. 48 (October 1924): 1. Emphasis in original.

[242]W. W. Sturdivan, "Andrew D. Urshan," *Gospel Tidings* (January 1968): 3. Urshan's report that he returned his credentials to the Assemblies of God in 1918 is mistaken. He returned them sometime between April 19, 1919 and May 17, 1919. See E. N. Bell, "Andrew Urshan's New Stand," *The Christian Evangel* (April 19, 1919): 9 and E. N. Bell, "The Urshan Trouble," *The Christian Evangel* (May 17, 1919): 7.

[243]"Editorial Comments and News," *The Witness of God* (August 1957): 1.

[244]"Editorial Comments and News," *The Witness of God* (August 1957): 1.

> ... we returned home via Stockton, Calif. While in Stockton we enjoyed immensely the graduation program of the Western Apostolic Bible College.[245]

In 1959, Urshan was still active in ministry in California.[246] In the spring of 1961, a long held dream came true for him.[247]

> Evangelist (Rev.) Andrew D. Urshan ... is on his way 'home' to Iran, to visit his hometown in Urmia and to 'weep at the graves of my mother and father.'. . . he was scheduled to spend some time in the Holy Land (Israel) attending a world Pentecostal Convention before continuing on to Iran. 'I am on my way to my native land,' he wrote shortly before departing by plane from Idlewild (New York), 'to visit with my remaining friends and relatives and to once more breathe the air of my old home town (Abadjaloo) and weep over the graves of my dear parents.'. . . Just a week before leaving the United States for his trip to Iran, Rev. Urshan delivered a sermon in Syriac at the Assyrian Presbyterian Church in Yonkers, N.Y.. . . Rev. Urshan returned to Iran for a brief visit in 1914, but had not been back to his native land until he decided to make the pilgrimage a few weeks ago.[248]

Urshan was exuberant when he arrived in Israel. The front page of the August 1961 issue of *The Witness of God* was headlined, "Greetings to all our readers from the Holy City . . . JERUSALEM!"[249]

Available evidence does not reveal the exact time that Urshan took this trip to Israel and Iran. The report in the *Assyrian Star* indicates that Urshan was on his way before the May-June 1961 issue went to press, and this seems to be confirmed by the August 1961 issue of *The Witness of God*. However, Urshan writes in the July 1962 issue:

> ... we have just returned from our two months long trip to Teheran, Iran. Our dreams came to pass well and good . . . to be able to visit several cities in Iran. It was upon my heart before passing out [sic] to visit my native land, and the streets where once I walked with my late parents, watching over young Andreous and other children some 70 years [ago] and [I] visited them also 48 years ago. It was upon me also to see the remaining relatives and the old time friends and give them the timely warning message to be ready to meet the soon coming great events in peace and with victory. This was done in the large Presbyterian Churches which were opened wide for my preaching where multitudes gathered and enjoyed the anointed preaching in the Name of the Lord.[250]

Aside from the two month trip to the Middle East, the available sources fail to document Urshan's ministerial activity during the years 1961-1965. There are indications in these materials, however, that suggest he had not been as active as he would have liked. This situation changed in the fall of 1965.

---

[245]"Our Recent Trip," *The Witness of God* (July 1958): 1.

[246]"Editorial – Adoration," *The Witness of God* (November 1959): 1.

[247]I am unable to reconstruct Urshan's ministry in 1960 for lack of documentation.

[248]"Assyrian Pastor Goes 'Home'," *Assyrian Star* (May-June 1961): 10, 14.

[249]"Editorial News from Jerusalem," *The Witness of God* (August 1961): 1.

[250]A. D. Urshan, "Editorial News," *The Witness of God* (July 1962): 1. The author's best guess is that the trip took place in the spring of 1961 and for some reason, Urshan failed to report on the trip until the July 1962 issue of *The Witness of God* was published.

When in our October 1965 General Conference in Grand Rapids, Michigan, the Lord spoke to me, saying, "Behold, I have set before thee an open door, and no man can shut it." When I said, yes, Lord, brethren in [the] Conference began to ask me for Bible teaching and preaching campaigns. . . . As I accepted urgent requests, I started in the Name of the Lord in Madison, Wisconsin, and on to Texas and Mississippi States.[251]

In January of 1966 Urshan ministered in Texas. By January 30 he was preaching in Jackson, Mississippi in a meeting that ended February 6.[252] All together, he preached in at least five states and fifteen churches during the year of 1966, the year he turned 82.[253]

Urshan began the year of 1967 with a meeting in Hammond, Indiana with Pastor Frank Munsey, followed by an engagement in Terre Haute, Indiana with Pastor Carl McKeller, who was Urshan's grandson-in-law.[254] During the month of June he ministered in San Diego, California for Pastor David Gray and in Napa, California for Pastor Paul Price. He concluded this evangelistic tour at Western Apostolic Bible College, where Clyde Haney was the founder and president.[255]

Going Home

Urshan preached nearly every night for a month during the fall of 1967. He concluded with an engagement in Bay City, Texas where R. E. Johnson was pastor. He passed from this life in Bay City at 11:55 a.m. on Monday, October 16, at the age of 83 years and five months.[256] He preached his last message on Thursday evening, October 12.

Stricken with a fatal heart attack, Urshan said to the pastor's wife: "I have fought a good fight, I have finished my course, I have kept the faith: Henceforth

---

[251]"Traveling for Jesus, Our Soon Coming King!" *The Witness of God* (June 1966): 1

[252]"June Greetings!" *The Witness of God* (June 1966): 1; Thomas L. Craft, "First Pentecostal Church," *The Witness of God* (June 1966): 8.

[253]*The Witness of God* (June 1966): 8; Urshan, *The Life Story,* 5th ed., 278; "Introduction," *The Witness of God* (September 1966): 8. These engagements included Birmingham, Alabama [Pastor Richard F. McCary]; Tupelo, Mississippi [James Moulter, president, Pentecostal Bible Institute]; Houston, Texas [Pastor C. L. Dees]; Alexandria, Louisiana [Pastor Gerald Mangun]; Minden, Louisiana [Pastor Tom Barnes]; Bossier City, Louisiana [Pastor McDaniel]; Baton Rouge, LA [Pastor Calvin Rigdon]; Stockton, California [Clyde Haney, president, Western Apostolic Bible College]; Deridder, Louisiana; DeQuincy, Louisiana; Oakdale, Louisiana; Dallas, Texas; Beaumont, Texas; Port Arthur, Texas; Jackson, Mississippi.

[254]"Season's Greetings," *The Witness of God* (October-December 1966): 1.

[255]*The Witness of God* (June 1967): 1. References to Napa, CA and Stockton, CA are taken from Urshan, *The Life Story,* 5th ed., 278. As a student at Western Apostolic Bible College I was in chapel services to hear his ministry for his 1966 and 1967 engagements at the school.

[256]*The Witness of God* (October-November 1967): 1, 2. It seems that Urshan had appointments that reached nearly to the end of November, for he wrote that he was not able to return home until November 25. This issue of *The Witness of God* reports Urshan's death to have occurred at "approximately 11:45 A.M." In the following memorial issue, Urshan's daughter Faith reported that he died at 11:55 A.M. (Faith Edith Schmidt, "Loving Memorial to Andrew David Urshan," *The Witness of God* [December 1967]: 7).

there is laid up for me a crown of righteousness, which the Lord, the righteous judge, shall give me at that day: and not to me only, but unto all them also that love his appearing."[257] (See II Timothy 4:7-8). Before the Johnsons took him to the hospital on Saturday morning, October 14, Urshan asked Pastor and Mrs. Johnson to sing with him the chorus, "Ready to go, ready to stay, ready my place to fill, Ready for service, lowly or great, ready to do Thy will."[258]

When he was taken to the Matagorda General Hospital in Bay City, he insisted before receiving any treatment that the nurses, the doctor, and Pastor and Mrs. Johnson kneel while Pastor Johnson led in prayer. Urshan witnessed to all who entered his hospital room, including the medical staff. He "taught one of the nurses a chorus and insisted that she sing each time she came to minister to his needs."[259]

His son, Nathaniel A. Urshan, his daughters, Grace Larson and Faith Schmidt, Pastor and Mrs. R. E. Johnson, Paul Gregory, James Kilgore, and Corliss Dees were all present during his waning hours. Among his final comments, Urshan told his son, "I am going to the International Convention in the New Jerusalem," making a play on the fact that the general conference of the United Pentecostal Church was to begin in two days, October 18, 1967. Then a man of God seen by many as a "mystic and seer" closed his eyes and went to be with his Lord.[260]

Thus died the man, but not his influence.

Summary

The life story of Andrew Bar David Urshan is a remarkable saga of a man who acknowledged his frailties, embraced his weakness, sought peace with those who disagreed with him, but never compromised convictions. David Reed chose well when he identified Urshan as one of the four most influential pioneers of nascent Oneness Pentecostalism.

Urshan was willing to change his mind if he thought God so directed him. He said he would never marry, but he did, twice. He had opposed medicine and doctors, but even though he always sought God's remedy first, he was willing to accept care from the medical field for his son and for himself. His decisions might invite mockery from skeptics, but although Urshan had strong opinions, he was not intransigent.

However, regardless of the consequence, unless so directed by God, he would not compromise. This led to the loss of fellowship with Trinitarian Pentecostals, a fellowship he treasured and enjoyed and which he would have continued, had he not been required to surrender his credentials in response to the rejection of his "Confession of Faith" by the Assemblies of God.

---

[257] J. Hugh Rose, "Farewell, Thou Man of God" *The Witness of God* (December 1967): 4.
[258] Faith Edith Schmidt, "Loving Memorial to Andrew David Urshan," *The Witness of God* (December 1967): 7.
[259] J. Hugh Rose, "Farewell, Thou Man of God," *The Witness of God* (December 1967): 6.
[260] J. Hugh Rose, "Farewell, Thou Man of God," *The Witness of God* (December 1967): 6.

Not only did Urshan grieve over his forced departure from the Assemblies of God and the doors of fellowship that were thereby closed to him; he also saw Satan at work in attempts to thwart the unification of Oneness groups.[261] In his comments on the merger of the Pentecostal Assemblies of the World and the Apostolic Church of Jesus Christ, Urshan wrote:

> . . . some are doing their utmost to destroy this needed merger, surely satan is at work. But what else can we expect since some men are determined to smash every good thing to build something for themselves. . . .

> . . . if you meet a minister that speaks against this timely merger, please remember that you have his or her number, avoid them, do not listen to their arguments but you stand by this good and pleasant thing that has happened[,] the merging of the P. A. of W. and A. C. of J. C. into this one great movement for God, the Pentecostal Assemblies of Jesus Christ. . . .[262]

In his opinion, those who shared a common experience should be able to find a level of fellowship in spite of doctrinal,[263] social, and cultural differences.[264]

Urshan died as he lived, active in the work of the Lord, proclaiming a simple gospel message while embracing divine mysteries, and loving his Pentecostal friends everywhere. In his words, written at the age of 79, Urshan declared:

> [W]e were forced to stop our ministry to all the Pentecostal faiths, blessing them, encouraging them to love one another, to have fellowship and worship together in such soul-saving campaigns, overlooking their difference on some Bible subjects.

> If that had not happened we would have been still preaching to thousands of different groups of the Pentecostals together to this very day.[265]

There was never a time when Urshan decided to be a Oneness pioneer. He knew what he believed, but he respected those with whom he did not agree. His destiny was shaped by those who did not share his willingness to seek unity in diversity. The distance to which he was willing to go in an effort to find unity gained little traction in his day, and the subsequent history of the relationship – or lack of it – between Trinitarian and Oneness Pentecostals indicates that Urshan's experience was prescient.

---

[261]Urshan, "The Grand and Good New Merger," *The Witness of God* (May 1932): 6.

[262]Urshan, "The Grand and Good New Merger," *The Witness of God* (May 1932): 6.

[263]Urshan, "The Story of My Life—28th Chapter," *The Witness of God* 6, no. 64 (May 1925): 3.

[264]The PAW consisted largely of black ministers, while the AC of J C consisted largely of white ministers.

[265]Urshan, "The Final and the Conclusion," *The Witness of God* (May 1963): 7. Urshan's reference to "soul-saving campaigns" alluded to his seven month campaign in Los Angeles in 1918.

Part 2: Theology, Christology, and Soteriology of Andrew D. Urshan

Chapter Six

Theological Influences

Introduction

Andrew D. Urshan's theological journey was rich and varied. Although he believed that he was divinely led to his ultimate home in Oneness Pentecostalism, he continued throughout his life to value his theological heritage and past experiences. Since he believed God had led him during his earlier journey, he could not disavow those earlier steps as he progressed.

Urshan described his life's journey as the turning of five leaves. The first leaf was his conversion as a student attending the American Presbyterian College in Urmia, Persia. This dramatic experience with God forever impacted his spiritual life. The second leaf was his arrival in America where he was exposed to a new world. His spiritual integrity was challenged as new values and experiences beckoned. The third leaf was his sanctification at a Nazarene church, at which point he declared he was "reclaimed and anointed to preach Christ." The fourth leaf was his introduction to Pentecostalism and his experience of baptism in the Holy Spirit. The fifth and final leaf was his baptism in the name of the Lord Jesus Christ with the accompanying insight of the theological significance of this formula as it relates to the nature of God.[1]

Although Urshan believed he had traveled farther on his spiritual and theological journey than some others who had also been baptized with the Holy Spirit, he could not reject those who had not had his experiences or "revelation."[2] In his view, the Pentecostal body was three-fold.

It seems that the great body of the baptized believers with the Holy Ghost who have

---

[1]Andrew David Urshan, *Why I was Baptized into the Name of the Lord Jesus Christ in Russia*, 1, 8. This little booklet consists of sixteen pages including the front and back covers. It does not include any publication information, but the front cover includes this statement: "Copied from 'The Story of My Life,' Chapter 27, which appeared in the 'Witness of God,' Sixty-second Edition, March, 1925, a Spiritual, Monthly Paper. Chicago, IL, U.S.A."

[2]Earlier, I have stated Urshan's understanding of the term "revelation." See footnote 35, page 27.

spoken with tongues is a three-fold body or three great parties. The first part of the body may be classified [as the] thousands of ministers and laity who have received the baptism of the Holy Ghost with the sign of tongues but do not hold on speaking with the other tongues to be the evidence, or the main sign of the Holy Spirit baptism. ... God is blessing the portion of His own truth preached to the hungry and honest church members.

The second part of the Spirit filled saints may be called the real Pentecostalists, for these stand firm on the evidence of speaking in other tongues of their baptism in the Holy Spirit. ... the third part of this great Spirit filled body and the later is nicknamed "The New Issue People" of whom I am glad to say I am one. These one God people, or "Jesus Only" folks have and are now going through terrible misrepresentations, persecutions and fiery trials.[3]

Although he does not include the Church of the East, Moody Bible Church, or the Brethren Church among his "leaves," these were definite influences in Urshan's theological journey. His father became a Presbyterian minister under the influence of American Presbyterian missionaries, but the pervasive theological and cultural milieu in which Andrew was raised owed much to the ancient traditions of the Church of the East, a form of Syrian Christianity frequently identified as Nestorianism.

Church of the East

Urshan appeals to the Church of the East's theology throughout the fifth edition of his autobiography which was published in 1967, the year he died. The entire first chapter is devoted to his perspective on the Assyrian-Chaldean people, the Aramaic (Syriac) language, the history of Assyria, and the "Nestorians," whom he described as "Apostolic Faith Christians."[4] As one works through his theology, it is apparent that Urshan was also influenced by the interpretive use of symbolism in eastern theology and by the place of mystery in one's theological vocabulary.[5] He saw the theology of the Church of the East as the New Testament antecedent of his own view.

> Those Eastern Christians were very fiery for the Bible fundamentals; particularly the Cross of Christ, representing the Atonement, and the absolute Deity of Jesus Christ.
>
> They taught the absolute depravity of human nature; hence the necessity of the atoning blood of Christ. They taught God is a mystery, the unapproachable Divine Being; hence the necessity of His manifestation in the flesh. They denounced strongly the worship of any picture, image of any divine being, or of the Saints.
>
> They believed in the God-head being a triunity of three Kenoomas[6] and never a

---

[3] Urshan, "Why I Was Baptized," 12-13.
[4] Urshan, *The Life Story*, 5th ed., 15.
[5] See pages 210-214 for a discussion of Ephrem's and Urshan's use of symbolism.
[6] The Syriac word Urshan transliterates as *kenooma* is usually rendered *qnoma*, which is the form we will use unless quoting from a source that does otherwise.

trinity of three separate distinct persons. "Ke-noo-ma" to them was an image, attribute, or a manifestation of God. For instance, they taught that Jesus, one Being, or His one person, contained two "Ke-noo-mas." That is: two distinct natures; one absolutely divine, the other perfectly human, though conceived by the Holy Spirit and born in the Virgin Mary.

Tri-unity of God to them was like mind, wisdom, and power. As mind produces wisdom, and wisdom and mind together produce power and action, so Father (the Supreme Mind) produces the Son (The Heavenly wisdom), and the Father in the Son produced the power (the Holy Spirit). All these three attributes of the one Divine Being were in Jesus of Nazareth; that is why He was not man-God, but the perfect God, and the perfect man; hence "Aman-El," the Lord over all, or the God-man with us.[7]

The solidarity Urshan felt with the theology of the Church of the East is seen in his appeal to the church's view of the "Bible fundamentals" and what he perceived to be a rejection of western Trinitarianism. He was willing to describe God as a triunity and even as the "three-one" God,[8] but he understood Trinitarianism to teach that God is "three separate and distinct persons," with the word "person" describing a self-conscious individual as it is used to describe individual human beings. This he could not believe.

According to Urshan, the term "Nestorians" was given to the Eastern Apostolic Church fathers as a "nickname" by the Western Roman Church. Previously, from the second to the fourth century, they were known as the Apostolic Church of the East or as Eastern Apostolic Christians. As Urshan describes it, the Roman Church fathers put an anathema on Nestorius, a one time bishop of Constantinople who was born in Syria,

"because they hated him for teaching in his diocese, this truth; 'Let no one call Mary, the mother of God; for Mary was a human being, and that God should be born of a human being is impossible.'"[9]

In Urshan's account, Nestorius, after being charged with heresy and exiled, withdrew to private life until 435 in his former monastery in Antioch and was then banished to Petra by the Roman emperor. After being captured and carried away from Petra by a roving band of nomads, he "finally escaped into Assyria, and found other Christians, still living, and dying for the true and unadulterated Apostolic teachings of the founders of the Church of Jesus Christ."[10]

Urshan denies that Nestorius was a heretic and says that when he went to Assyria, Nestorius "found thousands of pure and consecrated Apostolic Faith Christians, who believed as he did, in regard to the virgin Mary's position, on the subject."[11] In Urshan's view, "most of the Eastern Christians of Mesopotamia and

---

[7] Urshan, *The Life Story*, 5th ed., 16.
[8] Urshan, *The Almighty God*, 6, 10, 14, 42, 43, 44, 45, 47, 66, 74, 75, 77, 78, 82, 84, 87, 88, 93.
[9] Urshan, *The Life Story*, 5th ed., 14.
[10] Urshan, *The Life Story*, 5th ed., 14-15.
[11] Urshan, *The Life Story*, 5th ed., 15.

Persia were Apostolic in their doctrine."[12] After a brief discussion of their missionary zeal, he writes,

> If Mohammedanism had not risen to kill and oppress them, these ancient lands would have remained to this very day the crown and joy of the Christian world through the power of God, with those early Assyrian Christians. They have furnished thousands of holy martyrs for the Word of God, and the testimony of Jesus. The Bible lands are sprinkled with the blood of these faithful servants of God. The cry of their blood has not ceased; the Almighty still hears the cries of their afflicted children of today, and He has graciously left us a remnant to raise His glorious Apostolic Standard now before this present generation.[13]

It is quite clear that Urshan views the Pentecostal movement as a restoration of the faith once held by these early eastern Christians. They were, in his words, once "very fiery for the Bible fundamentals; particularly the Cross of Christ, representing the Atonement, and the absolute Deity of Jesus Christ."[14] The blood atonement was made necessary by "the absolute depravity of human nature."[15]

Urshan's restorationism is further developed than the restorationism typically seen among early twentieth century Pentecostals in the western world. From the western perspective, the Pentecostal experience was restored progressively as the end result of Martin Luther's discovery of justification by faith, John Wesley's preaching of sanctification as a second work of grace, and the late nineteenth century's holiness emphasis on the baptism of the Holy Ghost as a distinctive third work of grace.[16] By connecting restorationism with eastern Christianity, Urshan's Weltanschauung was a world apart.[17] His view of Pentecostalism as a restoration of the faith once held by eastern Christianity goes further than the typical western view; he saw also Oneness Pentecostalism as standing in solidarity with the eastern view of the Godhead.

The language used to describe this view is a challenge to those unaccustomed to wrestling with the subtleties of the Greek and Latin vocabularies typically used to describe the doctrine of the Trinity, but it should be recognized that the Syriac vocabulary has its own challenging subtleties. As Brock points out, "there were different understandings, not only of the term *qnoma,* but also of the term 'nature' (Greek *physis,* Syriac *kyana*)."[18]

In order to discern whether the understanding of the Godhead in the Church of the East is informative for the Oneness Pentecostal view, we must have clear comprehension of the Syriac terms and their possible connection to the Greek and

---

[12]Urshan, *The Life Story*, 5th ed., 15.
[13]Urshan, *The Life Story*, 5th ed., 15-16.
[14]Urshan, *The Life Story*, 5th ed., 16.
[15]Urshan, *The Life Story*, 5th ed., 16.
[16]See Donald W. Dayton, *Theological Roots of Pentecostalism* (Grand Rapids: Zondervan, 1987).
[17]Urshan, *The Almighty God,* 46.
[18]Brock, "The 'Nestorian' Church: A Lamentable Misnomer," 25. Urshan transliterates *qnoma* as "Ke-noo-ma."

Latin terms used in western Christianity. Then there is the need to fully explore Urshan's understanding of these vocabularies.

Urshan did not seem to distinguish between the meaning of *qnoma* in the context of the doctrine of the Trinity and in the context of Christology. This apparent error is critical and prohibits an accurate understanding of the theology and Christology of the Church of the East. In order to grasp the subtle distinctions between the Greek and Syriac words that are pertinent to this point, we should first consider the use of the Greek *hypostasis* in the Council of Chalcedon of 451:

> Therefore, following the holy Fathers, we all with one accord teach men to acknowledge one and the same Son, our Lord Jesus Christ, at once complete in Godhead and complete in manhood, truly God and truly man, consisting also of a reasonable soul and body; of one substance [*homoousios*] with the Father as regards his Godhead, and at the same time of one substance with us as regards his manhood; like us in all respects, apart from sin; as regards his Godhead, begotten of the Father before the ages, but yet as regards his manhood begotten, for us men and for our salvation, of Mary the Virgin, the God-bearer [*theotokos*]; one and the same Christ, Son, Lord, Only-begotten, recognized in two natures, without confusion, without change, without division, without separation; the distinction of natures being in no way annulled by the union, but rather the characteristics of each nature being preserved and coming together to form one person and subsistence [*hypostasis*], not as parted or separated into two persons, but one and the same Son and Only-begotten God the Word, Lord Jesus Christ; even as the prophets from the earliest times spoke of him, and our Lord Jesus Christ himself taught us, and the creed of the Fathers has handed down to us.[19]

The Church of the East rejected the Chalcedonian Definition due to perceived conflict between the Greek *hypostasis* and the Syriac *qnoma*, which is the Syriac word used to represent *hypostasis*. The Chalcedonian Definition declared that Christ had two natures that formed one person and *hypostasis*. For the Church of the East, this was impossible. The Syriac *qnoma* has a wider range of meaning than *hypostasis*, and it was the word used to represent both *hypostasis* and nature (*physis*). To say that Christ had two natures implied that he had two *qnome*, but the Syriac use of *qnoma* to translate *hypostasis* interpreted the Chalcedonian Definition to mean that Christ had only one *qnoma*. How could he simultaneously have one and two?

As Brock points out, this conundrum is due to the fact that "[w]hen the Church of the East uses *qnoma* in connection with 'nature' it usually speaks of 'the two natures and their *qnomas*", where *qnoma* means something like 'individual manifestation'."[20]

In addition, the Syriac word *kyana* and its relationship to *qnoma* further contribute to the rejection of the Chalcedonian Definition: "a *qnoma* is an individual instance or example of a *kyana* (which is understood as always abstract), but this

---

[19]Henry Bettenson, *Documents of the Christian Church*, 2nd ed. (London: Oxford University Press, 1967), 51-52. Emphases in original.

[20]S. P. Brock, "The 'Nestorian' Church: A Lamentable Misnomer," *Bulletin of the John Rylands University Library of Manchester*, 78: 28.

individual manifestation is not necessarily a self-existent instance of a *kyana*."[21] Thus, *kyana*, which corresponds to the Greek *ousia*, refers to "a general and immutable type in the sense of a species. So there is the usia [*ousia*] of God or the general species of human being."[22] Baumer's extended explanation of the philosophical terms 'nature,' 'hypostasis,' and 'person' is helpful:

> The fundamental basis is the definition of the Trinity from 381, which speaks of one *usia* [*ousia*] – understood as substance – in three hypostases – understood as persons. We can translate the Greek words *usia* and *physis* as 'nature', a universal category, a general and immutable type in the sense of a species. So there is the *usia* of God or the general species of human being. The Syriac word *kyana* corresponds to the Greek *usia*. The difficulty began with the term 'hypostasis'. Cyril and most non-Antiochene theologians interpreted the Greek word in the Neo-Platonic sense as a concrete realization of the *usia*, corresponding to the concrete person. Nestorius, however, when referring to a concrete person, used the term *prosopon*, in Syriac *parsopa*, and inserted the term 'hypostasis', Syriac *qnoma*, in between 'usia' and 'person'. Nestorius and the Church of the East understood the designation 'hypostasis' or 'qnoma' in the Aristotelian sense, as a material reality bound up with its species. The qnoma is an individual, representative realization of its nature, but does not necessarily exist for itself. The qnoma – that is – the hypostasis, is not yet the person, the *prosopon*. The prosopon is defined as the sum of accidental qualities that make the appearances of two hypostases different. Such qualities are, for instance, sex, hair colour, character traits, degree of intelligence, talents, etc. These qualities distinguish Peter from Paul or John from James. Applied to the example of the human being, usia/kyana refers to the general species of human, hypostasis/qnoma to a real, existing realization, and prosopon/parsopa to the appearance of the actual person. In brief, 'person' denotes the external appearance and 'hypostasis' the inner reality.[23]

The chart below shows a distinction in the language used in Alexandrine Christology (e.g., Cyril) and Antiochene Christology (e.g., Nestorius):

Alexandrine Christology	Antiochene Christology
Hypostasis: Concrete realization of *ousia* (e.g., concrete person)	*Prosopon (*Syriac *parsopa*): Concrete person Nestorius: *Usia* [Greek, *ousia*] *qnoma* [Greek, *hypostasis*] *parsopa*
Key Terms Applied to Human Species in Antiochene Christology	

Greek	Syriac	
Ousia	Kyana	General species of human
Hypostasis	Qnoma	A real, existing realization
Prosopon	Parsopa	Appearance of the actual person

---

[21]Brock, "The Nestorian Church," 28.
[22]Baumer, *The Church of the East*, 46.
[23]Baumer, *The Church of the East*, 46.

In a theological disputation between the Syrian Orthodox Church and the Church of the East which took place in 612, the official teaching of the Church of the East was for the first time declared to be "the two natures and two *qnome*" in Christ.[24]

> This terminology has been a bone of theological controversy ever since. Here ... much of the problem lies in the way that key terms in Greek and Syriac were understood by the various parties (and subsequent scholars). In particular, problems arose because the Greek term *hupostasis* (approximately "person") was regularly translated by the Syriac term *qnoma* (plural *qnome*; approximately "particular property", "characteristic"), even though the connotations of the two terms are quite different. For the Syriac theologians of Persia *hupostasis/qnoma* is the necessary individual manifestation of nature (*physis/kyana*), which is itself considered to be generic (e.g. humanity, divinity – closely associated in this Christology with Greek *ousia,* "essence"). As a consequence the Chalcedonian position that Christ had two natures but one *hupostasis/qnoma* appeared quite illogical to the Church of the East . . . . Instead Babai, and his succesors [sic] in the Church of the East, proclaimed that the *qnoma* of divinity (God the Word, perfect God) and the *qnoma* of humanity (Jesus, perfect man) are united in a single *prosopon* of sonship in an inseparable union from the very beginning of its fashioning.[25]

While the Christological formula declaring that there are two natures and two *qnome* in Christ appeared as an official statement for the first time in the early seventh century, the formula that God is a single being or nature consisting in three *qnome* [persons] appeared for the first time in the early fifth century.[26]

George David Malech, who had left Urmia on May 27, 1909 after serving as a teacher at the Presbyterian Mission College there – and who may have been teaching at the college when Urshan attended – offered a quotation from the Synod of Mar Akakios, who was the Patriarch of the Nestorian Church at the time of the synod in 486 a.d.

> We teach all believers according to the doctrine of the Apostles and our Father, which is accepted in the Church of Christ, that it is the faith and confession of us all, that there in God is one nature and three perfect personalities (*kenume*)[27] who are one true eternal Trinity, Who is Father, Son and Holy Spirit, which cleanses out paganism and judges Judaism.[28]

---

[24]David G. K. Taylor, "The Syriac Tradition," in *The First Christian Theologians: An Introduction to Theology in the Early Church,* ed. Gillian Rosemary Evans (Hoboken, NJ: Wiley-Blackwell, 2004), 214.

[25]Taylor, "The Syriac Tradition," 214-15.

[26]Christian Lange, *The Portrayal of Christ in the Syriac Commentary on the Diatessaron* (Leuven, Belgium: Peeters Publishers, 2005), 161, n. 26. For additional references to the one God in three *qnome* in the official documents of the Church of the East, see S. Brock, "Christology of Church of the East," in *Recent Studies in Early Christianity: A Collection of Scholarly Essays,* ed. Everett Ferguson (London: Taylor & Francis, 1999), 292-96.

[27]Variations in transliteration in Malech's book from current standards is probably due to the fact that Malech wrote the original work in Syriac, his son translated it from Syriac into Norwegian, and it was finally translated from Norwegian into English by Ingeborg Rasmussen, M.D. with stenography done by Cherrie M. Sly.

[28]George David Malech, *History of the Syrian Nation* (Minneapolis, MN: 1910), 343.

Malech also offers an extended treatment of his understanding of Christology.

> ... there are three Syrian words commonly used ... whose right signification it is very important to learn. These words are: 1) *Parsufa*[29] (Greek: *Prosopon*) which means: *a 'person.'* And the Syrians, and Nestorius, confess that Jesus Christ has *one parsufa,* or person, in the like manner as we confess in the western church. But they also teach that Jesus Christ has two *kejane*[30]or *natures*: the divine and the human, like as we confess. And besides, they teach that He has two *"kenume"*; or as they say: *"One person double in natures and their kenume."* ... To investigate the probable etymology of *kenuma,* sing., and *kenume,* plur., will not help us. The connection in which the word is used in the language will help us most. *"Kenuma"* signifies *"a person,"* ... but it is also used to denote the personal pronoun: *"self,"* .... And it may also mean: *"figure," "essence."* ... *kenuma* has several different meanings. In the early days the Syrians used this word when they spoke of the three persons of the holy Trinity, saying that there are three *kenume* in God, and one divine *"essence"* (Syriac: *"Ithutha"*). Now, the Syrians use more the word *"Parsufa,"* to signify *person,* when speaking of the three persons in God; and *kenume* when they speak of the two natures in Christ. But when they expressly confess ... in the Nicene Creed ... that there is *one parsufa,* or person, in Christ, they do not at the same time say that there are *two* persons in Christ, which would be a glaring contradiction. ... they mean by *kenume* of the natures of Christ about the same as what we mean by *"personality,"* i.e., the attributes, taken collectively, that make up the character of an individual, that which distinguishes and characterizes a "person".[31]

On February 22-27, 1996, the Second non-official Syriac Consultation organized by the foundation PRO ORIENTE met in Vienna. Participants from the Oriental Catholic Churches (Chaldean, Syrian, Maronite, Malabar, and Malankara), the Oriental Orthodox Churches (Syrian Orthodox from Antioch, Malankara Orthodox from India), and both jurisdictions of the Assyrian Church of the East worked out and agreed upon the following statement:

> It has ... become very clear ... that it is always essential to realize that, in the context of Christology (as opposed to the situation in Trinitarian theology), there is a clear and important difference between the understanding in the Church of the East of the term *qnoma* (i.e. individuated, but not personalized nature) and that of other Syriac Churches where *qnoma* is regularly understood as the equivalent of *hypostasis* in the sense of person.

Thus the following explanation of the term of *Qnoma* has been presented by the Assyrian, Chaldean and Syro-Malabar delegations of the Church of the East:

> "In Christology, as expressed in the synodical and liturgical sources of the Church of the East, the term *qnoma* does not mean *hypostasis* as understood in Alexandrine Tradition, but instead, individuated nature. Accordingly, the human nature which the Holy Spirit fashioned and the Logos assumed and united to Himself without

---

Malech says the same confession can be found in Mar Sabrishu's Synod, 596 A.D.

[29]Usually transliterated *parsopa.*

[30]Usually transliterated *kyane.*

[31]Malech, *History of the Syrian Nation,* 348-49.

any separation, was personalized in the Person of the Son of God. When we speak of the two natures and their *qnome*, we understand this very much in the same sense as two natures and their particular properties (*dilayatha*).

> It is important to note that the term *qnoma* is used in a different way in Trinitarian theology."[32]

Although the Church of the East employs a different vocabulary than is used in the theology of the Roman Catholic Church and the Syrian Orthodox Church, there may be no real difference in meaning. The fourteenth century Mar Odisho, "the last outstanding theologian of the Church . . . was convinced that the differences and disputes among the three great Christian communities of his time were founded only on words and terms, not in the religious ideas they expressed."[33] In 1994 Pope John Paul II and Patriarch Mar Dinkha IV signed the Common Christological Declaration, which read in part:

> As heirs and guardians of the faith received from the Apostles as formulated by our common Fathers in the Nicene Creed, we confess one Lord Jesus Christ, the only Son of God, begotten of the Father from all eternity who, in the fullness of time, came down from heaven and became man for our salvation. The Word of God, the second Person of the Holy Trinity, became incarnate by the power of the Holy Spirit in assuming from the holy Virgin Mary a body animated by a rational soul, with which he was indissolubly united from the moment of his conception. Therefore our Lord Jesus Christ is true God and true man, perfect in his divinity and perfect in his humanity, consubstantial with the Father and consubstantial with us in all things but sin. His divinity and his humanity are united in one person, without confusion or change, without division or separation . . . . The Lord's Spirit permits us to understand better today that the divisions brought about . . . were due in large part to misunderstandings.[34]

As it relates to our interest in Urshan's understanding of the Godhead as he perceived it to be formulated by the Church of the East, it is important to note that while the Church of the East makes a distinction between the meaning of *qnome* in the context of the doctrines of the Trinity and of Christology, Urshan makes no such distinction. Thus, he defines *qnoma* as "an image attribute [*sic*] or a manifestation of God"[35] and applies this definition both to the three *qnome* in the Godhead and the two *qnome* in Christ.

Urshan's commendation of the view of the Godhead held in the Church of the East and his conviction that this view harks back to the first century apostles and Christians leaves open a variety of questions that must be pursued: (1) Was his understanding accurate? (2) Aside from Christology and the *filioque* controversy,

---

[32]"Joint Communiqué of the Second Non-Official Consultation on Dialogue within the Syriac Tradition, Vienna February 1996," http://www.pro-oriente.at/dokumente/ 2SyrCons1996.doc (accessed June 27, 2009).
[33]Baumer, *The Church of the East,* 280.
[34]Baumer, *The Church of the East,* 280.
[35]Urshan, *The Life Story,* 5th ed., 16. I assume Urshan means "image, attribute, or a manifestation."

what is the real difference, if any, between the western and eastern branches of Christianity as to the doctrine of the Trinity? (3) Even if Urshan's understanding of the eastern view of the Godhead is not precise, how does his understanding shape his personal theology differently than the Oneness theologies developed within the western perspective?

It may seem presumptuous to question the accuracy of Urshan's understanding of the doctrine of the Godhead and Christology of the Church of the East. It was, after all, the cultural and religious milieu in which he grew up. But we must remember that his father was a Presbyterian minister, and we don't know the extent of his grasp on the subtle nuances of the Greek and Syriac languages on these subjects. Further, we know from common experience that many who claim to hold to the doctrine of the Trinity in the western world hold views that bear little resemblance to the historic creedal formulations, just as many who profess to a Oneness view of the Godhead and Christology embrace a variety of theological and Christological errors.

We offer a summary of the problem by Baum and Winkler.

> The creed of the Church of the East of 612 speaks of the inseparable unity of the God-Logos and the human nature, recognized in Jesus Christ as one person (*prosopon*). It is further expressed in Babai's terminology that "Christ is two *kyane* (natures) and two *qnome*." In the past, the Syriac term *qnoma* had been equated with the Greek *hypostasis* or even translated as "person." Thus the misconception developed that the Church of the East believed in two natures and two persons in Christ. However, for neither Babai nor the creed of 612 did *qnoma* denote a self-existent hypostasis. *Kyana* refers to the general, abstract nature, that is, the human being and the God being, while *qnoma* describes the concretization and individualization of this nature. Babai thus usually employed the formulation "the two natures and their *qnome*" which are united from the moment of conception. Both Babai's most important treatment of the matter, the *Book of Union* and the document of 612 clearly express that each nature needs a *qnoma* in order to exist concretely. Were one to equate *qnoma* with *hypostasis,* one would reach a faulty understanding of the statement; a translation of "person" is incorrect. Because of this terminology, the East Syriacs were also unable to comprehend the definition of the Council of Chalcedon, which speaks of two natures in one person and hypostasis.[36]

In 1908, shortly after Urshan's departure from Persia, W. A. Wigram's *The Doctrinal Position of the Assyrian or East Syrian Church* was published. Wigram attempted to explain why the Assyrian Church was considered heretical.[37]

> [T]he Assyrian church . . . acknowledges in Christ two Natures (*Kiani*),[38] two *Qnumi* and one *Parsopa* (πρόσωπον, *Persona,* or Person).

---

[36] Wilhelm Baum and Dietmar W. Winkler, *The Church of the East: A Concise History* (New York: Routledge Curzon, 2003), 38.

[37] The following claim of heresy is in addition to the refusal of the Church of the East to call Mary the "Mother of God."

[38] This is sometimes transliterated "Kyana."

The first and last of these terms present . . . no difficulty . . . It is the second, the word *Qnuma*, which needs examination.

The word, which is of somewhat uncertain derivation, occurs some twelve times in the New Testament; and there it is usually, though not always, the representative of the Greek αὐτός, either alone or in some one of its compounds. It is, however, by no means the exclusive rendering of that common word.

. . . we find it as the equivalent of ὑπόστασις in the Nicene sense, and used . . . in the translation of the Creed of the Council, as received in Persia in the year 411. Here it is the rendering of the word ὑπόστασις in the Anathema, ἐξ ἑτέρας ὑποστάσεως ἢ οὐσίας: and in this case . . . "two *Qnumi* in Christ" is not merely a permissible, but a necessary way of speaking.

. . . Later (450 A.D.) is the earliest date that the writer has noticed the use), *Qnuma* is used where a Westerner speaks of the "Persons" of the Holy Trinity. "One divine Nature, in three perfect *Qnumi*." The force, however, does not appear to be that of ὑπόστασις (as used e.g. by the Cappadocian fathers), but more "set of characteristics". The nearest English word would probably be "Personification."[39]

It is apparent that the theology of the Church of the East would be useful to Urshan if, in fact, *Qnuma* does not carry the same meaning as "person." But as it relates to the essential difference between Urshan's theology and western Trinitarianism, two questions arise: (1) Is Urshan's understanding of *Qnuma* accurate, and (2) how does his understanding of the English word *person* compare to its use in western Trinitarianism.

Presbyterianism

Although Urshan's theological and cultural heritage were first rooted in the Church of the East, his spiritual life had its origins in Presbyterianism through the influence of his father and his time as a student at the American Presbyterian College in Urmia. While attending this school, he was converted, an experience he described as being "born again and . . . made a new creature in Christ Jesus."[40] Although he later revised his understanding to having "truly . . . been blessed and [having] the branch of the Divine tree in the bitter water of my life . . . planted afresh,"[41] he never gave up the description of that event as "conversion."

---

[39]W. A. Wigram, *The Doctrinal Position of the Assyrian or East Syrian Church* (London: Society for Promoting Christian Knowledge, 1908), 49-50.

[40]Andrew D. Urshan, *The Story of My Life,* 1st ed. (St. Louis, MO: Gospel Publishing House, n.d.), 30.

[41]Urshan, "Third Chapter—Story of My Life: Andrew's Wonderful Conversion," *The Witness of God* 3, no. 35 (November 1922), 4. He continues, however, to use the language of regeneration: "It was here in this school that God met me one night in March 1900, convicted me of sin and regenerated my soul which transformed my character . . ." (Urshan, "Second Chapter—Story of My Life," *The Witness of God,* 3, no. 35 [November 1922]: 2). These revisions continue into the 3rd edition of Urshan life story.

Urshan also revised the description of his conversion's doxology, changing the phrase "burning even now as a clear blaze of glory of God the Father, God the Son, and God the Holy Ghost"[42] to state it was "burning even now as a clear blaze of glory of God, my Father, my elder Brother and my Comforter."[43] He did not, however, disavow the event itself. He treasured his conversion as a profound spiritual experience with radical, life-altering consequences.

Urshan's early sympathies with Presbyterian theology are confirmed by his willingness to teach in the village school associated with the Presbyterian Church in Abajalu, a ministry that included some pastoral responsibilities.[44] His self-identification as a Presbyterian is further demonstrated by the fact that he intentionally first attended a Presbyterian church upon his arrival in America.[45]

Furthermore, he considered Presbyterianism a primary theological checkpoint against which to measure other perspectives. This is demonstrated in the subsequent theological shifts he made throughout his life. He willingly abandoned strongly held beliefs when he received new "revelation" from God that caused him to understand Scripture in a new light.[46] He accepted joyfully any adverse consequences that might result. This becomes evident in the sections that follow.

---

[42]Urshan, *The Story of My Life*, 1st ed., 31.

[43]Urshan, "Third Chapter—Story of My Life: Andrew's Wonderful Conversion," *The Witness of God* 3, no. 35 (November 1922): 4. See also Urshan, *The Story of My Life*, 3rd ed., 22.

[44]Urshan, *The Life Story*, 5th ed., 31-33.

[45]Urshan, *The Life Story*, 5th ed., 54-56.

[46]An example of this is seen when Urshan's Brethren cousin challenged him to baptism by immersion. He was sure he could prove to his cousin from the Bible that baptism was accomplished by the sprinkling of babies. When he could not, however, he was willing to abandon what he now believed to be an error. His study of Scripture brought him to believe that baptism was by immersion and that it was only for those who had repented and believed the gospel. Sensing these words from God, "Arise, and go at once to your cousin and confess to him your doctrinal error and your unkind answer to him, and also ask him to baptize you," Urshan quickly obeyed. His willingness to abandon one theological view for another did not end with the transformation of his perspective on the biblical mode for baptism and believer's baptism; it would be demonstrated repeatedly. When he believed he had new biblical insight and divine confirmation, Urshan was willing to humble himself if necessary and to suffer whatever consequences might accrue from embracing newfound insight. (See Urshan, "Seventh Chapter—The Story of My Life: My first Few Months in Chicago—Cont.," *The Witness of God* 4, no. 40 [April 1923]: 8.) ¶His sanctification experience in a Nazarene church caused Urshan to further reevaluate his conversion at the Presbyterian college in Persia. He wrote, "I knew I had at last received that which I should have experienced in the beginning of my Christian life, namely this—that my old man with his lusts, and desires was nailed to the Cross with Jesus, and that Christ was made experimentally unto me, of God: wisdom, righteousness, sanctification, and redemption; and that I was complete in Him" (Urshan, *The Life Story*, 5th ed., 100-101). Urshan's explanation that he had received "experimentally" what he should have "experienced" in the beginning of his Christian life seems to indicate that he now believed he was sanctified at the point of conversion although he did not experience sanctification at that time. ¶When Urshan was first introduced to Pentecostalism with its supernatural perspective, it was again his Presbyterian orientation that provided his first theological checkpoint. He had been taught in the

The Brethren Church

Urshan's baptism in the Brethren Church may seem a minor point in his theological journey, but it influenced the development of Urshan's view that one must "walk in the light" as it was revealed. Even though his views about water baptism became much more specific, he always valued his Brethren baptism and believed God blessed him for taking that step.

Urshan's encounter with the theology of the Brethren Church came during a time of spiritual crisis. As he engaged in a lifestyle of music, dancing, and theatre-going, his cousin warned him regarding the direction his life was taking. He said, "Your feet are sliding into the degradation of black sins. If you do not quit this evil dancing you will fall into immorality!"[47]

Andrew took his cousin's warning seriously, gave up dancing, and began to accompany his cousin to American Brethren churches, interpreting for him when he preached in the Syriac language. He soon faced a theological challenge when he and his cousin argued over the mode of baptism. As a Presbyterian, Urshan believed that babies should be sprinkled; as a Brethren minister, his cousin was convinced that baptism was only for believers and that it was accomplished by immersion.

After studying his Syriac Bible, Urshan concluded that his cousin was right and submitted to baptism in a Brethren church, demonstrating a willingness to confess his error and embrace "new light."

Urshan believed that the Lord blessed him for this obedience. This experience also caused him to understand the importance of "walking in the light." He wrote, "To this very day I am so glad that I did not fail God in that new light regarding the mode of water baptism and as I walked in that light as He is in the light, the blood of Jesus Christ, his Son cleansed me from my error and stubbornness of spirit."[48] This became a pattern that would eventually lead him into his final home in Oneness Pentecostalism.

Presbyterian Church that the days of miracles were over with the end of the apostolic era, so he could not comprehend the possibility of anyone speaking in other tongues. Again, however, he went to Scripture to investigate the validity of what he had seen at his first Pentecostal service. (See Urshan, *The Life Story*, 5th ed., 112.) What he found there was sufficient to cause him to rethink what he had been taught. ¶Another challenge to Urshan's Presbyterian training involved his eschatology. He had never heard of the premillennial return of Christ, but his study of Scripture brought him to believe that the second coming of Jesus would occur before the millennium. (See Urshan, *The Life Story*, 5th ed., 224.) Urshan's continuing interest in his Presbyterian heritage was demonstrated by his 1961 visit to the Assyrian Presbyterian Church in Yonkers, N.Y., where he delivered a sermon in the Syriac language. See "Assyrian Pastor Goes 'Home,'" *Assyrian Star* (May-June 1961): 10, 14.

[47]Urshan, "Seventh Chapter—The Story of My Life: My First Few Months in Chicago—Cont.," *The Witness of God* 4, no. 39 (March 1923): 4. The misspellings and typographical errors in *The Witness of God* are so frequent that I will automatically correct them with no notice unless there seems to be some reason to note them.

[48]Urshan, "Seventh Chapter—The Story of My Life: My First Few Months in Chicago—Cont.," *The Witness of God* 4, no. 40 (April 1923): 8.

The Moody Bible Church

As a member of Moody Bible Church, Urshan was profoundly influenced by A. C. Dixon, the pastor of the church. Although Urshan resigned his membership when he was instructed to abandon the idea that baptism with the Holy Spirit is accompanied by speaking with tongues, he continued to respect Dixon and to value Dixon's theology so far as possible in conjunction with his Pentecostal convictions.[49]

Urshan's membership in The Moody Bible Church exposed him to the theology of fundamentalism. A. C. Dixon was the editor of the first six volumes of *The Fundamentals*. Although the the series did not begin publication until 1910 after Urshan had left The Moody Church, the volumes reflect the theology that characterized Dixon's preaching.

In its first iteration, fundamentalism "involved articulating what was fundamental to Christianity and initiating an urgent battle to expel the enemies of orthodox Protestantism from the ranks of the churches."[50] These enemies included "Romanism, socialism, modern philosophy, atheism, Eddyism, Mormonism, spiritualism, and the like, but above all liberal theology, which rested on a naturalistic interpretation of the doctrines of the faith, and German higher criticism and Darwinism, which appeared to undermine the Bible's authority."[51]

At first, *The Fundamentals* included a wide-ranging defense of traditional Christian doctrine. But the list of fundamentals soon shortened. In 1910, two years after Urshan's departure from The Moody Church, the General Assembly of the northern Presbyterian Church published a list of the five essential doctrines: "the inerrancy of Scripture, the virgin birth of Christ, the substitutionary atonement of Christ, Christ's bodily resurrection, and the historicity of miracles."[52] Other versions of fundamentalism offered different expressions of the essentials, replacing "miracles with the resurrection and the second coming of Christ" or "premillenarian doctrine as the fifth fundamental." One version put "the deity of Christ in place of the virgin birth."[53]

These themes influenced Urshan's view of genuine Christianity, appearing frequently in his writings. For example, he lost his job as a waiter at the Kenwood Hotel for writing a letter to one of the hotel's patrons, a prominent Christian Science practitioner, warning her that Christian Science was a delusion that threatened her with eternal damnation.[54]

In addition, such topics as higher criticism often appear in Urshan's writings, reflecting concerns addressed by Dixon.[55] Urshan also makes his own applica-

---

[49]Urshan printed an article by A. C. Dixon in his monthly publication.. See A. C. Dixon, "Power from on High by Prayer," *The Witness of God* 3, no. 30 (June 1922): 7.

[50]C. T. McIntire, "Fundamentalism," in Walter A. Elwell, ed., *Evangelical Dictionary of Theology* (Grand Rapids: Baker Book House, 1984), 433.

[51]C. T. McIntire, "Fundamentalism," *Evangelical Dictionary of Theology*, 433.

[52]C. T. McIntire, "Fundamentalism," *Evangelical Dictionary of Theology*, 433.

[53]C. T. McIntire, "Fundamentalism," *Evangelical Dictionary of Theology*, 433.

[54]Urshan, "Seventh Chapter—The Story of My Life: My First Few Months in Chicago—Cont.," *The Witness of God* 4, no. 41 (May 1923): 3.

[55]The term "higher criticism" refers to efforts to determine "authorship, date, sources,

tions of fundamentalism's issues. For example, he accused biblical scholars who rejected the didactic value of Acts as having engaged in higher criticism.

However, although Urshan deeply admired Dixon and teachers associated with Moody Bible Institute, he refused to abandon firmly held convictions that he believed to be biblical truth in order to retain their favor. For example, when he was ordered to suppress speaking with tongues in the meetings of the Persian mission being held in the Young People's Building of The Moody Church, Urshan resigned his membership in the church. He refused to compromise.

Holiness

At another moment of spiritual crisis, Urshan accepted the invitation of a patron in his restaurant to attend a meeting at a Nazarene church. There he experienced entire sanctification. By this time he had already been exposed to a "higher life" theology at The Moody Church that was similar to that held by the Church of the Nazarene. Dixon, following Moody, emphasized the importance of experiencing baptism with the Holy Spirit,[56] although this did not include the supernatural dimension of speaking with tongues.

What Urshan did gain at the Nazarene church beyond what he received at The Moody Church was an actual experience so dramatic and transforming that it redirected his entire life from that point. In his words, "My old man with his lusts and desires was nailed to the Cross with Jesus, and . . . Christ was made experimentally unto me, of God: wisdom, righteousness, sanctification, and redemption; and . . . I was complete in Him.[57]

Urshan's extended description of this event and its effect on his ministry leaves no doubt that it moved him substantially along the road of his spiritual journey from what he had experienced previously:

> My heart was hungry for more of God, seeking and searching for a more spiritual people than the Presbyterians, my mother church. The Lord led me to the 1st Pentecostal Nazarene church in Chicago, Ill. There consecrating and dedicating my life to God, I prayed through on one Sunday afternoon in June 1906. The power of God

---

and composition" of the biblical text. "Among conservative interpreters, the term *higher criticism* frequently implied the imposition of modern, 'scientific' presuppositions upon the study of Scripture" (Arthur G. Patzia and Anthony J. Petrotta, *Pocket Dictionary of Biblical Studies* [Downers Grove, IL: IVP Academic, 2002], 57).

[56]Marsden, *Fundamentalism and American Culture*, 70. Moody had introduced the "Keswick" form of the holiness movement to an American audience. "Keswick" theology, named for the town in the Lake District of Northern England where adherents held an annual convention, understood entire sanctification in relational terms. It occurred when and as long as persons yielded their lives completely to God. The Nazarenes followed the Wesleyan understanding in substantive categories. In this case, the "sinful nature" is transformed when a person submits completely to God's will. Both theologies equated entire sanctification with the Baptism in the Holy Spirit. (See David W. Faupel, *The Everlasting Gospel: the Significance of Eschatology in the Development of Pentecostal Thought* [Sheffield, England: Sheffield Academic Press, 1996], 85-87.)

[57]Urshan, *The Life Story*, 5th ed., 100-101.

fell on me so strong that a much deeper divine experience was mine, which they called sanctification. This experience changed my young passions to compassion for lost souls. Right then and there my heart began to burn for salvation of my Assyrian people in Chicago.

After much praying, fasting, testifying and doing personal work amongst them and preaching in [the] streets, the Lord began to convince those young Persians that I had something from heaven that they did not have and [they] began to let me pray for them. In two years time, the Lord had given me some sixty strong young married and single men.

I took them to that Nazarene church for their deeper consecration; they also were wonderfully sanctified.[58]

Although he later came to believe that conversion, sanctification, and baptism with the Holy Spirit could all occur simultaneously, Urshan continued to acknowledge the possibility that these experiences could occur sequentially, as they did for him.[59]

William H. Durham

Durham's theological influence on Urshan began with Urshan's first exposure to Pentecostalism by the testimony of a woman who operated the rooming house where "Mr. Morrison" lived. He encountered the woman when he attempted to find Morrison, the cook of the restaurant Urshan owned. Morrison's landlady, who attended Durham's church, shared her "Pentecostal" experience with Urshan.

After praying and studying Scripture, Urshan attended Durham's North Avenue Mission in Chicago. Shortly thereafter, he was baptized in the Holy Spirit at a lakeside prayer meeting and was then ordained by Durham in 1910.[60] Durham supported his work with the Persian Mission.

---

[58]W. W. Sturdivan, "Andrew D. Urshan," *Gospel Tidings* (January 1968): 2.

[59]Andrew D. Urshan, *Supreme Need of the Hour and the Source of the Mighty Revivals* (Cochrane, WI: 1922), 15.

[60]Authur L. Clanton, *United We Stand* (Hazelwood, MO: Pentecostal Publishing House, 1970), 190. Urshan does not refer to ordination by Durham but says that he was "legally ordained" at the World-Wide Camp Meeting in Arroyo Seco in 1913, "having been ordained a few years previous to this time by the Lord Himself." (See Urshan, *The Story of My Life,* 1st ed., 53.) In 1917, when Urshan applied for ordination with the Assemblies of God, he mentioned on his application that he had been ordained earlier by the "Rescue Mission Workers of America (Pentecostal)." (See Graham, *Conservative American Protestantism,* 44, n.1.) This was possibly a reference to ordination by Durham, who had founded the North Avenue Mission in 1901 as a holiness mission. Faith St. Clair, Urshan's daughter, says that she definitely heard her father talk about being ordained by Durham (Faith St. Clair, telephone interview by the author, September 24, 2009). Urshan's claim to have been "legally ordained" at Arroyo Seco could have reflected the idea that his earlier ordination by Durham "represented a general consensus that a person was 'called,' indicated by the laying on of hands of the mission leadership. . . . Ordination did not confer power or access to an authority structure, however; in theory, it simply recognized divine call" (Blumhofer, *Aimee Semple McPherson,* 80).

D. William Faupel comments on the connection between Durham and Urshan:

> Upon hearing Mable Smith's testimony in Chicago, William H. Durham left for Los Angeles to see for himself. After receiving the experience he returned to his North Avenue Mission. It quickly became the Azusa of the Midwest. Scores of future Pentecostal leaders including . . . Andrew Urshan . . . received their Pentecostal experience through his ministry.[61]

An early connection between Durham and Urshan is indicated by references to a street meeting sponsored by the North Avenue Mission. According to Blumhofer,

> A North Avenue Mission street meeting at the corner of Clark Street and Chicago Avenue (an intersection in a neighborhood favored by the city's Persian immigrants) brought Persian Americans to the mission. Almost immediately, some spoke in tongues. In the first few months of 1909, Durham baptized twenty-two Persian men, and three soon set out to evangelize their homeland. A Persian mission in Chicago acknowledged its indebtedness to Durham.[62]

Urshan refers to the influence of this same street meeting on his "new Assyrian converts":

> . . . I . . . asked them to join me in a special fasting and praying. On Sunday after church, while going home, we saw a humble couple, with their faces beaming with rays of sincerity, love, and earnestness, holding a street meeting at the corner of Chicago Avenue and North Clark Street. Though we never had seen or known this good man and his wife, we felt drawn to them, to sympathize and encourage them as they witnessed for our Lord and Saviour, Jesus Christ.
>
> Coming near to them, to our sorrow we saw some very unruly young men mocking them and laughing at them. . . . We felt embarrassed for that godly man, but what astonished us was his undisturbed countenance and manner. He kept on smiling and declaring the Word of God as though nothing had happened. We measured our patience and sanctification with that man's, and we found ourselves far below his standard. . . .
>
> Someone may ask, "Who were that godly couple?" I found out later that they belonged to the Pentecostal folks that I had visited once. Also because I had taken notice that they spoke a few phrases in "other tongues" when they got warm in Spirit. My converts also hearing these strange utterances said, "What is that?" I told them, "This is some kind of an expression of their Spirit-filled lives." Then two of the boys said to me, "Oh! We wish we were filled with the Spirit, as that couple seem to be." I then said, "Let's go home and pray that the Lord may fill us like He has filled them."[63]

---

[61]D. William Faupel, *The Everlasting Gospel: The Significance of Eschatology in the Development of Pentecostal Thought* (Sheffield: Sheffield Academic Press, 1996), 218.

[62]Blumhofer, "William H. Durham," 133-34.

[63]Urshan, *The Life Story*, 5th ed., 113-14 and Urshan, "Something New Happens," *The Witness of God* (October 1962): 2.

Urshan's reference to "the Pentecostal folks" that he had "visited once" apparently confirms that his first exposure to Pentecostalism was at the North Avenue Mission.

We may be sure Urshan was exposed to Durham's influence. He felt close enough to Durham to discuss with him his view of the deity of Jesus, and Durham was close enough to Urshan to try to discourage him from pursuing his ideas.[64] Thus, Urshan was certainly aware of Durham's views on sanctification. In contrast to the idea that sanctification was a second work of grace that occurred at a specific point in time after conversion and before baptism with the Holy Spirit, Durham proclaimed "the finished work of Calvary," which he interpreted to mean that sanctification occurred simultaneously with conversion, although it was also an ongoing and progressive work in the life of the believer. Durham's view reduced the notion of two works of grace down to one work of grace and two experiences (conversion [justification] and sanctification).[65] It may be that Urshan's exposure to Durham's view on sanctification was the reason for his assessment of his own sanctification experience in the Nazarene church:

> I knew I had at last received that which I should have experienced in the beginning of my Christian life, namely this—that my old man with his lusts, and desires was nailed to the Cross with Jesus, and that Christ was made experimentally unto me, of God: wisdom, righteousness, sanctification, and redemption; and that I was complete in Him.[66]

Urshan's explanation that he had received "experimentally" what he should have "experienced" in the beginning of his Christian life (i.e., at his conversion in the Presbyterian school in Persia) may indicate that, in retrospect, he believed he was sanctified at the point of conversion although he did not experience sanctification at that time.

That this is a valid way to understand Urshan's view subsequent to his exposure to Durham's influence may be indicated by his account of a revival meeting in Canada:

> After preaching on the "Three Loaves Blessing," a dear Sister blessed thereby stood up testifying said, "Oh, Praise The Lord, Brother Urshan preached just what I got from the Lord some years ago. I came to Him for JUSTIFICATION and prayed hard and got it, then I came to Him for the SECOND BLESSING, The Sanctification, and Prayed and I got that too. But, Glory, I came the third time and asked the Lord to Baptise me with the Holy Ghost and Fire. He gave me the third blessing also. So, I have the three Loaves now, Hallelujah." We were led to say "You all can see that Sister B— has what she claimed to have alright, but the only difference I

---

[64] Andrew D. Urshan to Nathaniel A. Urshan, November 9, 1964. Urshan also wrote, "I was warned by Pastor Wm. Durham and Ewart of Los Angeles and others not to preach and teach the doctrine of the New Birth of water baptism in the name of the Lord for remission of sins, in the name of Jesus and baptism of Spirit with tongues as the new birth of the Spirit" (W. W. Sturdivan, ed., "Andrew D. Urshan," *Gospel Tidings* [January 1968], 3).

[65] Walter J. Hollenweger, *The Pentecostals,* trans. R. A. Wilson (Minneapolis, MN: Augsburg Publishing House, 1972), 24-25. See also Reed, *"In Jesus' Name",* 87-94.

[66] Urshan, *The Life Story,* 5th ed., 100-101.

see of her experience from that of the importune man, is, that he got three loaves at once and in one course, but our Sister got her's by three definite and different courses, however, we are glad after all she made God to give her "The Threefold Blessing."[67]

There is unresolved tension in Urshan's varying statements on sanctification. On the one hand, he describes his sanctification as a definite experience that occurred several years after his conversion; on the other hand, he acknowledges that he should have experienced sanctification simultaneously with conversion. He accepted the genuineness of the experiences of a believer whose justification, sanctification, and Holy Spirit baptism occurred as three temporally distinct events, but interpreted Scripture to mean that these three experiences could occur at once.

That Urshan was sympathetic with Durham's views can be seen by the inclusion of an article by Durham in *The Witness of God*[68] and by Urshan's article on the finished work.[69] What we see here mirrors Urshan's later desire to honor genuine faith and experience wherever it is found. He had his convictions, which developed on his theological journey, but resisted any temptation to rush to judgment on those who differed with him. It may be difficult for those whose values are shaped by Enlightenment thought to tolerate this kind of tension, but that was not Urshan's heritage.

In 1912, Urshan discussed his understanding of Scripture with Durham and Frank Ewart.

> I was warned by Pastor Wm. Durham and Ewart of Los Angeles not to preach and teach the doctrine of the New Birth of water baptism in the name of the Lord for remission of sins, in the name of Jesus and baptism of Spirit with tongues as the new birth of the Spirit. I was also warned not to preach oneness of God in the person of Jesus Christ our Lord; saying, I was going into too deep things of Theology for a young man.[70]

---

[67]Andrew D. Urshan, *Supreme Need of the Hour and the Source of the Mighty Revivals* (Cochrane, WI: 1922), 15. This quote reproduces the typographical and spelling irregularities found in the source.

[68]W. H. Durham, "Salvation in Christ for All," *The Witness of God* 8, no. 71 (January 1926): 9-10.

[69]Urshan, "The Finished Work of the Cross of Christ Our Lord," *The Witness of God* (September 1955): 2. See also Urshan, *Supreme Need of the Hour,* 18.

[70]W. W. Sturdivan, "Andrew D. Urshan," *Gospel Tidings* (January 1968): 3. In a personal letter to his son, Nathaniel, Andrew dated this encounter as 1912. The same letter states that he had previously discussed these things with G. T. Haywood in 1910. Andrew Urshan to Nathaniel Urshan, November 9, 1964. In 1920, Urshan wrote of this event, "I was but a young man and young in the ministry, and when some older men, both in age and ministry learned that I was beginning to preach the . . . revelations, they advised me not to because they said those things were too deep and mysterious to anybody and how much more to me, being only a young minister. While listening to them I did not make my God-given revelations and scriptural illuminations known doctrinally, but I did exalt the Name and the Person of Jesus Christ just as much as I do now both in life and word but not in theology" (A. D. Urshan, "Our Personal Testimony Concerning the New Issue People," *The Witness of God* 1, no. 10 [September 1920]: 3).

Although he valued Durham's friendship and counsel, he was more concerned with following biblical truth. Urshan stated, "But the Lord showed me in the old and new [sic] *Testament* that that was pure Apostolic doctrine and the whole Gospel truth. Instead of quitting it, I published it in a magazine of mine and in tracts."[71]

Durham's influence included Urshan's revised opinion on sanctification. Durham collapsed the two works of grace typical of American Pentecostalism in the first decade of the twentieth century into one work of grace with the two experiences of justification and sanctification occurring simultaneously.[72] Urshan would go further, following the emerging Oneness teaching, including not only justification and sanctification but also Spirit baptism into one ideal work of the Spirit. Urshan was a pragmatist, however, recognizing that the ideal was not always the experience. He did not discredit the testimony of those who continued to claim three distinct works of grace.[73]

Although Urshan's association with Trinitarian Pentecostalism continued from his baptism with the Holy Spirit in 1908 until his disassociation from the Assemblies of God in 1919, he had the views that later became known as "New Issue" from the very first. He stated that it was in 1908 that "the Lord began to reveal" that Jesus was "the only embodiment [and] visible personality of the invisible incomprehensible divine Being – The Father in the Son, not a separate person as some teach, but the possessor and giver of the Holy Spirit." For Urshan, this revelation was "these three in one, and that one was my blessed Jesus."[74]

In 1910, as Urshan read the book of Acts, he noticed that the apostles baptized Jews, Samaritans, and Gentiles "in the Holy name of Jesus Christ the Lord," and he "began baptizing in that matchless Name."[75]

Without violating Urshan's own treatment of his life, then, it could be said that he experienced the turning of eight "leaves," six of which served to shape his theology: (1) Church of the East; (2) Presbyterianism; (3) Brethren Church; (4) Moody Bible Church; (5) Nazarene Church; and (6) Pentecostalism. Consistent with the idea of "walking in the light," Urshan continued to value these "leaves," integrating them into his developing theology.[76]

Summary

As Urshan worked through the various theological influences in his life to arrive finally at Oneness Pentecostalism, he developed an abbreviated version of what

---

[71] W. W. Sturdivan, "Andrew D. Urshan," *Gospel Tidings* (January 1968): 3.

[72] Reed, *"In Jesus' Name,"* 87-94. In the first decade of the twentieth century Pentecostal theology typically saw justification, sanctification, and Holy Spirit baptism as occurring sequentially. In Durham's "finished work of Calvary" theology, justification and sanctification occurred simultaneously. See also Hollenweger, *The Pentecostals,* 24-25.

[73] Andrew D. Urshan, *Supreme Need of the Hour and the Source of the Mighty Revivals* (Cochrane, WI: 1922), 15.

[74] W. W. Sturdivan, "Andrew D. Urshan," *Gospel Tidings* (January 1968): 2.

[75] W. W. Sturdivan, "Andrew D. Urshan," *Gospel Tidings* (January 1968): 2.

[76] See Urshan, "Seventh Chapter—The Story of My Life: My First Few Months in Chicago—Cont.," *The Witness of God* 4, no. 40 (April 1923): 8.

is commonly known as the Wesleyan Quadrilateral: Scripture, reason, tradition, and experience.[77] The missing ingredient for Urshan was tradition. He wrote, "I apply to sanctified reason as well as to providential occurrences, coupled with all the Scriptures before deciding definitely upon any divine matter."[78] Unlike most early Pentecostals, Urshan did value tradition, though he never stated it as such. He understood Syriac Christianity as representative of Apostolic – or first century – faith.[79] He further described the Christians of the Church of the East as "living and dying for the true and unadulterated Apostolic teachings of the founders of the Church of Jesus Christ."[80]

However, when he found traditional beliefs he had been taught that could not be supported by Scripture, he would change his theology. For example, when he could not square with Scripture the Presbyterian view of baptism as the sprinkling of infants, Urshan abandoned that view in favor of immersion. When he became convinced from Scripture that speaking in tongues was the initial sign that one had been baptized with the Holy Spirit, coupled with his observation of others speaking in what he understood as the Syriac language, Urshan withstood the pressure of the pastor he had admired, A. C. Dixon, and the best arguments of a member of the faculty of Moody Bible Institute. His experience with sanctification in a Nazarene church transformed his life and motivated him to lead many others to the same experience. As much as he valued the friendship and spiritual leadership of William Durham, Urshan did not heed his warning against the views that would later be known as "New Issue." He had read the Bible, and that was his ultimate authority. When in Russia God clearly responded to Urshan's "fleece," confirming that he should baptize in the name of the Lord Jesus, Urshan did so, even though he "did not want to take a definite step with – or against – either side" of the dispute that was brewing in the United States. Although he had come to the conclusion in 1910 that baptism should be administered in the name of the Lord Jesus Christ, he wished to return to the United States and "investigate thoroughly before coming to any conclusion" as he prayed "for God's definite leading in the matter."[81] Finally, when challenged by leaders of the Assemblies of God to declare his faith clearly and publicly, he did so, even at the cost of losing the associations he had cherished.

For Urshan, Scripture, providential occurrences, sanctified reason and his eastern heritage came together to form his theology. The various "leaves" in his life turned as Urshan embraced "more light,"[82] developing a theology that had a profound influence on the shape of what has been called the "third stream" of

---

[77]R. G. Tuttle, Jr., "The Wesleyan Tradition," in Walter A. Elwell, ed., *Evangelical Dictionary of Theology* (Grand Rapids, MI: Baker Book House, 1984), 1166.

[78]Urshan, "The Life Story of Andrew Bar-David [2nd section]," *The Witness of God* (August 1946): 11.

[79]Urshan, *The Life Story*, 5th ed., 15.

[80]Urshan, *The Life Story*, 5th ed., 15.

[81]Urshan, *The Life Story*, 5th ed., 234.

[82]Urshan, "The New Light or the More Light," *The Witness of God* 1, no. 10 (September 1920): 1.

Pentecostalism. In the chapters to come, we will examine Urshan's perspectives on the Godhead and salvation, noting also how he responded to his critics.

Chapter Seven

The Mystery of the Godhead

Introduction

Urshan's theology was a contributing influence during the shaping of the "Oneness" dimension of Oneness Pentecostalism in the first half of the twentieth century, but the concept of "mystery" he had embraced before 1921 was not to endure. If today's Oneness Pentecostals use the word "mystery," it is not in reference to a "threeness" in God, but to the Incarnation.

> There never has been a mystery as to "persons" in the Godhead. The Bible clearly states that there is only one God, and this is easy for all to understand. The only mystery about the Godhead is how God could come in flesh, how Jesus could be both God and man.[1]

> Trinitarians universally describe their doctrine as a mystery. . . . however, the only mystery relative to the Godhead is the manifestation of God in flesh, and even that has been revealed to those who believe. A mystery in Scripture is a divine truth previously unknown but now revealed to man. . . .

> The Bible never says that . . . the question of plurality in the Godhead is a mystery. Instead, it affirms in the strongest terms that God is one. Why resort to an explanation that the Godhead is incomprehensible mystery in order to protect a man-made doctrine with nonbiblical terminology when the Scriptures plainly give us a simple, unambiguous message that God is absolutely one? It is wrong to state that the Godhead is a mystery when the Bible clearly states that God has revealed the mystery to us.[2]

> The Godhead is no mystery, especially to the church. We cannot understand everything there is to know about God, but the Bible clearly teaches that God is one in number and that Jesus Christ is the one God manifest in flesh.[3]

---

[1] David K. Bernard, *The Oneness of God* (Hazelwood, MO: Word Aflame Press, 1983), 65.
[2] Bernard, *The Oneness of God,* 289.
[3] Bernard, *The Oneness of God,* 296.

In contrast to this late twentieth century expression of the "oneness" of God, Urshan had acknowledged mystery and incomprehensibility. He had developed a doctrine of God between the two poles of the strong affirmation of the deity of Christ and the equally strong affirmation of mystery. His commitment to the deity of Christ mirrored the nascent fundamentalism of the Moody Church and his assertion of mystery reflected the influence of his Syriac heritage.

The Almighty God in the Lord Jesus Christ

Urshan published his book *The Almighty God in the Lord Jesus Christ* in 1919 when he still lived in Los Angeles. It is a collection of seven "open letters" he had mailed to thousands of people upon his resignation from the Assemblies of God.[4] He said that more than 500 people were baptized in Jesus' name as a result of reading these letters. The ninety-five page book is a compendium of his thinking at that time combined with material which he perceived supported his point of view. These sources include the following:

- A selection from John Bunyan discussing the implications of Colossians 2:9[5]

- Brief quotations concerning the deity of Christ from a variety of historical figures dating from the second to the twentieth century

- A portion of a sermon preached by F. C. Jennings at the Fulton Street prayer meeting in New York City

- An excerpt from *More than One Hundred Scriptural and Incontrovertible Arguments for Believing in the Deity of Christ* by Samuel Green[6]

- Brief quotations from a variety of "German Protestant fathers"

- Lyrics from a variety of English hymn-writers

- An extended reprint from "Eusebia" (August 1898)

---

[4] Urshan, "The Story of My Life—28th Chapter," *The Witness of God* 6, no. 64 (May 1925): 4.
[5] John Bunyan, *The Whole Works of John Bunyan* (London: Blackie and Son, 1862), 671.
[6] Christian Resources & Links, doctrinal & practical writings, *Supreme Divinity of Our Lord and Saviour Jesus Christ,* http://www.wholesomewords.org/resources/deity-ofchrist.html (accessed April 16, 2010). Samuel Green was the pastor of the Union Church in Boston for eleven years, beginning March 26, 1823, although his health prevented him from active ministry during the final three of those years (Richard Salter Storrs, *Memoir of the Rev. Samuel Green: late pastor of Union Church, Boston* [Boston: Perkins and Marvin, 1836], 96, 399). Green's *More than One Hundred Scriptural and Incontrovertible Arguments* was a direct assault on Unitarianism, a common target of Green's (Storrs, *Memoir of the Rev. Samuel Green,* 125-28, 186, 190). Storrs' *Memoir* is available at http://books.google.com/. books?id=OQQFAAAAYAAJ &printsec=front-cover&source=gbs_ge_summary_r&cad=0#v=onepage&q&f=false.

- Selections from various sources ranging from the twelfth to the twentieth century

- An extended quotation from T. P. Douglas, *A Message to Christians and to the World*

- Quotations of varying length from Mark Lev ("a Hebrew Christian"); I. M. Haldeman (a Baptist pastor); William Bridge (a seventeenth-century English minister); Baruch Spinoza (a seventeenth-century Dutch philosopher); the *Christian Evangel*; J. Monro Gibson's *Christianity According to Christ*[7]; *The Sunday School Lesson Illustrator* (August 1919)

Urshan's selections from these sources are not always precise, nor does he always indicate where there are gaps in the quotations. Since he does not follow today's conventions for quotations, it is necessary to read carefully, comparing his work against original sources. Careful analysis often reveals that the sources simply argue for the deity of Christ rather than supporting Urshan's understanding of the Oneness of God. As we examine this book, we must keep in mind that Urshan's later writings sometimes correct his earlier thoughts as found in this work. For example, in *The Almighty God in the Lord Jesus Christ*, Urshan wrote, "I personally cannot refrain from believing that there is a plurality in God's mysterious Being, and that this plurality is shown as a three-ness, not three separate distinct Beings or Persons of God, but a mysterious, inexplicable, incomprehensible three-ness, as it is expressed by the Apostle in I Jno. 5:7 and Mat. 28:19 ...."[8] But within the next two years after the publication of the book, Urshan learned of the lack of early textual support for I John 5:7. In 1921 he wrote, "It is an evident fact that the Scriptures no where indicate the word 'Three' in connection with the Godhead, except in one place (1 John 5:7) which is no Scripture but was simply inserted into the Scriptures by Constantine during the third century, and you will not find it in any original writings at all."[9] That he had appealed to I John 5:7 in 1919 to support the idea of "three-ness" but later withdrew the textual variant from consideration alerts the reader to his willingness to revise his understanding with the discovery of new insights.

Another example is that in 1923, Urshan published the book *Doctrine of Trinity and the Divinity of Jesus Christ*.[10] The book seeks to find legitimate use for the word *trinity*: "While it is true that the word 'Trinity' is not found in the Bible, yet it is equally true that this word has been used most reverently by millions of believers during the last sixteen centuries. So we can not afford to ignore it and misconsider it altogether ... but for the sake of many earnest and zealous

---

[7] J. Monro Gibson, *Christianity According to Christ* (London: James Nisbet and Co., 1889), 80-85.

[8] Andrew D. Urshan, *The Almighty God in The Lord Jesus Christ* (Los Angeles: n.p., 1919), 77.

[9] A. D. Urshan, "Scriptural Facts Concerning the Godhead Question," *The Witness of God* 2, no. 19 (July 1921): 5.

[10] A.D.Urshan, *Doctrine of Trinity and the Divinity of Jesus Christ* (Cochrane, WI: n.p., 1923).

Christians we will give it a proper place ... to magnify the truth on our blessed subject, even the Absolute Deity of Jesus Christ our Redeemer."[11] But in 1953, Urshan wrote, "So please let us stand on the Word of God on this most solemn and sublime teaching, the Mystery of God. Let us use the Bible's words and no other terminology. Let our Phraseology be Bible phrases only."[12] These examples indicate we should not think without further evidence that *The Almighty God in The Lord Jesus Christ* represents Urshan's final perspectives.

In the preface of *The Almighty God in the Lord Jesus Christ,* Urshan prays that the reader's heart will be filled with "true worship and adoration toward God, our Heavenly Father, who dwelleth and manifesteth Himself in His only begotten Son."[13] This statement sets the agenda for the entire book. If Urshan meant only that the Father was *manifest* in the Son, it would be difficult to distinguish between this and the historic idea of circumincession,[14] wherein the persons of the Trinity indwell one another in a unity of being.[15] However, the words 'manifest' and 'incarnate' are synonymous for Urshan.

> The God who created the old world, things visible and invisible, by His WORD, now comes down in His incarnate WORD to create a new generation . . . . God the Father, by the power of His Spirit, comes with and in His Son, into the world, to give everlasting life unto all them that should believe on His NAME . . . .[16]

> "No man knows the Son but the Father; neither knoweth any man the Father save the Son, and He to whomsoever the Son will reveal Him." In this Scripture our Lord limits the revelation and the manifestation of the Father to that which is made **in and through Himself.** Therefore the Son is a great mystery, as is the Father.[17]

Western Trinitarianism sees the Trinity as *manifest* in the incarnate Son, but it is only the Son, the second person of the Trinity, who is *incarnate.* In the words of the Creed of Nicaea, it was "the Son of God . . . who for us men and for our salvation came down and was made flesh."[18]

While some of Urshan's terminology seems to retain Trinitarian concepts, other statements go beyond the pale of Trinitarianism. For example, Urshan declares

---

[11] Urshan, *Doctrine of Trinity*, 4.

[12] Andrew D. Urshan, "The Mystery of God, or Who Is God?", *The Witness of God* (December, 1953): 8.

[13] Urshan, *The Almighty God,* 5.

[14] Circumcincession "refers primarily to the coinherence of the persons of the Trinity in the divine essence and in each other" (Richard A. Muller, *Dictionary of Latin and Greek Theological Terms* (Grand Rapids: Baker Book House, 1985), 67. This theological concept is also referred to as *perichoresis* (Muller, 222) and *interpenetration* (Justo L. Gonzalez, *Essential Theological Terms* [Louisville, KY: Westminister John Knox Press, 2005], 36).

[15] Jean-Yves Lacoste, ed., *Encyclopedia of Christian Theology* (New York: Routledge, 2005), 315.

[16] Urshan, *The Almighty God,* 6.

[17] Urshan, *The Almighty God,* 6.

[18] Henry Bettenson, ed., *Documents of the Christian Church,* 2nd ed. (London: Oxford University Press, 1967), 25.

that we worship "three in one, the God of the Bible, who is the Father, the Son, and the Holy Ghost, who indwelleth, manifesteth Himself unto, and blesseth all His creatures **in** and **through** Jesus Christ."[19] He calls his readers to "worship God the Father, the Son, and the Spirit in our glorious Lord."[20] But in a chapter titled "The Fatherhood of God," Urshan identifies the Father with the Son.

> This glorious, divine relationship gives the Deity's most blessed and gracious title, FATHER, to Jesus Christ; thus Jesus Christ "**shall be called the Everlasting Father,**" as the prophet Isaiah said (Isa. 9:6). Some people shrink from confessing Jesus Christ as their Father. This shrinking is caused by the fear of men, who have concluded that Jesus Christ is the Son of God, therefore He cannot be called our Father-God. But if one is willing to suffer the contradiction of all, and go to the Bible, he will easily see that Jesus Christ is our Father . . . .[21]

Urshan denies, however, that this does away "with the identity of the Father of the Son" or that it "makes Jesus Christ His own Father." Rather, "it confirms His own saying, that 'the Father dwelleth in me,' and 'He that seeth me seeth the Father'."[22] As to why Jesus is never called the Father in the epistles, Urshan says,

> It is because the message of the Gospel is to believe on the Son of God; for the Son of God came in the flesh, to save us and reconcile and to bring us to a place where we shall be able, sometime in the coming age, to see this deep truth. Therefore Isaiah 9:6, and our Saviour's own declaration in Revelation 21:2, with Psalm 45:16 are prophecies **yet to be fulfilled.**[23]

Although at least to some extent Urshan identified the Father with the Son, he was reluctant to preach this idea. He explained,

> I, for one, am not led to preach Jesus Christ my Heavenly Father now; although I love to quote the . . . Scriptures and believe them with my whole heart; but I truly believe that, when we shall see our Saviour face to face and see the fullness of the Deity in Him and through Him shining forth with eternal glory, we shall not shrink then from calling Him "our Father" as well as "Lord God Almighty" in the ages to come."[24]

The preface of *The Almighty God in the Lord Jesus Christ* sets forth Urshan's emphasis "on the Infinite NAME of God and His Majestic Fullness."[25] For Urshan, God's name is connected inseparably with his identity and "fullness," and that name was born by the Messiah. This is set forth early in the book's introduction:

> To know the **Name** of God is to know **Him,** for He reveals His great power and majestic Person with His fathomless love and grace and all His infinite attributes, **by and through His great and holy name.**

---

[19]Urshan, *The Almighty God,* 87. Emphasis in original.
[20]Urshan, *The Almighty God,* 88.
[21]Urshan, *The Almighty God,* 94. Emphasis in original.
[22]Urshan, *The Almighty God,* 94.
[23]Urshan, *The Almighty God,* 95. Emphases in original.
[24]Urshan, *The Almighty God,* 95.
[25]Urshan, *The Almighty God,* 5.

God has revealed Himself at different times in past ages by His excellent Names given to His people, but "Yah-weh" (Jehovah), the Name of God, is the fullest explanation and manifestation of His great and infinite Being. "Yah-weh" therefore is the memorial Name of the T-h-r-e-e—O-n-e God, which literally means the **present** and **future** one self-existing, unchangeable **God,** the LORD "which is, which was, and which is to come," or the "I AM THAT I AM."

The "I AM" Name of God . . . applies to His then present revelation and active purpose revealed to His people Israel . . . . But the Lord gave Moses and Israel at the same time another great promise for another great deliverance, and that deliverance was to take place in the future. This promise is included also in His blessed revealed Name, viz., "THAT I AM." ("I AM THAT I AM' means a present and future God.)

The word "THAT" points to His other or future manifestation, when he should appear again . . . as David's Son . . . through the Seed of the woman, as **"God manifest in the flesh,"** becoming IMMANUEL . . . **"God with us."**[26]

The views in this introductory statement are reiterated throughout *The Almighty God* with some additional development. In summary, here are Urshan's points:

- The name of God and the person of God are inseparable.

- Yahweh is the ultimate name of God.

- Yahweh is a "three-one" God.

- Yahweh speaks of the present and the future.

- Yahweh indicates that God is self-existing and unchangeable.

- The phrase "that I am" points ahead to the Messiah.

The claim that Yahweh speaks of the present *and* the future is problematic. Typically, a translator would choose one possibility or the other. The notion that the relative particle "that" (*asher*) points to the Incarnation is not supported by current scholarship. *Asher* can be translated as who, which, when, whose, whom, and that. Since "that I am" is a relative (dependent) clause, it must refer back to the clause upon which it depends. It cannot refer ahead to something else.[27]

The problems in Urshan's understanding of *eheyeh asher eheyeh* – commonly translated "I am that I am" or "I am who I am" – do not mean necessarily that his theology is wrong. They do mean, however, that his theology cannot depend on these assumptions. Other evidence would need to be submitted to support his point of view.

It is unfortunate that Urshan includes quotations from *Eusebia* as supporting documents. Nearly fourteen full pages out of the ninety-five in the book consist of material lifted from this source. A monthly publication edited by William Lee

---

[26]Urshan, *The Almighty God,* 6. Emphasis in original.

[27]See C. L. Seow, *A Grammar for Biblical Hebrew* (Nashville, TN: Abingdon Press, 1987), 61-62.

Stroud, *Eusebia* was an Arian journal that arrived at its "oneness" view of God by denying the deity of Jesus Christ.[28] Claims that Jesus was not God are found throughout the publication. For instance: "Jesus was the Christ, the Son of God, and not God. If He were God, He was not a Son at all, and so could have no Father."[29] The journal also redefined several Christian doctrines, including the immortality of the soul, hell, and the nature of faith. Instead of faith being trust in God, it was defined as "the solid conviction of the truth of a proposition, distinctly stated and comprehended."[30] The Holy Spirit was identified as "that mediatory energy, or influence, that is shed forth by Jesus Christ from His holy Father . . . ."[31]

It is not only unfortunate that Urshan appealed to *Eusebia* for its anti-Trinitarian stance. It is further to be regretted that he adopted the use of "YAH-OSHUA" from *Eusebia* as a legitimate spelling for the Messiah's name.[32] It was claimed in *Eusebia* that Jesus' "proper Hebrew name is YAH-oshua, identical with that applied to 'Joshua, the Son of Nun.'"[33] This claim betrays a lack of familiarity with the Hebrew language. Although "Joshua" and "Jesus" are the same name with the transliteration reflecting Hebrew or Greek origins, it is not true that the name given Joshua by Moses in Numbers 13:16 should be transliterated as YAH-oshua. The correct transliteration is *Yehoshua*`.[34]

Finally, it is regrettable that Urshan, having quoted extensively from *Eusebia*, followed up with these words:

> You have read the masterpiece on God's NAME in His dear Son, spoken of by these eminent Christian men who knew the original languages, Hebrew and Greek. You are undoubtedly now ready to understand better the same blessed truth which is given to us by the Holy Ghost through revelation, backed up by an abundance of Scriptures.[35]

The treatment of God's name in *Eusebia* is not reliable and those who wrote in the journal apparently had limited or no knowledge of the Hebrew language. For Urshan to say that he had received the "same blessed truth . . . given . . . by the

---

[28]The selection of the title "Eusebia" for this journal is no doubt intentional. Eusebius of Nicomedia presented the case for Arianism at the Council of Nicaea, and Constantius, the emperor of the eastern branch of the Roman Empire, was, with his wife Eusebia, a defender of Arianism. See Justo L. Gonzalez, *A History of Christian Thought*, vol. 1, rev. ed. (Nashville, TN: Abingdon Press, 1970), 267, 277; De Imperatoribus Ro-manis, *An Online Encyclopedia of Roman Emperors*, "Eusebia Augusta (353-360 A.D.) and Faustina (360-361 A.D.)," Michael DiMaio, Jr., http://www.roman-emperors.org-/eusebia.htm (accessed April 19, 2010).

[29]"True and False Christianity," *Eusebius* 5, no. 1 (July 1892): 47-48.

[30]"True and False Christianity," *Eusebius* 5, no. 1 (July 1892): 35.

[31]"The Trinity," *Eusebius* 5, no. 6 (December 1892): 139.

[32]Urshan, *The Almighty God*, 6, 77. Urshan also spells the Messiah's name as "Yahsous," another error (Urshan, *The Almighty God*, 69).

[33]"True and False Christianity," *Eusebius* 5, no. 1 (July 1892): 42.

[34]To the untrained eye YAH-oshua and *Yehoshua*` may seem identical, but the *Yeh* of *Yehoshua*` is not YAH. YAH, the abbreviation for Yahweh, is an independent or terminal form that can stand alone or at the end of a word, but it cannot stand at the beginning. In the Hebrew Scriptures, YAH never appears at the beginning of a word as an abbreviation for Yahweh.

[35]Urshan, *The Almighty God*, 41.

Holy Ghost through revelation" suggests that he was not fully aware of the theological bias of *Eusebia*. His theology was certainly not that which was espoused by *Eusebia*. Indeed, he clearly rejected Arianism.[36]

A phrase that appears early in reference to Christ in *The Almighty God* is "absolute deity."[37] This term, which was often used by early twentieth century Oneness Pentecostals, was meant to distinguish the Oneness view of Jesus from the Trinitarian view. Oneness Pentecostals understood Paul's statement "in him dwelleth all the fullness of the Godhead bodily" (Colossians 2:9) to mean that the Father, Son, and Holy Spirit are known in and through Jesus. Urshan urged his readers to

> worship God, the Father, the Son, and the Holy Ghost in His new revealed NAME for this dispensation. . . . God was in Christ reconciling the world unto Himself! . . . He is yet with all His greatness, power and glory dwelling and manifesting Himself before the angels in that lovely Person of His Christ, the Son (see Col. 2:1-9).[38]

To speak of his "absolute deity" meant that Jesus was not only "God the Son" manifest in the flesh, but that he was "God manifest in the flesh" (I Timothy 3:16). For Urshan, God was "revealing to and energizing His people to proclaim, as never before, a full and glorified Saviour, who is God-man."[39] Urshan set out to do this in the first chapter of *The Almighty God* by offering "a brief exposition of the Deity o[f] Jesus Christ as it is recorded in the Epistle to the Hebrews."[40]

This "exposition" is limited to a few brief comments on the manner in which Hebrews proclaims the superiority of Christ over the angels, Moses, Joshua, and Aaron by calling him "**God, the Creator and Upholder** of all things by the power of HIS WORD."[41] Urshan declared,

> In these days of ours, not only are thousands of so-called Christians denying the absolute Deity of our Lord, but those who believe it are trying to preach Him feebly as God the Son, and by so doing they think they have gone to the limit in exalting "the Lord of Glory." But the Apostle in the above Epistle exalts Him above all human and angelic dignitaries and proclaims Him as God, in addition to proclaiming Him as the Son.[42]

After quoting Matthew 11:27, Urshan commented,

---

[36]Andrew D. Urshan, *Doctrine of Trinity and the Divinity of Jesus Christ* (Cochrane, WI: The Witness of God, 1923), 14, 28.

[37]Urshan, *The Almighty God*, 10.

[38]Urshan, *The Almighty God*, 44. This "new revealed NAME" was "Lord Jesus Christ" (Urshan, *The Almighty God*, 44) with 'Lord" representing 'Father,' 'Jesus' representing 'Son,' and 'Christ' representing 'Holy Spirit' (Urshan, *The Life Story*, 5th ed., 140).

[39]Urshan, *The Almighty God*, 10.

[40]Urshan, *The Almighty God*, 10.

[41]Urshan, *The Almighty God*, 10. Emphasis in original.

[42]Urshan, *The Almighty God*, 10. For Urshan, the phrase "absolute deity" refers not simply to the belief that Christ is God as confessed in Trinitarian Christology but to the belief that the entire Trinity is manifest in the Lord Jesus Christ. This is what it means for "all the fullness" of the Godhead to dwell in Christ (Urshan, "The Story of My Life—10th Chapter—Cont.," *The Witness of God* 4, no. 45 [September 1923]: 4; Urshan, *Doctrine of Trinity*, 26, 29; Urshan, *The Almighty God*, 10).

In this Scripture our Lord limits the revelation and the manifestation of the Father to that which is made **in and through Himself.** Therefore the Son is a great mystery, as is the Father. . . . So many of us, with our narrow minds, are apt to think that we know all about the person and the glory of Jesus Christ, and that He is the second person in the Trinity, or the Son of man and the Son of God, inferior to God the Father.[43]

In an apparent nod to his former associations in Trinitarian Pentecostalism and at The Moody Church with its "fundamentalism," Urshan concluded just before turning to a quotation from John Bunyan,

Our very traditions and so-called Bible fundamentals prove that we are so proud and so limited in our knowledge that we are not even able to listen to the doctrine of Jesus Christ as our **God, the Creator** . . . and as **God, our Saviour** . . . and the **God who bought us** . . . much less believe it. We shrink from falling on our faces before Him and crying out, **"My Lord and my God!"** as Thomas did . . . .[44]

Thus, in the first chapter of *The Almighty God* Urshan indicated that he wished to exalt Jesus beyond the concept of "God the Son." Although he was not opposed to that term and used it himself on occasion,[45] he believed Jesus was further exalted when identified simply as "God." Urshan was willing to use the word "mystery" not only of the "plurality in God's mysterious Being"[46] but also of the Son, in that the "revelation and manifestation" of the Father is "made in and through the Son," and of the Father for the same reason.

It is doubtful that many who embrace the doctrine of the Trinity would disagree with Urshan that Jesus is God, our Creator, our Savior, and the God who bought us. Few, if any, would shrink from calling Jesus Lord and God. But for Urshan, insistence upon the Trinitarian proclamation of three persons in the Godhead was synonymous with relegating Christ to a lesser position. One wonders, then, why he thought it strengthened his position to quote from a variety of historical figures who embraced Trinitarianism but who declared Jesus to be God.

Urshan's first extended quotation is from John Bunyan.[47] There is nothing in the quotation contrary to western Trinitarianism, and Bunyan quotes the biblical witness that God is in Christ, "reconciling the world unto Himself by Him." Perhaps the reason Urshan included this material from Bunyan is that Bunyan was wrestling with apparent conundrums concerning Christ.

[I]f in [the humanity of Christ] dwells all the fullness of the Godhead bodily, how then appears He before Him to make intercession? Or if Christ is the throne of grace, and mercy-seat, how doth He appear before God as sitting there, to sprinkle that now with His blood? Again, if Christ be the altar of incense, how stands He as a priest by that altar, to offer the prayers of all saints thereon, before the Throne?[48]

---

[43]Urshan, *The Almighty God,* 10. Emphasis in original.
[44]Urshan, *The Almighty God,* 11. Emphasis in original.
[45]Urshan, "Open Letter," 4.
[46]Urshan, *The Almighty God,* 77.
[47]Urshan, *The Almighty God,* 11-12.
[48]John Bunyan, *The Whole Works of John Bunyan,* vol. 1 (London: Blackie and Son, 1862), 671, quoted in Urshan, *The Almighty God,* 11.

Urshan titled his quotation from Bunyan "The Mysterious and Marvelous Christ." This is not Bunyan's title, so it is intentional on Urshan's part. Thus, his apparent reason for including this section from Bunyan was to point out that Bunyan believed there was something mysterious about Christ, as did Urshan. Perhaps Urshan's thinking ran like this: If Christ can be the altar of incense and yet stand by the altar of incense as a priest, he can also be indentified as both the Father and the Son.

The next group of quotations by Urshan is from a variety of sources declaring the deity of Christ. None of them are non-Trinitarian. The well-known second century statement by Pliny the Younger (62-113) that former Christians "asserted . . . that the sum and substance of their fault or error had been that they were accustomed to meet on a fixed day before dawn and sing responsively a hymn to Christ as to a god"[49] is offered by Urshan as early evidence of belief in the deity of Christ.[50]

Urshan is apparently following here a well-known litany of historic figures testifying to belief that Christ was God. His references are quite similar to A. B. Winfield's *Antidote to the Errors of Universalism,* published in 1850.[51] His next reference is to the second century claim by Justin Martyr that God "came from above, and became man among men, and who is again to return, when they who pierced Him shall see and bewail Him."[52] Four references in a row, including Justin Martyr, are lifted almost verbatim from an early work now preserved under the title *Scripture Testimony to the Deity of Christ* by Samuel Green.

The next reference is to the second century bishop Theophilus and his statement, "The Word **was God,** and sprung from God."[53] Urshan subsequently quotes Irenaeus (d. ca. 190) that "The Ebionites are vain, not receiving **the union of God and man,** by faith, into their souls."[54] The following quotation is taken from Clement of Alexandria (c. 150-211), who declared that Jesus was "**both man and God . . . adored as the living God.**"[55]

After quoting ante-Nicene fathers, Urshan returned to a contemporary source, following almost word-for-word a book published the year before his *The Almighty God in the Lord Jesus Christ.* This book, compiled and edited by Arthur Hamilton De Long and Allen P. De Long, was titled *Tributes of Great Men to Jesus Christ.*[56] The first quotation is from the fourth century Epiphanius: "My Christ

---

[49]Paul Halsall Mar, *Medieval Sourcebook: Pliny on the Christians* (1996), http://www.fordham.edu/halsall/source/pliny1.html (accessed April 19, 2010).

[50]Urshan, *The Almighty God,* 12. Urshan's quote is not precise: "They, Christians, sing in social worship a hymn to Christ as God."

[51]Aaron Burr Winfield, *Antidote to the Errors of Universalism* (Auburn, NY: Derby, Miller, & Co., 1850), 53.

[52]Urshan, *The Almighty God,* 12.

[53]Urshan's source read "came," not "sprung." Emphasis is Urshan's.

[54]Emphasis is Urshan's.

[55]Emphasis is Urshan's.

[56]Arthur Hamilton De Long and Allen P. De Long, comps. and eds., *Tributes of Great Men to Jesus Christ* (New York: Fleming H. Revell Company, 1918).

and God was exceedingly beautiful in countenance."[57] This is from an extended statement by Epiphanius claiming to describe the physical appearance of Christ.[58] Next Urshan quotes from an eighteenth century "Swedish philosopher" who said, "He is the Lord Jesus Christ, who is Jehovah the Lord, Creator from eternity, Saviour in time, and Reformer to eternity." This "philosopher" was Emanuel Swedenborg, and the rest of the quotation, not included by Urshan is "who is at once the Father, the Son and the Holy Spirit."[59] A poem about Christ follows by Thomas Chatterton which includes the phrases "**the Godhead wore**" and "**Man Almighty God.**"[60] Lord Byron is quoted as saying, "If ever man was God or God man, Jesus Christ **was both.**"[61] Thomas B. Macauley's words attesting to Christ as "**Deity embodied in human form walking among men**" are next,[62] followed by Cyrus D. Foss' declaration, "Thou art Christ, the Son of the Living God, **Thyself very man and very God.**"[63] Luther Tracy Townsend is quoted as saying, "The true soul, the ruler of nations, sinless and infinite, a God and a man, is an established fact."[64] Next are the words of Francis E. Willard: "**He is the incarnate God . . . How beautiful it is to be with God.**"[65] In the final quotation from *Tributes of Great Men,* Urshan offers the words of Richard Watson Gilder, "If Jesus Christ is a God, and the only God, I swear, I will follow Him through heaven and hell, the earth, the sea, and the air."[66]

Urshan next quoted from Spurgeon's sermon "The Exaltation of Christ": "In heaven, in earth, in hell, all knees bend before Him, and every tongue confesses that He is God."[67]

At this point stage in his argument, Urshan explains the purpose of his quotations.

> Some may be puzzled over such attributes given to Him, and question within themselves how Jesus Christ can be the Son of Jehovah, and yet Jehovah Himself; or how He can be the Son of God and yet the Almighty God. Such a question cannot be fully answered with a satisfactory explanation, because therein lies "the great mystery of Godliness," but believe it we must.[68]

---

[57] Urshan, *The Almighty God,* 12.
[58] De Long, *Tributes of Great Men,* 28.
[59] De Long, *Tributes of Great Men,* 39. Swedenborg was not a classical Western Trinitarian. In his view, "God is one in three principles, each of which are manifest in Jesus Christ" (H. F. Vos, *Dictionary of Christianity in America* (Daniel G. Reid, Robert D. Linder, Bruce L. Shelley, and Harry S. Stout, eds.; Downers Grove, IL: InterVarsity Press, 1990), 275.
[60] De Long, *Tributes of Great Men,* 46.
[61] De Long, *Tributes of Great Men,* 54.
[62] De Long, *Tributes of Great Men,* 58.
[63] De Long, *Tributes of Great Men,* 89.
[64] De Long, *Tributes of Great Men,* 94.
[65] De Long, *Tributes of Great Men,* 95.
[66] De Long, *Tributes of Great Men,* 101. In each of these quotes, the emphases are Urshan's.
[67] Urshan, *The Almighty God,* 13. See Charles Haddon Spurgeon, *Spurgeon's Sermons, Second Series* (New York: Sheldon & Company, Publishers, 1869), 149.
[68] Urshan, *The Almighty God,* 14.

Virtually all of the quotations offered by Urshan – Swedenborg would be an exception – are from Trinitarians. They confess Jesus to be God, but this would not persuade Urshan's Trinitarian readers of his view. They did not need to be convinced of the deity of Christ. Even Urshan's next statement would find few if any arguments from his Trinitarian readers:

> Jesus Christ, being of the same substance as that of the Father, and being His only begotten Son, who sprang forth from the bosom of the Deity, and by right inherits the Name of the His Father, and the Father being pleased that in Him should all His fullness dwell, –all these scriptural facts give Him the rightful title of Jehovah, just as He calls Himself the Almighty.[69]

It is Urshan's conclusions that would begin to raise the eyebrows of his readers:

> There are not three Almighties [sic], there is but one Almighty God. Jesus Christ being the Word, the **Son,** the **expression,** the **image,** the **Heir,** the **embodiment,** and the **revelation of the trione God,** makes Him the Almighty. So in Christ our Lord we have the Almighty God, the Father, the Son, and the Holy Ghost; for "in Him dwelleth all the fullness of the Godhead bodily."[70]

Even here, Urshan's Trinitarian readers would probably not stumble until they reached the phrase "the revelation of the tri-one God."[71] They would not question his claim that Jesus is "the Almighty," but they might balk at the phrase "in Christ our Lord we have the Almighty God, the Father, the Son, and the Holy Ghost." His more informed Trinitarian readers might, however, connect his claim with the historic doctrine of circumincession.

Urshan's next appeal is from a message preached by F. C. Jennings at the Fulton Street prayer meeting in New York City in 1908. Jennings declared the deity of Jesus: **"He is none other or less than God."** The baby Jesus **"is God with us."** He is **"God, our God."**[72]

The next quotation – about two and one-third pages – are selected paragraphs from Samuel Green's treatise *More than One Hundred Scriptural and Incontrovertibile Arguments for Believing in the Deity of Christ*.[73] As the title of the article indicates, it is a defense of the deity of Jesus. What Urshan does not point out is that Green wrote to oppose Unitarianism, a monotheistic perspective that denied the Trinity and the deity of Christ. Urshan cited only passages that defended Christ's deity. He did not include passages that defended Western Trinitarian understanding. For example, Green wrote:

> Do you say, I cannot comprehend God as existing in *three persons* — FATHER, SON, and HOLY SPIRIT? . . .

---

[69]Urshan, *The Almighty God,* 14.
[70]Urshan, *The Almighty God,* 14. Emphasis in original.
[71]Urshan spells this coined word as "trione," but I hyphenate it for ease of reading.
[72]Urshan, *The Almighty God,* 14. Emphases are Urshan's.
[73]Urshan, *The Almighty God,* 15-17. For the article in its original form see Christian Resources and Links, doctrinal & practical writings, *Supreme Divinity of our Lord and Savior Jesus Christ,* http://www.wholesomewords.org/resources/deityofchrist.html.

... You say, The terms *Trinity* and *Trinitarianism* are not found in the Bible. Where in the Bible are the words *Unity* and *Unitarianism* to be found (that is, in the sense of the Unitarian error which speaks of the "unity of God" to the denial of the Deity and personality of the Son and of the Holy Spirit)?[74]

Urshan quotes next from various German sources. They proclaim the deity of Christ, but none question the doctrine of the Trinity.[75] Quotations from five English hymns follow. Three assert Christ's deity; none address the doctrine of the Trinity.[76]

The next section of *The Almighty God* consists of an article by Urshan titled "The Necessity of Preaching Jesus Christ as God."[77] The article begins by declaring that those who are true Christians believe in the deity of Christ and are "free from the spirit of Unitarianism and Christian Science."[78] The term "the absolute deity of our Saviour" appears in the second paragraph, as well as this question:

> If the Holy Scriptures proclaim Jesus Christ as the Son of God and yet God, manifested in the flesh, and the fullness of the Godhead bodily dwelleth in Him, how then, can a minister of the Gospel, who is commanded by the Holy Spirit to preach the "Word," ignore so many chapters and Bible texts on this great theme if he be a faithful steward of the household of God?[79]

A casual reader with no knowledge of the debate between Trinitarian and Oneness Pentecostals might well think that Urshan's concern is with those who deny Christ's deity, like the Unitarians. But Urshan believed illumination of the Scriptures by the Holy Spirit would lead to a correct understanding of Jesus' identity.

> Again, we read of the specific office of the Holy Spirit, which is to reveal and glorify not the Father, not Himself, but the Lord Jesus Christ. How then can a Spirit-filled and Spirit-led man of God dare to grieve Him who came to teach and lead us into all the truth? No, he that is a faithful and obedient servant of the Lord Jesus, will have fresh revelations from heaven through the illumination of the Scriptures by the Holy Ghost, and he will declare the eternal truth concerning the "God-man" (Matt. 13:52).[80]

The insistence on "fresh revelations" lent credibility to early critics of Oneness Pentecostalism who claimed that the "New Issue" relied on extra-biblical revelation. But it is important to note that for Urshan, "illumination of the Scriptures by the Holy Ghost" was "fresh revelation." He did not have in mind "revelations" apart from Scripture. As Urshan said elsewhere, "I apply to sanctified reason as well as to providential occurrences, coupled with all the Scriptures be-

---

[74]Christian Resources and Links, doctrinal & practical writings, *Supreme Divinity of our Lord and Savior Jesus Christ*, http://www.wholesomewords.org/ resources/deityofchrist.html (accessed April 20, 2010).

[75]Urshan, *The Almighty God,* 18.

[76]Urshan, *The Almighty God,* 19.

[77]Urshan, *The Almighty God,* 19-23.

[78]Urshan, *The Almighty God,* 19. Unitarianism and Christian Science were among the early targets of fundamentalism.

[79]Urshan, *The Almighty God,* 19.

[80]Urshan, *The Almighty God,* 19-20.

fore deciding definitely upon any divine matter."[81] Somewhat like John Wesley, Urshan's intention was to study "all the Scriptures," to note "providential occurrences" (i.e., the confirmation of the word, cf. Wesley's "experience"[82]), and to apply "sanctified" reason. Nowhere here is there any suggestion that Urshan was willing to jettison Scripture. The only thing missing in Urshan's "trilateral" as opposed to Wesley's Quadrilateral was tradition. As noted at the beginning of this chapter, this is not to say that Urshan did not value tradition. His perspective on the tradition of Syriac Christianity as early Christianity suggests that he simply did not think of it as tradition.

Urshan further declared that Christ "is not less than the very **Almighty God.**"[83] He appealed to his readers to "preach the full Christ, not only the Son of God and the Son of Man, but the very God Almighty who fills all things."[84] "We must proclaim the Lord of Glory as the Jehovah God," he wrote, in order to prevent those in "so-called Christian countries" who have heard the humanity of Christ emphasized from becoming "the victims of Russellism, Unitarianism, Christian Science . . . Higher Criticism and the New Theology."[85]

Urshan connects belief in the deity of Christ with the new birth: "It is so little known that the sure foundation of 'The New Birth' or the birth by the Spirit is the **accepting** and **believing** in the Lord Jesus as God, the Creator!"[86] He foresees the day when all who are born again will understand the deity of Christ: "The day is coming . . . that all those who are truly born of God will sooner or later see that Jesus Christ is God, their Creator, as well as the Saviour, and that their miraculous new birth took place because of the Godhead, life and power in His **NAME.**"[87]

The next thirteen pages of *The Almighty God in the Lord Jesus Christ* are quoted directly from *Eusebia*, a late nineteenth-century Arian publication. It is regrettable that Urshan included material from this monthly journal in his publications – both here and in *The Witness of God*. The material is non-Trinitarian, but it denies the deity of Christ. Urshan believed that Jesus Christ was "the eternal supreme deity"; that was the whole point of his theology.[88]

---

[81]Urshan, "The Life Story of Andrew Bar-David [2nd section]," *The Witness of God* (August 1946): 11.

[82]See Steven L. Porter, "Wesleyan Theological Methodology as a Theory of Integration," *Journal of Psychology and Theology* 32, no. 3 (2004): 190-199.

[83]Urshan, *The Almighty God*, 20. Emphasis in original.

[84]Urshan, *The Almighty God*, 20.

[85]Urshan, *The Almighty God*, 20.

[86]Urshan, *The Almighty God*, 22. Emphasis in original.

[87]Urshan, *The Almighty God*, 22. Emphasis in original.

[88]We will probably never know why Urshan included *Eusebia*, but we can surmise at least two scenarios: (1) Someone besides Urshan typed the manuscript for this book and/or for the "open letters" from which the book is drawn. Phillip Dugas, Urshan's stepson, confirmed to me in a telephone conversation on April 20, 2010 that someone else typed Urshan's materials. Dugas never saw Urshan use a typewriter or knew of him using a typewriter. After Urshan married Dugas' mother, she and Dugas were both involved in typing material for *The Witness of God*. It is possible that Urshan handed someone the copy of *Eusebia* from which he wished to quote, indicating the article to be copied, but forgetting

The third chapter of *The Almighty God in the Lord Jesus Christ* returns to quotations from a variety of sources. First, Urshan returns to John Bunyan. In this case, Urshan calls attention to Bunyan's claim that Daniel prayed "**in the name of Christ**" and that those who come to God by Christ "**must first have the knowledge of Him**."[89] When quoting from other sources, Urshan indicated what he wished to emphasize by use of bold fonts or other typographical conventions. Bunyan was, of course, a Trinitarian; a chapter in defense of the doctrine of the Trinity is included in the book from which Urshan quoted.[90]

Next Urshan quoted a statement from John Wesley indicating that the "inspired writers" of Scripture called Jesus Jehovah. The statement is, however, Trinitarian in formulation. Wesley said, "They ascribed to Him all the attributes and all the works of God, so that we need not scruple to pronounce Him God of God, light of light, very God of very God: in glory equal with the Father, in majesty co-eternal."[91]

Urshan took his next quotation from the same source. In this case it was a poem by Charles Wesley exalting "Jesus, the name high over all."[92]

Then Urshan offers a quotation from a sermon by C. H. Spurgeon, "The Eternal Name": "[A]s God upon the throne He sits, the everlasting **One,** the Father, Son and Holy Ghost; –and if the Universe were all annihilated, **still would His Name be heard**."[93] Urshan ended the quotation in mid-sentence. The rest of Spurgeon's statement reads "for the Father would hear it, and the Spirit would hear it, and deeply graven on immortal marble in the rocks of ages, it would stand—Jesus the Son of God, co-equal with his Father."[94]

Urshan returned next to Lawson's *Greatest Thoughts* for a quotation by Bernard of Clairvaux. The poem declares that there is no sweeter sound than Jesus'

---

to mark out material that would express an Arian point of view; or (2) Urshan may have read *Eusebia* through his lens rather then from an Arian perspective. For Urshan, the deity of Christ was connected with his identity as the Father, as well as the Son and the Holy Spirit, manifest in the flesh.

[89] Urshan, *The Almighty God,* 37. See also *The Works of that Eminent Servant of Christ, John Bunyan,* vol. 2 (Philadelphia: T. W. Lord, 1834), 82. Emphases are Urshan's.

[90] In this chapter, Bunyan wrote, "[W]here thou readest, 'The Lord our God is one Lord,' there take heed that thou dost not thence conclude, Then there are not three persons in the Godhead" (*The Works of that Eminent Servant of Christ,* 284).

[91] Urshan, *The Almighty God,* 37. Urshan's source was James Gilchrist Lawson, comp., *Greatest Thoughts About Jesus Christ* (New York: George H. Doran Co., 1919), 21. The phrase "God of God, light of light, very God of very God" is from the Nicene Creed.

[92] Urshan, *The Almighty God,* 37. See Lawson, *Greatest Thoughts,* 57.

[93] Urshan, *The Almighty God,* 38. Emphases are Urshan's.

[94] The Spurgeon Archive, *The New Park Street Pulpit,* "The Eternal Name," http://www.spurgeon.org/sermons/0027.htm (accessed April 20, 2010).

name.[95] Next is a quotation from John Monro Gibson[96] declaring the name of Jesus to be that "**Name by which He has made Himself known to us.**"[97]

Urshan turns next to a quotation from W. W. Simpson in the *Latter Rain Evangel*.[98] At first Simpson seems to be endorsing the Jesus' name formula for baptism:

> The literal translation of Matt. 28:19 is, "baptizing them into the Name." etc., which means those baptized are to pass out of the dominion of self into the authority of the Father, Son, and Spirit. Acts 2:38 says, "Be baptized in the Name of Jesus Christ," which means that they were to be in His authority and no longer under the dominion of self. The reason why the Father and the Spirit are mentioned in the former but not in the latter is that Jesus had not ascended, taken His seat on the Throne of God, with "all authority in heaven and earth," in His hands. "Both Lord and Christ," therefore His authority was now commensurate with the authority formerly vested in Father, Son and Spirit. There was no change in personality but a real and radical change in authority. With "all authority given into His actual possession the "**Name of Jesus Christ" must include exactly as much authority as was formerly included in the "Name of the Father, and of the Son, and of the Holy Ghost.**"[99]

Simpson's purpose is, however, to defuse the argument over the baptismal formula. Prior to the words quoted by Urshan, Simpson wrote:

> But when saints turn away from considering the essential meaning of baptism to discussing the formula the logical result is that instead of escaping the toils of formalism we get deeper into them. When we teach that baptism, in order to be Scriptural and meet the Lord's approval, *must* be done while repeating the words "I baptize you in the name of Jesus Christ,'" or, "I baptize you in the Name of the Father, and of the Son and of the Holy Ghost," we are simply formalists of a most pronounced type. And in emphasizing the formula we draw attention away from the essential thing, i. e. the attitude of the heart toward God.[100]

---

[95]Urshan, *The Almighty God*, 38. See Lawson, *Greatest Thoughts*, 67.

[96]John Monro Gibson graduated from the University of Toronto in 1862. His theological education was from Knox College. After serving as a pastor in Montreal and professor at Montreal Theological College, he moved in 1880 to London, England where he became pastor of St. John's Wood Presbyterian Church. He served as moderator of the Presbyterian Church in England and wrote many books. The University of Toronto conferred the honorary degree of Doctor of Laws on him in 1902. Gibson died on October 13, 1921. See University of Toronto Monthly, http://www.archive.org/stream/ universityoftoro22univuoft/ universityoftoro22univuoft_djvu.txt (accessed April 21, 2010).

[97]Urshan, *The Almighty God*, 38. Emphases are Urshan's. See John Monro Gibson, *Christianity According to Christ*, 2nd ed. (London: James Nisbet & Co., 1889), 8.

[98]"The *Latter Rain Evangel* was an early Pentecostal periodical published by the Stone Church in Chicago Illinois. During its time (1908-1939) it enjoyed a wide distribution in the United States and around the world. The church played a critical role in the development of the Pentecostal movement as it hosted a number of important conferences including the second General Council of the Assemblies of God. Many of the sermons from the conferences were published in the pages of the *Latter Rain Evangel*," Flower Pentecostal Heritage Center, http://ifphc.org/index.cfm?fuseaction=products. agpublications (accessed April 21, 2010).

[99]Urshan, *The Almighty God*, 38. Emphases are Urshan's. See W. W. Simpson, "The Baptismal Formula," *Latter Rain Evangel* 11, no. 8 (May 1919): 19.

[100]Simpson, "The Baptismal Formula," 19.

Indeed, it was Simpson's opinion that the name of Jesus was not to be used as a formula: "In order to prove that the Name of Jesus is not intended to be used as a formula, or at least has no efficacy as a formula we have but to turn to Matt. 1:22, 23 and Acts 19:13."[101] According to Simpson, "[t]o do a thing in the name of Jesus is simply to do it in His authority."[102]

Urshan discontinued his quotation from Simpson in mid-sentence. The rest of the sentence reads "not because He is all there is of God, but because all the authority of God is now possessed by the glorified Son."[103]

Simpson's rejection of the significance of any formula is clear in his concluding words:

> It is not the form of words repeated over a man at baptism that makes that act valid and effectual; it is this passing out of the dominion of sin and the flesh and self into that of the Lord Jesus.
>
> I believe there is nothing more grieving to the Lord than this present division of His people over the baptismal formula. What difference does the formula make anyway? The important thing is to get the one baptized out of self into Christ, and the formula has nothing to do with that. It is the attitude of heart represented as "Repentance toward God and faith toward our Lord Jesus Christ," that is the important thing. Where there is genuine Bible repentance and faith, baptism will be a real passing out of the dominion of sin through a real death of self into the authority of the Lord Jesus where He exercises His lordship over us by the Spirit. All agitating the question of formula simply takes the mind away from the important thing.[104]

The Sunday School Illustrator is the next source for Urshan. He quotes from an article by "Pierson"[105] comparing the Jewish requirement for a quorum of ten in order to erect a synagogue with the New Testament requirement of "two or three . . . gathered together **in my name**" in order for Jesus to be in their midst.[106]

Urshan continues with an unknown source that cites also *The Sunday School Times*, attributed to its editor, Charles Gallaudet Trumbull.

> The name of Jesus carries with it all the power of the triune God, for "in Him dwelleth all the fullness of the Godhead bodily" (Col. 2:9). His disciple's request that He show them the Father brought from Jesus the startlingly definite reply, "He that hath seen me hath seen the Father" (John 14:9). When John in the Revelation prophesied "They shall see His face; and His name shall be in their foreheads" (Rev. 22:4) **that name and face will be Jesus', when we shall "see Him as He is."**
>
> It may well be, therefore, that the disciples in baptizing in the name of Jesus were carrying out the commission of Matt. 28:19. Certainly either form is a true bap-

---

[101] Simpson, "The Baptismal Formula," 19.
[102] Simpson, "The Baptismal Formula," 19.
[103] Simpson, "The Baptismal Formula," 19.
[104] Simpson, "The Baptismal Formula," 19.
[105] This was A. T. Pierson (1837-1911), a Fundamentalist leader who lectured at Moody Bible Institute. See Pleasant Places Press, "A. T. Pierson," http://www.pleasantplaces.biz/authors/pierson_a.php (accessed November 22, 2010).
[106] Urshan, *The Almighty God,* 39. Emphasis is Urshan's.

tism if the reality is back of the ceremony. In both cases there is one God and one Name. Some Christians who have felt that the spiritual reality was not in the form of baptism that they received have had the ordinance performed again and received rich blessing through it.[107]

Urshan's next quotation is from a leaflet published by the Free Tract Society. It is the story of a "rum victim" whose deliverance came through the name of Jesus. There is no theological content to the quotation, but Urshan uses it to speak of **"the precious name of Jesus."**[108]

The final quotation in chapter 3 is again from the Arian publication *Eusebia*. The quotation addresses "burial in water in the name of YAH-oshua" and states, "The apostles did nothing in three names. Rome and her daughters do everything in three appellatives, but **no name.**"[109]

The fourth chapter of *The Almighty God* is written by Urshan and titled "The Great Commission and the Name of God in Jesus Christ." He sought to build upon "the same blessed truth" which was spoken of in previous chapters by "eminent Christian men who knew the original languages, Hebrew and Greek,"[110] though in his case this truth was given by revelation and supported by Scripture. In order to determine whether the quotations he cites support his position, we must examine Urshan's understanding of Matthew 28:17-19; Mark 16:14-19; and Luke 24:45-49.

Urshan begins his discussion of the Great Commission by pointing out the singularity of the name in Matthew 28:19:

> "Go ye therefore and teach all nations, baptizing them IN THE NAME;" notice . . . it is not written **in the names,** but IN THE NAME. . . . [T]he divine commission from the beginning has been sent forth in the one great NAME of the Almighty God. . . . It is the one name of the T-H-R-E-E—O-N-E God (1 John 5:7) . . . the NAME of the Father, of the Son and of the Holy Ghost.[111]

---

[107]Urshan, *The Almighty God*, 39. Emphasis is Urshan's. In a recent dissertation discussing the early adherents' response to the fundamentalists' critique of the Pentecostal movement, Gerald King provides additional insight to the significance of this article by Trumbull. King demonstrates that the New Issue controversy became known beyond the movement, raising questions for the broader evangelical movement as well: "The 'New Issue' caught the attention of a Wisconsin Sunday school worker in 1916, raising the matter with Charles Trumbull, editor of the ever-popular *Sunday School Times*. The unnamed inquisitor feared that the heresy had become widespread in the Middle West and wanted clarification as to why the trinitarian formula was not used in Acts 2.38. Trumbull reasoned that 'the name of Jesus carries with it all the power of the triune God . . .' and saw no justification for believers to be re-baptized in a second ceremony" (Gerald Wayne King, "Disfellowshiped: Pentecostal Responses to Funda-mentalism in the United States, 1906-1953 [PhD diss., University of Birmingham, March 2009], 113-14). King references "Baptized into What Name?" *Sunday School Times* 58, no. 21 (May 20, 1916): 322.

[108]Urshan, *The Almighty God,* 40. Emphasis in original.

[109]William Lee Stroud, ed., *Eusebia* (1900), quoted in Urshan, *The Almighty God,* 40.

[110]Urshan, *The Almighty God,* 41.

[111]Urshan, *The Almighty God,* 42. Emphasis in original.

For Urshan, this means that the Father has a name which is also the name of the Son and of the Holy Spirit. This is a name for "this Gospel dispensation."[112] The name is not "Father," or "Son," or "Holy Spirit," for Jesus commanded his disciples to baptize in the name "of the" Father, Son, and Holy Spirit. According to Urshan, "These words '**of the**' should make us understand that Father is not a proper noun, but a common noun, and that the Heavenly Father has a name which makes Him properly to be known . . . ."[113] Since "a **proper noun** is the name of a *particular person, place, or thing*", whereas "a **common noun** is the name of *any one* of a class of *persons, places, or things*",[114] Urshan means that 'Father' is not the name that specifically identifies the "T-H-R-E-E—O-N-E God."

Urshan uses the term "T-H-R-E-E—O-N-E God" eight times in this chapter. Although he wishes to identify a singular name for Father, Son, and Holy Spirit, he also wants to acknowledge a plurality, a "threeness" within the one God.

By comparing Matthew 28:19 with Mark 16:14-19 and Luke 24:45-49, Urshan believes he has discovered that "Jesus Christ is that one NAME of the T-H-R-E-E—O-N-E God."[115] He believes his view is legitimated by Colossians 3:17.

> His proper NAME is not Father, nor Son, neither Holy Ghost, but the Lord Jesus Christ. That does not do away with the loving Fatherhood of the Almighty, nor with the gracious Sonship of the Lord, and neither does it do away with the blessed existence of the excellent Spirit of God, but it makes clear and harmonizes all the scriptures with all the fullness of this T-H-R-E-E—O-N-E Godhead summed up in this dispensation for all the human race in that sweetest of all names, JESUS, the anointed Jehovah Lord.[116]

Urshan urges his readers to "worship God, the Father, the Son, and the Holy Ghost in His new revealed NAME for this dispensation."[117] He sees this "scriptural revelation" as making Matthew 28:19 and Acts 2:38 equivalents. He believes that Jesus Christ "is all of God for us [and the] visibleness [*sic*] of the invisible T-H-R-E-E—O-N-E God."[118]

As chapter four draws toward a conclusion, Urshan offers a list of Scriptures indicating words or terms that are used of God in the Old Testament and of Jesus in the New Testament. These include "Creator," "Redeemer," "Saviour," "Shepherd," "Rock," "King," "I AM," "I AM HE," and texts in the Old Testament stating that God was worshiped and in the New Testament that Jesus was worshiped.[119] The chapter ends with Urshan's interpretive statement of the Great Commission: "Go ye therefore and teach all nations, baptizing them **In The** NAME **of the**

---

[112]Urshan, *The Almighty God,* 42.

[113]Urshan, *The Almighty God,* 32. Emphasis in original.

[114]Madeline Semmelmeyer and Don Bolander, *Instant English Handbook* (Mundelein, IL: Career Institute, 1968), 44-45.

[115]Urshan, *The Almighty God,* 43.

[116]Urshan, *The Almighty God,* 44.

[117]Urshan, *The Almighty God,* 44.

[118]Urshan, *The Almighty God,* 47.

[119]Urshan, *The Almighty God,* 50.

Father, **of the** Son and **of the** Holy Ghost . . . which is JESUS CHRIST, THE LORD."[120]

Chapter five of *The Almighty God in the Lord Jesus Christ* is appropriately titled "Some Scriptures Worthy of Special Consideration Concerning the Name of God." The chapter consists largely of verses of Scripture that mention the name of God in a variety of contexts. There is little in the chapter to further advance Urshan's theology, but there are some statements that reiterate his views. For example, in response to those who said to him, "Don't play always on one string, and don't make the name of the Lord a hobby," Urshan said, "Such remonstrances [*sic*] are nothing less than a dishonoring and insulting of the Name of the triune God in our only Saviour, Christ."[121]

Urshan's disappointment over his inability to heal the breach between Trinitarian and Oneness Pentecostals is seen near the end of the chapter:

> [T]he Holy Ghost did not come into us Christians only to make us speak in tongues and to organize religious bodies, neither came He in us to cause us to fight one another; but He came to reveal to us the excellent glory of the Father, the Son, and the Holy Ghost, in the Person of JESUS CHRIST, our LORD, and to make all our thoughts, ambitions, works of faith, spiritual dreams and revelations, and all our life, to be gathered in ONE, even CHRIST JESUS.[122]

It was widely believed among early twentieth century Pentecostals that the reason for the outpouring of the Holy Spirit was to signal the nearness of Christ's return.[123] Urshan agreed with this and frequently warned his readers of the nearness of the rapture, the necessity for world evangelization, and the dangers awaiting those who were not prepared for Christ's return.[124] But he also taught that the Holy Spirit was given to reveal the manifestation of the Father, Son, and Holy Spirit in the Lord Jesus Christ. He further thought that all who were baptized with the Holy Spirit would eventually come to understand this.[125]

Chapter six of *The Almighty God in the Lord Jesus Christ* is titled "The Great Conflict of Our Day against God and His Word." In it Urshan sets forth the reasons for the theological conflict within Pentecostalism and explains his withdrawal from the Assemblies of God. The chapter also includes an extended quotation from a booklet titled *A Message to Christians and to the World* by T. P. Douglas.

For Urshan, the conflict within Pentecostalism was part of a broad cosmic issue. He wrote this book as World War I was coming to a close. He did not believe this

---

[120]Urshan, *The Almighty God*, 50. Emphases are Urshan's.

[121]Urshan, *The Almighty God*, 54.

[122]Urshan, *The Almighty God*, 57.

[123]See D. William Faupel, *The Everlasting Gospel: The Significance of Eschatology in the Development of Pentecostal Thought,* Journal of Pentecostal Theology Supplement Series, eds., John Christopher Thomas, Rickie Moore, Steven J. Land, no. 10 (Sheffield: Sheffield Academic Press, 1996).

[124]See, e.g., Andrew D. Urshan, *Timely Messages of Warning: Five pointed messages to the saints of God admonishing them to be prepared for the return of their soon coming Lord* (1917; repr., Portland, OR: Apostolic Book Corner, 1973).

[125]Urshan, *The Almighty God*, 22.

was simply a conflict between nations. Rather, it was a "**war of man against God's WORD and God's plan.**"[126] By this he meant that the Central Powers sought to set up a King of Kings and Lord of Lords in opposition to the only "King of Kings and Lord of Lords, whose name is the Word of God."[127] Furthermore, he opposed the League of Nations, seeing it as an attempt to establish peace apart from Jesus Christ. He believed these efforts would lead to the appearance of the Antichrist.

A second "army" also stood in opposition to God. This army was divided into two components: the first consisted of theological liberals who denied the deity of Christ, practiced higher criticism, and sought to introduce the millennium by their own efforts; the second was made up of those who spiritualize the Scriptures, like Christian Scientists and Spiritualists.

Urshan also saw the "world-wide Church Federation" as a "subtle satanic conflict against God."[128] Yet another enemy of God consisted of "lukewarm Christians," identified by Urshan with the church of Laodicea. Those who are lukewarm are divided into two "forces," post-millennialists and foolish virgins. Those who hold to post-millennialism "work hand-in-hand" with higher critics, and the "foolish virgins" are those who believe in the doctrines that came to be known as the fundamentals, but who resist "**the Apostolic baptism of the Holy Ghost.**"[129] These people have no oil in their lamps.

For Urshan, the theological division in Pentecostalism was caused by the same "invisible armies in the high places" that were working in the political realm, in false religions, and in the non-Pentecostal expressions of Christianity.

> [I]t is evident that already many of us Pentecostal people have been influenced in a great measure by the same invisible demoniac forces that have captured the present-day politics, false religions and lukewarm Christians, and have raised them up against Jesus Christ, and these very evil spirits are causing us, also, to fight one another, and God's advanced dealings with some individuals among us.[130]

The fate of these lukewarm Christians (e.g., postmillennialists) and the foolish virgins (e.g., fundamentalists) would not be as severe as the fate of the higher critics, but they would miss the rapture of the saints, the marriage supper of the Lamb, and the rewards to be given to those who "fought a **good fight of faith** and kept His WORD and **denied not His** Holy and Sacred NAME."[131] By missing the rapture, they would "find themselves in the midst of the great tribulation."

In an obvious nod to the view of some dispensationalists that the seven churches of Asia Minor represented seven church "ages," Urshan identified the last days "remnant of God" as the Church of Philadelphia.[132] This church consisted of those who had stood "loyal to their Saviour and His NAME," an evident reference to

---

[126]Urshan, *The Almighty God, 59.*
[127]Urshan, *The Almighty God,* 59.
[128]Urshan, *The Almighty God,* 63.
[129]Urshan, *The Almighty God,* 66. Emphasis in original.
[130]Urshan, *The Almighty God,* 67.
[131]Urshan, *The Almighty God,* 67. Emphasis in original.
[132]Urshan, *The Almighty God,* 70.

those who had embraced Urshan's views. He urged his readers to "proclaim His matchless NAME alone and renounce every man-made theory and theology on the God-head." He obviously had his own experience in mind when he continued that those who would do this would "soon see that the doors of all assemblies or churches organized and controlled by rules, regulations and creeds invented and confirmed by the vote of their conferences will soon be shut to him." If there is any doubt about this, it is removed by Urshan's own words:

> Permit us ... to be a little personal. We wish we did not have to be, but the occasion compels us to do so. Since we have come forth publicly speaking that which God wants us, and mean to be loyal to the words of our Lord through His prophets and apostles (as recorded in the Book of Acts) and have taken a stand for the name of the Lord Jesus Christ, the General Council [of the Assemblies of God], which is a Pentecostal people's organization, are trying to close the doors of their assemblies and to prejudice the hearts of all the people of God against this glorious message of the Church of Philadelphia ... by accusing us through their magazines of wrong doing, seeking to stain our God-given character.[133]

Urshan claimed that many Pentecostal people were defecting to "Russellism" and Unitarianism. The reason for this was that Pentecostals "did not preach the deity of our Lord and Saviour."[134] Many Pentecostals were also in the grip of "legalism." Again, we need not guess who he had in mind.

> The organization of the General Council has rules, regulations and a creed (fundamentals) which have been formulated and confirmed by a vote set forth in print, just like all other denominations, and no one can join that organization **now** if he does not keep within the borders of their set doctrines. If one should go ahead of their creed, as he is led by the Holy Spirit he is cast out and pronounced dangerous.[135]

Further, "worldliness" had crept into the ranks of Pentecostalism. Here, Urshan pulls no punches:

> Let a man of God go and visit the Assemblies of God, so-called, and he will see not only a great deal of fanaticism on one side and formality and dryness on the other, but the worldly dressing, worldly conversation and worldly pride, in some cases exceeding the other religious movements.[136]

Urshan also took on what he viewed as "higher criticism" among Pentecostals. This had to do with those who elevated the doctrinal authority of the four gospels above the book of Acts and the epistles, especially as it relates to the baptismal formula.

Urshan anticipated great persecution for Pentecostals that would remove "[e]very bit of worldly spirit and all the higher and lower criticism of His Holy Word." The purpose of this persecution would be to cause people to "hear and do every command up to the last letter. . . . to the last jot and tittle before He can lead us into perfection." This included the use of the right formula in water baptism.

---

[133] Urshan, *The Almighty God*, 71.
[134] Urshan, *The Almighty God*, 72.
[135] Urshan, *The Almighty God*, 73.
[136] Urshan, *The Almighty God*, 73.

Christ never commanded His apostles to baptize those that believe in His name into the Father, the Son and Holy Ghost, but into "THE NAME" of the T-H-R-E-E—O-N-E GOD. He is going to make us quit thinking that the Apostles baptized as the modern Theologians do. But He will humiliate us, so much that we will be glad to do exactly like His chosen and commissioned Apostles, exactly as it is written in the book of Acts, the pattern of God's church.[137]

Chapter seven of *The Almighty God in the Lord Jesus Christ* is titled "The Complete Fullness of the Deity in Jesus Christ." Here Urshan seeks to show that "Jesus Christ not only has the Name of the Deity in Him, but also the **fullness of the Deity** dwelleth in him, and that He is the **embodiment and visibleness** [*sic*] **of the invisible God.**"[138] By this he means Jesus is not only God the Son manifest in the flesh, but that He is the manifestation of "the Three-One god, or the Deity." It is here that Urshan sets forth his belief in a plurality within "God's mysterious Being."

> ... I personally cannot refrain from believing that there is a plurality in God's mysterious Being, and that this plurality is shown as a three-ness, not three separate, distinct Beings or Persons of God, but a mysterious, inexplicable, incomprehensible threeness, as it is expressed by the Apostle in I Jno. 5:7 and Mat. 28:19, and that the triune office of this one God is shown in I Cor. 12,—not three offices of three Gods but one office of one God with three branches (I Cor. 12:4-6). Again, in Eph. 4:4-6, we find this three-one God, who is called "One Spirit," "One Lord," "One God (the Deity) and Father of all, who is above all, and through all, and in you all." And the first expression or image of this Three-One God was Adam and Eve and that which was in them, a foreshadow of the coming One. We find this Three-in-One all through the Old Testament Scriptures, expressed by types and shadows pointing to God in Christ.[139]

Urshan saw no reason for confusion "concerning the Three-One God, **our Father, our Creator, our Saviour, and our All.**"[140]

> God the Father is light; the Son is light; the Holy Spirit is light,—not three lights, but one self-same Light with three rays (manifestations or revelations); and this great Triune Being of the excellent light of eternal life can be seen, and His blessings, gifts, and promises received, only **in and through Jesus Christ, "the Son of the Father."**[141]

Jesus Christ is the "visible embodiment of the invisible **three-one God.**"

At this point, Urshan appeals to other authors to buttress his view that the "threeness" of God was manifest in Jesus Christ. The first appeal is to I. M. Haldeman, pastor of the First Baptist Church of New York.

---

[137]Urshan, *The Almighty God,* 74.

[138]Urshan, *The Almighty God,* 75. Emphasis in original.

[139]Urshan, *The Almighty God,* 77. Urshan found "foreshadows" of "three-in-one" in Noah's ark and the tabernacle of Moses. Within two years after the publication of *The Almighty God in the Lord Jesus Christ* Urshan stopped appealing to I John 5:7, having discovered that it was a textual variant. See Urshan, "Scriptural Facts Concerning the Godhead Question," *The Witness of God* 2, no. 19 (July 1921): 5.

[140]Urshan, *The Almighty God,* 78. Emphasis in original.

[141]Urshan, *The Almighty God,* 78. Emphasis in original.

The first Ray is neither seen nor felt; the third Ray is not seen but is felt; the second Ray **is both seen and felt.**

Likewise the Father can neither be seen nor felt . . . The Spirit can never be seen, but is felt; while **the Son can both be seen and felt.**

The second Ray is the revelation and **manifestation of the first and third Rays, therefore the embodiment and fullness of the Light.**

The Son of God is the **revelation** of both the Father and the Spirit, therefore the embodiment and the fullness of God; as it is written, "In Him dwelleth all the fullness (Deity) of the Godhead bodily." Col. 2:9.[142]

The context in which this quotation is found indicates that Haldeman's use of this analogy was intended to fit within the framework of western Trinitarianism. Here are Haldeman's words prior to the phrase "the first ray is neither seen nor felt," with which Urshan began his quotation.

> Light is constituted of three rays. These rays are distinct from each other. They do not form three lights but three rays and one light . . . no one ray without the other two is light. If one ray is light it is because the other two are conjoined with it . . . . The three rays are never confounded, neither is the one light divided, but remains one light. Each ray has its separate function. The first originates, the second formulates, illuminates or manifests; the third consummates.[143]

The words "distinct," "never confounded," and "separate function" indicates that Haldeman had western Trinitarianism in view.

Urshan's next appeal is to William Bridge's comparison of the way in which the fullness of the Godhead dwells bodily in Christ to the one hive into which the bees bring "all the sweets that are in the flowers of the field." [144]

Next Urshan quotes Baruch Spinoza: "This is the highest thing which Christ said of Himself, namely **that He is the temple of God,** since God chiefly ministered Himself in Christ; as St. John said, that He might **express** it more **efficaciously**, clothed in the expression that 'The Word was made flesh.'"[145] To be precise, Spinoza used the word "manifested," not "ministered."[146] Apparently Urshan was not aware of Spinoza's rejection of the uniqueness of the Incarnation.

---

[142]Urshan, *The Almighty God,* 78-79. Emphases are Urshan's. According to Urshan, this quote is from Haldeman's tract "God's Only Begotten Son." The correct title is "Wherein was Jesus God's Only Begotten Son?" See The First Baptist Church in the City of New York, "Haldeman," http://firstbaptist-nyc.org/litesite.cfm?id=316 (accessed April 26, 2010).

[143]I. M. Haldeman, "Wherein Was Jesus God's Only Begotten Son?" quoted in Mary E. McDonough, *God's Plan of Redemption* (Anaheim, CA: Living Stream Books, 1999), 11.

[144]Urshan, *The Almighty God,* 79. This was apparently a well-known sentiment. It also appears in Thomas M. Iden, *The Upper Room Bulletin 1920-21,* vol. 7 (Ann Arbor, MI: Ann Arbor Press, 1921), 194.

[145]Urshan, *The Almighty God,* 79. Emphases are Urshan's.

[146]Frederic William Farrar, *The Life of Lives* (London: Cassell and Company, Limited,

Spinoza, a seventeenth century Dutch Jewish philosopher, has been characterized as "militantly anti-supernatural" and as a "modal" pantheist[147] who "identified God with the entire cosmos."[148] Spinoza did not mean by the statement quoted by Urshan that Jesus Christ was uniquely God manifest in the flesh. Rather, from the perspective of Spinoza's pantheism, Christ was God because everything is God.

Urshan undoubtedly found this quotation from Spinoza in Lawson's *Greatest Thoughts about Jesus Christ*, published in 1919, the same year as Urshan's *The Almighty God in the Lord Jesus Christ*. The next quotation by Spinoza could have helped Urshan understand Spinoza's view: "To know the ideal Christ, namely, the eternal wisdom of God, which is manifest in all things, . . . especially in Jesus Christ,—this alone is necessary."[149]

It is somewhat ironic that Urshan's next appeal is to answers written by E. N. Bell in the "Questions and Answers" column of *The Christian Evangel*, an official publication of the Assemblies of God. Urshan refers to Bell's answers as "proper." The two questions ask for an explanation of I John 2:23 and John 14:19. Bell's explanation of John 14:19 may seem troubling from current Oneness perspectives. However, Bell's answers appear to have fit with Urshan's understanding. Bell wrote, "He [Jesus] did not say, 'I am the Father.' There is a world of difference between saying He was in the Father and the claim that He is the Father. Until people learn the difference between **Is** and **In** there is no hope of their understanding this deep matter."[150]

It is interesting that Urshan appealed to Bell's explanation since in this same column Bell also wrote in opposition to "the New Issue doctrine" when responding to two other questions. In less than three months after this article was published, Bell's article titled "The Urshan Trouble" appeared in the May 17, 1919 issue of *The Christian Evangel*.

Following Bell, Urshan returned to J. Monro Gibson to seek support for his theological views. Although Gibson seems to come closer to Urshan's views than any of the other sources from which Urshan draws, he is still clearly Trinitarian. In an unreferenced portion of the chapter from which Urshan quotes, Gibson wrote, "The doctrine of the Trinity is involved throughout in the language of the

---

1900), 56.

[147]Norman L. Geisler and Paul D. Feinberg, *Introduction to Philosophy: A Christian Perspective* (Grand Rapids: Baker Book House, 1980), 260, 279.

[148]Edmund J. Thomas and Eugene G. Miller, *Writers and Philosophers: A Sourcebook of Philosophical Influences on Literature* (New York: Greenwood Press, 1990), 247.

[149]J. Gilchrist Lawson, comp., *Greatest Thoughts about Jesus Christ* (New York: George H. Doran Company, 1919), 142. See also Stanford Encyclopedia of Philosophy, "Baruch Spinoza," http://plato.stanford.edu/entries/spinoza/#Oth (accessed May 22, 2010) and The New York Times Sunday Book Review, "The Heretic Jew," by Harold Bloom, June 18, 2006, http://www.nytimes.com/ 2006/06/18/books/review/18bloom.html (accessed May 22, 2010).

[150]E. N. Bell, "Questions and Answers," *The Christian Evangel* nos. 276 and 277 (February 22, 1919): 5. Quoted in Urshan, *The Almighty God,* 79.

New Testament."[151] A close examination of the text from which Urshan quotes indicates that he avoided statements that would not have supported his views. Here, for example, is Urshan's first quotation:

> The Father, Son and Holy Ghost are all in **Jesus Christ.** "I am the Way, the Truth and the Life." Father, Son and Holy Ghost are **all here, each found in Him**, so that our thoughts are not to leave Christ when they pass to the Father or to the Holy Spirit. **Christ is all**—in Him dwelleth all the fullness of the Godhead bodily.[152]

This is a brief representation of a paragraph from Gibson, but it omits Gibson's Trinitarian language. Here is Gibson:

> Father, Son, and Holy Ghost, then, are all here; but in no perplexing separation or confusion; they are all in Christ Jesus; "I am the Way, the Truth, and the Life." The Father is here; but we do not see Him in His infinite majesty, we see Him as He is revealed in the man Christ Jesus; the eternal Son is here, but we do not see Him in His eternal glory, for it is veiled in mortal flesh. The Spirit is here, but only as the stream is in the fountain—the Holy Spirit is not yet given, but the promise of the gift is even now on the Saviour's lips, the promise of the Comforter, the Life Giver, ready to be sent as soon as His work as Opener up of the Way and Revealer of the Truth is done. Yes, Father, Son, and Holy Ghost are all here, each found in Him, so that our thoughts are not to leave Christ when they pass to the Father, or to the Holy Spirit—Christ is all—"In Him dwelleth all the fullness of the Godhead bodily."[153]

The title of the chapter from which this quotation is drawn is "The Trinity as Taught by Christ." Although Gibson's words may be an acceptable description of circumincession, he is still of the opinion that there is an "eternal Son" who, together with the Father and Holy Spirit, are found in Christ. This is not typical current Oneness language.

In the final paragraph of his quotation from Gibson, Urshan again omits evidence of Gibson's Trinitarianism. Urshan quotes: "Light shining out of darkness suggests the Father; shining in our hearts suggests the Spirit; shining reflected from the face of Jesus Christ—there is the Son."[154] On the other hand, Gibson's full sentence is as follows: "Here is another of those passages where the Trinity is in the background: for light shining out of darkness, suggests the Father; shining in our hearts, suggests the Spirit; shining reflected from the face of Jesus Christ, there is the Son."[155]

---

[151]John Monro Gibson, *Christianity According to Christ* (London: James Nisbet & Company, 1889), 78.

[152]Urshan, *The Almighty God,* 79-80. Emphases are Urshan's.

[153]Gibson, *Christianity According to Christ,* 80.

[154]Urshan, *The Almighty God,* 81.

[155]Gibson, *Christianity According to Christ,* 84. As noted earlier, throughout *The Almighty God*, today's conventions for quoting from other sources are not followed. Authors are sometimes not identified, titles may be overlooked or changed, places and dates of publication are not provided, and page numbers are ignored. The quotations themselves are often amended, with no indication that something has been omitted or revised. This was not unusual for the times; it should not be taken to reflect negatively on the character or motives of the author. But the fact remains that this treatment lends itself to a less than

Urshan next returns to his own observations. He develops the idea that God has but one face into which we can look, he wrote, "If God is three separate and distinct persons, then He must have three distinct, separate faces. But the Scriptures are contrary to such misleading teaching."[156] At this point he reflects the popular misunderstanding of the doctrine of the Trinity; he views Trinitarianism as holding to three "separate and distinct persons." Although this phrase can certainly be found in popular portrayals of the doctrine such as the *Dake's Bible,* it does not represent western Trinitarianism. The word "distinct" is typically used of the three "distinct persons," but the word "separate" is not.[157]

Urshan then sets forth Jesus Christ as the only object of worship. His divergence from western Trinitarianism is evident.

> We worship God the Father when we worship His Son Jesus Christ, for the Father dwells in His dear Son and His Son is His living and Holy Temple; and it is written: "Whosoever denieth the Son, the same hath not the Father: but he that acknowledgeth the Son hath the Father also" (1 John 2:23). . . . Have we two or three separate Gods to worship? No; but three in one, the God of the Bible, who is the Father, the Son, and the Holy Ghost, who indwelleth, manifesteth Himself unto, and blesseth all his creatures in and through Jesus Christ.[158]

In Urshan's view, the one God is Father, Son, and Holy Ghost, and this one God is manifest in Jesus Christ. He wrote,

> We do not preach Jesus Christ beyond the scripture when we call Him the Heavenly Father, neither do we call Him the Father apart from His own Father, which dwelleth within Him. Yes, Christ Jesus is our Father since the Father dwelleth in Him and since He is the only perfect visible Embodiment of our Heavenly Father.[159]

---

precise representation of sources. When analyzed today, we must do the work that Urshan did not feel compelled to do.

[156] Urshan, *The Almighty God,* 81.

[157] The well known Pentecostal evangelist Jimmy Swaggart holds this view. He was correctly castigated when he wrote the following confession: "I believe that in this divine Godhead there are three separate and distinct persons—each having His own personal spirit *body,* personal *soul,* and personal *spirit* . . . . Many people conclude that the Father, the Son, and the Holy Spirit are all one and the same. Actually, they are not . . . . The word 'one' in this passage means one in *unity.* . . . You can think of God the Father, God the Son, and God the Holy Spirit as three different persons exactly as you would think of any three other people—their oneness pertaining strictly to their being one in purpose, design, and desire" (Quoted in Michael Horton, ed., *The Agony of Deceit: What Some TV Preachers are Really Teaching* [Chicago: Moody Press, 1990], 277-8.) The "distinction" between the "three persons" has been described in a variety of ways. (See Edmund J. Fortman, *The Triune God: A Historical Study of the Doctrine of the Trinity* (Grand Rapids: Baker Book House, 1972), 140, 143-4, 160, 200, 207, 209, 212, 222-3, 228.) In the early formulation of Trinitarian vocabulary by Tertullian, the "three persons of the Trinity are distinct, yet not divided (*distincti non divisi*), different yet not separate or independent of each other (*discreti non separate*)" (Alister E. McGrath, *Christian Theology: An Introduction* [Oxford: Blackwell, 1994], 252].

[158] Urshan, *The Almighty God,* 86-7.

[159] Urshan, *Doctrine of Trinity,* 33.

Not only is Jesus the "embodiment" of the Father; he is "the embodiment of the Trinity."[160] Since "incarnation" is one of the possible definitions of "embodiment," there is little reason to think that Urshan meant something radically different than incarnation by use of the word.[161]

Although trinitarianism sees Jesus as the manifestation of the Trinity, often using language identical to Urshan's, the context of this usage and the parallel use of "embodiment" indicates that by "manifestation" he meant something different.

On the other hand, Urshan's view also differs from the more common Oneness perspective that rejects a preexistent Son. In addition, the term "three in one," is not so frequently used in Oneness theology.[162] For example, David Bernard does not think that God is limited to "three [roles, titles, or manifestations], nor" does he believe that the number three has "a special significance with respect to God."[163]

For Urshan, however, to worship Jesus was to "worship God the Father, the Son, and the Spirit."[164] Jesus was the "image of the living Three-One God."[165]

The final chapter in *The Almighty God* is titled "The Fatherhood of God." Urshan continues to use the term "three-one God" and states, "We have a Father-God, and He is found in His Son, Jesus Christ our Lord."[166] His closing statement reveals his pragmatism:

> I . . . am not led to preach Jesus Christ my Heavenly Father now; although I love to quote the above Scriptures and believe them with my whole heart; but I truly believe that, when we shall see our Saviour face to face and see the fullness of the Deity in Him and through Him shining forth with eternal glory, we shall not shrink then from calling Him "our Father" as well as "Lord God Almighty" in the ages to come. In the meantime . . . let us preach the Gospel that the Apostles preached, and also believe all such Scriptures making Jesus Christ even our **divine Father,** and worship His Father and our Heavenly Father in Him, putting away theological controversy on the Godhead, using only the terms that the Apostles used concerning the Deity. I have no doubt that, in doing so, we shall please God, the Father, the Son, and the Holy Ghost, and that He will bless us all in and through Jesus Christ, our All. Amen.[167]

---

[160]Urshan, "Unification of the Body of Christ," *The Witness of God* 7, no. 62 (March 1925): 1.

[161]*The American College Dictionary*, s.v., "embodiment."

[162]Urshan was comfortable using terms like "triune," "three in one," "triunity," and even "tri-one." He would not, however, say that God was "one in three." It is interesting that E. N. Bell was also comfortable using "triunity," "three-one-ity," and "three in one." He also, however, used the term "one in three." See E. N. Bell, "Questions and Answers," *Christian Evangel* nos. 276 and 277 (February 22, 1919): 5.

[163]Bernard, *The Oneness of God,* 142.

[164]Urshan, *The Almighty God,* 88.

[165]Urshan, *The Almighty God,* 88.

[166]Urshan, *The Almighty God,* 94.

[167]Urshan, *The Almighty God,* 95. Emphasis in original.

Doctrine of Trinity and the Divinity of Jesus Christ

Urshan's 1923 book *Doctrine of Trinity and the Divinity of Jesus Christ* consists largely of articles previously printed in *The Witness of God.* Although the book is exclusively focused on issues relating to Urshan's understanding of the Godhead, it is promoted as "a timely message to the church of Jesus Christ defending the truth against modern higher criticism."[168] However, one reads in vain if hoping to discover any discussion of the issues usually associated with higher (i.e., historical) criticism.

The book is further introduced in the preface as intended "to encourage the unity of faith among God's saints everywhere and to educate them against the darts of Satan of nowadays which are attacking **the absolute deity of Jesus Christ.**"[169] In this book, Urshan does not explain the Godhead or minimize the word Trinity. Rather, he simply declares "the mystery of the Godhead in the name and person of Jesus Christ."[170]

As noted above in our treatment of *The Almighty God in The Lord Jesus Christ*, it must be kept in mind as we examine *Doctrine of the Trinity and the Divinity of Jesus Christ* that Urshan later changed his view of the usefulness of the word *trinity*. In 1953 he wrote, "So please let us stand on the Word of God on this most solemn and sublime teaching, the Mystery of God. Let us use the Bible's words and no other terminology. Let our Phraseology be Bible phrases only."[171]

Although five years have passed since he withdrew from the Assemblies of God and joined the Pentecostal Assemblies of the World, Urshan's interest in building bridges and tearing down walls between Trinitarian and Oneness Pentecostals is still evident.

> The doctrine of the Godhead has been and is today among many people of God, a theme of controversy, over which many have been offended, others have separated themselves from their brethren in Christ and have become a new sect [of] Christians and still some have gone so extremely on the question that they pronounce eternal damnation upon those who do not see like them on this teaching. (Isa. 66:5.)
>
> We do not wish to stir up more strife or theological discussion on **the Trinity** and **Christ's Divinity** . . . .[172]

---

[168] Andrew D. Urshan, *Doctrine of Trinity and the Divinity of Jesus Christ* (Cochrane, WI: Andrew D. Urshan, 1923), front cover.
[169] Urshan, *Doctrine of the Trinity,* 2. Emphasis in original.
[170] Urshan, *Doctrine of Trinity,* 3.
[171] Urshan, "The Mystery of God, or Who Is God?", 8.
[172] Urshan, *Doctrine of Trinity,* 3. Emphasis in original. Urshan's reference to Isaiah 66:5 makes it clear that his description of the division among "many people of God" is informed by his rejection by the Assemblies of God: "Hear the word of the Lord, you who tremble at His word: Your brethren who hated you, who cast you out for My name's sake, said, 'Let the Lord be glorified, that we may see your joy,' but they shall be ashamed" (Isaiah 66:5).

Because the word Trinity has been used reverently by believers for 1,600 years, Urshan wishes to give it its "proper place" even though it is not found in Scripture. This place is to use it to magnify the "absolute deity of Jesus Christ," or, in other words, to show how the Trinity is in Christ. Urshan wants to use the word Trinity as an "instructive word to magnify God's own word concerning His majestic personality, glorious attributes and His blessed manifestations."[173]

Urshan's desire to build bridges is seen again in his statement, "We . . . will stand in the middle road on this delicate subject and . . . [recognize] and [honor] individuals' honest convictions and interpretations . . . we will lovingly and boldly take all the good words and expressions of men including our phraseology to make them all serve and glorify our Creator."[174]

For Urshan, Trinity means tri-unity (i.e., threeness of one unit), not tri-units (i.e., three units): "The word Tri-unity proves, when applied to God, a divine threeness of one Divine Being. We wish therefore to use the word Trinity, when it means Tri-unity, because with this definition the scriptural teachings on the God-head question are confirmed and magnified without any contradiction whatever."[175] Urshan did not believe that anyone could deny, on the basis of Scripture, that "there is a threeness both in the Old and New Testament connected with God's One Glorious **Being** and God's one **Name.**"[176] God has a "three-fold **relative-nature.**"[177] By "relative-nature," Urshan means there are relationships between the Father, Son, and Holy Spirit.

The second chapter of *Doctrine of Trinity* consists of an extended quotation from John Monro Gibson. Once again, Gibson seems to approximate Urshan's views on the Godhead, while remaining aligned with western Trinitarianism. He uses terms like "Eternal Son" and claims that "[t]he doctrine of the Trinity is involved throughout in the language of the New Testament."[178] Urshan describes Gibson's work as a "splendid article."[179]

The third chapter of *Doctrine of Trinity* is titled "The Divinity of Jesus Christ, or the Absolute Deity of the Son of God According to the Old and New Testament." The chapter consists primarily of biblical references indicating the deity of Christ. For the most part, those who adhere to the doctrine of the Trinity would find no argument with Urshan's claims.

However, many Trinitarian and Oneness adherents might find Urshan's interpretation of Genesis 1:1 to be odd. In his view, the first word in the Bible, *berē'shiyth* ("in the beginning") is "the eternal and personal Christ, the Lord who is, and always was, the personal and mysterious embodiment of the Deity."[180] Urshan arrives at this conclusion by pointing to the self-identification of Jesus

---

[173] Urshan, *Doctrine of Trinity*, 4.
[174] Urshan, *Doctrine of Trinity*, 4.
[175] Urshan, *Doctrine of Trinity*, 4.
[176] Urshan, *Doctrine of Trinity*, 4. Emphasis in original.
[177] Urshan, *Doctrine of Trinity*, 5. Emphasis in original.
[178] Gibson, *Christianity According to Christ*, 78.
[179] Urshan, *Doctrine of Trinity*, 6.
[180] Urshan, *Doctrine of the Trinity*, 11.

as "the Beginning" (Revelation 1:8). For Urshan, this makes Genesis 1:1 mean something like, "In Jesus Christ God created the heavens and the earth."[181]

In Urshan's view, the Father, Son, and Holy Spirit are one in similarity to the way a person is body, soul, and spirit.[182] Further analogies are offered in chapter four, titled "The Blessed Trinity of God Revealed in Nature and Demonstrated or Personified in Jesus Christ Our Lord." The first analogy offered in this chapter is that of the sun's three rays with their three-fold function of light, heat, and power. Urshan appealed to this analogy by Haldeman in *The Almighty God.* However, as noted earlier, his use of the analogy is to explain western Trinitarianism, not to endorse a view like Urshan's.

Other analogies offered by Urshan include fire with its heat, light, and power; trees, with their body, root, and sap; fountains, with their fountain head, body, and invisible power causing the fountain to leap forth; and one office with three branches. Each analogy supports the notion of some kind of plurality and relationality.

In Urshan's reading of church history, it was the "western Presbytery" of the church that wrongly described God as a trinity of persons in the third century.[183] This was a "daring attempt . . . that caused such havoc in the church that [it] ought to be brought to an end."[184] Urshan does not specifically identify this "third century" event that introduced "heretical teaching," but it is probably safe to assume that he has in mind the fourth century Council of Nicaea (A.D. 325). His reference to events in the "western" world is probably meant to distinguish the theology of western Christianity from eastern Christianity which was, in Urshan's view, the "Apostolic Faith."[185]

Urshan found it consistent to use both the term "Trinity," as he defined it, and "Jesus Only" to describe his theology.[186] He recognized the inadequacy of his analogies from nature, but declared that "Jesus our glorious Lord is perfection and complete manifestation of the Triune Being in His **absolute deity** to men and angels."[187] From the perspective of western Trinitarianism and current Oneness

---

[181]The mainstream of current Oneness Pentecostalism would not agree that "Christ . . . always was, the personal and mysterious embodiment of the Deity." The "embodiment" or Incarnation began in Mary's womb. Norris speaks of Jesus' "alleged" preexistence and explains verses that seem to "ascribe some sort of preexistence to Jesus Christ" as cases of God "creatively speak[ing] forth redemption, words that would find their fulfillment in the man Christ Jesus" (Norris, *I Am*, 362, 63). In Bernard's words, "[W]e can say the Spirit of Jesus pre-existed the Incarnation, but we cannot say the Son pre-existed the Incarnation in any substantial sense" (Bernard, *The Oneness of God*, 182-3).

[182]Urshan, *Doctrine of Trinity*, 16.

[183]Urshan understood the word "person," from the Latin *persona,* to imply personality, so the doctrine of the Trinity with its three persons indicated to him three personalities.

[184]Urshan, *Doctrine of Trinity*, 24-25.

[185]Urshan, *The Life Story,* 5th ed., 14-16. If Urshan had Nicaea in mind, he was mistaken to identify it with the western presbytery, for Nicaea and all of the ecumenical councils were eastern councils.

[186]Urshan, *Doctrine of Trinity*, 25.

[187]Urshan, *Doctrine of Trinity*, 26. Emphasis in original.

theology, to juxtapose "Trinity" and "Jesus only" as synonymous terms is jarring. However, for Urshan this was possible because of his redefinition of "Trinity" and his view that Jesus was not only the manifestation of God the Son but of the Father, Son, and Holy Spirit.

Urshan then offers analogies of both the "threeness" and "oneness" of God from Scripture.[188] The first is Noah's ark. The three stories of the ark were distinct but not "entirely separated." Instead, they were connected by internal doorways. The ark was one unit, "not three separate and distinct units." Urshan was convinced that "Noah's Ark could illustrate nothing other than the triune God manifested in Jesus."[189] By making this analogy, Urshan was responding to the claim that the ark typified "three separate and distinct persons." Instead, he saw in it the symbolism of "the unity of God's threefold person."[190]

Urshan also saw symbolism in the Ark of the Covenant. It was one receptacle, but it contained three items: the tables of the law, the pot of manna, and Aaron's rod. This foreshadowed the way in which the Word would dwell in Christ and his fulfillment of the symbolism of the manna from heaven. The rod represented the power of his resurrection.

Additional symbolism was seen "in the tabernacle in the wilderness and the temple of Solomon, both types of the Triune God in Jesus Christ."[191] The three "distinct and separate" divisions were "component parts of the whole." The veil provided the only division, signifying that people are separated from God by sin. The removal of this veil by Christ's death "proved Him to be the All of God for man and the All of Men for God."[192]

Urshan's passion was to know Christ better. In this, Paul was his example, who "confessed that he knew not perfectly the Christ, His Lord . . . and he was running forward counting all things but loss for this deeper knowledge of Jesus Christ."[193]

> Some of our Trinitarian friends think that the question of the absolute Deity of Jesus is exhausted when He is proved to be the eternal Son of God. It may be so to those who have no further revelation of Christ's Deity, but the great apostle knew Him better and called Him the Son of God and yet said there was much more to say of Him, God, the Son.[194]

Subsequent developments in Oneness theology would find these observations to be problematic. First, Urshan does not seem to object to the use of the term "eternal Son of God," although he sees it as a limited revelation of Christ's deity.[195] Bernard's comments on this term represent a current Oneness perspective:

---

[188]Urshan calls these analogies "illustrations."
[189]Urshan, *Doctrine of Trinity*, 26.
[190]Urshan, *Doctrine of Trinity*, 27.
[191]Urshan, *Doctrine of Trinity*, 27.
[192]Urshan, *Doctrine of Trinity*, 27.
[193]Urshan, *Doctrine of Trinity*, 28-29.
[194]Urshan, *Doctrine of Trinity*, 29.
[195]Other evidence that Urshan did not reject the phrase "eternal Son" includes his endorsement of Gibson's *Christianity According to Christ*. See also Urshan, *The Almighty*

> [M]any people use the phrase "eternal Son." Is this . . . correct? No. The Bible never uses it and it expresses a concept contradicted by Scripture. The word *begotten* . . . indicates a definite point in time—the point at which conception takes place. By definition, the begetter (father) always must come before the begotten (offspring). . . .
>
> . . . Since "Son of God" refers to humanity or deity as manifest in humanity, the idea of an eternal Son is incomprehensible. The Son of God had a beginning.[196]

The second term not used in today's Oneness theology is "God the Son." As explained by Bernard, "the term 'God the Son' is inappropriate because it equates the Son with deity alone, and therefore it is unscriptural."[197]

Chapter five of *Doctrine of Trinity and the Divinity of Jesus Christ* consists of answers to a series of questions.[198] The first question is "What is the use of writing and commenting on the question of the Godhead, since it is so obscure and mysterious?"[199] In response, Urshan concurred that "the God-head question is the mystery of mysteries" and states that he has "not attempted to explain the 'Unknown God' . . . but [has] declared Him . . . in and through Jesus Christ, who **is the embodiment** and **solution** of all unknown mysteries and the divine knowledge and wisdom."[200]

The second question concerns the use of plural pronouns in Genesis 1:26-27, 3:22-24, 11:5-8, and Isaiah 6:8. Urshan explains these in terms of angelic coope-ration with God.[201] Then, in an evident appeal to his theological roots in the Church of the East, Urshan offered this explanation:

> It is true indeed that the Father, Son and Holy Ghost created all things including man, but that does not necessarily make our one God three distinct and separate divine persons or beings. God has put in man, whom He created in His own image, three distinct but inseparable attributes to represent or to foreshadow His own mysterious TRI-ONE Being, namely **Mind, Wisdom, and Power.** Mind begets wisdom, and when wisdom is applied it produces powerful accomplishments, but the fact should never be forgotten that though mind produces wisdom, yet wisdom is still in the mind, and so with the power; though it proceeds from mind and wisdom accomplishing what mind desires and what wisdom supplies, yet that power still remains in mind and wisdom, while mind and wisdom are actually working in and through that power. So it is with **Our Wonderful GOD,** the supreme mind (the Father) begot the word (the Son) and the word produced the power (the Holy Spirit) and created all things visible and invisible. So the Father, the Son and the Holy Ghost, the **One Incomprehensible Spiritual Being** will remain a mystery, yet to

---

God, 86-87.

[196]Bernard, *The Oneness of God*, 104.

[197]Bernard, *The Oneness of God*, 99.

[198]The first four chapters of this book first appeared in issues of *The Witness of God* published in 1923. I have not located any previous appearance of the material in chapter five.

[199]Urshan, *Doctrine of Trinity*, 30.

[200]Urshan, *Doctrine of Trinity*, 30.

[201]Urshan, *Doctrine of Trinity*, 31.

be comprehended in all eternity, in and through the Person of Jesus Christ, who is the wisdom of God or tangibleness of the invisible Supreme mind and power.[202]

Urshan held this view throughout his life. First published in 1923, he included it intact in the final version of his autobiography, published in 1967, the year of his death.[203]

As noted earlier, Urshan identified "persons" with "beings." This is why he consistently speaks of Trinitarianism as a belief that God is three "separate and distinct" persons.[204] The analogy of mind, wisdom, and power – like Urshan's other analogies – is non-personal, underscoring plurality and relationality without implying personality. His analogical use of mind, wisdom, and power is similar to Augustine's memory, understanding, and will. It is even more similar to Augustine's earlier image of the Trinity as mind, knowledge, and love.[205]

Urshan's relational terms are not intended only to indicate relationality among the various components of the analogy, but also to show the relationship between the components of the analogy and human beings. For example:

> There is a threefold relationship of God to humanity manifested through the person of Jesus Christ. Father, Son and Holy Spirit are the three fold relationship, and not three persons. I am a "father" to my daughter, "son" to my mother, and "husband" to my wife. You would not call me my wife's "son," or my daughter's "husband," or my mother's "father." I am spoken of according to the relationship I bear to the one spoken of. So it is with the relative standing of Christ. It all depends upon from what point of view we speak of Him.[206]

The third question reads, "I think you are exalting Jesus more highly than the Bible does when you call Him the FATHER. Why not call Him the Eternal Son of God only?"[207] Urshan responds:

> We do not preach Jesus Christ beyond the Scriptures when we call Him the Heavenly Father, neither do we call Him the Father apart from His own Father which dwelleth within Him. Yes, Christ Jesus is our Father since the Father dwelleth in Him and since He [is] the only perfect visible embodiment of our Heavenly Father.[208]

---

[202]Urshan, *Doctrine of Trinity*, 32. Emphasis in original.

[203]Urshan, *The Life Story*, 5th ed., 16.

[204]Ushan uses the word "person" only in the context of the Incarnation. There is but one divine "person" in whom the Father, Son, and Holy Spirit are manifest, and this "person" also has a human personality that is distinct from all other humans. As noted earlier, Urshan's view of a "preexistent Son" is not accepted in current Oneness theology.

[205]*Augustine: Later Works*, trans. John Burnaby (Philadelphia: Westminster Press, 1955), 25. His analogical use of mind, wisdom, and power is similar to Augustine's memory, understanding, and will. It is even more similar to Augustine's earlier image of the Trinity as mind, knowledge, and love.

[206]Urshan, *Doctrine of Trinity*, 35.

[207]Urshan, *Doctrine of Trinity*, 33.

[208]Urshan, *Doctrine of Trinity*, 33.

In 1919 Urshan wrote, "I, for one, am not led to preach Jesus Christ my Heavenly Father now."[209] His practice changed during the four years that intervened between the publication of *The Almighty God in the Lord Jesus Christ* and *Doctrine of the Trinity and the Divinity of Jesus Christ.* Although he may not have used the term, his description of the Father as dwelling within Jesus Christ and Jesus as the embodiment of the Father as well as the manifestation of the "T-H-R-E-E—O-N-E God" would fit within the idea of perichoresis. However, since he understands "manifest" and "embodied" as synonyms for "incarnate," this is not the case.

The fourth question, apparently written by someone who embraced a form of Oneness theology, suggested that if God were three persons, "we must . . . expect to see three separate distinct divine faces in heaven."[210] Urshan's response focuses on the singularity of the word "face" in Scripture when used of God. But he also included an account of a vision experienced by Sadhu Sundar Singh, an Indian Christian mystic (1889-1929). Since Urshan writes that "[t]his vision of this holy man of God is in perfect harmony with the Scriptures," we will reproduce the entire vision as reported by Urshan:

> At one time I was a good deal perplexed about the doctrine of the trinity. I had thought of three separate persons sitting as it were on three thrones, but it was all made plain to me in a vision. I entered into an ecstasy in the third heaven. I was told that it was the same to which St. Paul was caught up. And there I saw Christ in a glorious body sitting on a throne. Whenever I go there it is the same. Christ is always in the center, a figure ineffable and indescribable. His face shining like the sun, but in no way dazzling, and so sweet that without any difficulty I can gaze at it—always smiling a loving, glorious smile. I felt, when first I saw Him, as if there were some old forgotten connection between us, and as though He had said, but not in words, "I am He, through whom you were created." I felt something the same, only far more intensely, as I felt when I met my father again after an interval of many years. My old love came back to me: I knew I had been his before.
>
> The first time I entered Heaven I looked around and asked, "But where is God?" And they told me, "God is not to be seen here any more than on earth, for God is Infinite. But there is Christ. He is God. He is the Image of the Invisible God, and it is only in Him that we can see God, in Heaven as on Earth." And streaming out from Christ I saw, as it were, waves shining and peace-giving, and going through and among the Saints and Angels, and everywhere bringing refreshment, just as in hot weather water refreshes trees. And this I understood to be the Holy Spirit.[211]

Urshan's presentation of this story and the same story told by B. H. Streeter, a fellow of Queen's College, Oxford, reveals one significant difference. In Streeter, Sadhu Sundar Singh saw Christ sitting on a throne in "a glorious spiritual body."[212] In Urshan's account, Singh saw Christ sitting on a throne in "a glorious body." Frank Bartleman's *The Deity of Christ*, published in 1926 also omits "spiritual"

---

[209] Urshan, *The Almighty God,* 95.
[210] Urshan, *Doctrine of Trinity,* 34.
[211] Urshan, *Doctrine of Trinity,* 34-35.
[212] B. H. Streeter, *The Message of Sadhu Sundar Singh: A Study in Mysticism on Practical Religion* (New York: The Macmillan Company, 1922), 44.

in his account of the vision.²¹³ By "spiritual," Singh could have meant "spirit," thereby denying the bodily resurrection of Christ. By omitting the word, Urshan (and Bartleman) undoubtedly sought to remove that ambiguity. Urshan continued his objection to finding three faces of God in heaven by stating:

> There is a threefold relationship of God to humanity manifested through the person of Jesus Christ. Father, Son, and Holy Spirit are the three fold relationship, and not three persons. I am a "father" to my daughter, "son" to my mother, and "husband" to my wife. You would not call me my wife's "son," or my daughter's "husband," or my mother's "father." I am spoken of according to the relationship I bear to the one spoken of. So it is with the relative standing of Christ. It all depends upon from what point of view we speak of Him.²¹⁴

This analogy may seem to push toward modalism, however, modalism sees the various "modes" (i.e., Father, Son, and Holy Spirit) as successive.²¹⁵ In Urshan's view, the "modes" were simultaneous. The fifth question came from a Jewish rabbi who questioned the idea that Jesus is God in view of Jesus' prayers. Urshan's answer was that "Jesus prayed in order to teach us to follow in His steps." As our example, "and as a son of man He prayed to the Spirit . . . which was in heaven as well as in Himself."²¹⁶

The sixth question is drawn from I Corinthians 11:3. In the questioner's view, the phrase "the head of Christ is God" indicates that "God the Father was higher than Jesus Christ." The questioner also asked "about the three distinct Persons manifested at Christ's baptism."²¹⁷ Urshan responded, "[s]ince the Father is the head of His Son then the Son must be the body of the Father."²¹⁸ Concerning the baptism of Jesus, "[t]hese manifestations were not in the mind of God to teach us a God of three separate persons (beings), but three manifestations of one Spiritual Being who was in Heaven and on earth and yet between Heaven and earth . . . ."²¹⁹ Further, "the three manifestations at the baptism of Christ were simply a wonderful divine drama . . . ."²²⁰

For the seventh question, an explanation was requested for John 17:11, 21-23, 26. Urshan answered, "I can see clearly the distinct identity of the Son from that of the Father, and that does not necessarily make the Son a separate being or person from that of the Father, except as to the matter of office or manifestation in the flesh."²²¹ This statement does not seem to be in harmony with Urshan's declaration elsewhere that the entire "T-H-R-E-E—O-N-E God" is manifest or embodied in Jesus Christ. The statement "except as to the matter of . . . manifestation in the

---

²¹³Frank Bartleman, *The Deity of Christ*—Chapter II, http://frankbartleman-deity.blogspot.com/2010/01/chapter-ii_01.html (accessed May 2, 2010).
²¹⁴Urshan, *Doctrine of Trinity*, 35.
²¹⁵See C. A. Blaising, "Monarchianism," *Evangelical Dictionary of Theology*, 727.
²¹⁶Urshan, *Doctrine of Trinity*, 38.
²¹⁷Urshan, *Doctrine of Trinity*, 38.
²¹⁸Urshan, *Doctrine of Trinity*, 38.
²¹⁹Urshan, *Doctrine of Trinity*, 39.
²²⁰Urshan, *Doctrine of Trinity*, 39.
²²¹Urshan, *Doctrine of Trinity*, 41.

flesh" seems to limit the Incarnation to the Son and in that sense make "the Son a separate being or person from that of the Father." This is the only time in his writings that the incarnate Christ is said to be "a separate being or person from that of the Father." Whatever he may have had in mind, as expressed here, is inconsistent with his assertions elsewhere.

Urshan explained Jesus' prayer for believers to be one as Jesus praying "that they all may receive the Spirit of life of which the Father and Son are one. That believers, though many individuals, [would] yet be one in Christ and in spirituality, as Son and Father are one spirit-being."[222] He then defined oneness as follows:

> The oneness of God is not . . . the unity in will, in fellowship and in purpose only, which is true as to the triune manifestation, but divine oneness is beyond this. Divine oneness is one in Being, one in spiritual form, and one in substance, therefore one in personality, manifested in and through Christ. That is why Jesus said, "He that seeth me, seeth the Father," also in Heaven we shall see His face, not **their** faces.[223]

Urshan's engagement with mystery surfaces again: "[T]he Father and Son are one God and one spiritual being with three mysterious and inseparable identities."[224]

Question eight is multifaceted. First, the questioner asked, "Is it wrong to preach and sing, 'God in three persons, blessed trinity'?"[225] Urshan answered, "Yes, for there is no such radical conclusion on the God-head written in the Bible." Next, the questioner asked, "But why do you baptize into the name of Jesus Christ and not into the name of the Father, Son, and the Holy Ghost?"[226] Urshan's answer: "When we baptize into the name of Jesus Christ, we baptize into the name of the Father, Son, and the Holy Ghost."[227] In Urshan's view, Jesus "is the dispensational name of the Deity,"[228] just as Elohim was God's name during the dispensation of promise and Jehovah was God's name during the dispensation of law. So when Urshan baptized believers, he did not say that "Jesus is the Father, Son, and Holy Ghost" but that "Jesus is the **name of God** the Father, the Son and the Holy Spirit."[229]

There may be a fine line to draw here, but it seems that Urshan is suggesting a personification of the name. In other words, Jesus is not the Father, Son, and Holy Spirit, but Jesus is the *name* of the Father, Son, and Holy Spirit. That this may be the case is suggested by Urshan's use of the words of Thomas Ken to conclude his answers to question eight:

> Praise God from whom all blessings flow

---

[222]Urshan, *Doctrine of Trinity*, 41.
[223]Urshan, *Doctrine of Trinity*, 42. Emphasis in original.
[224]Urshan, *Doctrine of Trinity*, 42.
[225]Urshan, *Doctrine of Trinity*, 43.
[226]Urshan, *Doctrine of Trinity*, 43.
[227]Urshan, *Doctrine of Trinity*, 43.
[228]Urshan, *Doctrine of Trinity*, 43.
[229]Urshan, *Doctrine of Trinity*, 43.

Praise Him all creatures here below

Praise Him above, ye heavenly host

Praise Father, Son, and Holy Ghost

Amen

Questions ten and eleven are answered by G. T. Haywood, so will not be analyzed here. Question twelve asks for an explanation of John 1:1 and John 17:5. Urshan responds with a series of conundrums: Jesus is both the door of the sheepfold and the food for the sheep; He is the Lamb of God, but also God and the shepherd; He is at the right hand of God, but makes intercession before God, and the fullness of the Godhead is in Him; He is the right arm of God, the Son of God, the throne of God, the slain Lamb in the midst of the throne, and the Lion from the tribe of Judah.

After continuing further in this vein, Urshan states,

> We cannot explain these things fully though we may attempt to. The solution of the problem is that since God is almighty and . . . omnipresent, He can be a man on the earth and remain God in the high heavens; He has the right to call Himself the Father and the Son and the Holy Spirit and yet at the same time [to] be **One Being and One God**, and it is not our business to try to fully explain these wonderful, yet mysterious things that are hidden in the wisdom of God.[230]

The Witness of God

The essence of Urshan's theology can be seen in articles that he excerpted from *The Witness of God* and reprinted in book form. There are, however, statements in *The Witness of God* that are not precisely reproduced elsewhere that help illuminate his perspective. For example, after a discussion of the singularity of the word "name" in Matthew 28:19, Urshan concluded:

The Lord—stands for the Father.

Jesus—stands for the Son.

Christ—stands for the Holy Spirit.

Our God's Divine Threeness in One Person even

---

[230] Urshan, *Doctrine of Trinity,* 46. Emphasis in original. The book *Doctrine of Trinity and the Divinity of Jesus Christ* continues beyond the number of pages in the copy in my possession. I have not located an entire copy, so I am not sure how far the book runs beyond page 48. But Urshan's tendency to reprint articles from *The Witness of God* in book form assures us that we have access to the full scope of his theology.

In		Jesus (1)
		Christ (2)
		The Lord (3)

This was indeed a wonderful revelation to me of the Trinity in Christ. . . .

This blessed revelation of Christ's Absolute Deity has been a crowning truth of all other portions of truth the Lord has so graciously granted me, though unworthy I am. Naturally, seeing the great value of the baptism invested in faith in the One Name of the triune God, made very clear to me John 3:1-6, namely—the water birth was the baptism of water and the Spirit birth was the baptism of the Holy Spirit.[231]

In 1924, Urshan published an article titled "The Fundamentals of Faith." The first of these articles is titled "The One God":

The one Lord God of the Old Testament, whose primeval names are Elohim, El-shaddai, El-Elyon, El-Olam, Jehovah and Adonai, **IS the Lord Jesus Christ.** And that there are not three Gods, but one invisible, unapproachable, in-comparable and incomprehensible Supreme Being, who can be seen and touched only in the Person of Jesus Christ the Son, who alone is the visible embodiment of the Father, the Son, and the Holy Spirit.[232]

The view that the Father, Son, and Holy Spirit are Incarnate in Jesus Christ is at odds with Oneness theology as it has developed since Urshan's days. In today's Oneness theology, the Son did not preexist the Incarnation as the Son. Some of today's Oneness thinkers would, however, agree that Jesus, the Son of God, is the Incarnation of the Father, although some would nuance this idea further by saying that Jesus is Yahweh Incarnate.[233] In 1925 Urshan was still describing Jesus as "the embodiment of the Trinity."[234]

It may be thought that Urshan's infrequent use of the word "incarnate" in favor of the terms "manifest," "indwelling," and "embodiment" means that his view of the manifestation of the "T-H-R-E-E—O-N-E" in Jesus Christ can be

---

[231]Urshan, "The Story of My Life—10th Chapter—Cont.," *The Witness of God* 4, no. 45 (September 1923): 4.

[232]Urshan, "The Fundamentals of Faith," *The Witness of God* 6, no. 52 (May 1924): 1.

[233]See David K. Bernard, *The Glory of God in the Face of Jesus Christ: Deification of Jesus in Early Christian Discourse* (Blandford Forum, England: Deo Publishing, 2016), 87-89; Bernard, *The Oneness of God*, 66-70. In one recent scholarly contribution to Oneness theology as of this writing, David Norris does not say that the Father is Incarnate in the Son. He views this language as anachronistic, since in order to be a father, one must have progeny. Instead, Norris prefers to say that the Son is Yahweh Incarnate. He acknowledges, of course, that Yahweh is the Father. See Norris, *I AM*, 77. This description of Norris' view is drawn from *I AM* and from a personal telephone conversation on May 4, 2010.

[234]Urshan, "Unification of the Body of Christ," *The Witness of God* 7, no. 62 (March 1925): 1.

explained in terms of perichoresis rather than incarnation. But Urshan does use the word "incarnate" in a way that suggests something beyond perichoresis. The use of "incarnate" twice in the Introduction to *The Almighty God in the Lord Jesus Christ* is significant and serves to shape the conversation from that point, making the use of various terms more stylistically than theologically significant.

> The God who created the old world, things visible and invisible, by His WORD, now comes down in His incarnate WORD, to create a new generation, making manifest "the mystery hid for ages," even **"the great mystery of godliness."** God the Father, by the power of His Spirit, comes with and in His Son, into the world, to give everlasting life unto all them that should believe on His NAME; the Name which is above every name, in heaven, in the earth, and under the earth, the lofty Name of the Father given to His Son, the Name at which every knee shall bow and which every tongue shall confess, JESUS, the Lord.[235]
>
> The "I AM" Name of God . . . applies to His then present revelation and active purpose revealed to His people Israel . . . . But the Lord gave Moses and Israel at the same time another great promise for another great deliverance, and that deliverance was to take place in the future. This promise is included also in His blessed revealed Name, viz., "THAT I AM." ("I AM THAT I AM" means a present and future God.)
>
> The word "THAT" points to His other or future manifestation, when he should appear again . . . as David's Son . . . through the Seed of the woman, as **"God manifest in the flesh,"** becoming IMMANUEL . . . **"God with us."**[236]

In Urshan's view, the name Yahweh applied to God as he was revealed to Israel, but in a future manifestation Yahweh would be revealed as "God manifest in the flesh." He celebrates this manifestation poetically with the language of incarnation:

> O, Hark the voice of love and grace,
>
> Sounding in the names of God,
>
> Down the blessed God incarnate
>
> Comes to shed for men His blood.
>
> Hallelujah! It is finished,
>
> Christ has triumphed by His Name "JAH!"[237]

---

[235]Urshan, *The Almighty God,* 6-7. Emphasis in original.
[236]Urshan, *The Almighty God,* 6. Emphasis in original.
[237]Urshan, *The Almighty God,* 7.

Over thirty years later, concluding an article emphasizing the mysteriousness of God, Urshan wrote, "Let us cleave to Him who is the Son, yet the Mighty God and the Everlasting Father, and stop right there and dare not go any further."[238]

As Oneness theology has developed to this point, the acknowledgement of mystery is usually limited to the Incarnation.[239] Urshan, however, never abandoned his belief that God is mysterious. In 1953 he wrote that there is "one blessed mysterious God."

> Who was or is He? No one knows, not even the angels. . . . the mysterious One, Elohim the creator of all. He is incomprehensible and unknown—One and far beyond any human imagination or words. . . .
>
> No one knows who God's Son really is, no, not even the angels. The Son alone knows who God the Father is, and the Father alone knows who the Son is just as Matt. 11:27 declares. Even Paul did not know the Son of God as he desired to about this. . . . The only begotten of the Father came to us in the flesh, and from then on, and for the first time from all the beginn[ing] God was and is to be more fully and really known, as to His perfect likeness, His divine nature and His mysterious personality. . . .
>
> The Lord Jesus Christ, as to His mysterious relationship, and as Logos the word of God, he is the only begotten Son of God, how long, where, and how, no one knows. . . .
>
> Two or three in offices, or manifestations of Himself, known as the Father, the Son, and the Holy Ghost.
>
> He is three distinct, but not separate in His divine being and personality, hence wherever one part of His being is the other two are there also. Wherever one is at work, the other two are at work at the same place and a[t] precisely the same time. . . .
>
> Here we see the Father or Elohim at work creating all things, but He is working in His Word by His Spirit; not as three Gods or divine spirits, but as One divine mystery, known as the Father, the Son, and the Holy Spirit.[240]

This description, with its language of mystery, uncertainty, and "threeness," is substantially at odds with what Oneness theology became as it followed other trajectories that focused more on Oneness in opposition to plurality and on what has been revealed in contrast to what is yet unknown.

Urshan's view of the preexistence of Christ is also at odds with that which is more commonly held in today's Oneness theology.

> [B]efore Adam and his family were created . . . even before the foundation of the

---

[238]Andrew D. Urshan, "The Mystery of God, or Who is God?" *The Witness of God* (December 1953): 8.

[239]See Bernard, *The Oneness of God*, 65.

[240]Urshan, "The Mystery of God, or Who is God?," *The Witness of God* (December 1953): 4-5.

world, there was one who is, was, and ever will be, "Jesus," or the Lord and Savior. This being so, a spirit that confesseth not that Jesus Christ came in the flesh is not of God. The Bible shows plainly that there was a Christ Jesus in glory long before He actually came in a human form.[241]

Since "Christ" is a messianic designation and the Messiah was given the name "Jesus" in conjunction with the Incarnation, today's Oneness theologians would not say "there was a Christ Jesus in glory" before the Incarnation. From the Oneness perspective, to speak of Christ Jesus or of Jesus Christ is to speak of God as he is manifest in human existence. In Bernard's view, to speak of the preexistence of Jesus is to acknowledge "that God was the author of the Incarnation, the source from which He [Jesus] as a human being came."[242] According to Norris, Scriptures that seem to speak of the pre-Incarnate existence of the Son "demonstrate how God not only spoke the cosmos into existence; He also creatively spoke forth redemption, words that would find their fulfillment in the man Christ Jesus. It is only in this way, and precisely in this way, that Jesus Christ may be said to 'preexist.'"[243]

Perhaps we can understand Urshan's claim that "there was a Christ Jesus in glory long before He actually came in human form" in terms of his idea of dispensational names of God. Since "Lord Jesus Christ" was the name of the "T-H-R-E-E—O-N-E God" for this dispensation, it could be said that Christ existed before the Incarnation though not yet with this dispensational name. In other words, the God we now know as the Lord Jesus Christ existed before the foundation of the world.

The Church of the East

We pointed out earlier that in order to assess the usefulness of Urshan's explanation of the theology and Christology of the Church of the East for his claim that these ancient expressions informed his personal theology and Christology, it would be necessary to examine the accuracy of his understanding of the vocabulary used by that tradition. We also said that it would be important to examine Urshan's understanding of the meaning of the word "person" as it relates to the use of the word in western Trinitarianism. We now turn to address these issues.

In simple terms, the Church of the East rejected Chalcedonian Christology because of the conflict between the Greek *hypostasis* and the Syriac *qnoma,* used to represent *hypostasis*. The Church of the East could not accept the Chalcedonian assertion that Christ was one person and one *hypostasis* with two natures. Since *qnoma* represented both *hypostasis* and nature (*physis*), the Chalcedonian Definition's statement that Christ had one *hypostasis* seemed to mean that he had only one *qnoma* or nature.

---

[241]Urshan, "Jesus the Name," *The Witness of God* (September 1966): 1.

[242]David K. Bernard, *The Oneness View of Jesus Christ* (Hazelwood, MO: Word Aflame Press, 1994), 76.

[243]Norris, *I AM,* 63.

In order to examine Urshan's understanding of the theology and Christology of the Church of the East in an orderly fashion, we will look closely at his explanation.

> They believed in the God-head being a triunity of three Kenoomas and never a trinity of three separate distinct persons.[244]

The first problem we see here is the use of the term "separate distinct persons." This is not the language of western Trinitarianism, regardless of creedal affinities. While western Trinitarianism does speak of "distinct persons," it does not speak of "separate persons." From the perspective of Oneness theology, this may seem almost irrelevant, but in order to understand a theological position accurately, precision is necessary. At this point in Urshan's description of the theology of the Church of the East, the introduction of a term used in an aberrant expression of Trinitarianism clouds the issue. Of course the Church of the East did not confess three "separate distinct persons" in the Godhead; neither did western Christianity. Without attempting here to parse the intended meaning of "distinct" as it relates to the Trinitarian view of three persons, it is evident that the word "separate" strengthens and radicalizes the meaning of "distinct" beyond what is intended in Trinitarian theology.[245]

Urshan understood "person" in the modern sense of a self-conscious individual rather than in the sense of the Greek *hypostasis, prosōpon,* or the Latin *persona* or *subsistentia.* This is indicated by Urshan's description of the western

---

[244] Urshan, *The Life Story,* 5th ed., 16.

[245] A search of Questia, an online research library offering more than 70,000 full text books and two million journal articles reveals the paucity of the term "separate and distinct" in connection with theology. Only five books contain the phrase "separate and distinct persons." Three of these five contain the term in a discussion of the same document, the "Treaty Between Spain and Portugal Concluded at Tordesillas, June 7, 1494" (W. Keith Kavenagh, ed., *Foundations of Colonial America: A Documentary History,* vol. 3 [New York: Chelsea House, 1973], 1684; N. Andrew and N. Cleven, *Readings in Hispanic American History* [Boston: Ginn, 1927], 72; Frances Gardiner Davenport, ed., *European Treaties Bearing on the History of the United States and Its Dependencies* [Washington, DC: Carnegie Institution of Washington, 1917], 94. One of the books uses the term in a discussion of William Penn's rejection of Trinitarianism (William I. Hull, *William Penn: A Topical Biography* [London: Oxford University Press, 1937], 168. The last of the five uses the term in connection with a quote from Joseph Smith, the founder of Mormonism (Robert L. Millet, *Joseph Smith: Selected Sermons and Writings* [New York: Paulist Press, 1989], 125, n. 5). No journal article includes the term "separate and distinct." On the other hand, 507 books and seventy journal articles include the term "distinct persons." Not all of these are used in a theological context, but many are. Even the phrase "distinct persons" does not appear in Philip Schaff, *The Creeds of Christendom with a History and Critical Notes,* vol. 2, The Greek and Latin Creeds, with Translations (New York: Harper & Brothers, Franklin Square 1919). It is also interesting that David K. Bernard, prolific late twentieth and early twenty-first century Oneness author, uses the phrase "separate and distinct persons" only twice in his book *The Oneness of God.* Once is when presenting quotes from Finis Dake, Jimmy Swaggart, and Carl Brumback to demonstrate what Bernard calls "outright tritheism"; the other is in a glossary definition of Ditheism (David K. Bernard, *The Oneness of God* [Hazelwood, MO: Word Aflame Press, 1983], 258-9, 314.

Trinitarian view as three "separate and distinct persons" and by the equating of "person" with "being."[246] His rejection of the notion of three "separate and distinct persons" was apparently in response to this fundamental misconception that he found among some of his fellow Pentecostals. Although the phrase "separate and distinct" is not found in the Articles of Faith of the Assemblies of God which were adopted in response to the "New Issue," the phrase was apparently used by some Trinitarian Pentecostals, including those in the Assemblies of God during the second and third decades of the twentieth century. For example, Finis Jennings Dake (1902-87), who attended Central Bible Institute in the mid 1920s and who was ordained by the Assemblies of God in 1927, used the phrase in his reference Bible and his book *God's Plan for Man*.[247] Although Dake's publishing career began later than Urshan's, it would be reasonable to assume that Dake's theology, including the terms he used to describe it, reflected his earlier training in the Assemblies of God and his continued association with Pentecostals not only in the Assemblies of God but also in the Church of God (Cleveland, TN) and among those not affiliated with any organization.

Urshan did embrace the idea that "the Father and Son are one God and one spiritual Being with three mysterious and inseparable identities."[248] This may have been implied for him by the Syriac *qnoma*.[249]

The second problem in this sentence is that the use of the word "triunity" and the phrase "never a trinity" suggests that the Church of the East was non-Trinitarian. This is not accurate. The cause for the separation of the Church of the East from the Trinitarian churches that confessed the historic creeds was not its doctrine of the Godhead but its Christology. Although the Church of the East declared its independence at the synod of 424, this "did not imply a schism, since the creed of Nicea provided a common foundation with the Western patriarchates."[250] The theological rift between the Church of the East and western Christianity had its roots not in 325 but in 451 with the Christology of the Council of Chalcedon.[251] Mar Odisho (d. 1318), identified by Baumer as "the last outstanding theologian of the Church," "was convinced that the differences and disputes among the three great Christian communities of his time [the Church of the East, the Syrian Orthodox Church, and the Roman Catholic Church] were founded only on words and terms, not in the religious ideas they expressed."[252]

The evidence, both ancient and modern, indicates that it is an error to understand the Church of the East as non-Trinitarian. The use of *qnoma* in the Christol-

---

[246] Urshan, *The Almighty God*, 77.

[247] Finis Dake, *Dake's Annotated Reference Bible*, NT (Lawrenceville, GA: Dake's Bible Sales, 1963), 280; Leon Bible, "Theological Summary of the Writings of 'Finis Jennings Dake,'" 1998, www.dakebible.com/WebPages/dake-theology.htm (accessed November 20, 2010); P. H. Alexander, "Finis Jennings Dake," in *NIDPCM*, 569.

[248] Urshan, *Doctrine of Trinity*, 42.

[249] Urshan transliterates *qnoma* as "Kenooma."

[250] Baumer, *Church of the East*, 81.

[251] Baumer, *Church of the East*, 82.

[252] Baumer, *Church of the East*, 280.

ogy of the Church of the East must not be confused with the use of the word in the theology of the church. When used of the three *qnomas* in the Godhead, the word meant something different than when used of the two *qnomas* in Christ.

> ... It is always essential to realize that, in the context of Christology (as opposed to the situation in Trinitarian theology), there is a clear and important difference between the understanding in the Church of the East of the term *qnoma* (i.e. individuated, but not personalized nature) and that of other Syriac Churches where *qnoma* is regularly understood as the equivalent of *hypostasis* in the sense of person.
>
> Thus the following explanation of the term of *Qnoma* has been presented by the Assyrian, Chaldean and Syro-Malabar delegations of the Church of the East:
>
> In Christology, as expressed in the synodical and liturgical sources of the Church of the East, the term *qnoma* does not mean *hypostasis* as understood in Alexandrine Tradition, but instead, individuated nature. Accordingly, the human nature which the Holy Spirit fashioned and the Logos assumed and united to Himself without any separation, was personalized in the Person of the Son of God. When we speak of the two natures and their *qnome*, we understand this very much in the same sense as two natures and their particular properties (*dilayatha*).
>
> It is important to note that the term *qnoma* is used in a different way in Trinitarian theology."[253]

Contrary to Urshan's understanding of *qnoma* in the Trinitarian theology of the Church of the East, the use of the word did not mean that the Church of the East denied that there were three "persons" in the Godhead.

> "Ke-noo-ma" to them was an image, attribute, or a manifestation of God.[254]

I have found no evidence that the Church of the East understood *qnoma* as an image or attribute. The closest that I have found to indicate that the Church of the East understood *qnoma* to mean "manifestation" is Brock's comment that "[w]hen the Church of the East uses *qnoma* in connection with 'nature' it usually speaks of 'the two natures and their *qnomas*", where *qnoma* means something like 'individual manifestation'"[255] and Taylor's observation that "[f]or the Syriac theologians of Persia *hupostasis/qnoma* is the necessary individual manifestation of nature (*physis/kyana*), which is itself considered to be generic (e.g. humanity, divinity – closely associated in this Christology with Greek *ousia*, "essence").[256] This is a critical point indicating Urshan's failure to distinguish between the meaning of *qnoma* when used in the context of Trinitarian theology and when used in

---

[253]"Joint Communiqué of the Second Non-official Consultation on Dialogue within the Syriac Tradition, Vienna February 1996," http://www.pro-oriente.at/dokumente/ 2Syr-Cons1996.doc (accessed May 9, 2010).

[254]Urshan, *The Life Story*, 5th ed., 16.

[255]S. P. Brock, "The 'Nestorian' Church: A Lamentable Misnomer," *Bulletin of the John Rylands University Library of Manchester*, 78: 28.

[256]Taylor, "The Syriac Tradition," 214-5.

the context of Christology.[257] It is when *qnoma* is used in connection with "nature" in a generic sense that it carries the meaning of "individual manifestation." As Baumer points out in a discussion of the differences in Christology between Cyril (c. 375-444) and Nestorius (b. 382), "Nestorius and the Church of the East understood the designation . . . 'qnoma' in the Aristotelian sense, as a material reality bound up with its species. The qnoma is an individual, representative realization of its nature . . . . The qnoma . . . is not yet the person, the *prosopon*."[258]

According to *A Compendious Syriac Dictionary*, published the year after Urshan's arrival in the United States, when *qnoma* is used in the context of theology, the word represents "the persons of the Godhead." When used in the context of Christology, "Christ is two natures and two qnumi united in the person of the Son."[259] Since the Church of the East used *qnoma* to represent "person" in its Trinitarian theology and said that Christ had two *qnomas,* the church was misunderstood by others to believe that in Christ there were two persons. This was an error from the beginning.

As it relates to the Christology of the Church of the East, *qnoma* means individuated or individualized nature, but nature in this context doesn't mean person. Just as human nature is distinct from a specific human person, so an individuated nature is not yet an *hypostasis.* So in the Incarnation there were two *qnomas* (individualized natures), each with its own set of properties (divine nature [deity] for one; human nature [humanity] for the other). These two *qnome* are instantiated in the personal identity of Jesus Christ, the Son of God. In the Trinitarianism of the Church of the East, *qnoma* means personal identity but not individuated nature, because Father, Son, and Holy Spirit are not individuated natures in the way the divine nature and human nature are in Christ. Rather, *qnoma* underscores the personal identity in the sense that Father, Son, and Holy Spirit each have personal properties analogous to how an individuated nature has its own set of properties. Whether *qnoma* is used in Christology or theology, the connection seems to be *unique set of properties* with the difference being the application of this unique set to an individuated nature or a personal identity.

> For instance, they taught that Jesus, one Being, or His one person, contained two "Ke-noo-mas." That is: two distinct natures; one absolutely divine the other perfectly human, though conceived by the Holy Spirit and born of the Virgin Mary.[260]

---

[257]The context in which Urshan discussed the meaning of *qnoma* indicates that he made no distinction in meaning whether the word was used in the Christology or theology of the Church of the East: "They believed in the God-head being a triunity of three Kenoomas and never a trinity of three separate distinct persons. 'Ke-noo-ma' to them was an image attribute [*sic*] or a manifestation of God. For instance, they taught that Jesus, one Being, or His one person, contained two 'Ke-noo-mas.' That is: two distinct natures; one absolutely divine, the other perfectly human, though conceived by the Holy Spirit and born of the Virgin Mary" (Urshan, *The Life Story,* 5th ed., 16).

[258]Baumer, *The Church of the East,* 46.

[259]Robert Payne Smith, *A Compendious Syriac Dictionary* (Oxford: Clarendon, 1903), 510.

[260]Urshan, *The Life Story,* 5th ed., 16.

At this point Urshan's understanding of *qnoma* is imprecise but perhaps not erroneous. When used in the context of Christology, "*qnoma* is the necessary individual manifestation of nature (*physis/kyana*), which is itself considered to be generic (e.g. humanity, divinity—closely associated in this Christology with Greek *ousia* "essence")."[261] In other words, when the Church of the East said that "two natures and two qnumi [are] united in the person of the Son,"[262] it meant more than to say that generic human nature and a generic divine nature were united in Christ; it meant that there was a specific, individual manifestation of humanity united with his human nature and a specific, individual manifestation of deity united with his divinity.[263]

In Baumer's discussion of a nature, the term *nature* is used generically in reference to the species. Human *nature* refers to a species distinct from non-human species. The common human *nature* is manifested in individual human beings so that a particular human is a unique manifestation of a common (i.e., generic) human nature. Another way of using the term *nature* is in reference to an individualized nature that comprises each human. It is an instance of the generic human nature concreted and individualized.

Mar Babai the Great (d. 628) explains:

> A singular essence (*ousia*) is called a "*qnoma.*" It stands by itself, singular in number, being one and distinct from many. It is not, therefore, joined [to anything else]—except, with such things as are rational and free creatures, when it receives various accidents, either of excellence or evil, or of knowledge or ignorance, but with the irrational there are also here various accidents . . . a *qnoma* is fixed in its natural state . . . it is differentiated from its fellow *qnome* in the unique property which it possesses in its *parsopa* – that of Gabriel is not that of Michael, and Paul is not Peter. However, in each and every *qnoma* the whole common nature is recognized, and it is known intellectually what the one nature is which encompasses the *qnome* in general.[264]

With this explanation, *nature* means common (i.e., generic) nature and *qnoma* means a concrete instance or manifestation of that common nature. Urshan uses the term "distinct nature," which implies that by *qnoma* he means a concrete instantiation of a generic nature, whether human or divine. According to Mar Babai, the common nature is known *intellectually*, that is, by abstracting in our minds from all concrete forms of that nature. We look at all humans and call what they all have in common a nature. Once again we can see that *qnoma* refers to *unique set of properties* or attributes.

As it relates to *parsopa,* Mar Babai the Great offers this insight:

> *Parsopa* is also the characteristic of a certain *qnoma* which distinguishes it

---

[261]Taylor, "The Syriac Tradition," 214-5.
[262]Smith, *A Compendious Syriac Dictionary,* 510.
[263]See Baumer, *The Church of the East,* 46.
[264]Mar Babai the Great, *Liber de Unione*, I.17, quoted by Fr. Andrew Younan. http://www.kaldu.org/Theology_Course_2007/06_B_PChristology_03_Video.html. (accessed May 10, 2010).

from others. Therefore the *qnoma* of Paul is not that of Peter, even though in nature and *qnoma* they are the same, for each of them possesses a body and soul, a[n]d is living and rational and fleshly, yet parsopically they are distinguished from one another by the singular uniqueness which each of them possesses, whether in stature, or in form, or in temperament, or in wisdom . . . .[265]

In a lecture titled "Christology in the Patristic Period," Fr. Andrew Younan explains the use of *qnome* by the Church of the East as it relates both to the Trinity and to Christology:

> God—as in Father, Son, and Holy Spirit—did not become man. Only the Son became man. The Father did not become flesh. The Holy Spirit did not become man. Only the Son. One *qnoma* of the three became man . . . . [N]or was it human nature that was united perfectly to God the Son, but Christ the man. So this is a new kind of category. It's not the kind of thing you're going to find in the West. . . . Particular nature versus abstract nature—this is the contribution of the term *qnoma*. . . . *Qnoma* does not mean hypostasis, but individuality. . . . *Qnoma* does not mean individual, but individuality. Christ is not two individuals. . . . Distinct doesn't mean separate.[266]

To further explain the difference between "distinct" and "separate," Fr. Younan referred to the black color of his coat and to the softness of the fabric of his coat. The blackness and the softness are distinct from each other, but not separated from one another.

In his explanation of the Christology of the Church of the East, Urshan is correct to say that Christ has two distinct natures and two *qnomas*. It is incorrect, however, to identify generic nature with *qnoma*. According to the Christology of the Church of the East, the *qnoma* of humanity in Christ was a specific, individual manifestation of humanity—Christ the man. The *qnoma* of deity in him was a specific, individual manifestation of deity—God the Son.

Urshan connects the meaning of *qnoma* to a distinct set of properties or attributes that manifest some form of existence. This is an essentially correct understanding of the term as it relates to Christology. It would not be correct to read *qnoma* as a reference to common (i.e., generic) nature.[267] In the Christology of the Church of the East, the distinct set of human properties possessed by Christ is a manifestation of common human nature. Likewise, the distinct set of divine properties possessed by Christ is a manifestation of the common divine nature. *Qnoma*

---

[265]Mar Babai the Great, *Liber de Unione*, I.17, quoted by Fr. Andrew Younan. http://www.kaldu.org/Theology_Course_2007/06_B_PChristology_03_Video.html. (accessed May 10, 2010).

[266]Fr. Andrew Younan, lecture: "Christology in the Patristic Period," Part III—Christ in the East. http://www.kaldu.org/Theology_Course_2007/06_B_PChristology_03_Vi-deo.html (accessed May 10, 2010).

[267]Urshan refers to "two distinct natures" in his use of *qnoma*, but he does not specifically say that these *natures* are distinct sets of properties *within* a specific nature (e.g., humanity or deity). The distinction he makes is between humanity and deity, not between common humanity and a distinct manifestation of humanity or between common deity and a distinct manifestation of deity.

does not mean *hypostasis* in Christology but a concrete, individualized form of common (i.e., generic) human nature or divine nature. But as applied to the Trinitarianism of the Church of the East, *qnoma* refers to the distinct set of *personal* properties possessed by the Father, Son, and Holy Spirit. In this case, *qnoma* means *hypostasis* because the *hypostases* of the Father, Son, and Holy Spirit are the unique set of properties by which each manifests the common divine nature.

Although Urshan resisted the use of the word *person,* he apparently retained what he understood to be the theology of the Church of the East. As it relates to Christology, he embraced the essential meaning of *qnoma,* but he gave no notice of the change in meaning of this term when applied to the doctrine of the Trinity. He made no connection between the words *qnoma* and *person.* Indeed, he saw these two words as expressing different concepts of the plurality within God.

> Tri-unity of God to them was like mind, wisdom, and power. As mind produces wisdom, and wisdom and mind together produce power and action, so Father (the Supreme Mind) produces the Son (the Heavenly wisdom), and the Father in the Son produced the power (the Holy Spirit).[268]

Urshan offers no documentation of his claim that eastern Christianity views the Father as "supreme mind," the Son as "heavenly wisdom," and the Holy Spirit as "power." The analogy of mind, wisdom, and power is, however, similar to Augustine's analogy of the Trinity as memory, understanding, and will or as mind, knowledge, and love.[269] If the Church of the East did use the analogy of mind, wisdom, and power, it must nevertheless be kept in mind that it also accepted the canons of the Council of Nicaea in 410.[270] With the language of mind, wisdom, and power, the "persons" of the Trinity become instead impersonal principles, ideas, forces or, in Urshan's word, "attributes."

In Urshan's understanding of the theology of the Church of the East, the Father [Supreme Mind] "produces" the Son [Heavenly Wisdom], and the Father [Supreme Mind] and Son [Heavenly Wisdom] produce Power [Holy Spirit]. He may have understood this in connection with his view of what it meant for the Son to be the *only-begotten*[271] and in conjunction with the idea of *qnoma* as *unique set of properties.* If so, the unique set of properties comprising the Son [Heavenly Wisdom] is in some sense begotten by the unique set of properties comprising the Father [Supreme Mind] in a manner analogous to the way in which wisdom or understanding comes about from the mind as memory. The parallel here is that one must put information into the storehouse of memory before insights can begin to emerge and understanding occurs.

---

[268]Urshan, *The Life Story,* 5th ed., 16.

[269]*Augustine: Later Works,* trans. John Burnaby (Philadelphia: Westminster Press, 1955), 25.

[270]See Brock, "The 'Nestorian' Church," 33 and Julian Faultless, "The Two Recensions of the Prologue to John," in *Christians at the Heart of Islamic Rule: Church Life and Scholarship in Abbasid Iraq,* ed. David Thomas (Boston: Brill, 2003), 183.

[271]See Urshan, "The Mystery of God, or Who is God?," *The Witness of God* (December 1953): 4-5.

All these three attributes of the one Divine Being were in Jesus of Nazareth; that is why He was not man-God, but the perfect God, and the perfect man; hence "Aman-El", the Lord over all, or the God-man with us.[272]

Finally, in our examination of Urshan's understanding of *qnoma* as used by the Church of the East and the word "person" in comparison to western Trinitarianism, it must be remembered that Urshan understood "person" in the modern sense of a self-conscious individual as opposed to in the sense of the Greek *hypostasis, prosōpon,* or the Latin *persona* or *subsistentia*. Urshan describes the western Trinitarian view as three "separate and distinct persons" and equates "person" with "being."[273] Muller points out that in theological usage, *persona* does not

> have the connotation of emotional individuality or unique consciousness that clearly belongs to the term in contemporary usage. It is quite certain that the Trinitarian use of *persona* does not point to three wills, three emotionally unique beings or . . . three centers of consciousness; such implication would be tritheistic. . . . [T]he patristic, medieval, Reformation, and Protestant scholastic definitions of the term *persona* are united in their distinction from colloquial modern usage. In brief, the term has traditionally indicated an objective or distinct mode or manner of being, a subsistence or subsistent individual, not necessarily substantially separate from other like *personae*. Thus, in trinitarian usage, three *personae* subsist in the divine *substantia* or *essentia* . . . without division and, in christological usage, one *persona* has two distinct *naturae*, the divine and the human.[274]

As it relates to the use of *qnoma,* Urshan perceives himself to be theologically connected with the Church of the East, but a precise understanding of the way the word is used by the Church of the East suggests that although he understood the basic meaning of *qnoma* and applied this meaning in a way that allowed him to resist modern notions of person, he did not grasp the conceptual difference between the application of *qnoma* to the Christology and the Trinitarianism of the Church of the East.

Another link between Urshan's theology and that of the Church of the East is seen in a comparison of the symbolic theology and the theology of divine names of Ephrem the Syrian, a fourth century Syriac Christian, and Urshan's use of symbolism and name theology.

To speak of Ephrem's "symbolic theology" and "theology of divine names" does not indicate two distinct approaches to his theology. Rather, "God has provided the types and symbols, the names and titles, all pointing to Christ."[275] For our purposes, Ephrem's influence on Syriac Christianity becomes immediately interesting in the context of Urshan's theological roots, his appeal to symbols, and his unique emphasis on the divine name. This sets Urshan apart from the early twentieth century Oneness Pentecostal thinkers whose western worldview emphasized logic, reason, and "facts" rather than mysterious symbols – whether in

---

[272]Urshan, *The Life Story,* 5th ed., 16.
[273]Urshan, *The Almighty God,* 77.
[274]Muller, *Dictionary of Latin and Greek Theological Terms,* 226-7.
[275]S. H. Griffith, "The Thorn among the Tares," in *Studia Patristica*, M. F. Wiles and E. J. Yarnold, eds., vol. xxxv (Leuven: Peeters, 2001), 419.

nature or Scripture – and whose focus on "name," while sounding on the surface much like Urshan's focus, was informed by different presuppositions than his.

Much of the difference between Urshan's perspective and that of other Oneness thinkers like Ewart and Haywood centers on the meaning of "mystery." From the Enlightenment standpoint of the West, biblical "mystery" was something previously unknown that was now revealed. As this worked out in later twentieth century Oneness Pentecostal theology, little room was left for mystery:

> A mystery in the New Testament is simply a plan of God that was not understood in the Old Testament but which *has* been made known to us. We "may under-stand... the mystery of Christ which in other ages was not made known unto the sons of men, as it is now revealed unto his holy apostles and prophets by the Spirit" (Ephesians 3:4-5).
>
> We can know the mystery of God and the Father, which is Christ. . . . The mystery of God *has* been revealed to us by God's Spirit. . . . There is therefore no biblical mystery about the Godhead and certainly no mystery about the number of persons in the Godhead. The only mystery is Christ, and He has been revealed to us! The mystery of God and the mystery of Christ converge in the Incarnation. It is simply that the one God of Israel came to the earth in flesh. This mystery has been revealed and God's Word declares that it has been made known to us today.[276]

As it relates to the identity and work of Christ, David Norris views mystery as having been revealed in Paul's time. This mystery was not beyond the comprehension of ordinary believers who chose to believe in Jesus. Norris' understanding of I Timothy 3:16 is that the mystery to which Paul refers is not about the mystery related to the makeup of the Godhead as it is speaking more broadly about the life of faith now available to believers because of the Incarnation.[277]

The widespread use of *The Scofield Reference Bible* in Pentecostalism, including Oneness Pentecostalism, has influenced the understanding of "mystery" in the Pentecostal mind. Scofield defined "mystery" thus: "A 'mystery' in Scripture is a previously hidden truth, now divinely revealed, but in which a supernatural element still remains despite the revelation."[278] Although Scofield left room for "a supernatural element," this element did not always get transferred in the popular use of Scofield's thought.[279]

In the context of Syriac theology, however, revelation does not purge mystery of the unknown. Seely Joseph Beggiani explains, "While mystery manifests truth communicated in the revelation of Christ, still even after the communication, the unfathomable nature of the divine utterance remains concealed and cannot be

---

[276]Bernard, *The Oneness of God*, 65-66.

[277]This statement was confirmed to the author in an email from David Norris dated May 24, 2010.

[278]C. I. Scofield, *The Scofield Reference Bible*, 1014.

[279]As a student doing undergraduate work in a Oneness Pentecostal Bible college where the *Scofield Reference Bible* was in common use, I clearly remember being taught that a "mystery" was something previously unknown that was now revealed. I don't recall ever hearing that there was still a "supernatural element" involved.

fully understood, but is apprehended by faith."²⁸⁰ Type and mystery are bound up with each other to the extent that "type and symbol are embodiments of the divine presence in Creation."²⁸¹

For Ephrem, typology was "the main vehicle of doing theology."²⁸² He had no confidence in rationalism as a guide to truth, as can be seen in his rejection of Arianism:

> Blessed is the one who has not tasted
>
> the bitter poison of the wisdom of the Greeks
>
> Blessed is the one who has not let slip
>
> the simplicity of the apostles.²⁸³

Griffith points out that Ephrem

> rejected the idea that the articles of faith could be determined by academic research, or by intellectual scrutiny that put dialectic ahead of believing. . . . He spoke of the "accursed dialectic" . . . as "a hidden worm from the Greeks." . . . Ephraem . . . thought that the proper posture for a Christian was an attitude of prayer and praise, arising from the contemplation of the mysteries God has strewn in both nature and scripture to lead the human mind to divinity.²⁸⁴

There are times when reading Urshan that one could wonder if he did not take his cue directly from Ephrem. This is not to suggest that he actually did so, but it seems too much to think that Urshan's embrace of typology and mystery, when compared to Ephrem, was merely coincidental. The best explanation may simply be that Urshan's theological roots in eastern Christianity exposed him to a perspective informed by the wide-spread appreciation Ephrem had garnered in that theological milieu.

Possekel points out that Ephrem "approaches the trinitarian mystery symbolically. The two most prominent trinitarian images in Ephrem's works are both taken from nature: the plant (or tree) and its fruit; and the sun (or fire), its light, and its warmth."²⁸⁵ Here is Urshan in 1919:

---

²⁸⁰Seely Joseph Beggiani, "The Typological Approach of Syriac Sacramental Theology," *Theological Studies* 64, no. 3 (2003): 547.

²⁸¹Beggiani, "The Typological Approach of Syrian Sacramental Theology," 544.

²⁸²Beggiani, "The Typological Approach of Syrian Sacramental Theology," 544.

²⁸³E. Beck, *Des heiligen Ephraem des Syrers Hymnen de Fide* (CSCO, vols. 154 & 155; Louvain: Secrétariat du CorpusSCO, 1955), II:24 E. Beck, *Des heiligen Ephraem des Syrers Hymnen de Fide* (CSCO, vols. 154 & 155; Louvain: Secrétariat du CorpusSCO, 1955), II:24, quoted by Sidney Griffith, "A Spiritual Father for the Whole Church: the Universal Appeal of Saint Ephraem the Syrian," *Hugoye: Journal of Syriac Studies* 1, no. 2 (July 1998), http://syrcom.cua.edu/Hugoye/vol1No2/ HV1N2 Griffith.html#FN46 (accessed May 23, 2010).

²⁸⁴Sidney Griffith, "A Spiritual Father for the Whole Church: the Universal Appeal of Saint Ephraem the Syrian," *Hugoye: Journal of Syriac Studies* 1, no. 2 (July 1998), http://syrcom.cua.edu/Hugoye/vol1No2/HV1N2Griffith.html (accessed May 23, 2010).

²⁸⁵Ute Possekel, "Ephrem's Doctrine of God," in Andrew B. McGowan, Brian E. Dal-

God the Father is light; the Son is light; the Holy Spirit is light,—not three lights, but one self-same Light with three rays (manifestations or revelations); and this great Triune Being of the excellent light of eternal life can be seen, and His blessings, gifts, and promises received, only **in and through Jesus Christ, "the Son of the Father."**[286]

Fire is another wonderful illustration of God's three-fold unity because it is like the sun, consist[ing] also of three distinct but inseparable elements, viz: heat, light, and power.[287]

God not only reveals Himself through light and fire, but a most beautiful example of God's triune being is found in that of a tree. There are three principal parts to a tree, the root, the body, and the sap. The root is the source of the tree's life and represents God the Father as **"the root of David"** and the author of all life. The body of the tree illustrates Christ, the visible part of the tree which can be seen and felt and which bears the fruit.

. . . The sap represents the Holy Ghost or quickening spirit: that invisible agent of God's person which does the actual work of creating and sustaining life both natural and supernatural in and through the word of God which is Christ.[288]

Many of those who receive their training to do biblical exegesis in the western world learn to focus on the "literal," "grammatical," "historical," and "contextual" meaning of words and texts. But for Ephrem,

> If there were [only] one meaning for the words [of Scripture] the first interpreter would find it, and all other listeners would have neither the toil of seeking nor the pleasure of finding. But every word of our Lord has its own image, and each image has many members, and each member possesses its own species and form. Each person hears in accordance with his capacity, and it is interpreted in accordance with what has been given him.[289]

This perspective opens Scripture up to multiple levels of meaning. If Urshan read Scripture this way, and it seems certain he did, it is understandable that he could see evidence of the "threeness" of the one God in such diverse biblical pictures as Noah's ark and Moses' tabernacle.

Ephrem warned against pressing too far into the investigation of the names of God, since the divine names are the boundary marking the limits for human

---

ey, S.J., and Timothy J. Gaden, eds., *God in Early Christian Thought: Essays in Memory of Lloyd G. Patterson,* Supplements to Vigiliae Christianae (Leiden, The Netherlands: Brill, 2009), 233-34.

[286]Urshan, *The Almighty God,* 78. Emphasis in original.

[287]Urshan, *Doctrine of Trinity,* 22.

[288]Urshan, *Doctrine of Trinity,* 23.

[289]Syrus Ephraem, *Saint Ephrem's Commentary on Tatian's Diatessaron: An English Translation of Chester Beatty Syriac MS 709 with Introduction and Notes by Carmel McCarthy* (Oxford: Oxford University for the University of Manchester, 1993) 139, quoted by Angela Kim Harkins, "Theological Attitudes toward the Scriptural Text: Lessons from the Qumran and Syriac Exegetical Traditions," Theological Studies 67, no. 3 (2006): 511.

investigation.²⁹⁰ Although Urshan focused much of his study on the name of God, he did believe there were limits to the investigation of God:

> We cannot explain these things fully though we may attempt to. The solution of the problem is that since God is almighty and . . . omnipresent, He can be a man on the earth and remain God in the high heavens; He has the right to call Himself the Father and the Son and the Holy Spirit and yet at the same time [to] be **One Being and One God**, and it is not our business to try to fully explain these wonderful, yet mysterious things that are hidden in the wisdom of God.²⁹¹

Ephrem would have agreed:

> Let us not allow ourselves to go astray
> and to study our God.
>
> Lest us take the measure of our mind,
> and gauge the range of our thinking.
>
> Let us know how small our knowledge is,
> too contemptible to scrutinize the Knower of All.²⁹²

Urshan, like Ephrem, viewed water baptism as a birth rather than emphasizing the imagery of death and resurrection. In early Syriac tradition, baptism was "a new womb giving birth to new children bearing the image of the New Adam."²⁹³

Urshan's description of his conversion as having "the branch of the Divine tree in the bitter water of my life . . . planted afresh"²⁹⁴ certainly resonates with the Syriac view that the Cross of Christ was the antitype of the Tree of Life in the Garden of Eden.²⁹⁵ For Syriac Christianity, the Garden of Eden was a type of divinization,²⁹⁶ a concept embraced by Urshan.²⁹⁷

Summary

This examination of Urshan's theology demonstrates that it was on a different trajectory than other Oneness expressions. Although Urshan was more prolific than other early twentieth century Oneness thinkers, including Frank Ewart and G. T. Haywood, his theology tended to respond to Trinitarianism as he understood it. At the same time, he sought to build bridges between Oneness and Trinitarian Pentecostals.

---

²⁹⁰Ute Possekel, *Evidence of Greek Philosophical Concepts in the Writings of Ephrem the Syrian,* CSCO subsidia, 102 (Louvain: Peeters, 1999), 45.

²⁹¹Urshan, *Doctrine of Trinity,* 46. Emphasis in original.

²⁹²Sidney Griffith, "A Spiritual Father for the Whole Church: the Universal Appeal of Saint Ephraem the Syrian," *Hugoye: Journal of Syriac Studies* 1, no. 2 (July 1998).

²⁹³Beggiani, *Typological Approach of Syriac Sacramental Theology,* 552-53.

²⁹⁴Urshan, "Third Chapter—Story of My Life: Andrew's Wonderful Conversion," *The Witness of God* 3, no. 35 (November 1922), 4.

²⁹⁵Beggiani, *Typological Approach of Syriac Sacramental Theology,* 554.

²⁹⁶Beggiani, *Typological Approach of Syriac Sacramental Theology,* 554.

²⁹⁷Urshan, *Apostolic Faith Doctrine,* 7.

Urshan's emphasis on mystery is not retained in today's Oneness theology. But this emphasis is not surprising in view of the uniqueness of his theological roots. Ewart, Haywood, and Small were westerners who imbibed in the common cultural Enlightenment milieu of logic, reason, and science. They had little room for mystery as embraced by Urshan. This is not to say that Haywood, Ewart, and Small rejected the concept of mystery altogether, but their use of the idea was unlike Urshan's.

For Haywood and Ewart, the mystery was not in the plurality of God but in the Incarnation. Consider, for example, Haywood's response to the question "Is it possible for us to understand the mystery of the Godhead?" He answered,

> The invisible things of Him from the creation of the world are clearly seen, being "understood" by the things that are made, even His eternal power and Godhead; so that, they are without excuse. (Rom. 1:20.) Man is a trinity; is made in God's image with a spirit, soul, and body, but he is but one person, and not three. They that believe and teach that doctrine are "without excuse." God has winked at the time of this ignorance"[298]

In Haywood's view,"[t]he Mystery of the FATHER, SON and HOLY GHOST is fully comprehended in Christ Jesus. As Father, He was the Creator, Begetter of all things. . . . As Son, He was our example in the days of His flesh, from His baptism in the Jordan up to His ascension on the resurrection morning. . . . As Holy Ghost He comes within and abides forever."[299] Urshan's "incomprehensible" and Haywood's "comprehended" reflect different perspectives on the "mystery."

For Ewart, only those to whom truth has not been revealed face "inexplicable mystery."[300] In connection with his reading of Colossians 2:2, Ewart declared that those who have the "hidden wisdom" of I Corinthians 2:7-8 can solve "The mystery of God—even Christ." The Incarnation is a "revealed mystery" that Jesus "explained."[301] In other words, "The mystery was God expressing Himself in terms of human life."[302] Ewart quoted C. I. Scofield as saying, "The peculiarity of Bible mysteries is that after you get the scriptural or apostolic revelation of them there is still a mystery involved."[303] Thus Ewart was willing to embrace or, as he said, "fellowship" the mystery, even though he could "neither explain nor understand it,"[304] but it was not the same mystery as Urshan's.

Urshan, the easterner among the most influential Oneness thinkers in the early twentieth century, sometimes used Enlightenment language—he spoke of "facts" and "experience"—but this language was tempered by his deep-rooted Persian

---

[298]G. T. Haywood, "The Witness of God Question Box," *The Witness of God* 10, no. 93 (April 1928): 11.

[299]G. T. Haywood, *Divine Names and Titles of Jehovah* (Portland, OR: Apostolic Book Publishers, n.d.), 22.

[300]Frank J. Ewart, *The Revelation of Jesus Christ* (Hazelwood, MO: Pentecostal Publishing House, n.d.), 10.

[301]Ewart, *The Revelation of Jesus Christ,* 12-13.

[302]Frank J. Ewart, *The Name and the Book* (Hazelwood, MO: Word Aflame Press, 1947, reprinted 1986), 84.

[303]Ewart, *The Name and the Book,* 170. I have not been able to verify this quote from Scofield.

[304]Ewart, *The Name and the Book,* 170.

heritage that was shaped by the theology of the Church of the East. In his view, the Church of the East "taught God is a mystery, the unapproachable Divine Being; hence the necessity of His manifestation in the flesh."[305]

For our purposes, the important issue is Urshan's conception of the theology and Christology of the Church of the East, even if his conception was not entirely accurate. He brought this perceived theology and Christology into consideration for what he thought it contributed to his personal theology and Christology. The subtle nuances of the ancient Syriac vocabulary used by Nestorius and the Church of the East in comparison to the Greek and Latin vocabularies used in the west require a sophisticated mastery of these languages to discern the differences between the theologies. Urshan knew modern Syriac and studied ancient Syriac during his one semester in high school in Persia, but he may not have gained sufficient mastery of the ancient language during that time to grasp the full significance of the delicate shades of meaning that divided the Church of the East from western Christianity. This possibility is heightened since Urshan did not formally study the Greek and Latin languages. And regardless of the level of his mastery of ancient Syriac, it would have been quite another thing to master the theological vocabulary of that language. His misunderstanding of the difference in the way *qnoma* was applied to the Christology and Trinitarian theology of the Church of the East suggests that Urshan had not mastered that theological vocabulary. As Muller points out, "The ability to work productively in the field of theology . . . rests in no small measure upon the mastery of the vocabulary."[306]

Urshan's understanding of theology and Christology reflects his eastern cultural and theological heritage as influenced by the Church of the East. Even though he did not fully grasp the subtleties of *qnoma*, a key term in the theological and Christological vocabulary of the Church of the East, his views nevertheless represent a largely Syriac trajectory of thought with its implicit suspicion of western forms of Trinitarianism. For Urshan, these suspicions focus on the term *person* and its implications of tritheism.

When we look beyond the theological vocabulary of the Church of the East to the conceptual insights of symbolic theology and theology of divine names, as seen in the works of Ephrem the Syrian, we can discern a historic influence that is reflected in Urshan's search for symbols and his emphasis on name theology. Although his conclusions are not Ephrem's, his methodology is, at least to a recognizable extent.

---

[305]Urshan, *The Life Story*, 5th ed., 16.

[306]Richard A. Muller, *Dictionary of Latin and Greek Theological Terms* (Grand Rapids: Baker Book House, 1985), 7.

Chapter Eight

Doctrine of Salvation

Introduction

Urshan's soteriology is set forth in a variety of articles in *The Witness of God*, some of which were reproduced in booklet format. The articles were written not only by Urshan, but also by other early twentieth century Oneness Pentecostals like George Farrow and Garfield T. Haywood. We can assume that the articles written by Farrow and Haywood were included in *The Witness of God* because they reflect Urshan's views. This is a safe assumption not only because he selected these articles for inclusion in his publication but also because a comparison of the ideas set forth in these articles with other articles he authored show a commonality of perspectives.

As we survey Urshan's views, we will note that although he built his soteriology around Acts 2:38 as the "new birth" of water and Spirit set forth by Jesus in John 3, he did so with sensitivity to the genuineness of the faith experience of those who had not been baptized having the name of Jesus called over them and who had not experienced baptism with the Holy Spirit with the "sign" of speaking in tongues. He did this in the context of nuance and by embracing some of the dispensational notions of the *Scofield Reference Bible*. Specifically, Urshan nuanced the meanings of the terms "saved" and "born again" so that they were not synonymous, distinguished between the experiences of being "begotten" and "born," and suggested distinctions between the "kingdom of Heaven" and the "kingdom of God."

Bernard summarizes Urshan's soteriology:

> Andrew Urshan . . . made a distinction between being begotten and born. He described his status at repentance as "a happy, blood-washed, newly conceived child of the King!" He spoke of people being "saved" before they were born again and wrote of some who had died in the faith before baptism in Jesus' name. Nevertheless, he taught that baptism in Jesus' name is for the remission of sins. It is necessary to go in the Rapture and escape the Tribulation. He also believed strongly that the baptism of the Holy Spirit is necessary. People who believed in God and lived righteous lives "without ever coming to the light of being born again according to Acts 2:38" will rise in the second resurrection, presumably to live on the new earth.[1]

---

[1] David K. Bernard, *A History of Christian Doctrine: The Twentieth Century*, A.D. 1900 – 2000, vol. 3 (Hazelwood, MO: Word Aflame Press, 1999), 122-3.

The accuracy of this summary will be demonstrated as we examine Urshan's soteriology in a chronological fashion, beginning with the earliest articles in *The Witness of God* that specifically address this subject.

The Witness of God

Urshan first approached the subject of the new birth in the September 1921 issue of *The Witness of God* in an article entitled "Introductory Questions on the Doctrine of the New Birth." The article is set up as a series of questions and answers.[2]

The first questions the motivations of those who "dispute on the doctrine of the new birth" as taught by Jesus in John 3. It calls for speculation on Urshan's part and does not inform us of his views. However, it does tell us what he thought about the motives of those who disagreed with him. Urshan believed his understanding of the new birth was the "clear and plain" teaching of Scripture. Those who agreed with him were "hungry to know God's word more perfectly," while those who disagreed were establishing "their own ideas" with a desire to gain followers. Those who disagreed were either knowingly "wresting" the Scripture and would be destroyed, or they were deceived by Satan.[3]

The second question requests a definition of the new birth. In response, Urshan offers John 3:5. The third question asks, "What is it to enter into the Kingdom of God?" Urshan responds, "It is to get into the place or state where the Kingdom of God is." The fourth question is, "Where is that place, or what is that state?" Urshan defines the kingdom of God as being "in the power," based on I Corinthians 4:20. To enter the kingdom, one must "get first in that state of the power of God." This statement enables us to begin to understand Urshan's hermeneutic. Urshan uses this definition taken from Paul and applies it to interpret the words of Jesus in the Gospels when he finds the term "kingdom of God" expressed. His logic suggests that "enter the kingdom in the power" is "to enter the church." However, elsewhere in his writing, he denies that the church and the kingdom should be equated or that Jesus should be called "King" by those who are in the church. This appears to leave us with a contradiction.[4]

Urshan maintained that in order to experience the new birth, one must be baptized with the Holy Spirit. This requires that one must not only speak in tongues but also embrace Urshan's understanding of the Godhead and Christology. For example, in response to the question, "Have we got anything to do with the person of Jesus Christ in order to enter into the Kingdom of God?", he replies,

> Yes! Indeed. We must receive Him as the Son of God (the incarnate word John 1:14) and also as God our maker. And also we must believe on His Name. John 1:10-13. Otherwise our birth of water would be good for nothing without a thorough turning toward God, and faith in Him through His death and resurrection

---

[2]There is no indication as to whether the questions originated with readers of *The Witness of God* or whether Urshan composed them to serve as an outline for the article.

[3]Urshan, "Introductory Questions on the doctrine of the New Birth," *The Witness of God* 2, no. 21 (September 1921): 1.

[4]Urshan, "Jesus the King of Jews," *The Witness of God* 10, no. 103 (March 1929): 11-12.

reconciles us to God. See Acts 2:38; 8:36-37; and 19:1-7. It is our faith in Christ's resurrection and the fullness of the Godhead in His name that brings the Holy Spirit from above upon us and causes us to be born from above. Compare Luke 24:45-49 with John 14:26.[5]

The response to the next question reveals a critical point in his understanding of soteriology. Although he sets a high bar for the new birth and thus for inclusion in the kingdom of God, he sees an experience with God short of the new birth. This experience is conversion—as he experienced while enrolled in the American Presbyterian College in Urmia, Persia. In his conversion experience, Urshan understood that he was "begotten of God." In his new birth experience, he understood that he was "born again by the Spirit of God."[6] Thus, in answer to the question, "Is there any difference between the words 'begotten' and 'born,'" Urshan responded:

> Sometimes these two words in English mean the same thing and sometimes the word "begotten" means "conceived". Begetting belongs to God . . . but birth belongs to the Spirit of God. . . . . Just as in [the] natural, the Father begets, but the Mother conceives and brings forth. Experience proves this; many of us when we were converted we were only conceived, or the Word of life which we accepted was planted into our hearts by God which dwelt with us, but when the Holy Spirit came in us by the divine baptism, the word was energized so powerfully that it came forth with supernatural shouts, crying in other tongues, Abba Babba, Abba, Babba or, Ba-Ba . . . which literally means, "The Father my Father." It is the same Aramaic language which Jesus actually used when He was on the earth; when He talked to His Father. This is the real and the full Bible sign of the new birth . . . .[7]

Not only does Urshan distinguish between "begotten" and "born"; he also broadens the meaning of "salvation" so that it includes all of those who walk in the "light," an idea common among early twentieth century Pentecostals, both Trinitarian and Oneness. In what may be a unique contribution to this concept, Urshan thinks that the person who walks faithfully in the "portion of the divine light" he or she has received will be baptized with the Holy Spirit upon being resurrected and that this baptism will be indicated by the resurrected person speaking "in the Heavenly language" or in tongues. This experience will not, however, qualify the resurrected person to "share . . . the glory" with those who experienced the "normal and full New Testament birth" of water and Spirit. Urshan responds to the question, "Please tell me if a man is saved when [he] has been conceived or converted without the Holy Ghost utterances?"

> The word saved or "salvation" has very great and broader meaning in the Bible. It begins at the conversion and it ends with the coming of the Lord. But you [are asking] if that person is going to Heaven if he should pass away without the baptism in

---

[5]Urshan, "Introductory Questions on the Doctrine of the New Birth," *The Witness of God* 2, no. 21 (September 1921): 1.

[6]This distinction is not embraced by contemporary Oneness theologians.

[7]Urshan, "Introductory Questions on the Doctrine of the New Birth," *The Witness of God* 2, no. 21 (September 1921): 1.

the Holy Ghost. To this we will say, "Yes." If that person had only a certain portion of the divine light and he walked in it faithfully, at the resurrection morning the Holy Spirit will fall on him and will fill him and he will come out of the grave with the Old Testament saints shouting glory in the Heavenly language and will go to meet his Lord. But the share of such believers will be with the Old Testament saints and not with the glory of those who have been born of water and the Spirit and have had the normal and full New Testament birth.[8]

Although the bar for the new birth is high, it is not so high to simply become a child of God. As a follow-up, the next question reads, "Is that person a child of God before he receives Spiritual baptism?" Urshan answers:

> Yes! Just as you were a child of your parents when you were yet in your mother's womb just as much as when you were born. The difference is not in the relationship but in the fullness of life, or in the development of the Spiritual condition. The disciples of Christ before Pentecost and the Old Testament saints are called God's children though they were outside of the Kingdom, yet they all (the old prophets) died in the faith [and] received not the promise of the Spirit, that they may not be perfect without us. . . . Nevertheless they will have their share in the Kingdom at the coming of their King. But we who believe on the Name of Christ and [are] baptized into His name and His life are privileged of more and greater things. . . .[9]

Urshan rejects the idea that to be born of water is to be born of the word apart from water baptism. Since water baptism is found in Scripture, to be born of water is to be born of the word. Those who reject water baptism reject the word of God.[10]

It is somewhat shocking to discover that, in Urshan's view, Spirit baptism that is not accompanied by water baptism is false: "[N]either [will] Spirit baptism . . . stand the test if it is not completed with water baptism of repentance and faith in Christ. Such partial baptism is false, it is man-made, though apparently wonderful; God's real twofold baptism [only will] stand the test of the fire."[11]

On the surface, it would appear from this statement that Urshan believed that unless a person obeyed Acts 2:38 in the way he understood, one would be lost. This was not Urshan's understanding. One must keep in mind that Urshan had redefined a number of theological categories. Thus he can go on to say:

> One can be saved, yet not born again. Old Testament saints were saved but they were not born again. The new birth experience is exclusively New Testament

---

[8]Urshan, "Introductory Questions on the Doctrine of the New Birth," *The Witness of God* 2, no. 21 (September 1921): 1.

[9]Urshan, "Introductory Questions on the Doctrine of the New Birth," *The Witness of God* 2, no. 21 (September 1921): 1.

[10]Urshan, "Introductory Questions on the Doctrine of the New Birth," *The Witness of God* 2, no. 21 (September 1921): 1.

[11]Urshan, "The One Christian Baptism," *The Witness of God* 2, no. 22 (October 1921): 7. Once again, it is regrettable that Urshan includes an article from the late nineteenth century Arian journal *Eusebia* in defense of water baptism, including the sacred name theology that requires pronouncing the Messiah's name as "Yah-sous" (Urshan, "Baptism," *The Witness of God* 2, no. 22 [October 1921]: 8).

teaching. . . . We . . . must be conceived by the Word first, and be brought forth of the water and the Spirit.

> The word "salvation" means deliverance. Many are delivered from many bad habits and sins, yet not born of water and the Spirit. He that is born again is not only delivered but also born of God. Salvation makes us God's own people. The new birth experience makes us God's own children in Christ. This being the truth, our Lord could say to the Pharisees, "For I say unto you, among those that are born of woman there is not a greater prophet than John the Baptist, but he that is least in the kingdom of God is greater than he." John was a prophet and friend of God, but the least in the kingdom of God is the one who is born of water and Spirit and he is a child of God.[12]

Thus, those who are "saved" are God's "people." Those who have the new birth experience are God's "children." Those who experience the new birth are thus in the kingdom of God and are greater than John the Baptist because they are God's children, whereas John was one of God's people.

Urshan included two articles in the November-December 1930 issue of *The Witness of God* that set forth clearly the soteriology to which he subscribed. George R. Farrow was the author of the article "The New Birth: What it Is, What it Does." The second article, titled, "The Mysteries of the Kingdom," was written by G. T. Haywood. Both articles, drawing on Scofield's distinction between the kingdom of heaven and the kingdom of God, find a place of salvation for people of faith who do not experience the new birth. First, we will look at Farrow's article.

For Farrow, the "confusion" and "error" in understanding John 3:3-5 comes from reading the key terms as metaphors.

> Most confusion and error on the subject of the new birth has come from the common but erroneous practice of giving these words a metaphoric meaning; saying that when Jesus said "water" He meant the Word; when He said "SPIRIT" He meant the wind, and when He said "the Kingdom of God" He meant heaven, the eternal abode of the redeemed . . . .[13]

The most significant statement here as it relates to soteriology is the disconnection between heaven and the kingdom of God. In Farrow's view, Jesus did not refer to the requirements for entrance into heaven in his conversation with Nicodemus. The kingdom of God is the church, not heaven. Like Urshan, Farrow understands Jesus' statement about the inferiority of John the Baptist to mean that the most insignificant person in the church is greater than John because the "least believer" in the church "occupies a closer and more intimate relationship with God than did John." Otherwise, in Farrow's view, if "kingdom of God" means "heaven," either "John did not go to heaven, or if he did, [he] was the most insignificant person there, and this would not likely be the case with the one who was

---

[12]Urshan, "There is a Difference," *The Witness of God* 10, no. 10 (November-December 1930): 8.

[13]George R. Farrow, "The New Birth: What it Is, What it Does," *The Witness of God* 10, no. 10 (November-December 1930): 15.

the predestined forerunner of the Lord Jesus Himself."[14] Farrow draws the following implications from his understanding of this passage of Scripture:

> [E]ntering the kingdom of God does not mean entering heaven, but rather it means entering into that relationship with God which is experienced and enjoyed only by those Spirit-filled believers in Christ who come into the Pentecostal experience in the Pentecostal way; in other words it means entering the kingdom of God by the water and Spirit birth route.
>
> ... to take any other view of the new birth teaching ... and be consistent, we must either take the one extreme of teaching that born of water and Spirit and baptized in water and Spirit are two different experiences, or the other radical extreme of un-Christianizing and barring from heaven everyone who has not been saved through the Acts 2:38 experience. To take this last radical position means that we must bar from heaven all the Old Testament saints, patriarchs and prophets, and multiplied thousands of holy, God-fearing men and women of the church age, many of whom walked with God in a life of consecration and prayer and served Him with a devotion that would put most of us to shame, yet they knew nothing of the Acts 2:38 experience.[15]

Those of the church age who have not "had light" are judged by God on the same basis as the Old Testament saints: Though not receiving the birth of the Spirit, they will be saved because they "walked with God by faith and served Him to the best of their light."

Farrow anticipated objections to his view: "I think I hear someone say, 'To teach thus we will be lowering the standard and people will be satisfied with an experience short of a Pentecostal one.' We reply, 'Must the truth be presented from a false basis or lose its effect?' God forbid!"[16]

Haywood's article "The Mysteries of the Kingdom" develops Scofield's kingdom of God/kingdom of heaven dichotomy further. According to Haywood, there was great conflict "among the ministerial ranks" because of the following differences of opinion: (1) No one is born of God until he or she is baptized with the Holy Spirit; (2) a person is baptized with the Holy Spirit when saved, but without speaking in tongues; (3) one can be in the bride of Christ without being baptized with the Holy Spirit; (4) there are only two kingdoms, the kingdom of light and the kingdom of darkness, and everyone is in one or the other.[17]

Haywood insisted that throughout Scripture it is evident that God has "two classes of people." This claim was based on Psalm 114:2: "Judah was his sanctuary, and Israel his dominion." Haywood commented, "Though there was a 'sanctuary' and a 'dominion,' yet they were all God's people. So it is with the people of

---

[14] Farrow, "The New Birth," *The Witness of God* 10, no. 10 (November-December 1930): 16.

[15] Farrow, "The New Birth," *The Witness of God* 10, no. 10 (November-December 1930): 16-17.

[16] Farrow, "The New Birth," *The Witness of God* 10, no. 10 (November-December 1930): 17. This article appeared originally in the *Apostolic Herald*. George Farrow was the author of the Oneness Pentecostal anthem "It's All in Him."

[17] G. T. Haywood, "The Mysteries of the Kingdom," *The Witness of God* 10, no. 10 (November-December 1930): 17.

God today. Those who are converted are in His 'dominion' while those who are baptized with the Holy Ghost are in the 'sanctuary.'" Adopting Scofield's perspective, Haywood states, "There is a difference between the Kingdom of God and the Kingdom of Heaven. Many failing to see this have greatly erred and have confused the two terms endeavoring to make them mean one and the same thing."[18]

Haywood testified that he came to his conclusions by "a close study of the scriptures and prayer." His study was informed by the notes in the *Scofield Reference Bible*, as is evident by his many direct quotations, paraphrases, and allusions to Scofield. Sometimes Haywood offers extensive verbatim quotations from Scofield; at other times he revises Scofield somewhat to make use of Scofield's views from the perspective of Oneness Pentecostalism.[19]

The Kingdom of Heaven "embraces the whole Christian profession of this age, or the visible congregated body of God's people." It is truly entered only by conversion. Based on his understanding of the parables of Matthew 13, Haywood asserts that children of the devil are found in the Kingdom of Heaven, but not in the Kingdom of God. The Kingdom of God, which is in the midst of the Kingdom of Heaven, can be entered only by being "born again." The church, also known as the bride and the body, is called out from the Kingdom of Heaven. After declaring that the church is the "pearl of great price," Haywood offers a lengthy quotation from Scofield to prove his point. Without identifying Scofield, Haywood introduces his quotation with these words: "We hereby quote the notes on this parable by a well known authority on such things." When the quotation is concluded, he states, "Thus we have given the words of one of the most prominent Bible teachers of modern times."[20]

It is the children of the Kingdom of Heaven who are eligible to be baptized with the Holy Spirit. This claim by Haywood is based on Jesus' statement that the world cannot receive him. Thus, a distinction is made between the "world" and the Kingdom of Heaven. As soon as a person hears and believes, God counts him or her righteous.

In addition to the distinction between Judah as God's sanctuary and Israel as his dominion, Haywood offers the physical layout of the Tabernacle as a further example of distinctions in relationships with God. The court of the Tabernacle represents the Kingdom of Heaven; the Tabernacle itself represents the Kingdom of God. People of faith have, so to speak, entered the court, while only those who are

---

[18] G. T. Haywood, "The Mysteries of the Kingdom," *The Witness of God* 10, no. 10 (November-December 1930): 18.

[19] Compare G. T. Haywood, "The Mysteries of the Kingdom," *The Witness of God* 10, no. 10 (November-December 1930): 17-19 with *The Scofield Reference Bible*, 1003, 1014-18.

[20] An interesting thing about the use of Scofield by early twentieth century Pentecostals, whether Trinitarian or Oneness, is that Scofield was not sympathetic with Pentecostalism. This problem has been explored by various Pentecostal scholars. See, e.g., Gerald T. Sheppard, "Pentecostals and the Hermeneutics of Dispensationalism: The Anatomy of an Uneasy Relationship," *Pneuma: The Journal of the Society for Pentecostal Studies*, Fall (1984): 5; F. L. Arrington, "Dispensationalism," in *NIDPCM*, 585; Kenneth J. Archer, *A Pentecostal Hermeneutic for the Twenty-First Century: Spirit, Scripture and Community*, Journal of Pentecostal Theology Supplement Series 28, eds., John Christopher Thomas, Rickie D. Moore, and Steven J. Land (London: T & T Clark International, 2004), 57.

"purged by blood and washing in water in the laver" can enter the sanctuary. Here Haywood offers scriptural support from John 3:3-5, Acts 2:38, and Mark 16:16.

Haywood draws heavily on Scofield in making a distinction between the Kingdom of God and the Kingdom of Heaven:

> (1) The Kingdom of God is *spiritual,* including all moral intelligences willingly subject to the will of God, whether angels, the Church, or saints of past or future dispensations . . .; while the Kingdom of Heaven is *earthly, visible,* Messianic, mediatorial, and Davidic, and *will culminate into the "millennium." Christ's visible reign on* earth. (2) The Kingdom of God *consists of none but the true, Spirit-filled children of God . . . while* the Kingdom of Heaven, during this age, is the sphere of a profession which may be real or false. . . . (3) Since the Kingdom of *God (the spiritual sphere of God's dominion), and the Kingdom of Heaven (the earthly sphere) are to terminate in one at the close of this age, the two are often spoken of interchangeably. They* have almost all things common. For this reason many parables and other teachings are spoken of the Kingdom of Heaven in Matt. and of the Kingdom of God in Mark and Luke. The parable of the wheat and tares, and of the net . . . are not spoken of the Kingdom of God. In that kingdom (of God) there are neither tares nor bad fish. But the parable of leaven is spoken of in the Kingdom of God also . . . for *in the midst of the Spirit-filled life there is much error, so much so that many of the baptized saints are led astray by the doctrines of false teachers.* (4) The Kingdom of God "comes not with outward show" . . . but is chiefly that which is inward and spiritual . . . while the Kingdom of Heaven is organic, and is to be manifested in glory on earth.[21]

Haywood then departs from reliance on Scofield and continues: "[A]nd will have the privilege of walking on earth and arising and going into the heavens as free as the angels. It is the Bride of Christ that will share this privilege—the Wise Virgins—those who are "baptized by one Spirit into one body."

To further demonstrate his point, he offers this analogy:

> Every man in Indiana is in the United States, but [all that are in the United States are not in Indiana,] every one in the house is in the yard, but all that are in the yard are not in the house. All who were in the Sanctuary were in the Court, but all that were in the Court were not in the Sanctuary. So it is with the Kingdom of Heaven and the Kingdom of God. One may be in the Kingdom of Heaven and yet not in the Kingdom of God, while he that is in the Kingdom of God is in the Kingdom of Heaven also.[22]

Haywood believed that there would be "tribulation saints"—those who missed the rapture of the church—who would wrestle "with the powers of the devil in the anti-christ." They are represented by the nine disciples at the foot of the Mount of Transfiguration who could not cast out an evil spirit.[23] Urshan concurred with

---

[21]G. T. Haywood, "The Mysteries of the Kingdom," *The Witness of God* 10, no. 10 (November-December 1930): 18-19. See also Scofield, *Scofield Reference Bible,* 1003. Italized words are Haywood's development of Scofield's notes.

[22]G. T. Haywood, "The Mysteries of the Kingdom," *The Witness of God* 10, no. 10 (November-December 1930): 19. The bracketed portion of the quote above is inserted to replace an obvious omission from the original text.

[23]G. T. Haywood, "The Mysteries of the Kingdom," *The Witness of God* 10, no. 10

Haywood on these matters and went on to state that one must be "baptized into the revealed Name of the dispensation of the fullness of times [in order to] escape the terrible hour of tribulation."[24]

Thus Urshan was not alone among early Oneness theologians in believing those who had not been baptized in Jesus' name would enter the Kingdom of Heaven. Beyond this, he not only believed that it was possible to be a child of God before experiencing Spirit baptism, he taught that it was possible to have the Holy Spirit *with* us before he is *in* us. These Christians experience faith and great joy since they are "judicially" children of God before becoming his sons "experimentally" by being baptized with his Spirit. Receiving the promise of the Spirit is "the seal of our salvation," which must be "wrought and examined before it is sealed." Before giving his Holy Spirit, God cleanses and puts within a new heart and a new spirit.[25]

Apostolic Faith Doctrine of the New Birth

In 1941 Urshan published a booklet titled *Apostolic Faith Doctrine of the New Birth*. The booklet had its origins in a series of four messages he preached in September 1941 at the Apostolic Faith Church in New York where Urshan was pastor. Before being published in booklet form, the articles were printed in a special Christmas issue of *The Witness of God*.[26] Although the book contains no further development, it provides an excellent summary of his understanding of this doctrine. The publication of this booklet in 1941 is an indication that his soteriology had not changed in the years that had passed since his departure from the Assemblies of God. This has already been seen in the previous quotation from the April 1950 issue of *The Witness of God*.[27]

He begins by declaring that the teaching that one experiences the new birth at the point of believing on the Lord Jesus and accepting his "finished work on the cross" is an "incomplete man-made teaching" that offers no experience. It does, however, prepare the way "for the forth-coming of this matchless supernatural experience into those that repent, believe, and get baptized in the name of Jesus, our Lord."[28] Conversion is "conception, to be developed into this Bible new birth." Entrance into the church is gained by believing the "Apostolic teaching," being baptized in water in the name of the Lord Jesus and receiving the Holy Spirit.[29]

A glimmer of Urshan's theological roots in the doctrine of deification or theosis as taught by the Church of the East can be seen in this statement: "Just as sure as we are human in the Adamic nature, we can equally be sure to become divine in

---

(November-December 1930): 19.

[24]Urshan, "The Life Story of Andrew Bar David," *The Witness of God* (August 1946): 12.

[25]Urshan, "The Holy Spirit, Works, and Gifts," *The Witness of God* (April 1950): 4.

[26]Urshan, *Apostolic Faith Doctrine of the New Birth* (Cochrane, WI: The Witness of God, 1941), 3.

[27]Urshan, "The Holy Spirit, Works, and Gifts," *The Witness of God* (April 1950): 4.

[28]Urshan, *Apostolic Faith Doctrine*, 4.

[29]Urshan, *Apostolic Faith Doctrine*, 5.

Christ Jesus."[30] Nestorius said, "The Word of God became flesh, so that in him humanity might be transformed into divinity and the nature of humanity renewed."[31]

Urshan, like Haywood, is deeply influenced by the *Scofield Reference Bible*. In this instance he follows Scofield's understanding that in the Abrahamic Covenant, Abraham's descendants would be as numerous as the sand on the sea shore and the stars of heaven, indicating two kingdoms or two families. There is Abraham's earthly family, Israel, represented by the sand, and his heavenly family, the church, represented by the stars.[32] The heavenly family is also known as the Kingdom of God, into which entry is gained by being born of water in baptism and of the Spirit. In Jesus Christ there are two seeds, "the seed of the woman, His earthly part, and the seed of God or the Word of God, His heavenly or divine part."[33] To experience the new birth is to become "a real Jew, a child of Abraham according to the promises."

In order to commence his kingdom, "God had to beget God." This resulted in the "two-fold Deity of Christ." Indeed, Jesus is "twice, yea thrice . . . God because the Father and the Holy Ghost are all in Him, by Him, and through Him to compose the divine family, the stars like family or the heavenly family."[34]

On page 13, Urshan states, "Believe, obey, and delay not for you must be born again or be lost!" Directly across the page, in response to the question, "Would these folks [who have believed in Christ but have never been immersed in Jesus' name, and have not received the Holy Ghost with the sign of tongues] be lost if they had not gone on to the water and Spirit birth," Urshan answers, "No, for when they continued to walk in the light they had, they consequently entered into the deeper and higher divine experiences."[35] Perhaps these statements can be reconciled if we remember that Urshan tended to redefine words. In the final section of the booklet, titled "Twenty Seven Questions and Answers on the New Birth Teaching," Urshan's responses provide an outline of his soteriology.

Like Haywood, Urshan follows the *The Scofield Reference Bible* when explaining the difference between the kingdom of God and the kingdom of heaven.

> [T]he kingdom of God is strictly the kingdom or life belonging to celestial beings converted ones and the holy angels; but the kingdom of heaven means the Lord ruling among men on the earth, especially His people Israel. For instance, the kingdom of heaven contains both wheat and tares, good and bad fish; that is, such are found where this kingdom is; but nothing unrighteous or unclean can enter, appear in, or inherit the kingdom of God.[36]

Those who believe in Christ but are not baptized in Jesus' name and who have not been baptized with the Holy Spirit with the sign of tongues belong to the kingdom of heaven. They are the good seed in the kingdom and are eligible to be born of water and Spirit in order to enter the kingdom of God. They would not be lost, however,

---

[30] Urshan, *Apostolic Faith Doctrine*, 7.
[31] Baumer, *The Church of the East*, 1.
[32] Urshan, *Apostolic Faith Doctrine*, 10. See also Scofield, *The Scofield Reference Bible*, 25.
[33] Urshan, *Apostolic Faith Doctrine*, 10.
[34] Urshan, *Apostolic Faith Doctrine*, 11.
[35] Urshan, *Apostolic Faith Doctrine*, 13.
[36] Urshan, *Apostolic Faith Doctrine*, 13. See also *The Scofield Reference Bible*, 1003, 1014-6.

if they had not been "born of water and Spirit." Their spiritual progress indicates the genuineness of their faith, and on the basis of their faith they would not be lost.

There is also a difference between being "begotten" and "born." Just as a baby is begotten or conceived in the mother's womb, so a person who hears the word and embraces it is conceived or begotten by the word. Conception is not the new birth.

A person who has faith in Christ and who is thus conceived or begotten can be called a child of God before being born of the Spirit. Urshan sees biblical proof for this claim in Galatians 4:6: "And because ye are sons, God hath sent forth the Spirit of his Son into your hearts, crying, Abba, Father."

Those who believe on Christ's name and repent but who are not baptized by water and Spirit "stand on the same ground that the saints of the Old Testament stood; they were saved by faith not receiving the promise of the Spirit. They are not the real Spirit born children of God, but they are the people of God and adopted children."[37] Before being baptized into the body of Christ, believers are "in the womb of the church conceived."

In answer to the direct question "Can one be saved and not be born again," Urshan responded:

> The word "saved" conveys a greater meaning than generally known. It implies deliverance from sin and also God Himself coming into our life. . . . Yes, some can be delivered from hell though not being born of God, just like the Old Testament saints were saved through faith though not being born again. The thief on the cross may represent this class of saved ones who had no knowledge of the doctrine of the full salvation neither had a chance to perform it. His recognition of Christ and faith in Him saved him.[38]

Urshan did not wish, however, to minimize the importance of being baptized in the name of the Lord Jesus Christ and with the Holy Spirit with the sign of speaking in tongues. He believed that "[t]he apostolic teaching and experiences in the book of Acts are the sure New Testament pattern" and that only those with these experiences would constitute the Bride of Christ.

Summary

Urshan's soteriology calls those who believe in Jesus Christ to repentance, water baptism in the name of the Lord Jesus Christ for the remission of sin, and the gift of the Holy Spirit with the sign of speaking with tongues. This is the new birth. Those who have this experience enter the Kingdom of God, becoming the children of God, members of the body of Christ, the bride of Christ, and the church. They are "wise virgins."[39]

On the other hand, those who believe in Jesus Christ but who are not baptized in his name and who do not experience baptism with the Holy Spirit with the sign of speaking in tongues are in the Kingdom of Heaven. They have been conceived

---

[37] Urshan, *Apostolic Faith Doctrine*, 14.
[38] Urshan, *Apostolic Faith Doctrine*, 14.
[39] Urshan, *Apostolic Faith Doctrine*, 15.

or begotten and are thus in the womb of the church, but since they are not born again, they are not in the church. They are the people of God and adopted children, like Old Testament saints.

Chapter Nine

Responses to Theological Criticism

Introduction

David Reed, foremost historian of Oneness Pentecostalism, dates the birth of the Oneness movement as April 15, 1914 when Frank Ewart and Glenn Cook baptized each other in Jesus' name. Almost immediately division arose among Pentecostals over this issue. Urshan was on his missionary trip to Persia when the controversy erupted. He was deeply grieved over the division among Pentecostals into what he called the "Old Issue" and "New Issue" camps. This division arose after he departed from the United States for his missionary trip to Persia. Urshan arrived back in his home village of Abajalu on March 1, 1914. Frank Ewart and Glenn Cook baptized one another in Jesus' name on April 15, 1914, the date viewed by David Reed as the birth of the Oneness Pentecostal movement.[1] Although Urshan had baptized converts in the name of Jesus from the time of his baptism with the Holy Spirit on July 4, 1908, he was not so baptized until his ministry in Russia in 1915. Although he was fully aware of the developing schism in America, he determined to wait until his return to the United States to do further research into the matter. In the meantime, he intended to adhere to his earlier conviction not to rebaptize anyone. Due to the insistence of the believers in Russia, however, who had previously been baptized with the traditional formula and because of what he considered divine intervention, Urshan changed his mind.

When he arrived back in the United States on June 25, 1916, Urshan insisted that he did not identify with the "New Issue," although he had been baptized in Jesus' name. On September 13, 1917, he was ordained by the Assemblies of God, even though he did not fully endorse the statement of fundamental truths of the organization. He wrote at that time, "I do not object [to] the formula which is written in Acts 2:38, not as the New Issue folks explain it but simply because it is [the]

---

[1]Reed, *"In Jesus' Name"*, 143-4.

written word of God."² After disassociating himself from the Assemblies of God in 1919, however, he openly owned the label.

Urshan had hoped to be an agent of healing between Trinitarian and Oneness Pentecostals. For his efforts he received only criticism from both sides.

> We naturally thought when we came forth boldly proclaiming the name of the Lord that all the New Issue so-called ministers would not only rejoice over our new step, but would encourage us at least with a word of congratulation. While many did that and rejoiced over our new and firm stand for One God in Christ, yet there were those who were supposed pioneers of that message who began to throw slurs at us in their writings and their personal conversations.
>
> The Old Issue people began to publish that we had gone into error and that we had some carnal intentions for gain, [and] that is why we stepped out of their ranks taking the New Issue doctrine, and some of the New Issue preachers denounced us as being compromisers, saying [that] we knew the truth long before we fully preached it [and that] for the sake of some personal gain we stood with the opposers long enough to do a great deal of harm to the truth.³

Urshan felt isolated, wondering whether he had a future in the Oneness movement. He also gained a deeper appreciation for Jesus' words recorded in Matthew 10:22: "Ye shall be hated of all men for my name's sake." It occurred to him that "all men" included those with whom he was in theological and experiential agreement.⁴

As Urshan reflected on his separation from Trinitarian Pentecostals, he identified two causes for this turn of events: he was misunderstood, and the "enemy" was at work.

Misunderstood

When Urshan's seven-month Los Angeles crusade was in full swing, he was asked by officials in the Assemblies of God to submit a "Confession of Faith" for publication in *The Weekly Evangel*. His "confession" appeared in the April 20, 1918 issue:

> It has been reported lately from this city something that may create a wrong impression that I am supporting the advocators of the "New Issue" so-called in our great blessed revival meetings in this city. This is absolutely not so, but rather contrary. I personally believe and stand on the blessed written word of God concerning the great mystery of godliness, not on the conclusions of men, nor in their words of strife concerning God-head teaching, therefore I prayerfully and humbly confess that I believe in **one God, the Father, the Son and the Holy Ghost.** Matthew 28:19.

---

²Stephen Ray Graham, "Conservative American Protestantism and the Origins of Pentecostalism: A Case Study of Andrew D. Urshan" (MA thesis, Wheaton College, 1982), 47.

³Urshan, "The Story of My Life—29th Chapter: Between Two Fires for 'Jesus Only'," *The Witness of God* 7, no. 65 (June-July 1925): 2.

⁴Urshan, "The Story of My Life—29th Chapter: Between Two Fires for 'Jesus Only'," *The Witness of God* 7, no. 65 (June-July 1925): 2.

I believe in Jesus Christ, the Son of the Father, who is the true God and the eternal life. 1 John 5:20. 2 John 5.

I believe that there are three that bear record in heaven, the Father, the Word **(Jesus Christ)** and the Holy Ghost, and these three are one. 1 John 5:7.

I believe in the Spirit by which we are all baptized into one body, whether we be Jews or Gentiles, whether bond or free and have been all made to drink in one Spirit; yea, one Lord, one faith, one baptism, one God and Father of all, who is above all, and in you all. 1 Cor. 12:13, and Eph. 4:5-6.

I believe this adorable Three-One God can be only approached and seen in and through the person or face of Jesus Christ, the Son. 1 Timothy 6:16. Matthew 11:27. John 1:18. John 14:7-11. "For in Him dwelleth all the fullness of the Godhead bodily." Col. 2:9.

I believe in one most glorious, eternal, incomprehensible and mysterious Being of God; and that Jesus Christ the Son, is the only true and full express image of His glorious and bright Being. Heb. 1:3. Col. 1:15-19.

I believe also and practice the emphatic and definite commandment of God through the lips of the great apostle to the Gentiles who said, "and whatsoever ye do **in word or deed**, do all in the name of the Lord Jesus, giving thanks to God and the **Father** by Him." Col. 3:17.

Now, "The grace of the Lord Jesus Christ and the Love of God, and the communion of the Holy Ghost be with you all. Amen." 2 Cor. 13:14.[5]

In Urshan's opinion, this "confession" was made necessary because of jealousy among some of the ministers who were welcomed on the platform during the Los Angeles crusade. These ministers were "hunting to find some reason to down us."[6] They thought he was "teaching the so-called New Issue doctrine" because he was "exalting fervently the Name of Jesus." As a result, the state chairman of the Assemblies of God "called a conference for the purpose of condemning" Urshan on doctrinal grounds, "but they were shamefully disappointed for they could not find a cause." This was not the end, however. The state chairman sent a letter to the Assemblies of God headquarters stating that although Urshan appeared to agree with the teachings of the organization, he seemed to encourage the New Issue teachings. The letter insisted that Urshan must take a stand either with the Assemblies of God or with those who taught the New Issue.

Urshan was grieved over being "forced to do something that if [he] were left free [he] would not have done, because [he] loved God's baptized people without respect of persons and their particular differences in some of their doctrines." He believed his "evangelistic ministry . . . could have benefited both schools and .

---

[5] Andrew D. Urshan, "Confession of Faith," *The Weekly Evangel* (April 20, 1918): 13. Emphasis in original.

[6] Urshan, "The Story of My Life—28th Chapter," *The Witness of God* 6, no. 64 (May 1925): 3.

. . wished to remain neutral," but this was not to be. For three months, he quit preaching for Trinitarian or Oneness Pentecostals, praying and waiting for the mind of God.

During his three-month sabbatical from preaching for others (he conducted his own independent ministry during this time in a local theater[7] and for a small group known as the House of Light[8]), Urshan received "greater revelation" on the deity of Christ. He wrote to the officials of the Assemblies of God explaining his belief that the name of the Father, Son, and Holy Ghost was "Jesus Christ our Lord" and asking whether the Assemblies of God wished for him to continue in fellowship with them. They responded that his position was not acceptable. Urshan then withdrew, sometime during the six-week period of April 1 – May 17, 1919. He then proceeded to write and circulate his seven open letters.[9]

From Urshan's perspective, he was misunderstood. Under the subheading "Yes, Misunderstood," he wrote,

> Some of our friends think we do not believe in the Sonship of Jesus Christ and [that we are] doing away with the Fatherhood of God. We answer that such a report is erroneous and a misrepresentation. There is nothing sweeter to us [than] the sentence "Jesus the blessed Son of God" or "Our heavenly Father." We see the word proceeding from God the Father becoming flesh, and yet that very word is still eternally in the Father and the Father is in that incarnate, crucified, buried, risen and glorified WORD. . . . the Father is in the Son, [the] Son [is] in the Father, two, yea, three, but never more than ONE SINGLE DIVINE being or person.[10]

As elsewhere in his writings, Urshan describes the relationship between the Father, Son, and Holy Spirit in terms with which western Trinitarianism would concur. Theologically, they call this relationship circumincession, interpenetration, or perichoresis.[11] However, in Urshan's understanding, the words "being" and "person" are synonyms, so that to say that there are three "persons" in the Godhead means that there are three "beings." This misunderstanding of the Trinitarian position led Urshan to believe that Trinitarians were guilty of believing in three Gods.

---

[7]Urshan, "The Story of My Life—29th Chapter," *The Witness of God* 7, no. 65 (June-July 1925): 2.

[8]"The House of Light," *The Witness of God* 1, no. 10 (September 1920): 4-5.

[9]Urshan, "The Story of My Life—28th Chapter," *The Witness of God* 6, no. 64 (May 1925): 3. E. N. Bell wrote in the April 19, 1919 issue of *The Christian Evangel*, "Brother Urshan has offered to turn in his credentials held from the General Council, if they cannot endorse his teaching, and I am sure they cannot endorse it" (E. N. Bell, "Andrew Urshan's New Stand," *The Christian Evangel* [April 19, 1919]: 9). Then, in the May 17, 1919 issue of *The Christian Evangel*, Bell reported that Urshan had "given up his credentials and left us" (E. N. Bell, "The Urshan Trouble," *The Christian Evangel* [May 17, 1919]: 7).

[10]Urshan, "The Story of My Life—26th Chapter, *The Witness of God* 7, no. 62 (March 1925): 5.

[11]Circumcincession "refers primarily to the coinherence of the persons of the Trinity in the divine essence and in each other" (Richard A. Muller, *Dictionary of Latin and Greek Theological Terms* (Grand Rapids: Baker Book House, 1985), 67. This theological concept is also referred to as *perichoresis* (Muller, 222) and *interpenetration* (Justo L. Gonzalez, *Essential Theological Terms* [Louisville, KY: Westminster John Knox Press, 2005], 36).

The Work of the Enemy

In addition to being misunderstood, Urshan believed "the enemy" was behind his rejection by Trinitarian Pentecostals.

> [T]he enemy was made angry over our God-given victory in this revival [the Los Angeles crusade of 1918] and . . . we were forced to stop our ministry to all the Pentecostal faiths, blessing them, encouraging them to love one another, to have fellowship and worship together in such soul-saving campaigns, overlooking their difference on some Bible subjects.
>
> If that had not happened we would have been still preaching to thousands of different groups of the Pentecostals together to this very day, but Satan interfered, inserting jealousy in some hearts. This proves again that our worst enemies are those within our own camps as Judas was among the eleven.[12]

During the early days of the Los Angeles crusade, Urshan wrote an article that appeared in *The Weekly Evangel* accusing unnamed Pentecostal believers of "carnality."

> Many are full of harsh judgment, bitter criticism, pride and envy in their life and practice because they are planted in the evil soil of carnality, and they are so rooted in that hard, unproductive soil that it takes weeks of revival meetings to unroot them. We meet such strife and trouble creators everywhere, but some of them though they are ignorant, are honest, and when they hear of God's **fullness** they begin to seek the same.[13]

The following month, Urshan wrote, "It is a sad fact that many Pentecostal ministers are busy preaching and fighting over theological doctrines and are neglecting such messages as this [confession of faults]."[14] Then, the next month, his "Confession of Faith" was printed in the same publication.

Although the Los Angeles crusade was considered a great success in terms of attendance and the number of people reported to have come to faith in Christ,[15] discontent rumbled among the ministers attending the meeting. In retrospect, Urshan wrote that those who embraced the "new light" were "slandered, misrepresented and cast out by their Pentecostal brethren," fulfilling Isaiah 66:5, but that the day was coming soon when "there will be no more scoffers and mockers of these **one God people** for they shall be put to shame for their rejection of the new or more light of Christ which the Holy Spirit has tried to show them." In his opinion, the Pentecostals who rejected the "new light" had chosen "darkness or the

---

[12]Urshan, "The Final and the Conclusion," *The Witness of God* (May 1963): 7.

[13]Andrew D. Urshan, "The Fullness of God," *The Weekly Evangel* (February 2, 1918): 3. Emphasis in original. For Urshan, the word "fullness" was connected with his understanding of the Godhead. (See Urshan, "The New Light or the More Light," *The Witness of God* 1, no. 10 [September 1920]: 2.)

[14]Andrew D. Urshan, "The Confession of our Faults," *The Weekly Evangel* (March 2, 1918): 4.

[15]It was reported that 500 people came to new faith in Christ during the Los Angeles crusade. See Urshan, "Our Farewell Meeting in Los Angeles," *The Witness of God* (May 1963): 7.

false light (the traditions of men), instead of the Heavenly revelation of the Lord God Almighty."[16] In contrast, Urshan asserted, "We cannot believe the theory of the three distinct and separate persons of the Godhead. . . . We do, however, believe in **one God,** who reveals Himself to us as the Father, the Son, and the Holy Spirit, with three distinct manifestations, operations, in three dispensations."[17]

Urshan counted as enemies not only those who rejected his views out of hand, but also those who had once embraced them and later turned away: "Our worst enemies are those who once stood firm for the truth as it is in Christ Jesus and [who] have left our ranks, joining the opposing parties for the sake of popularity, etc. However, we are glad the Lord is the avenger of His elect, who cry unto Him day and night."[18] Those who fought immersion as the right mode of water baptism were "goat-like Christians," while to fight immersion "solely into the name of the Lord Jesus Christ" was evidence of "the anti-Christ spirit."[19]

Within two years of withdrawing from the Assemblies of God, Urshan was convinced that "half of the Pentecostal movement has gone into denominationalism and legalism . . . fast losing the Holy Spirit power, the Holy Spirit love and unity, being in danger of complete collapse . . . struggling to keep God's work . . . together by commercial and political schemes and power." Meanwhile, those with whom Urshan agreed had "finally caught the glimpse of the apostolic doctrine" and were living "holy, unselfish, and consecrated lives."[20]

Accusations flew in both directions. E. N. Bell described Urshan's membership in the Assemblies of God as "playing 'possum." He further claimed that Urshan's statements before the General Council of the Assemblies of God at a meeting in St. Louis deceived the council and that some of those who sent missionary funds to Urshan were "misled" and wanted their money returned. Bell wrote,

> [W]e cannot . . . approve . . . of his present teaching or of the methods which have really deceived both us and some of our people.
>
> . . . We owe it to our people to let them know we have been deceived. Through the Evangel, unknowingly, we let our readers be misled, and now it is only common honesty to confess it, and let our people know the truth that they no longer be misled. If anyone desires to approve of his teaching and continue to send him money to waste

---

[16]Urshan, "The New Light or the More Light," *The Witness of God* 1, no. 10 (September 1920): 1. Emphasis in original.

[17]Urshan, "The New Light or the More Light," *The Witness of God* 1, no. 10 (September 1920): 2. Emphasis in original. The reference to "three dispensations" may sound at first like Sabellianism, but Urshan elsewhere explained his view in such a way that the manifestations were simultaneous, and he specifically rejected Sabellianism. Urshan apparently misunderstood Sabellianism, however, to teach that in the Godhead there were "three beings" and that these "beings" were only "attributes." (See "The Historical Facts," *The Witness of God* 2, no. 19 [July 1921]: 1; "How and When Paganism Entered Christianity," *The Witness of God* 10, no. 105 [May 1929]: 4-5.)

[18]Andrew D. Urshan, "Editorial," *The Witness of God* 8, no. 71 (January 1926): 3.

[19]Urshan, editorial note on "Sheep Should Be Dipped," *The Witness of God* 10, no. 92 (March 1928): 7.

[20]Urshan, "The Historical Facts," *The Witness of God* 2, no. 19 (July 1921): 1.

in flooding the country with circulars costing over $100 an issue, telling of his new doctrines and what he confesses is a new revelation, I have not a word to say. . . . .

. . . We love Bro. Urshan and our hearts are bleeding over him, but

Bro. Urshan Went to the Public.

We tried PRIVATELY not long ago, when questions arose, to get Bro. Urshan to take his stand for the truth which his holding credentials with us implied he held. His final answer was to rush publicly into print and try to spread his errors all over the country.[21]

From Urshan's perspective, the reason he did not clearly and publicly state his convictions earlier was that God did not lead him to do so and that the "conditions were not favorable." He believed it was a mistake for many who did not exercise his restraint.

[M]any have failed to understand God's plan for them in the Holy Ghost and they have given out Spirit-inspired revelations and divine lessons too soon, before the full development of the same, and by their human knowledge and zeal, have gone before the Lord instead of following His leadings; thus, having missed the mark and perfect approval of God, they have caused confusion, divisions, and trouble among God's saints instead of building up the Church of God. I solemnly believe this has been one of the biggest causes of creating so much strife, debate, misunderstanding, and the grieving of each other over what is called "Old" and "New" Issues.[22]

Summary

The second decade of the twentieth century was a troubled time for Pentecostalism. First the movement divided in two over Durham's doctrine of "The Finished Work of Christ." While this controversy divided the movement into "Second Work" and "Finished Work" camps, both expressions were considered acceptable within the broad scope of Christian orthodoxy. Now the "Finished work" camp divided again over the "New Issue" which Christian orthodoxy considered heretical. In addition, Oneness adherents believed that the baptism with the Holy Spirit evidenced by speaking in tongues was the birth of the Spirit to which Jesus referred in John 3. Within Oneness Pentecostalism there was also the view, like Urshan's, that water baptism in Jesus' name was the "birth" of water to which Jesus referred in the same text.

In retrospect, it is clear that more than the Holy Spirit was at work. Clearly the baptism with the Holy Spirit did not overrule human nature. Nor is it likely that the Spirit would lead Christians to such startlingly different conclusions or to hurl bitter accusations at each other.

---

[21]E. N. Bell, "The Urshan Trouble," *The Christian Evangel* (May 17, 1919): 6-7. Emphasis in original.

[22]Urshan, "Republication of our First 1918 Open Letter to All Pentecostal Saints," *The Witness of God* (n.d.): 1.

Urshan yearned for acceptance from both Trinitarian and Oneness Pentecostals. At the same time, given enough time and in the right spiritual environment, he hoped he could be an instrument to bring all Pentecostals together theologically and experientially. When this did not happen, he chose to stand with those who shared the theological understanding he believed God had revealed to him.

Chapter Ten

Conclusion

Pentecostal scholars testify to the significant and lasting contribution Andrew D. Urshan has made not only to Oneness Pentecostalism but also to Pentecostalism at large.[1] Urshan's influence was due to the abundance of his literary output as well as to his strength of character and depth of spirituality. Even those who disagreed with him theologically admired the genuine trust in God and the sterling courage that enabled him to face almost indescribable danger and hardship during his mission to Persia.

Urshan's unwillingness to compromise his deeply held convictions was balanced by his love and concern for those with whom he disagreed. His reluctant departure from the Assemblies of God was made all the more painful because it signaled the end of his hope to build bridges of fellowship between Trinitarian and Oneness Pentecostals. He grieved over this until the end of his life.

---

[1] Works referencing Urshan by non-Oneness authors include, but are not limited to the following: Robert Mapes Anderson, *Vision of the Disinherited: The Making of American Pentecostalism* (New York: Oxford University Press, 1979), 112, 129, 187, 295; Stanley M. Burgess and Gary B. McGee, eds., *Dictionary of Pentecostal and Charismatic Movements* (Grand Rapids: Zondervan Publishing House, 1988), 866; Stanley M. Burgess, ed., *NIDPCM*, 1167; D. William Faupel, *The Everlasting Gospel: The Significance of Eschatology in the Development of Pentecostal Thought*, Journal of Pentecostal Theology Supplement Series 10, John Christopher Thomas, Rickie D. Moore, Steven J. Land, eds. (Sheffield: Sheffield Academic Press, 1996), 218, 220, 233, 234, 245, 282, 285-87; Walter J. Hollenweger, *The Pentecostals* (Minneapolis, MN: Augsburg Publishing House, 1972), 269; Douglas Jacobsen, *Thinking in the Spirit: Theologies of the Early Pentecostal Movement* (Bloomington, IN: Indiana University Press, 2003), 14, 196-197, 232-234, 235-259, 354, 358, 390 n. 88, 390-391 nn. 97, 107, 109, 392-393 nn. 116, 124; David A. Reed, *"In Jesus' Name": The History and Beliefs of Oneness Pentecostals,* Journal of Pentecostal Theology Supplement Series 31, John Christopher Thomas, Rickie Moore, Steven J. Land, eds. (Blandford Forum: Deo Publishing, 2008), passim.; David Reed, "Aspects of the Origins of Oneness Pentecostalism," in Vinson Synan, ed., *Aspects of Pentecostal-Charismatic Origins* (Plainfield, NJ: Logos International, 1975), 143-168; Vinson Synan, *The Century of the Holy Spirit: 100 Years of Pentecostal and Charismatic Renewal* (Nashville, TN: Thomas Nelson Publishers, 2001): 146; Grant Wacker, *Heaven Below: Early Pentecostals and American Culture* (Cambridge, MA: Harvard University Press, 2001), 80, 188.

As if he had not already faced enough suffering to prove his trust in God during the Armenian Genocide and by the rejection of those he counted as dear brothers and sisters in Christ, his failed marriage proved to be the culminating blow. Understandably, he identified with Job. In an article entitled, "The Fiery Furnace of Testing," he wrote:

> Our move to Chicago must have angered Satan much against myself and family. He must have challenged God to let him turn loose on us, to afflict our very lives; for we did go through some awful tests, trials, temptations, afflictions and heartbreaking sorrows. The things which happened in our family circle, we do not feel led to write about, but we can say, that even in those very dark hours of unexpected and unforeseen battles with the "powers of darkness," we held on to the Holy Name of Jesus, and He (blessed be His glorious name) hid us in that strong tower again, from the wrath of our enemies.[2]

Thus, Urshan did not simply develop a theoretical approach to doctrine and praxis, but also had his faith tested by the most severe trials imaginable. He found that faith sufficient to sustain him through it all. He was not perfect, and he was the first to admit that.[3] But his personal imperfections did not cause him to give up hope. He found his God to be sufficient for the trials without and the struggles within.

Urshan's contribution to Pentecostalism in North America was unique. He alone of the four most influential shapers of early twentieth century Oneness Pentecostalism brought to the table the perspective of the Christianity of the East.[4] Although he had no formal training in its theology and may have misunderstood its finer points, Urshan brought this influence along with its cultural milieu with him to the United States. of America. Though this early influence was filtered through the Presbyterian lens of his home and limited formal education, and eventually through his experiences with broader Evangelicalism (i.e., Brethren, The Moody Church, the Nazarene Church, and Pentecostalism), Urshan never gave up his confidence in mystery and a hermeneutic that valued symbolism.

As Urshan's theology developed, he never recanted his assessment of the value of his earlier spiritual experiences, including conversion as a student attending the American Presbyterian College, his baptism by immersion in the Brethren Church, or his sanctification in the Nazarene Church in Chicago. Even though he decided upon later reflection that his experience as a Presbyterian student was not the new birth as he had previously thought, he still acknowledged it as a dramatic, life-changing event. He continued to describe it as conversion and said, in terms

---

[2]Urshan, *The Life Story,* 5th ed., 260.

[3]See, e.g., Urshan, "My Last Personal Remarks Concerning the Story of My Life," *The Witness of God* (October 1946): 3; Urshan, "When We Are Ashamed of Ourselves," *The Witness of God* (April 1963): 3-5.

[4]David Reed identifies the four most influential shapers of Oneness Pentecostalism as Frank Ewart, G. T. Haywood, Andrew D. Urshan, and Franklin Small. See David A. Reed, *"In Jesus' Name": The History and Beliefs of Oneness Pentecostals,* Journal of Pentecostal Theology Supplement Series 31, John Christopher Thomas, Rickie Moore, Steven J. Land, eds. (Blandford Forum: Deo Publishing, 2008), 168-9.

reminiscent of the language of Eastern theology, "The Spirit witnessed with my spirit that I had truly been blessed and the branch of the Divine tree in the bitter water of my life was planted afresh."[5]

Urshan's baptism in the Brethren Church, which would certainly have been done having the words "in the name of the Father, and of the Son, and of the Holy Ghost" called over him, and which was no doubt triple immersion, did not represent his final understanding of water baptism. Nevertheless, he did not renounce the experience but rather continued to value it as an event that revealed to him the importance of "walking in the light."[6]

His sanctification experience in a Nazarene Church continued to be a spiritual highlight in Urshan's life, even after he came to the conclusion that conversion, sanctification, and Holy Spirit baptism should ideally occur simultaneously.[7] He never claimed that this experience was anything less than sanctification, and he didn't disregard the sanctification of others whose experience, like his, followed conversion and preceded Holy Spirit baptism.[8]

Urshan's interest in name theology, identified by Reed as the attempt to retrieve the early Jewish Christian theme of the name of God, mirrors Ephrem of Syria's theology of divine names, an integral expression of Ephrem's symbolic theology. Although Urshan comes to different conclusions than Ephrem, the methodology is similar. Urshan's conclusions are linked to his exaltation of Jesus to the place of "absolute deity," the one in whom dwelt the Father, the Son, and the Holy Spirit.

After Urshan's withdrawal from membership in The Moody Church and baptism with the Holy Spirit, he founded a successful Persian mission in Chicago. This mission grew out of the ministry he had already begun as a member of The Moody Church and had been considered the mission of The Moody Church to the growing Persian community in Chicago. After Urshan's departure from The Moody Church the mission grew rapidly and became the first base for his ministry. While serving as pastor of the Persian Pentecostal Mission, Urshan attended the 1913 World-Wide Camp Meeting at Arroyo Seco, near Los Angeles, California. There he participated as a speaker, sitting on the front row of the platform with the leading preachers.[9]

While attending the World-Wide Camp Meeting, Urshan was "legally ordained" and received a call from God to go on a mission trip to Persia.[10] After further ministry in North America, he arrived at his home village of Abajalu on

---

[5] Urshan, *The Life Story,* 5th ed., 27. Cf. Urshan, *The Story of My Life,* 1st ed., 30.
[6] Urshan, *The Life Story,* 5th ed., 87-88.
[7] Sturdivan, "Andrew D. Urshan," *Gospel Tidings* (January 1968): 2.
[8] Andrew D. Urshan, *Supreme Need of the Hour and the Source of the Mighty Revivals* (Cochrane, WI: 1922), 15.
[9] It remains a curiosity, in light of later developments, that he makes no reference in his autobiography to the issue of Jesus' name baptism in connection with this camp meeting. Whatever happened there regarding baptism in Jesus' name seems to have made no impact on him. He had been baptizing in the name of the Lord Jesus Christ since 1910.
[10] Urshan, *The Story of My Life,* 1st ed., 52-53.

March 1, 1914.[11] From then until his departure from Russia in 1916, he faced untold hardship in connection with the beginning of World War I, the Armenian Genocide, and religious persecution. But in the midst of this adversity his ministry was accompanied by signs, wonders, and outpourings of the Holy Spirit, resulting in the establishment of Oneness Pentecostal churches that endure to this day. As his ministry in Russia drew to an end, Urshan was baptized in the name of the Lord Jesus Christ.

Upon his return to the United States in 1916, Urshan attempted to continue the ministry he had among Trinitarian Pentecostals when he left for Persia two years earlier. In 1917 he was married to Mildred H. Hammergren and ordained by the General Council of the Assemblies of God. But in 1918, when he emphasized his understanding of the "absolute deity" of Jesus Christ during a successful seven month campaign in Los Angeles, questions about his theological orthodoxy arose among other ministers attending the meeting. This resulted in Urshan returning his credentials to the Assemblies of God in 1919 and identifying himself unreservedly with the "New Issue," also known at that time as the "Jesus Only" movement. His separation from the Assemblies of God was a painful episode in Urshan's life; had he been allowed to hold his convictions while remaining in that fellowship, he would have done so.

Urshan's ministry among Oneness Pentecostals flourished, but his suffering was not over. Andrew and Mildred had four children, and Mildred stayed at home with the children while Andrew travelled frequently as an evangelist. Andrew was able to provide a beautiful home for his family at 3219 Osgood St. in Chicago. The home still stands, but with a renaming and renumbering of the streets in the area, it is now located at 3210 N. Kenmore Avenue in Chicago's Lakeview District.[12]

During Urshan's absences from home his wife became romantically involved with another man. The marriage ended in divorce in 1935, bringing Urshan's evangelistic ministry to a temporary halt. Gaining custody of his children, Andrew accepted the pastorate of a church in New York City where he raised his family.

In 1950 Urshan remarried, moved to California, and resumed his evangelistic ministry. Although this signaled a new and hopeful day in his ministry, he was yet to face another experience of deep sorrow. In 1951, his youngest child, "Andy," died at the age of twenty-two. He had suffered for many years with muscular dystrophy.

Urshan died in 1967 in the midst of a preaching campaign at the age of eighty-three. He left a rich family, spiritual, and theological legacy that continues to enrich Oneness Pentecostalism.

---

[11] Urshan, *The Story of My Life,* 1st ed., 52-55.

[12] Faith St. Clair, Urshan's daughter, remembers that the family lived in a "beautiful home" (September 24, 2009 telephone interview with Faith St. Clair. As of this writing, it is for sale for $885,000, but the real estate agent handling the home places its true value at over $1,000,000, attributing the current asking price to weakness in the real estate market. (This information was provided by Dennis Mosten, Urshan's step-grandson, who lived and pastored a church in the Chicago area and who did research for this project in the Chicago Public Library.)

Although Urshan's writings touched many areas of faith and Christian living, his primary emphases were on the doctrine of the God-head, Christology, and soteriology. As a Oneness theologian, the doctrine of the God-head and Christology were one and the same for Urshan. His understanding of the doctrine represented both the "Apostolic Faith" and the theology of the Church of the East.[13] This set his approach to these subjects apart from the approach of such other early Oneness thinkers as Ewart, Haywood, and Small, creating a unique contribution to Oneness thought in the first half of the twentieth century.

Urshan's description of the Incarnation differed from that of other Oneness thinkers. For Urshan, Jesus was the manifestation of the Father, Son, and Holy Spirit. This differed from western Trinitarianism, which sees Jesus as the Incarnation of God the Son, but it also differed from the more common Oneness view in the western world, which sees the Incarnation as the manifestation of God, resulting in the Son of God, who is both God and man. Responding to a common Oneness misunderstanding of western Trinitarianism, Urshan frequently insisted that there were not three "separate and distinct persons" in the Godhead. As late as 1953, Urshan published the following statement in *The Witness of God*.

> Who was or is He? No one knows, not even the angels. . . . the mysterious One, Elohim the creator of all. He is incomprehensible and unknown—One and far beyond any human imagination or words. . . .
>
> No one knows who God's Son really is, no, not even the angels. The Son alone knows who God the Father is, and the Father alone knows who the Son is just as Matt. 11:27 declares. Even Paul did not know the Son of God as he desired to about this. . . . The only begotten of the Father came to us in the flesh, and from then on, and for the first time from all the beginn[ing] God was and is to be more fully and really known, as to His perfect likeness, His divine nature and His mysterious personality. . . .
>
> The Lord Jesus Christ, as to His mysterious relationship, and as Logos the word of God, he is the only begotten Son of God, how long, where, and how, no one knows. . . .
>
> Two or three in offices, or manifestations of Himself, known as the Father, the Son, and the Holy Ghost.
>
> He is three distinct, but not separate in His divine being and personality, hence wherever one part of His being is the other two are there also. Wherever one is at work, the other two are at work at the same place and a[t] precisely the same time. . . .
>
> Here we see the Father or Elohim at work creating all things, but He is working in His Word by His Spirit; not as three Gods or divine spirits, but as One divine mystery, known as the Father, the Son, and the Holy Spirit.[14]

---

[13]Urshan, *The Life Story*, 5th ed., 15.

[14]Urshan, "The Mystery of God, or Who is God?," *The Witness of God* (December 1953): 4-5. In the phrase "He is three distinct, but not separate," Urshan may have intended to write,

Urshan's theology did not survive to become normative in late twentieth and early twenty-first century Oneness theology in North America. His soteriology was to fare better.

From early in the twentieth century, Oneness Pentecostalism has been characterized by the belief that Peter's proclamation in Acts 2:38 was normative for Christian initiation in the first century church and that it should remain so. Two streams of thought developed, the one seeing water baptism as identification with Christ and the other viewing water baptism as the "birth of water" to which Jesus referred in John 3. Those who saw baptism as identification with Christ believed that baptism was performed "because of" the remission of sins, or in response to the forgiveness that had already occurred, while those who saw baptism as the birth of water believed that baptism accomplished the remission of sins.

According to Reed, Urshan, Ewart, Haywood, and Small had much in common.

> They all agreed on the necessity of re-baptism in the name of Jesus, the revelational character of the name of Jesus, and the radical oneness of God with its attendant rejection of the doctrine of the Trinity. But they did not agree on the meaning of Acts 2:38. Ewart and Small remained closest to Durham's initial vision of Acts 2:38 as full identification with Christ. Haywood and Urshan interpreted the same text as the new birth. This difference led to a divergence that produced two distinct streams of thought within the Oneness movement, which in turn has had repercussions both internally and externally for nearly a century.[15]

When the Pentecostal Church, Inc. merged with the Pentecostal Assemblies of Jesus Christ to form the United Pentecostal Church, Inc., these diverse views had to find common ground. Church historian, Robin Johnston highlights the issue:

> The most critical area of concern was over the function of baptism and the language of the new birth. On the whole, the members of the PA of JC tended to equate the new birth with John 3:5, which references the birth of water and Spirit. They held that the birth of the water was Jesus Name baptism and birth of the Spirit was the baptism of the Holy Spirit. As a result the majority of the PA of JC maintained that baptism in Jesus name was "for" the remission of sins. Conversely a significant portion of the PCI believed that baptism was "because of" the remission of sins.[16]

Urshan was affiliated with the Pentecostal Assemblies of Jesus Christ and held to the view most common in that organization. He says nothing in the various editions of his autobiography about the status of his affiliation after the merger, but the first time his name appears in the ministerial directory of the United Pentecostal Church, Inc. was 1956, eleven years after the merger. The most specific statement by Urshan about his organizational affiliation after the formation of the United Pentecostal Church, Inc. is this: "Later I took membership with this good

---

"He is three distinct, but not separate [attributes]." Elsewhere, he wrote, "God has put in man, whom He created in His own image, three distinct but inseparable attributes to represent or to foreshadow His own mysterious TRI-ONE Being" (Urshan, *Doctrine of Trinity,* 32).

[15]Reed, 169.

[16]Robin M. Johnston, "Howard A. Goss: A Pentecostal Life" (PhD diss., Regent University, 2010), 150.

organization."[17] He was able to affiliate with the United Pentecostal Church even though the fundamental doctrine of that organization did not specifically mention the "birth of water" or "birth of spirit."[18]

Urshan died as a man who had cut a bold swath across the religious landscape not only of North America, but also of Persia, Russia, Norway, and Great Britain. He was not deterred by threats of death, suffering, rejection, or failure. Had he been born in another time, but not in another place, his name may have been found with another list of heroes, one that begins with Abel and ends with Urshan's fellow-sufferers of another era.[19]

---

[17]Sturdivan, "Andrew D. Urshan," *Gospel Tidings* (January 1968): 3.

[18]Johnston points out that at the request of Howard Goss, who would become the first general superintendent of the United Pentecostal Church, Inc., W. T. Witherspoon composed the statement that was adopted as the fundamental doctrine without using the words "birth of water and Spirit" (Johnston, "Howard A. Goss," 150).

[19]See Hebrews 11:4-38.

Appendix

Review of Relevant Literature: A Bibliographic Essay

Primary Sources Related to Urshan

A substantial assortment of primary sources written by Urshan is available for research. This includes five editions of his autobiography, collections of sermons, treatises on a variety of subjects, and articles appearing over a period of nearly fifty years in his monthly periodical, *The Witness of God*. Urshan wrote on many topics, not all of which are pertinent to this study. For our purposes, our research is confined to those resources that tell the story of his life and the shaping of his theology.

A review of the primary literature reveals that Urshan used the language of Eastern Christianity during his theological journey: (1) Nestorius is appealed to for his rejection of a Trinity of "three separate and distinct persons"; (2) the idea of mystery in the "threeness" of the one God is embraced in 1919, including the description of the triune God as an "incomprehensible Being" and a mysterious "tri-one" Being whose threeness is seen as "mind, wisdom, and power"; (3) Urshan's views of marriage reflect the monastic theology of the Church of the East; (4) the language of the Church of the East is employed to describe his conversion; (5) the condemnation of kneeling before idols and pictures reflects the view of Eastern Christianity; (6) Urshan's "way of watchfulness and prayer" resonates with the language of Evagrius; (7) the sympathetic treatment of astrology is in harmony with astrology's acceptance by the Church of the East.

Autobiographies

A comparison of the five editions of Urshan's autobiography is particularly significant in revealing the ongoing theological reshaping of his story. This does not mean the story changes, but that Urshan understands parts of his story differently from the perspective of his developing theological journey. Because of the significance of the changes as Urshan retold his story, it is important to examine each edition of his autobiography.

The first edition of Urshan's autobiography, *The Story of My Life*, was published by the Gospel Publishing House, the official publishing house of the Assemblies of God, when it was located in St. Louis, Missouri.[1] This version, which chronicles events in Urshan's life from his birth (May 17, 1884) to his marriage to Mildred Harriet Hammergren (August 9, 1917) includes no notice of his practice of baptizing in the name of the Lord Jesus Christ or of his view of the Oneness of God. Although Urshan attended the Arroyo Seco camp meeting in 1913, where he heard God's call to return to his homeland of Persia to preach the gospel, nothing is said about the controversy that arose at that camp meeting about baptizing in the name of the Lord Jesus Christ.[2] Urshan describes his conversion experience as being "born again" and distinguishes it from his later experience of baptism in the Holy Spirit with the evidence of speaking with tongues. The second edition, a revision of the first, was printed as chapters in *The Witness of God* from the October 1922 issue through the combined June-July 1925 issue. To save the cost of printing the second edition in book form, Urshan had 400 extra copies of each issue of *The Witness of God* printed so that when the project was finished all thirty chapters could be collected and sent to those who wanted the complete autobiography. This second edition contains two concluding chapters that are omitted from the third edition.[3]

The most immediate difference between the second edition and the previous edition is the addition of a first chapter concerning the Assyrian-Chaldean race and religion. It becomes quickly apparent that this chapter was added for theological purposes. Urshan discusses the Syriac language, which he claims to have heard spoken on occasion by those who were speaking in tongues. The Assyrians are identified as "Nastorians" (Nestorians) who rejected a "trinity of three separate distinct persons" in favor of "a tri-unity of three Kenoomas," a "Ke-noo-ma" being "an attribute, and not a person." Further, these Nestorian Assyrians saw the "tri-unity of God" as being "like mind wisdom [*sic*] and power."[4]

This chapter is an indication of the influence of Eastern Christianity – and specifically Syrian Christianity – on Urshan. His description of Nestorianism is approving.[5] Also, although Urshan later married, he had earlier declared he would remain single in order to devote his life more fully to God. Even though he decided to marry, he continued to espouse Paul's admonition that the man who has a wife should be as though he had none. In Urshan's view, after a married man is

---

[1]Although undated, internal evidence and evidence found in other editions indicates publication in 1917.

[2]In cases where Urshan claims to have received direction from God, I will report his claims at face value rather than using words like "alleged" or "claimed" or using typographical conventions like quotation marks. This will aid in providing a straightforward reading and prevent unnecessary cluttering of the text.

[3]Urshan, *The Witness of God* 7, no. 65 (June and July 1925): 1.

[4]Urshan, *The Life and Experiences of Andrew David Urshan*, 4th ed. (N.P), 3.

[5]Urshan, "First Chapter—Story of My Life: The Assyro-Chaldean's Race, And the Life Story of Andrew David Urshan, the Assyro-Chaldean," *The Witness of God* 3, no. 34 (October 1922): 2-4.

filled with the Holy Spirit, he may still love his wife and children, but they will not be so "intense" about each other. They will be like "shadows" around him. In his view, marriage is "good," to marry and raise a family for God's glory is "better," but "to remain single for God, and avoid much suffering in the flesh" is "best." These ideas resonate with monastic theology.[6]

Additional revisions for theological purposes are found in numbers of parallel accounts with the first edition. Where the first edition uses the word "saved," the third edition consistently replaces "saved" with "blessed." On at least one occasion, the word "saved" is replaced by "convicted." In some cases, the changes are even more remarkable. For example, in the account of Urshan's conversion while attending an American Presbyterian school in Persia, the first edition reads, "I had been born again and had been made a new creature in Christ Jesus."[7] In the account of the same event in the third edition, these words are replaced with these: "I had truly had been blessed and the branch of the Divine tree in the bitter water of my life was planted afresh."[8]

Another theologically motivated change is seen in Urshan's recollection of his conversion. In the first edition, he reports that the memory "is burning even now as a clear blaze of glory of God the Father, God the Son, and God the Holy Ghost."[9] The second edition revises this to read, "is burning even now as a clear blaze of glory of God, my Father, my elder Brother and my Comforter."[10] Regardless of these kinds of changes, Urshan continues to use terms like "the Trinity in Christ" and "the One Name of the triune God"[11] in the second edition. As in the previous edition, there is no mention of the idea of baptism in Jesus' name in connection with his visit at the 1913 Arroyo Seco camp meeting, even though Urshan reveals that his profile at the camp meeting was quite high; he sat on the platform with about seventy ministers and spoke in some of the sessions being held simultaneously.[12]

---

[6]See Urshan, *Timely Messages of Warning* (1917; repr., Portland, OR: U.P.C., 1973), 52 and Andrew Bar David Urshan, *The Life Story of Andrew Bar David Urshan: An Autobiography of the Author's First Forty Years*, 5th ed. (Stockton, CA: W. A. B. C. Press, 1967), 255-260. It would become clear that Urshan's understanding of Christian marriage was not fully shared by his first wife and ultimately became a major factor in their divorce.

[7]Andrew D. Urshan, *The Story of My Life*, 1st ed. (St. Louis, MO: Gospel Publishing House, [1917]), 30.

[8]Urshan, "Third Chapter—Story of My Life: Andrew's Wonderful Conversion," *The Witness of God* 3, no. 35 (November 1922), 4. He continues, however, to use the language of regeneration: "It was here in this school that God met me one night in March 1900, convicted me of sin and regenerated my soul which transformed my character . . ." (Urshan, "Second Chapter—Story of My Life," *The Witness of God*, 3, no. 35 [November 1922]: 2). These revisions continue into the 3rd edition of Urshan's life story.

[9]Urshan, *The Story of My Life*, 1st ed., 31. This reference to "the Divine tree" is connected to the theology of the Church of the East that identifies the Cross of Christ with the "Tree of Life."

Urshan, "Third Chapter—Story of My Life: Andrew's Wonderful Conversion," *The Witness of God* 3, no. 35 (November 1922): 4. See also Urshan, *The Story of My Life*, 3rd ed., 22.

[11]Urshan, "The Story of My Life—10th Chapter—Cont.," *The Witness of God* 4, no. 45 (September 1923): 4. See also Urshan, *The Story of My Life*, 3rd ed., 94, 179.

[12]See Urshan, "The Story of My Life—13th Chapter," *The Witness of God* 4, no. 48

Throughout this second edition, Urshan discusses his practice of baptizing in the name of the Lord Jesus Christ. He understands this phrase to be the revealed name of the Father, Son, and Holy Ghost for this dispensation. It is clear that Urshan saw the fulfillment of Christ's command in Matthew 28:19 as requiring the use of the words "Lord Jesus Christ."[13] In his "Open Letter," Urshan wrote, "Since the Father has given His Name and Title to His Son to bear, therefore it is right and scriptural for us to do all things, which includes the Baptism in Water, in the Name of Jesus Christ, the LORD; why? because JESUS is the name of God the Son, CHRIST stands for the fullness and name of the Holy Ghost . . . and the Name of the Father . . . is JEHOVAH, the LORD . . . ."[14] Indeed, Urshan may have taken issue with those who baptized in the name of Jesus only, for he wrote:

> The Enemy knew all these Holy Ghost things were coming, and he came like an Angel of Light unto some of the saints, and made them to make a hobby of Water Baptism in the Name of Jesus, and try to explain the incomprehensible Mystery of the Godhead wrongly. Well, that should not stop us from proclaiming the Truth, and THE WHOLE TRUTH as it is in CHRIST JESUS; beloved, my heart and soul is filled with such good things about our great God, the Father, the Son and the Holy Ghost, in and through the Person of the Glorified Lord . . . the kernel of the Message is the FULNESS OF THE TRIUNE GOD DWELLING AND REVEALING HIMSELF IN CHRIST JESUS . . . .[15]

The third revised and enlarged edition of Urshan's autobiography is still titled *The Story of My Life*. It is self-published. Although it is undated, internal evidence indicates that it was printed in 1933.[16] In the introduction, Urshan explains the reasons for this revision. First, he sees this edition as a witness for the Lord. Second, the first edition was out of print. Third, the previous editions were "too brief and imperfect" in that they include "only hints of God's wonderful dealings with us."[17] Urshan wishes in the third edition to "tell the rest which did not appear that Jesus may get the full glory" out of his life. For the first time Urshan reveals that he was baptized in 1915 by a Russian elder while ministering in Russia.[18]

This version of the autobiography concludes, like the first edition, with Urshan's marriage to his first wife, Mildred H. Hammergren, who writes a brief final epilogue to the book. It does not include the two final chapters found in the second edition.

(December 1923): 3-4.

[13] He sometimes reordered the words as "Jesus Christ, the Lord." The word "Lord" represented "Father," Jesus" represented "Son," and "Christ" represented "Holy Ghost." See, e.g., Andrew D. Urshan, "Republication of our First 1918 Open Letter to All Pentecostal Saints," *The Witness of God* (1941), 2-5 and Andrew D. Urshan, *Apostolic Faith Doctrine of the New Birth* (Cochrane, WI: n. p., 1941), 12.

[14] Urshan, "Open Letter," 4. Emphases in original.

[15] Urshan, "Open Letter," 4. Emphases in original.

[16] See *The Story of My Life*, 3rd ed., rev. and enlarged (Chicago), Introduction, 108.

[17] Urshan, *The Story of My Life*, 3rd ed., Introduction.

[18] Urshan, "The Story of My Life—26th Chapter: Why I Was Baptized in Jesus' Name," *The Witness of God* 7, no. 62 (March 1925): 2-5.

Beginning with the January 1962 issue of *The Witness of God* and continuing through the May 1963 edition, Urshan again serialized his life story: *The Life and Experiences of Andrew David Urshan*, the fourth edition of his life story.[19] This edition includes concluding material not found in the second edition or the third edition which appears in book form, including a veiled reference to Urshan's divorce from his first wife.[20] It also includes theological revisions. For example, in his discussion of the reasons for his baptism in Jesus' name in the third edition as it appeared in book form, Urshan wrote, "The question is then what that one name of the Deity (Trinity) is into which we are commissioned to baptize."[21] In the fourth edition, this line is revised to read, "The question is then: 'What was that one name of the Diety [sic] used in practice by all of His faithful Apostles, or Christian Pioneers, or Trail-blazers?'"[22]

The final version of Urshan's autobiography was printed in 1967.[23] The most significant difference between this edition and the third edition is that it concludes with a selection of pictures that do not appear in previous editions and with a chapter that reprints some material not seen since the second edition.

The successive editions of Urshan's life story reveal more than the events of his life. They disclose a man who is on a theological journey while honoring all of his spiritual experiences even as he redefines them. What he once understood to be salvation becomes a blessing.[24] The baptismal formula he consistently used ceases to be an option and becomes a necessity. His understanding of the Godhead can at first continue to be expressed in selected Trinitarian terms, but those terms eventually fall away. The developments in his theological perspectives do not, however, lead him to reject any of his experiences that were once understood differently. Nor do they lead him to reject the experiences of others who continue to understand them as once he did.

There is tension in the idea that Urshan was on a theological journey even as he honored his redefined spiritual experiences. But this is tension that should be understood in view of the value he placed on his ancient Syrian heritage. He was a man going in two directions. He went forward as he experienced new dimensions of spiritual life, even as he found himself looking back to a perceived recovery of the theological vision of his forebears.

This tension is seen in the final version of Urshan's autobiography. In a discussion of the relationship between Nestorius and the Apostolic Church of the

---

[19]Urshan, *The Life and Experiences of Andrew David Urshan*, 4th ed. (N.P.), 1. Urshan referred to this serialization as the third edition.

[20]Urshan, "My Arrival in the United States," *The Witness of God* (April 1963): 2.

[21]Urshan, *The Story of My Life*, 3rd ed., 179.

[22]Urshan, "Andrew in Russia," *The Witness of God* (March 1963): 5.

[23]Andrew D. Urshan, *The Life Story of Andrew Bar David Urshan* (Stockton, CA: W. A. B. C. Press, 1967). This version is identified on the inside title page as originally printed in *The Witness of God*.

[24]Urshan does not define what he means by "blessing," but the context in which he uses the word on his theological journey suggests he is is referring to a work of God in his life that is short of the ultimate work of salvation. In other words, it is a legitimate work of God leading to salvation.

East, Urshan describes "Nestorians" as Christians who lived and died "for the true and unadulterated Apostolic teachings of the founders of the Church of Jesus Christ."[25] Nestorius was welcomed by these Christians "as their brother in the original Apostolic Faith."[26] Church history, according to Urshan, indicates "that most of the Eastern Christians of Mesopotamia and Persia were Apostolic in their doctrine . . . ."[27] The "Bible fundamentals" for which the Eastern Christians were passionate included the atonement, the deity of Christ, the depravity of human nature, the mysteriousness of God's being, the Incarnation, the rejection of the use of pictures and images in worship, and the belief "in the God-head being a triunity of three Kenoomas and never a trinity of three separate distinct persons."[28]

Urshan's description of Eastern Christianity was not intended to be a mere retracing of history. Instead, he believed that the blood of the martyrs – Eastern Christians whose lives had been taken by Islamic oppressors – was still crying out with the result that God had "graciously left us a remnant to raise His glorious Apostolic Standard now before this present generation."[29] He saw his own spirit leading him to recapture the authentic voice from the past and bringing with him the "remnant" who still clung to the vestiges of that voice. Thus, Urshan was a renewal theologian. By redefining his spiritual experiences, he saw himself rebuilding a crumbling edifice. His task to "raise [the] glorious Apostolic Standard" anew.

Sermon Collections

Urshan published a book titled *Timely Messages of Warning* in 1917. It included "five pointed messages to the saints of God admonishing them to be prepared for the return of their soon coming Lord."[30] These messages were originally written during a ministry trip to Canada. The chapter titles are "True and False Holiness," "Anathema Maranatha," or "At the Coming of the Lord," "Fervent in Spirit, Serving the Lord," "Overcoming Life," and "The Timely Message." These messages were published before Urshan's departure from the Assemblies of God in 1919. They hint at his desire to remained affiliated with this denomination. For example, in the chapter "Fervent in Spirit," He writes, "So . . . to be a real normal Christian is to be filled with the Holy Ghost and fire. I don't say you are not saved before you have the baptism; you are saved that you might get the baptism – you are saved to get the

---

[25]Urshan, *The Life Story*, 5th ed., 15.
[26]Urshan, *The Life Story*, 5th ed., 15.
[27]Urshan, *The Life Story*, 5th ed., 15.
[28]Urshan, *The Life Story*, 5th ed., 16.
[29]Urshan, *The Life Story*, 5th ed., 15-16. The original wording of this phrase indicates forcibly Urshan's conviction that the Church of the East had a substantial role in the restoration of first century Christianity: "He has graciously left us a remnant to raise His glorious standard through them before this present generation" (Urshan, "First Chapter – Story of My Life," *The Witness of God* vol. 3, no. 34 [October 1922]: 3.)
[30]Andrew D. Urshan, *Timely Messages of Warning* (1917; repr., Portland, Ore.: Apostolic Book Corner, 1973), front cover.

fire and have it blazing." In addition, the book includes his view that when a person is baptized with the Holy Spirit he/she can expect to "shake under the power."[31]

In 1918, Urshan published *Timely Messages of Comfort*, a book consisting of "eight heart-comforting, soul-supporting and spirit-sustaining gospel messages given by Andrew D. Urshan, Persian evangelist, in Los Angeles, California, year 1918."[32] These messages were "preached before large audiences in Los Angeles, Cal., during the Old Time Gospel Revival and All Saints' Convention in Ice Skating Palace, 1041 South Broadway."[33] The first message, titled "The Great Purpose of Redemption and the True Worship with Its Blessed Benefits" includes terminology quite common in Urshan's writings when discussing the Godhead, like "[t]hat great God, that incomprehensible Being of Heaven, the Triune God . . . ."[34] This message includes his insistence that "[i]f you do not believe in the atonement of Jesus Christ you are still in your sins and you are doomed for eternal loss . . . ."[35] It also reflects Urshan's use of the Syriac translation of Scripture – something frequently seen in his sermons and writings – and underscores the importance of the influence of his religious and cultural heritage in Syrian Christianity.

In his second message, "Knowing God in All Our Ways and Honoring Him in Our Hearts," Urshan continues to distinguish his conversion from his experience with Spirit baptism. Further reference to the Assyrian language is included. A glimpse into the "holiness" view of the times is seen in the notion that for a person who was baptized in the Spirit to go to an ice skating rink was "an insult to the Son of God."[36] To be baptized with the Holy Ghost is "to have God the Father, the Son and the Holy Ghost in us . . . ."[37] As the message closes, this same experience is described as having "God our Father, our Elder Brother, and our Comforter to lead and guide us through life, directing our paths."[38]

The third message, "What Happened After the Baptism of the Holy Spirit," contains references to other physical phenomena, besides tongues, that Urshan expects to accompany Holy Spirit baptism. He writes, "When I first went to the Pentecostal meetings in Chicago I saw the shaking, heard the speaking in tongues

---

[31] See, e.g., Urshan, *Timely Messages of Warning*, 37, 38, 50. See also Urshan, *Timely Messages of Comfort* (1918; repr. Portland, OR: Apostolic Book Corner Press, 1973), 36, 37. "Shaking under the Power" is mentioned so frequently in Urshan's various writings that it almost, if not quite, rises to the place of importance given to speaking with tongues as the "sign" of Holy Spirit baptism. Six years later, Urshan distinguished between tongues as the "sign" of Spirit baptism and the other "evidences" of Spirit baptism like the fruit of the Spirit. See Andrew D. Urshan, *My Study of Modern Pentecostals* (1923; repr. Portland, OR: Apostolic Book Publishers, 1981), 48-49.

[32] Urshan, *Timely Messages of Comfort* (1918; repr., Portland, Ore.: Apostolic Book Corner, 1973), front cover.

[33] Urshan, *Timely Messages of Comfort*, 5. Attendance at these meetings is said to have reached as high as 5,000.

[34] Urshan, *Timely Messages of Comfort*, 11.

[35] Urshan, *Timely Messages of Comfort*, 13.

[36] Urshan, *Timely Messages of Comfort*, 22-23.

[37] Urshan, *Timely Messages of Comfort*, 25.

[38] Urshan, *Timely Messages of Comfort*, 33.

and other manifestations . . . ."[39] He continues, "I felt there was something glorious behind that shaking and speaking in other tongues which I lacked then."[40] This led him to pray, "Oh, Lord these people are not only worshipping Thee with their spirits but with their very bones also."[41] However, following his own Spirit baptism, Urshan experienced such spiritual "dryness" that he began to doubt God's existence and the inspiration of Scripture. He was kept from suicide only by Bible reading and prayer. He experienced victory only when he testified publically about God, Jesus, and the Bible. In retrospect, Urshan viewed his post-Spirit baptism struggle as his "wilderness" experience, similar to the temptation of Jesus which preceeded the Messiah's ministry in the power of the Spirit.

In his fourth message, "Perfect Liberty in God through Jesus Christ," Urshan contrasts his pre- and post-Spirit baptism experiences: "Before I had the Baptism of the Holy Spirit I was greatly blessed, but did not have full liberty in my nature or body to praise the Lord, testify, pray, and give not only my money but all my life to the Lord."[42] His eagerness for people to be baptized with the Holy Spirit is "not so much after tongues, but for God to take control of our lives and our tongues too."[43]

In his fifth message, "The Gracious Dealings of God Misunderstood," Urshan makes a strong connection between suffering and holiness. In his view, it is not enough for us to be "washed by the blood of His Son," because "wrinkles do not go by washing."[44] For the wrinkles to go, God must use "the heavy hot irons of afflictions and [stretch] us in all directions and so severely that we think we will be torn to pieces."[45]

The sixth message, "First Persian Christian Martyr," recounts the story of Sophia, a Persian girl who died for her faith. In the seventh message, "Compassion of Jesus – Are the Days of Miracles Passed [sic]?," Urshan explains that "the source of miracles of grace is the compassion of Jesus Christ."[46] Since Christ still has compassion, and since we are to emulate that compassion, miracles have not ceased.

The final message is titled "Continual Prayer is Continual Victory." It explains Urshan's quite literal understanding of Paul's command to "pray without ceasing." He believes this is important because "we are nearing the hour of temptation which shall come upon the whole earth. The only way to escape it and be caught away with Christ for His soon-coming marriage supper, is the way of watchfulness and prayer."[47] This idea evokes a similar theme in the monastic theology of Eastern Christianity, especially as developed by Evagrius of Pontus, whose idea of praying without ceasing described watchfulness against demonic forces that

---

[39] Urshan, *Timely Messages of Comfort,* 36.
[40] Urshan, *Timely Messages of Comfort,* 37.
[41] Urshan, *Timely Messages of Comfort,* 37.
[42] Urshan, *Timely Messages of Comfort*, 51.
[43] Urshan, *Timely Messages of Comfort*, 52.
[44] Urshan, *Timely Messages of Comfort,*61.
[45] Urshan, *Timely Messages of Comfort*, 61.
[46] Urshan, *Timely Messages of Comfort,* 96.
[47] Urshan, *Timely Messages of Comfort,* 102.

assaulted the mind through imaginative thoughts. This state of prayer was arrived at through constant mental training and "guarding."[48]

Treatises

In 1919, still living in Los Angeles, Urshan published a book titled *The Almighty God in the Lord Jesus Christ*, which was first written in the form of a series of open letters.[49] The book includes extended quotations from a variety of sources. The Preface explains that "in order to confirm the truth of God in this book, we have taken the writings and testimonies of many eminent Christian men on the great theme, that the Scripture might be fulfilled, 'In the mouth of two or three witnesses every word shall stand.'"[50] These "witnesses" include John Bunyan, F. C. Jennings, "German Protestant Fathers," John Wesley, Charles Wesley, Spurgeon, Bernard of Clairvaux, J. Monro Gibson, W. W. Simpson, Charles Gallaudet Trumbull, William Lee Stroud, and the theological journal *Eusebia*. Urshan believes that the theology understood by these thinkers on the basis of their knowledge of the original languages has been shown to him by direct revelation.

> You have read the masterpiece on God's NAME in His dear Son, spoken of by these eminent Christian men who knew the original languages, Hebrew and Greek. You are undoubtedly now ready to understand better the same blessed truth which is given to us by the Holy Ghost through revelation, backed up by an abundance of Scriptures.[51]

Throughout the book, Urshan frequently uses the term "the Three-One God" to explain his view. Other terms he uses favorably include "the triune God," "three in One," and "God the Father, the Son, and the Spirit in our glorious Lord."[52] He is opposed, however, to the idea that "God is One in Three."[53] Urshan is willing to embrace the concept of mystery, which reflects the value he places on his roots in the religious worldview of Syriac Christianity.

> . . . I personally cannot refrain from believing that there is a plurality in God's mysterious Being, and that this plurality is shown as a three-ness, not three separate, distinct Beings or Persons of God, but a mysterious, inexplicable, incomprehensible threeness . . . and that the triune office of this one God is shown . . . not three offices of three Gods but one office of one God with three branches . . . .[54]

---

[48] See *Evagrius of Pontus: The Greek Ascetic Corpus* (trans. Robert E. Sinkewicz; Oxford: Oxford University Press, 2003), 150, 190, 197.

[49] As noted above, in 1921 Urshan rejected the use of the word "three" as it relates to theology after discovering that I John 5:7 is a textual variant. In 1953 he appealed for the use of biblical terms only in theological discussion.

[50] Urshan, *The Almighty God*, 5.

[51] Urshan, *The Almighty God*, 41. Emphasis in original.

[52] See, e.g., Urshan, *The Almighty God*, 6, 42-44, 45, 47, 54, 66, 74-75, 77-78, 82, 84, 87, 88, 93.

[53] Urshan, *The Almighty God*, 87.

[54] Urshan, *The Almighty God*, 77. See footnote 49, above.

This acceptance of mystery is at odds with some later developments in Oneness theology.[55] Although Urshan believed that the "Father-God . . . is found in His Son, Jesus Christ our Lord,"[56] his continuing desire for unity among Pentecostal believers – even after his departure from the Assemblies of God – is seen in the concluding words of the book:

> I, for one, am not led to preach Jesus Christ my Heavenly Father now; although I love to quote the . . . Scriptures and believe them with my whole heart; but I truly believe that, when we shall see our Saviour face to face and see the fullness of the Deity in Him and through Him shining forth with eternal glory, we shall not shrink then from calling Him "our Father" as well as "Lord God Almighty" in the ages to come. In the meantime, brethren, let us preach the Gospel that the Apostles preached, and also believe all such Scriptures making Jesus Christ even our **divine Father**, and worship His Father and our Heavenly Father in Him, putting away theological controversy on the Godhead, using only the terms that the Apostles used concerning the Deity. I have no doubt that, in doing so, we shall please God, the Father, the Son, and the Holy Ghost, and that He will bless us all in and through Jesus Christ, our all. Amen.[57]

In 1922, while living in Cochrane, Wisconsin, Urshan published the book *Supreme Need of the Hour and the Source of the Mighty Revivals*.[58] The book consists of twenty-four sermons on prayer and Holy Ghost revivals which had been published previously in Urshan's monthly paper *The Witness of God*. Urshan continues to make a distinction between conversion and being filled with the Holy Spirit.[59] He also distinguishes between justification, sanctification, and baptism with the Holy Spirit and fire, although he believes that it is possible for a person to get all "three loaves at once and in one course."[60] In chapter 5 Urshan deals with what he calls "secrets" of the Welsh revival, which are primarily the result of an eye-witness account by J. M. Jones. The chapter begins with the declaration that "one of the greatest revivals next to Pentecost was that which took place in Wales" and continues with a discussion of the international impact of the revival.[61] In chapter 6, Urshan writes that "we are living in the last days of this dispensation." Further, he claimed that "[g]igantic battle is almost to burst forth both in the air and on the earth, of which not only the Spirit of prophecy is foretelling and call-

---

[55]For example, David K. Bernard writes, "The Bible never says that the Godhead is an unrevealed mystery or that the question of plurality in the Godhead is a mystery. . . . Why resort to an explanation that the Godhead is an incomprehensible mystery . . . ? . . . It is wrong to state that the Godhead is a mystery when the Bible clearly states that God has revealed the mystery to us." David K. Bernard, *The Oneness of God* (Hazelwood, MO: Word Aflame Press, 1983), 289.

[56]Urshan, *The Almighty God*, 94.

[57]Urshan, *The Almighty God*, 95. Emphasis in original.

[58]Andrew D. Urshan, *Supreme Need of the Hour and the Source of Mighty Revivals* (Cochrane, WI: n.p., 1922).

[59]Urshan, *Supreme Need*, 13, 16, 31.

[60]Urshan, *Supreme Need*, 15.

[61]Urshan, *Supreme Need*, 30.

ing our attention to it, but even the scientific men of the world are tremblingly proclaiming it."

As scientific proof of the impending doom, Urshan offers an article from the December 20, 1921 edition of the *Montreal Quebec Gazette*, titled "World to Be Shaken," and subtitled, "Almost every kind of disaster prophesied for 1926." The article, taken from a news service in London on December 19, refers to the *British Journal of Astrology*, which had published the horoscope for 1926. According to this journal, the alignment of Mars and Mercury indicated not only "a succession of plagues, famines, floods, shipwrecks, rioting and revolution" for 1926, but also that Armageddon would take place in 1932 in "a final conflict between Mohammedanism, allied with Bolshevism, against the united Anglo-Saxon world." This would end in "a 'universal peace' in 1932." Urshan follows this astrological forecast by saying, "Surely the Almighty is on the job, finishing the work and cutting it short in righteousness."[62]

According to this chapter, the supreme need of the hour is watching and praying. As an expression of his other-worldly concerns, Urshan writes, "So many of God's people are sick now days and most of them have some kind of stomach trouble; eating too much of pastry, candy, and drinking much of tea and coffee is the main cause."[63] In his view, his readers should "spend more time in prayer instead of an afternoon tea or coffee."[64] He advises that "when you are invited for a dinner, don't let people force you to eat and drink the things that you know are not good for you."[65]

Urshan's disapproval of what he considers to be non-spiritual methods is apparent in chapter 13, "Days and Nights of Prayer and Fasting." He writes, "And we are so blinded even in our own day that we resort to everything, however shameful, to carry on the work. We have the holy circus and the clown. Oh, the awful reproach! Our religion has become a huge joke."[66] In his opinion, "What we call a revival is a glimpse of normal, everyday Christianity."[67] In chapter 19,

---

[62]Urshan, *Supreme Need*, 32. The legitimacy Urshan gives to astrology and his identification of it with science seems at first to be incredible. But we must remember that he was a man of his times whose cultural heritage was deeply rooted in ancient Chaldean thought. The Chaldeans were renowned for the practice of astrology, which influenced Syrian and Nestorian Christianity. Benson Bobrick points out that "[a]ccording to an ancient tradition, common to both Gnostic and Syriac Christians as well as to the Persians and Jews, Adam received the doctrines and mysteries of astrology directly from the Creator, and by knowledgeably scanning the constellations in the skies foretold that the world would one day be destroyed by water, then by fire. As a memorial to those who came after him, he (or his descendants, Seth and Enoch) had this knowledge engraved upon two pillars, one of brick, the other of stone. According to Flavius Josephus . . . the second pillar could still be seen in Syria in A.D. 63." Benson Bobrick, *The Fated Sky: Astrology in History* (New York: Simon & Schuster, 2005), 5.

[63]Urshan, *Supreme Need*, 34.
[64]Urshan, *Supreme Need*, 34.
[65]Urshan, *Supreme Need*, 36.
[66]Urshan, *Supreme Need*, 71.
[67]Urshan, *Supreme Need*, 72.

titled "Sweet Bitterness," Urshan's disapproval of a concern for external appearance can be seen: "If our dear sisters in the Christian circle would spend the time that they spend curling hair, painting and powdering their faces, in prayer they would win more people to Christ by their beautiful shining faces filled with Christ's beauty."[68] In view of Urshan's belief that physical signs like shaking should accompany baptism with the Holy Spirit, it is somewhat surprising to find in chapter 20, titled "Mourners Benches and the Mark of God," a disapproval of some physical expressions of worship. It is his opinion that "some saints want the platform small and low, so they can easily jump on it and down from it when they hope to dance."[69] The reason some folks "come to meetings not to mourn for the lost world, but to have 'a good time,' so as to hear fast music and dance" is that "worldly sensations and pleasures cost too much, . . . was injurious to their health, prosperity and daily circumstances."[70] Since it was too expensive and problematic to have a "good time" in the world, these folks come to church instead. It is Urshan's view that Jesus never appeared "smiling or laughing, but rather groaning and weeping."[71] We are to emulate His example. This theme continues in the final chapter of the book, "The Last Prophetic Words of Our Lord to His True and Faithful Church." Urshan writes that everyone

> who lives close to God will choose a weeping spell for God's cause before the throne of mercy far more than dancing and shouting for this belongs to the unmatured [sic] state; it is allright [sic] for the little children spiritually speaking, but God wishes us to forget these things behind and grow into divine manliness of the full stature of the man Christ Jesus, getting under the burden of the Lord like a faithful wife who is generally a real help-mate of her dear husband.[72]

In 1923, Urshan released a book titled *My Study of Modern Pentecostals*.[73] To a large degree, it is an autobiographical retelling of information previously published in *The Witness of God*. In addition to recounting his introduction to Pentecostalism, Urshan explains the difference between the speaking with tongues that accompanies Holy Spirit baptism and the gift of tongues. He refutes the idea that tongues were for the purpose of preaching the gospel with the logic that if that were the case, women would not need the gift "because women were not to be Apostles."[74] The speaking with tongues that occurs with the baptism of the Holy Spirit is due to the "Spirit giving utterance," resulting in "possibly. . . a few sentences."[75] But a person with the gift of tongues is one who has already been baptized with the Holy Spirit, and who can speak with tongues or stop speaking at will.

---

[68]Urshan, *Supreme Need*, 101.
[69]Urshan, *Supreme Need*, 102.
[70]Urshan, *Supreme Need*, 102.
[71]Urshan, *Supreme Need*, 102.
[72]Urshan, *Supreme Need*, 124.
[73]Andrew D. Urshan, *My Study of Modern Pentecostals* (1923; repr. Portland, OR: Apostolic Book Publishers, 1981).
[74]Urshan, *My Study*, 36.
[75]Urshan, *My Study*, 37.

Urshan then turns to his understanding of Divine Healing. He believes that the genuineness of one's faith is attested by whether or not one is healed. Next, in contrast to his earlier reflections, he describes favorably the experience of "shaking under the power of God, speaking in unknown tongues, falling on the floor prostrate, shouting, weeping, singing, praying and dancing sometimes."[76] Then, he offers scriptural support for the practice of "trembling" and "shaking." A distinction continues to be made between conversion and Holy Spirit baptism.[77] Further, Urshan declares that we are "judicially the children of God before we receive the promise of the Father, and then [we] become experimentally His sons . . . ." To receive "the promise of the Spirit is called 'the seal of salvation.' Surely the thing must be wrought and examined before it is sealed."[78] It is here, in chapter 4, that Urshan gives his most complete explanation of the difference between the "sign" and the "evidence" of Holy Spirit baptism. The sign is tongues; the evidence is the fruit of the Spirit.[79] Moreover, in chapter 7 Urshan clearly states that twentieth century Pentecostalism has its origins, not in Topeka or on Azusa Street, but in Wales: "It is noteworthy that since 1904 there has been a special religious earthquake throughout Christiandom [sic], all over the earth beginning with the Welsh revival and spreading abroad everywhere in different manners of divine operations. And it is within this period that speaking in other tongues and shaking of the bodies of believers has universally made its appearance."[80] Further, Urshan asserts that "this Pentecostal revival fell in two years time all over the world, in many places where there was not a single mission or Christian worker."[81] Finally, without offering documentation, Urshan claims that Martin Luther, John Wesley, Dwight Moody, Charles Finney, and other notable Christians spoke with tongues.[82]

In 1923, Urshan published *Doctrine of Trinity and the Divinity of Jesus Christ*, "a timely message to the church of Jesus Christ defending the truth against modern higher criticism."[83] The purpose of this work is "to promote the unity of the faith among God's Spirit-filled people every where."[84] Urshan's ecumenical interest is seen in the statement of his motive. He writes, "We do not wish or even try to explain the question of the Godhead . . . neither are we endeavoring to minimize the word Trinity; but our chief purpose is to declare . . . the mystery of the Godhead in the name and person of Jesus Christ."[85] He hopes that "the Holy Father, our glorious Saviour and our blessed Comforter" will "unite us all in one accord in truth."[86] He decries the fact that "some have gone so extremely on the

---

[76]Urshan, *My Study*, 41.
[77]Urshan, *My Study*, 44.
[78]Urshan, *My Study*, 45.
[79]Urshan, *My Study*, 48-49.
[80]Urshan, *My Study*, 62.
[81]Urshan, *My Study*, 63.
[82]Urshan, *My Study*, 84-85.
[83]Andrew D. Urshan, *Doctrine of Trinity and the Divinity of Jesus Christ* (Cochrane, WI: Andrew D. Urshan, 1923), front cover.
[84]Urshan, *Doctrine of Trinity*, 3.
[85]Urshan, *Doctrine of Trinity*, 3.
[86]Urshan, *Doctrine of Trinity*, 3.

question that they pronounce eternal damnation upon those who do not see like them on this teaching."[87] He does "not wish to stir up more strife or theological discussion on **the Trinity** and **Christ's Divinity** . . . ."[88] Although the word "trinity" is not found in Scripture, Urshan points out that "this word has been used most reverently by millions of believers during the last sixteen centuries. So we cannot afford to ignore it and misconsider [sic] it altogether like mohammedans [sic], Jews and Unitarians do, but for the sake of many earnest and zealous Christians we will give it a proper place . . . to magnify the truth . . . ."[89] To Urshan, the word "trinity" means "tri-unity," never "tri-units." Here is the difference: "Tri-unity means threeness of one **Unit** . . . but Tri-units means threeness of three **Units**." He explains, "The word Tri-unity proves . . . a divine threeness of one Divine Being. We wish therefore to use the word Trinity, when it means Tri-unity, because with this definition, the scriptural teachings on the God-head question are confirmed and magnified without any contradiction whatever." In his view, no one can deny "that there is a threeness both in the Old and New Testament connected with God's One Glorious **Being** and God's one **Name**."[90] Chapter 2, titled "Trinity in Christ" consists of an article by John Monro Gibson," which Urshan describes as a "splendid article."[91] As is typical of early Pentecostals who seemed to enjoy poking fun at preachers who had earned seminary degrees, but who cheerfully appealed to such educated clergy when it served their purposes, Urshan lists Gibson's M.A. and D.D. after his name. In his search for analogies to explain the "threeness" of God, in chapter 4, titled "The Blessed Trinity of God Revealed in Nature and Demonstrated or Personified in Jesus Christ Our Lord," he draws threefold comparisons from the sun's rays (light, heat, and power), fire (heat, light, and power), trees (root, body, and sap), fountains (fountain head, fountain proper, and the invisible power causing the fountain the leap forth), and the threefold character of man (spirit, soul, and body). He does not note that these same analogies are often used in an attempt to explain the historic doctrine of the Trinity. In spite of his willingness to use the word "Trinity" as he has defined it, Urshan also uses the term "Jesus Only" to describe his faith.[92] He prefers to "use Bible terms only."[93] When responding to questions about the Godhead, Urshan uses terms that hint at an understanding of the Godhead informed by Syrian Christianity. He describes God's "mysterious TRI-ONE Being" as "**Mind, Wisdom, and Power.**"[94]

---

[87]Urshan, *Doctrine of Trinity*, 3.
[88]Urshan, *Doctrine of Trinity*, 3. Emphasis in original.
[89]Urshan, *Doctrine of Trinity*, 4.
[90]Urshan, *Doctrine of Trinity*, 4. Emphases in original. See footnote 49, page 253.
[91]Urshan, *Doctrine of Trinity*, 6.
[92]Urshan, *Doctrine of Trinity*, 25.
[93]Urshan, *Doctrine of Trinity*, 29.
[94]Urshan, *Doctrine of Trinity*, 32. Emphasis in original. As noted earlier, this is the same term he uses in the first chapter of his revised autobiography to describe the view of God in Syrian Christianity.

In 1925, Urshan published *The Doctrine of Redemption and the Redemption of the Body*.[95] It addresses the idea that it is possible for Spirit-filled people to avoid death altogether by experiencing the "redemption" of the body in this life. This was sometimes described as the "never die" doctrine. Urshan rejected this idea, pointing out that those who held this view died just like everyone else.

In 1932, Urshan published the "American-Assyro Unique Song Book," with a foreword written by his wife, Mildred H. Urshan.[96] A duplicate in the Syriac language was published to provide a "spiritual uplift of the Assryians in Persia, Russia, Iraq and America."[97] The book contains 35 songs, 14 of which were written or adapted by Urshan. One was written by G. T. Haywood. William E. Booth-Clibborn's Oneness anthem "Down From His Glory" is included. Other Oneness writers who have a song included are L. R. Ooton and R. C. Lawson. The rest of the songs were written by a variety of trinitarian authors. Most of those written by Oneness authors are obviously intended for theological purposes. For example, the first song in the book, written by Urshan and titled "Jesus, Fairest Jesus," includes the words, "Glory, hallelujah to the Lamb once slain, now in heav'n exalted over all to reign. Father, Son and Spirit, in Thee we adore . . . ." Urshan's adaptation of "I Was Lost But Jesus Found Me," the second song in the book, includes a third verse with the words, "Just repent and be baptized, and receive the Holy Ghost." Lawson's "Praise Thy Name" includes the words, "I have called thee, 'Abba Father.' I have stayed my heart on thee, Son of God, Thou Holy Spirit, Thou art all in all to me." Urshan's "Hallelujah to His Name" declares, "All the fullness of the Godhead, dwelleth in Him bodily." Urshan's triumphalistically titled "Everything That's Not of Jesus Shall Go Down" asserts, "There is only one Name that you need, and that Name is Jesus, 'Lord of Hosts,' for in Him dwells the 'Father, Son and Holy Ghost.'"

In 1941, while pastoring the Apostolic Faith Church in New York, New York, Urshan published a small book titled *Apostolic Faith Doctrine of the New Birth*.[98] The book, consisting of a series of four messages, distinguishes conversion and new birth.[99] Conversion occurs when a person is "conceived" by the Word;[100] the new birth consists of water baptism in the name of the Lord Jesus Christ and baptism in the Holy Spirit with the sign of speaking with tongues.[101] He also distinguishes between the kingdom of heaven and the kingdom of God. People who have genuine faith in Christ but who have not been baptized in the name of Jesus and who have not received the Holy Ghost with the sign of tongues are in the kingdom of heaven, standing "on the same ground that the saints of the Old Testament stood; they were saved by faith not receiving the promise of the Spirit.

---

[95]Andrew D. Urshan, *The Doctrine of Redemption and the Redemption of the Body* (Chicago: The Witness of God, 1925).

[96]Andrew D. Urshan, *American-Assyro Unique Song Book* (Chicago: 1932).

[97]Urshan, *Song Book*, inside front cover.

[98]Andrew D. Urshan, *Apostolic Faith Doctrine of the New Birth* (Cochrane, WI: 1941).

[99]Urshan, *Apostolic Faith Doctrine*, 5.

[100]Urshan, *Apostolic Faith Doctrine*, 13.

[101]Urshan, *Apostolic Faith Doctrine*, 10, 13.

They are not the real Spirit born children of God, but they are the people of God and adopted children."[102] Only those who have experienced both water baptism in the name of the Lord Jesus Christ and baptism in the Holy Spirit with the sign of speaking with tongues are in the kingdom of God, also identified as the church and the bride of God.[103] In addition, Urshan distinguishes between being begotten and being born. To be begotten is to be spiritually conceived by the word, another description for conversion. At this point, a person can be called a child of God and is "in the womb of the church conceived."[104] Those who are not baptized in the name of Jesus and who have not received the Holy Ghost with the sign of tongues would not be lost "if they had not gone on to the water and Spirit birth."[105] Urshan gave the following response to the question, "Can one be saved and not be born again?"

> The word "saved" conveys a greater meaning than generally known. It implies deliverance from sin and also God Himself coming into our life. . . . Yes, some can be delivered from hell though not being born of God, just like the Old Testament saints were saved through faith though not being born again. The thief on the cross may represent this class of saved ones who had no knowledge of the doctrine of the full salvation neither had a chance to perform it, his recognition of Christ and faith in Him saved him.[106]

Periodicals

For nearly fifty years, beginning in 1919, Urshan published the monthly paper *The Witness of God.* This periodical included articles written by Urshan on the topics of theology, Christology, soteriology, eschatology, and holiness.

In addition to articles written by Urshan, *The Witness of God* also included articles written by such other Oneness thinkers as G. T. Haywood and George R. Farrow. He also included articles by non-Pentecostals that seemed to address the Oneness perspective.

In addition to his articles that appeared in *The Witness of God,* Urshan wrote for a number of other periodicals. This includes *Confidence*, edited by Alexander A. Boddy; *Latter Rain Evangel,* published by Evangel Publishing House; *Pen-

---

[102]Urshan, *Apostolic Faith Doctrine*, 13, 14.

[103]Urshan, *Apostolic Faith Doctrine,* 5, 12, 13.

[104]Urshan, *Apostolic Faith Doctrine*, 13, 14.

[105]Urshan, *Apostolic Faith Doctrine*, 13.

[106]Urshan, *Apostolic Faith Doctrine*, 14. It should be noted that in an undated reprinting of *Apostolic Faith Doctrine of the New Birth* released by the Apostolic Book Corner in Portland, Oregon, seven of the questions and answers in the section titled "Twenty Seven Questions and Answers on the New Birth Teaching" were deleted with no notice that this had been done. The section still bears the same title, but only twenty questions and answers remain. Here are the deleted questions: (1) Would these folks be lost if they had not gone on to the water and Spirit birth?; (2) Can one be called a child of God before he is born of the Spirit?; (3) Were the apostles the children of God before the day of Pentecost?; (4) The folks that believe on Christ's name and repent but are not baptized by water and the Spirit, where do they stand?; (5) What is the difference between the adopted and born children of God?; (6) What is the new birth?; (7) Can one be saved and not be born again?

tecostal Outlook, the official periodical of the Pentecostal Assemblies of Jesus Christ, edited by S. G. Norris; *The Christian Evangel*, edited by E. N. Bell and published by the Gospel Publishing House; *The Pentecostal Evangel*, the official periodical of the Assemblies of God, edited by Stanley H. Frodsham; *The Weekly Evangel*, published by the Gospel Publishing House and edited by E. N. Bell; and *Word and Witness*, edited by E. N. Bell.

Secondary Sources Related to Urshan

Urshan's importance in the development of Oneness theology is indicated by the secondary literature that is beginning to explore his life and thought.[107]

Urshan's Life and Theology

In *Thinking in the Spirit: Theologies of the Early Pentecostal Movement* (2003), Douglas Jacobsen devotes 28 pages to "Andrew David Urshan's Spiritual Theology."[108] He concludes that the "Oneness theologies of Urshan and Haywood gave the early pentecostal movement a new breadth and depth of vision."[109] The breadth came from Haywood; the depth from Urshan. Their theologies were "more distinctively pentecostal than anything that preceded them; at the very least, they were less dependent on previous forms of Christian theology."[110] Jacobsen takes note of Urshan's emphasis on holiness, his view of the new birth as being an almost physical event which included not only speaking with tongues but also bodily shaking, and his continuing desire to be a peacemaker among both Trinitarian and Oneness Pentecostals. Jacobsen's observations concerning the theological influence on Urshan of his Persian and Nestorian background are helpful.[111]

Some inaccuracies in Jacobsen's account underscore the need for greater care in research. For example, in a discussion of Urshan's first marriage, Jacobsen writes that "he married a woman named Ethel (he does not provide her last name)" and that "his wife left him sometime in the late 1920s or early 1930s under circumstances that are not clear."[112] Actually, the name of Urshan's first wife was Mildred Harriet Hammergren, who left Urshan for another man, resulting in divorce. Although she later repented, the marriage was not restored. In 1950, Urshan married Ethel Dugas.[113] In another case, Jacobsen quotes Urshan's expla-

---

[107]Unfortunately, this literature contains some historical inaccuracies which are noted here in order to correct the historical record. In addition, this literature does not explore the formative influence of the theology of the Church of the East on Urshan's beliefs.

[108]Douglas Jacobsen, *Thinking in the Spirit: Theologies of the Early Pentecostal Movement* (Bloomington, IN: Indiana University Press, 2003), 232-259.

[109]Jacobsen, *Thinking*, 259.

[110]Jacobsen, *Thinking*, 259.

[111]Jacobsen, *Thinking*, 235, 256.

[112]Jacobsen, *Thinking*, 240-241.

[113]Andrew D. Urshan married Mildred Harriet Hammergren on August 9, 1917. (See *The Weekly Evangel*, August 25, 1917, p. 13.) His second wife, Ethel Dugas, was a licensed minister with the United Pentecostal Church, Inc. Urshan himself was not licensed with the United Pentecostal Church until 1956.

nation of Nestorian theology as "a triunity of three Kenoomas [personalities] and never a trinity of three separate persons."[114] Jacobsen's explanation does not correspond with Urshan's own statement that a Kenooma is an "image attribute [*sic*] or a manifestation of God"[115] and not a personality.

However, Jacobsen's notion that the creative theologians of early Pentecostalism "felt compelled to improvise language, bending the meanings of old words and inventing new phrases, to help their readers ... better understand the elusive yet powerful ways in which God's Spirit may be present in the world"[116] connects accurately with Urshan's attempt to communicate his views. Urshan's redefinition of "trinity," his use of "triunity," and "the THREE-ONE God" demonstrate a desire to keep one hand on the valuable vocabulary of the past while reaching ahead to the new revelations he had received.

D. William Faupel's *The Everlasting Gospel: The Significance of Eschatology in the Development of Pentecostal Thought* (1996)[117] includes a treatment of Andrew D. Urshan from Faupel's perspective that Pentecostalism's rapid growth was due to its eschatological hope. This was certainly the case with Urshan, who frequently warned his readers of the nearness of the rapture, the necessity for world evangelization, and the dangers awaiting those who were not prepared for Christ's return.

Stephen Ray Graham's MA thesis, "Conservative American Protestantism and the Origins of Pentecostalism: A Case Study of Andrew D. Urshan,"[118] concludes that Urshan "is one Pentecostal who stood solidly in the tradition of nineteenth-century conservative American Protestantism, who borrowed from that tradition and who ... carried that tradition with him as he exerted a great influence on one group of the heirs of that tradition."[119] While Graham claims that Urshan looked at Scripture in a "scientific" way in his search for "exact" meaning, he fails to convey an awareness of Urshan's embrace of "incomprehensible mystery." Although Graham argues accurately that Urshan was engaged with fundamentalism, common sense philosophy, restorationism, revivalism, and the notion of the "age of the Spirit" – all characteristics of nineteenth-century conservative American Protestantism – no notice is given to the continuing influence of Syrian Christian-

---

[114]Jacobsen, *Thinking*, 256.

[115]Urshan, *The Life Story*, 5th ed., 16. The closest Urshan comes to defining Kenoomas as personalities is in a discussion of "Nastorians" [he means "Nestorians"]: "They do not call the Trinity, a trinity of three persons but of three 'Qnumi,' an obscure word which portrays [pertains?] to personalities and yet does not. They say in Christ Jesus were and are now two of these 'Qnumi'" (Urshan, "When Paganism Crept into Apostolic Christianity," *The Witness of God* (October 1965): 3.

[116]Jacobsen, *Thinking*, xiii.

[117]D. William Faupel, *The Everlasting Gospel: The Significance of Eschatology in the Development of Pentecostal Thought,* Journal of Pentecostal Theology Supplement Series, eds., John Christopher Thomas, Rickie Moore, Steven J. Land, no. 10 (Sheffield: Sheffield Academic Press, 1996).

[118]Stephen Ray Graham, "Conservative American Protestantism and the Origins of Pentecostalism: A Case Study of Andrew D. Urshan" (MA thesis, Wheaton College, 1982).

[119]Graham, "Conservative American Protestantism," 82.

ity on Urshan's thought. Thus while accurate in detail, failure to understand the influence the Eastern Church had on Urshan limits the value of Graham's thesis.

Histories of Oneness Pentecostalism

David A. Reed, Professor Emeritus of Pastoral Theology and Research Professor at Wycliffe College, Toronto, Canada, has contributed significantly to the study of the third stream of Pentecostalism, known early in the 20th century as the "New Issue" or "Jesus Only" teaching but more commonly known today as "Oneness Pentecostalism." His perspective is from the viewpoint of one whose earliest church experiences were in the Oneness Pentecostal movement in New Brunswick, Canada.[120] Born into a family prominent in the United Pentecostal Church in eastern Canada,[121] his first memory of reading was "staring at the large wall poster behind the pulpit" in the Full Gospel Assembly upon which were emblazoned the words of Acts 2:38: "Repent, and be baptized every one of you in the name of Jesus Christ for the remission of sins, and ye shall receive the gift of the Holy Ghost" (KJV).[122]

Reed rejects the claim of heresy for Oneness Pentecostalism. He identifies the movement's theology as an historic Christian heterodoxy that deserves ongoing engagement from the larger Christian community. After locating the origin of Oneness Pentecostalism in its religious and social location, Reed examines the soteriology of the four theological pioneers, Frank Ewart, G. T. Haywood, Franklin Small, and Andrew Urshan. For Ewart and Small, Acts 2:38 represented full identification with Christ. For Haywood and Urshan, this verse described the new birth.[123] Reed believes that the Oneness focus on the name of God was an attempt to retrieve the early Jewish Christian theme of the name of God, an emphasis weakened with the Gentilization of Christianity. This "Jewish Christian theology of the Name" emerged "within the context of its American heritage in Jesus-centric Pietism and the early Pentecostal movement."[124] He argues that Oneness Pentecostalism must be taken seriously for the following reasons: (1) its global strength; (2) the increasing favor it has gained in academia; (3) its spiritual resonance with those outside the movement; and (4) the institutional and theological maturing of the movement.[125]

Early in his research, Reed described the Oneness movement as "evangelical unitarian pentecostalism."[126] He believes that "[t]he oneness movement is unitarian in the sense that it is one of the many anti-trinitarian protests within the his-

---

[120]David A. Reed, *"In Jesus'Name": The History and Beliefs of Oneness Pentecostals*, ix.

[121]David Reed, "Aspects of the Origins of Oneness Pentecostalism," in Vinson Synan, ed., *Aspects of Pentecostal-Charismatic Origins* (Plainfield, NJ: Logos International, 1975), 143.

[122]Reed, *"In Jesus' Name"*, ix.

[123]See Reed, *"In Jesus'Name"*, 191-201.

[124]David Arthur Reed, "Origins and Development of the Theology of Oneness Pentecostalism in the United States," *Pneuma*, vol. 1, no. 1 (1979): 31.

[125]This paragraph follows a review by Daniel L. Segraves of *"In Jesus' Name": The History and Beliefs of Oneness Pentecostals* by David A. Reed in *Religious Studies Review* 35, no. 1 (March 2009): 44.

[126]Reed, "Aspects," 143.

tory of the Church."[127] For Reed, Oneness Pentecostals belong to the segment of "evangelical unitarians" who "place great emphasis on revelation instead of reason, and on redemption through the shed blood of Christ . . . affirm[ing] both His deity and His humanity."[128] Further, Reed asserts that "[a]lthough there may be theological deficiencies in the evangelical unitarian scheme, it should be pointed out that there appears to be nothing *substantially* different from trinitarianism that would endanger the Gospel."[129] Following a discussion of evangelical unitarians who predated Oneness Pentecostalism, Reed writes, "That oneness pentecostals, therefore, be regarded as 'hopeless heretics' is an obvious overreaction in light of the evangelical tradition to which they belong."[130]

Reed is not content to reject the heresy label. Instead, he offers an alternate interpretive scheme. First, he suggests that "*the end result of an orthodox position may in fact be distorted by over-reaction to a perceived threat.*"[131] Calvin's reaction to Servetus is offered as an example. In Reed's view, "what was later identified as orthodoxy evolved out of first-century diversity, not embryonic homogeneity."[132] This diversity included "three early theological traditions—Greek, Latin and Hebrew [Christianities] . . . ."[133] Hebrew Christianity, the theological tradition Reed associates with today's Oneness Pentecostalism, "disappeared completely."[134] Suggestions for this disappearance include "[l]ack of theoretical and linguistic development, the influence of Hellenism, and an anti-Semitic spirit."[135]

Second, Reed suggests that "*heterodox beliefs and practices should at least initially be regarded as family matters rather than as intrusions by strangers.*"[136] First, if heterodox beliefs are banished prematurely, "we miss what God may be saying to the church in their often garbled, coded dialect."[137] Second, "even when there is evidence of unfaithfulness, exclusion is not necessarily the appropriate action."[138] Reed notes George Lindbeck's point that in the rejection of heretical groups the example of the ancient prophets is missed; the Lord may cast out the "adulterous spouse" of ancient Israel for a time without divorce. Third, "the matter of faithfulness may be compromised by cultural imperialism, as unintentional as it may be. Each person hears the other through his or her particular social and linguistic history."[139] Reed notes that "[w]ith the demise of Hebrew Christianity, a world of understanding was lost between Gentile Christianity and its Jewish

---

[127] Reed, "Aspects," 163.
[128] Reed, "Aspects," 163.
[129] Reed, "Aspects," 164.
[130] Reed, "Aspects," 164.
[131] David A. Reed, "Oneness Pentecostalism: Problems and Possibilities for Pentecostal Theology," *Journal of Pentecostal Theology* 11 (1997): 75. Italics are Reed's.
[132] Reed, "Oneness Pentecostalism," 76.
[133] Reed, "Oneness Pentecostalism," 77.
[134] Reed, "Oneness Pentecostalism," 77.
[135] Reed, "Oneness Pentecostalism," 77.
[136] Reed, "Oneness Pentecostalism," 77. Italics are Reed's.
[137] Reed, "Oneness Pentecostalism," 77.
[138] Reed, "Oneness Pentecostalism," 78.
[139] Reed, "Oneness Pentecostalism," 78.

roots."[140] Fourth, "patience with new ideas provides fledgling movements opportunity to experiment and mature within the context of family conversation."[141]

Furthermore, Reed believes that Oneness Pentecostalism is "a twentieth-century . . . adaptation of themes drawn from specifically Jewish Christian New Testament materials."[142] The singular name of Jesus "reveals a God who is one, in ways more compatible with the Jewish monotheism of the OT."[143] Acknowledging the incipient tritheism of much of popular trinitarianism, Reed sees Oneness Pentecostalism as passionately seeking "to preserve a witness to the radical unity of God . . . ."[144] It is not that Oneness Pentecostalism denies fully the "trinitarian" aspect of God, but that this is "limited to God in his revelation, an economic Trinity" which is seen as "three manifestations, functions, or offices, rather than distinct persons within the Godhead."[145]

Reed identifies four doctrinal challenges faced by Oneness Pentecostalism:

> First, the Oneness doctrine of God oversteps the boundary of orthodox, creedal formulations. Second, its Christology is awkward and carries overtones of Nestorian separation of the two natures. Third, its theology of the name of Jesus is almost totally unfamiliar to other Christians, and understood less! Finally, its insistence upon baptism and rebaptism in Jesus' name is offensive to most trinitarian Christians, especially when defended on Oneness theological grounds.[146]

Reed develops his "Jewish Christian" paradigm in five theses. First, *Both trinitarian and Oneness theologians can find common ground in a kerygmatic understanding of revelation.*"[147] Reed defines kerygmatic theology as "a theology of revelation grounded in Scripture" which stands over against dogmatic theology and scholasticism and fundamental theology.[148] Reed appeals to James Dunn and Karl Barth to illustrate the value of kerygmatic theology.

Second, *"The New Testament materials contain theologically legitimate ideas and practices identified as 'Jewish Christian' regarding God and the person and work of Jesus."*[149] The works of Jean Danielou, Richard Longenecker, James Dunn, and Larry Hurtado are referenced by Reed as enabling one to trace the contours of earliest Jewish Christianity, seen among the first Christians who "knew themselves to be the People of God, and to be in continuity with Israel"[150] and who drew upon "a conceptual frame of reference and expressions rooted in semitic thought generally and Judaism in particular."[151]

---

[140]Reed, "Oneness Pentecostalism," 78.
[141]Reed, "Oneness Pentecostalism," 78-79.
[142]Reed, "Oneness Pentecostalism," 79.
[143]Reed, "Oneness Pentecostalism," 79.
[144]Reed, "Oneness Pentecostalism," 79.
[145]Reed, "Oneness Pentecostalism," 79-80.
[146]Reed, "Oneness Pentecostalism," 80-81.
[147]Reed, "Oneness Pentecostalism," 81. Italics are Reed's.
[148]Reed, "Oneness Pentecostalism," 81-82.
[149]Reed, "Oneness Pentecostalism," 83. Italics are Reed's.
[150]Reed, "Oneness Pentecostalism," 83.
[151]Richard Longenecker, *The Christology of Early Jewish Christianity* (SBT Second

Third, "*Within this theologically legitimate Jewish Christian reality there is a theology of the Name of God.*"[152] This "theology of the name" has to do with the ancient Near East view that "one's name revealed and embodied the character and personality of the person."[153]

Fourth, "*The Name of Jesus is a discernible and valid Christological designation within New Testament Jewish Christian materials.*"[154] Reed appeals to Dunn's point that "[t]he name of Jesus was used in the same way as the name of God or of a heavenly being."[155]

Fifth, "*Water-baptism in the name of Jesus (or one of its variations) is biblically legitimate, and ought to be accepted as a genuine alternative to the trinitarian formula in Mt. 28.19.*"[156] Reed affirms that "[i]t is generally recognized in current New Testament scholarship that the first Christians baptized using some form of the name of Jesus."[157] He points out that Karl Barth affirms and perhaps prefers "the theological appropriateness of the phrase 'into Jesus Christ'."[158] He also notes that James Dunn argues "that Acts 2.38 is the text *par excellence* of conversion-initiation . . . ."[159]

Reed concludes that there are possibilities for dialogue between Oneness Pentecostals and other Christians. This is based on the theological space made possible by "the interpretive lenses and motifs of earliest Jewish Christianity."[160] This dialogue should take note of Oneness Pentecostal praxis rather than being based exclusively upon a reading of their exclusivistic teachings.[161] For this to occur, however, not only must the broader Christian community be willing to engage in this dialogue; Oneness Pentecostals must be willing to come out from behind their own wall of isolation and to reconsider the confession "that they alone are the one people of God."[162]

Reed's irenic treatment of Oneness Pentecostalism – in the face of frequently strident calls for the condemnation of the movement as cultish and heretical – has done much to lay the groundwork for the possibility of dialogue between Oneness and Trinitarian Pentecostals. Four years before the Oneness-Trinitarian Dialogue began, Reed and another scholar "attempted to initiate a dialogue directly among various Trinitarian and Oneness organizations, but neither the timing nor

---

Series, 17; Naperville, IL: Allenson, 1970), 3; cited in Reed, "Oneness Pentecostalism," 83.

[152] Reed, "Oneness Pentecostalism," 85. Italics are Reed's.

[153] Reed, "Oneness Pentecostalism," 86.

[154] Reed, "Oneness Pentecostalism," 87. Italics are Reed's.

[155] James Dunn, *Jesus and the Spirit: A Study of the Religious and Charismatic Experience of Jesus and the First Christians as Reflected in the New Testament* (London: SCM Press, 1975), 194; cited in Reed, "Oneness Pentecostalism," 88.

[156] Reed, "Oneness Pentecostalism," 89. Italics are Reed's.

[157] Reed, "Oneness Pentecostalism," 89.

[158] Reed, "Oneness Pentecostalism," 90.

[159] Reed, "Oneness Pentecostalism," 90.

[160] Reed, "Oneness Pentecostalism," 92.

[161] Reed, "Oneness Pentecostalism," 93.

[162] Reed, "Oneness Pentecostalism," 93.

the hosts was right."[163] Reed's characterization of Oneness theology's emphasis on the name and practice of water baptism in the name of the Lord Jesus Christ as a valid and early Jewish Christian theology of the name extends to Oneness Pentecostalism the possibility of a legitimate link with first century Christianity and questions the stigma associated with the claim that Oneness Pentecostals arrived at their conclusions by means of extra-biblical revelation.

Thomas A. Fudge's *Christianity Without the Cross: A History of Salvation in Oneness Pentecostalism*[164] is largely an oral history that begins about twenty years after the origin of the Oneness movement. Fudge's work is valuable in that it preserves the results of his interviews with many people who have been involved in the development of Oneness Pentecostalism, but it is largely limited to the history of the United Pentecostal Church International.[165] The title of Fudge's book is misleading and offensive to Oneness Pentecostals. Certainly, Oneness Pentecostals do not preach a "Christianity" devoid of the cross of Christ.[166]

The two most recent histories of Oneness Pentecostalism written by insiders are David K. Bernard's *A History of Christian Doctrine: The Twentieth Century A.D. 1900 – 2000*[167] and two works by Talmadge L. French, his M.A. thesis at Wheaton College, published under the title *Our God Is One: The Story of the Oneness Pentecostals*[168] and *Early Interracial Oneness Pentecostalism*, adapted from his Ph.D. thesis from the University of Birmingham UK.[169] Bernard sees Urshan as one of the "key thinkers" in the development of Oneness theology, along with Frank Ewart and G. T. Haywood.[170] He points out that the Oneness pioneers, including Urshan, "did not proclaim dogmatically that all who had not experienced Acts 2:38 would go to the lake of fire." Instead, "most felt that there still could be a type of salvation outside the New Testament church, similar to that of Old Testament saints, particularly for people who walked in all the 'light' they had received."[171]

---

[163]David Reed, "An Anglican Response," *Pneuma* 30 (2008): 263. This is Reed's assessment of his efforts in his response to the Oneness-Trinitarian Final Report, 2006-2007. The Oneness-Trinitarian Dialogue was sponsored by the Society for Pentecostal Studies.

[164]Thomas A. Fudge, *Christianity Without the Cross: A History of Salvation in Oneness Pentecostalism* (Boca Raton, FL: Universal Publishers, 2003).

[165]Just for clarification, I initially regretfully questioned the possible accuracy of interview records in Fudge's book, but I have since learned that the first and formal interview was recorded and that my responses were accurately reported by Fudge.

[166]In his critique of the prospectus I presented for this dissertation, David Reed, who was a reader for Fudge's work, informed me that the original title was *Christianity without the Cross?* As Reed pointed out, the omission of the question mark was "major and unfortunate."

[167]David K. Bernard, *A History of Christian Doctrine: The Twentieth Century a.d. 1900 – 2000*, vol. 3 (Hazelwood, MO: Word Aflame Press, 1999).

[168]Talmadge L. French, *Our God Is One: The Story of the Oneness Pentecostals* (Indianapolis, IN: Voice & Vision Publishers, 1999).

[169]Talmadge L. French, *Early Interracial Oneness Pentecostalism* (Eugene, OR: Pickwick Publications, 2014).

[170]Bernard, *A History*, 87.

[171]Bernard, *A History*, 122.

French's *Our God Is One* includes his research into more than 300 Oneness Pentecostal organizations worldwide. Chapter 2 of *Our God Is One* includes a section titled "Andrew D. Urshan and the Impossibility of Neutrality." French traces the events leading up to Urshan's departure from the Assemblies of God, describing the Assemblies of God leadership as "outraged."[172] *Early Interracial Oneness Pentecostalism* is the story of G. T. Haywood and the Pentecostal Assemblies of the World from 1901 to 1931, focusing especially on "its unparalleled interracial commitment to an all-flesh, all-people, counter-cultural Pentecost."[173] French includes a discussion of Urshan's role as a "Oneness apologist and evangelist" (p. 121).

Other histories of Oneness Pentecostalism include Arthur L. Clanton's *United We Stand*[174] and Fred J. Foster's *Think It Not Strange*.[175] Although including Pentecostal history before the rise of Oneness Pentecostalism, these works essentially are organizational histories of the United Pentecostal Church International.

Frank J. Ewart's *The Phenomenon of Pentecost* is a now-classic history of early 20th century Pentecostalism, including the Oneness movement.[176] Ewart acknowledges Urshan as one "who was mightily used of the Lord" in the propagation of the Oneness message and who attempted, but failed, to reunify the trinitarian and Oneness factions.[177] He does not, however, include Urshan in his final chapter titled "Early Pentecostal Leaders."

The history of the Pentecostal Assemblies of the World (PAW) has been documented by Morris E. Golder and James L. Tyson.[178] Urshan, described as "charismatic," "caring," and "scrupulously honest,"[179] was one of seven men chosen at the October 4-6, 1923 general conference of the PAW as presbyters who would "have oversight over the affairs of the general body" and whose authority superseded that of the previous "offices of chairman and secretary."[180] At this same conference, "A. D. Urshan, 866 N. State Street, Chicago, was elected secretary-treasurer of foreign missions."[181] Urshan was also a member of a commission charged with introducing "a new magazine that would serve as the one official

---

[172]French, *Our God Is One*, 76.

[173]French, *Our God is One*, back cover.

[174]Arthur L. Clanton, *United We Stand: A History of Oneness Organizations* (Hazelwood, MO: Pentecostal Publishing House, 1970).

[175]Fred J. Foster, *Think It Not Strange* (Hazelwood, MO: Pentecostal Publishing House, 1965), reprinted and revised in 1981 as *Their Story: 20th Century Pentecostals*.

[176]Frank J. Ewart, *The Phenomenon of Pentecost* (Hazelwood, MO: Word Aflame Press, 1975).

[177]Ewart, *The Phenomenon of Pentecost*, 108.

[178]Morris E. Golder, *A History of the Pentecostal Assemblies of the World* (1973); James L. Tyson, *The Early Pentecostal Revival: History of Twentieth-Century Pente-costals and the Pentecostal Assemblies of the World, 1901-30* (Hazelwood, MO: Word Aflame Press, 1992).

[179]Tyson, *Early Pentecostal Revival*, 220.

[180]Tyson, *Early Pentecostal Revival*, 241-42.

[181]Tyson, *Early Pentecostal Revival*, 216.

monthly organ for the body. [The commission] christened the new magazine *The Christian Outlook*."[182]

Urshan's leadership in the foreign missions work of PAW was significant:

> Urshan and Haywood would raise the level of the missions board to new heights. Their strong missions-minded leadership would set the standards, criteria, and pattern that enabled the P.A.W. to emphasize the importance of world evangelism. A Persian by birth, Urshan was in a unique position to understand not only the need but also the complexities of ministering to peoples draped in superstition and false dogmas.
>
> Through the efforts of many dedicated men and women the Foreign Missions Board took root, but A. D. Urshan, G. T. Haywood, and Sister Hilda Reeder must be singled out as those individuals who gave the ministry true direction and clarity in the 1920s and 1930s.[183]

At the July 8, 1924 meeting of the presbyters in Chicago, it was Urshan who "related the cause for the proposed division between the colored and white . . . on the grounds of the Southern Brethrens' [*sic*] conditions in the south."[184] By 1925, "Andrew Urshan had left the P.A.W."[185]

Conclusion

A survey of the primary and secondary literature indicates the significance of Andrew D. Urshan not only for Oneness Pentecostalism but also for Pentecostalism at large. First, the primary sources demonstrate the vast quantity and substantial scope of his work. No other Oneness Pentecostal thinker in the first half of the twentieth century comes close to Urshan for the sheer quantity of literary output. Second, the primary sources provide clear evidence of the multicultural influence that helped shape Urshan's thinking. This includes his early years in Persia in the Assyrian-Chaldean milieu, Syrian Christianity, Presbyterianism, and – in America – continued exposure to a variety of expressions of Christianity, including Presbyterian, evangelical, Brethren, fundamentalist, holiness, and Pentecostal churches.

Although Urshan's understanding of his spiritual experiences was reshaped as he continued his spiritual journey, he continued to acknowledge the legitimacy of those transforming events, whether he identified them as conversion, blessing, salvation, sanctification, or Spirit baptism. And he continued to confess the authenticity of these events in the lives of others who used different terms to identify them.

As his understanding of his experiences was transformed, Urshan's soteriological language developed. But he sought to describe his understanding of God in ways that honored mystery and valued his traditional vocabulary while incorporating the content of his new insights. He was not on a mission to reshape the

---

[182] Tyson, *Early Pentecostal Revival*, 210.
[183] Tyson, *Early Pentecostal Revival*, 211.
[184] Tyson, *Early Pentecostal Revival*, 240.
[185] Tyson, *Early Pentecostal Revival*, 201.

language of God; his mission was to reshape Christology so as to elevate Christ to the place of ultimate supremacy as the one in whom the fullness of God dwells.

The current interest in Urshan, as seen in the work of Jacobsen, Faupel, and Reed, further demonstrates the importance of Urshan not only for the study of early twentieth century Pentecostalism, but for Pentecostalism's ongoing search for its self-identity. From Jacobsen's description of Urshan as one who gave early Pentecostalism "depth of vision," to Faupel's recognition of the eschatological hope of the nascent movement, a hope emphasized by Urshan, to Reed's claim that Urshan was one of the four most significant thinkers in the retrieval of the early Jewish Christian theme of the name of God, Urshan's important contributions are seen.

The primary and secondary literature makes it clear: Urshan is a figure worthy of continued and intensified study. It could be that his desire for ongoing dialogue between those who disagree but who have so much in common may yet find fulfillment.

Bibliography

Primary Sources

Books

Urshan, Andrew D. *The Almighty God in the Lord Jesus Christ.* Los Angeles: 1919. Reprint, Portland, OR: Apostolic Book Corner, n.d.

———. *Apostolic Faith Doctrine of the New Birth.* Cochrane, WI: 1941.

———. *The Doctrine of Redemption and the Redemption of the Body.* Chicago: The Witness of God, 1925.

———. *Doctrine of Trinity and the Divinity of Jesus Christ.* Cochrane, WI: 1923.

———. *The Life and Experiences of Andrew David Urshan.* 4th ed. N.p.: n.d.

———. *The Life Story of Andrew Bar David Urshan: An Autobiography of the Author's First Forty Years.* Stockton, CA: W.A.B.C. Press, 1967.

———. *My Study of Modern Pentecostals.* N.p.: 1923. Reprint, Portland, OR: Apostolic Book Publishers, 1981.

———. *Pentecost as it was in the Early 1900's.* Portland, OR: Apostolic Book Publishers, 1987.

———. *A Religious Timely Debate.* New York, NY: Apostolic Faith Christian Church, n.d.

———. *The Story of My Life.* 1st ed. St. Louis, MO: Gospel Publishing House, n.d.

———. *The Story of My Life.* 3rd ed. Chicago: n.d.

———. *Supreme Need of the Hour and the Source of the Mighty Revivals.* Cochrane, WI: 1922.

———. *Timely Messages of Comfort.* Los Angeles, CA: Author, 1918. Reprint, Portland, OR: Apostolic Book Corner, 1981.

———. *Timely Messages of Warning.* St. Louis, MO: The Gospel Publishing House, 1917. Reprint, Portland, OR: Apostolic Book Corner, 1973.

———. *Why I Was Baptized in the Name of the Lord Jesus Christ in Russia.* Chicago: IL: n.d.

Song

Urshan, Andrew D. *American-Assyro Unique Song Book.* Chicago, IL: Author, 1932.

Journal Articles

Urshan, Andrew D. "Acts 2:38 and Matt. 28:19 in History." *The Witness of God* 10, no. 10 (November-December 1930): 27-28.

———. "The Almighty God in the Lord Jesus Christ." *The Blessed Truth* 4, no. 18 (October 1, 1919).

———. "An Open Letter on the Absolute Deity of our Lord and Saviour Jesus Christ." *The Witness of God* 9 (November 1941): 2-5.

———. " 'Anathema Maran-Atha,' Or 'at the Coming of the Lord'." *The Witness of God* (February 1962): 5-7.
———. "Andrew D. Urshan Arrives in Persia." *The Christian Evangel* (n.d.): 6.
———. "Andrew in Russia." *The Witness of God* (March 1963): 5.
[Urshan, Andrew D.?] "Andy's Brief Biography." *The Witness of God* (October 1951): 3.
[Urshan, Andrew D.?] "Announcing." *The Witness of God* (July 1932): 1.
———. "Another Revelation." *The Witness of God* (November 1962): 2-8.
———. "Apostolic Faith Christian Church Articles of Faith." *The Witness of God* (October 1937): 7-8.
———. "Are You Ready?" *The Pentecostal Herald* (June 1961): 17, 21.
———. "Assurian Lad from Iran Seeking the True Americanism." *The Witness of God* (February 1962): 2-4.
———. "The Baptism of the Holy Ghost." *Glad Tidings* 1, no. 5: 10-12.
———. "Bend Oregon." *The Witness of God* 10, no. 96 (August 1928): 3.
———. "A Bible Revival." *Historical News* 10, no. 1 (October-December 1990): 1, 3.
———. "The Bible Truth Versus Social Purity Doctrines: Ungodly Marriages and Excessive Fleshly Indulgences." *The Witness of God* no. 6 (September 1924): 1-8.
———. "Born again." *Pentecostal Witness of the Grace and Truth* 1, no. 1 (October 1911): 4-6.
———. "Chapter Five—Story of My Life: My First Six Months in America." *The Witness of God* 3, no. 35. (December 1922): 6-7.
———. "Chicago and Mrs. Crawford's Revival Campaign." *The Witness of God* 3, no. 29 (May 1922): 7-8.
———. "Chicago's Second International Bible Conference." *The Witness of God* 3, no. 32 (August 1922): 1.
———. "A Christian Disciple." *Pentecostal Witness of the Grace and Truth* 1, no. 1 (October 1911): 8-9.
———. "Christian Battlefield's [sic]: Old and New Lines." The Witness of God (October 1947): 5.
———. "The Christian in Iran." *The Witness of God* (February 1963): 2-8.
[Urshan, Andrew D.?] "Columbus for Jesus." *The Witness of God* (January 1933): 2.
———. "Coming Revival Campaign in Los Angeles." *The Witness of God* 1, no. 2 (January 1920): 5.
———. "Concerning Our Books." *The Witness of God* 1, no. 1 (December 1919): 8.
———. "Concerning the Name of our Lord." *The Witness of God* 1, no. 4 (March 1920): 7.
———. "Confession of Faith." *The Latter Rain Evangel* 10, no. 8 (May 1918): 15.
———. "Confession of Faith." *Weekly Evangel* no. 236-237 (April 20, 1918): 13.
———. "Confession of Faith Concerning the God-Head." *Glad Tidings* 1, no. 5: 6.
———. "Confession of Our Faults." *The Weekly Evangel* (March 2, 1918): 4.
———. "Dear Reader." *The Witness of God* (June 1967): 1.
———. "Deity of Jesus Christ, the Son of God." *Glad Tidings* 1, no. 5: 8-9.

———. "Denominationalism and the World-Wide Pentecostal Movement." *The Witness of God* 2, no. 18 (June 1921): 1.

———. "The Divine First of all." *The Witness of God* (February-March, 1967): 3, 8.

———. "Divine Healing." *Pentecostal Witness of the Grace and Truth* 1, no. 1 (October 1911): 6-7.

———. "Doctrinal Questions." *The Witness of God* (August 1962): 2-4.

———. *The Doctrine of Redemption and the Redemption of the Body*. Chicago, IL: The Witness of God, 1925.

———. *The Doctrine of the New Birth Or the Perfect Way to Eternal Life*. Cochrane, WI: The Witness of God, 1921.

———. *Doctrine of Trinity and the Divinity of Jesus Christ*. Cochrane, WI: The Witness of God, 1923.

———. "Editorial." *The Witness of God* 2, nos. 14-15 (February and March 1921): 14.

———. "Editorial." *The Witness of God* 10, no. 81 (February 1927): 13.

[Urshan, Andrew D.?] "Editorial – Adoration." *The Witness of God* (November 1959): 1.

[Urshan, Andrew D.?] "Editorial Comments and News." *The Witness of God* (August 1957): 1.

[Urshan, Andrew D.?] "Editorial Message and News." *The Witness of God* (April 1950): 12.

———. "The Editorial Message on the Deity of Christ." *The Witness of God* (March 1963): 124-125.

[Urshan, Andrew D.?] "Editorial News." *The Witness of God* (August-September 1948): 2.

[Urshan, Andrew D.?] "Editorial News." *The Witness of God* (July 1962): 1.

———. "Editorial News." *The Witness of God* (June and July 1950): 1.

[Urshan, Andrew D.?] "Editorial News and Comments." *The Witness of God* (January 1949): 2.

[Urshan, Andrew D.?] "Editorial News and Comments." *The Witness of God* (June 1952): 8.

[Urshan, Andrew D.?] "Editorial News and Comments." *The Witness of God* (January 1957): 4.

[Urshan, Andrew D.?] "Editorial News and Comments." *The Witness of God* (September 1955): 1.

[Urshan, Andrew D.?] "Editorial News and Comments." *The Witness of God* (November 1953): 1.

———. "Editorial News and Notes." *The Witness of God* 10, no. 104 (April 1929): 2.

———. "Editorial News and Notes." *The Witness of God* 10, no. 108 (August 1929): 2.

———. "Editorial News and Notes." *The Witness of God* 10, no. 110 (October 1929): 2.

[Urshan, Andrew D.?] "Editorial News and Notes." *The Witness of God* (January 1932): 2.

[Urshan, Andrew D.?] "Editorial News and Notes." *The Witness of God* (April 1933): 2.

[Urshan, Andrew D.?] "Editorial News and Notes." *The Witness of God* (June 1931): 2.

[Urshan, Andrew D.?] "Editorial News of Interest." *The Witness of God* 6, no. 48 (October 1924): 1.

———. "Editorial Pen Points on the New Birth." *The Witness of God* 11, no. 9 (October 1930): 15-16.

———. "Editorials." *The Witness of God* [10], no. 94 (May 1928): 6.

———. "Eighth Chapter—The Story of My Life." *The Witness of God* 4, no. 41 (May 1923): 4-5.

———. "Eighth Chapter—Cont., The Story of My Life—Cont." *The Witness of God* 4, no. 42 (June 1923): 5.

———. "The Emanuel Gospel Mission of Montreal." *The Witness of God* 4, no. 46 (October 19232): 1.

———. "The Essentiality of Water Baptism." *The Witness of God* (January-February 1976): 2-4.

———. "Faith and Knowledge." *Pentecostal Witness of the Grace and Truth* 1, no. 1 (October 1911): 3.

———. "The Final and the Conclusion." *The Witness of God* (May 1963): 7-8.

———. "The Finished Work of the Cross of Christ Our Lord." *The Witness of God* (September 1955): 2.

———. "Fire! Fire!" *The Witness of God* (October 1935): 5, 8.

———. "First and Second Resurrections." *Pentecostal Outlook* no. 10 (April 1941): 3, 12.

———. "First Chapter—Story of My Life: The Assyro-Chaldean's Race, and the Life Story of Andrew David Urshan, the Assyro-Chaldean." *The Witness of God* 3, no. 34 (October 1922): 2-4.

[Urshan, Andrew D.?] "For Your Information." *The Witness of God* 11, no. 2 (February 1930): 10.

———. 'The Fulness [sic] of God." *The Weekly Evangel* (February 2, 1918): 3.

———. "The Fundamentals of Faith." *The Witness of God* 6, no. 52 (May 1924): 1.

[Urshan, Andrew D.?] "God's Acknowledgment and Our Trip East!" *The Witness of God* (October and November 1951): 3, 8.

———. "Going Forward." *Pentecostal Witness of the Grace and Truth* 1, no. 1 (October 1911): 16.

———. "The Grand and Good New Merger." *The Witness of God* (May 1932): 6-7.

———. "The Historical Facts." *The Witness of God* 2, no. 19 (July 1921):1.

———. "The Historical Facts Concerning Ecclesiastical Dispute in the Church of Christ Chiefly Over Trinitarianism." *The Witness of God* (August-September 1976): 2-3.

———. "The Holy Spirit, Works, and Gifts." *The Witness of God* (April 1950): 4.

[Urshan, Andrew D.?] "The House of Light." *The Witness of God* 1, no. 10 (September 1920): 4-5.

———. "How and When Paganism Entered Christianity." *The Witness of God* 10, no. 105 (May 1929): 4-5.

———. "The Human and Heavenly Parentship." *The Witness of God* (May 1933): 3.

[Urshan, Andrew D.?] "Important!" *The Witness of God* (May 1935): 1.

———. "Important Camp Announcement." *The Witness of God* 10, no. 104 (April 1929): 2.

———. "Important Editor's Comments." *The Witness of God* (1962): 8.

———. "Important News and Information." *The Witness of God* 1, no. 10 (September 1920): 8.

———. "Important Timely Questions and Answers." *The Witness of God* (May 1946): 9-11.

———. "Indianapolis Visit." *The Witness of God* 7, no. 61 (January and February 1925): 8.

———. "Indwelling of Christ." *Pentecostal Witness of the Grace and Truth* 1, no. 1 (October 1911): 9-11.

———. "Interesting News." *The Witness of God* 6, no. 55 (July 1924): 4.

———. "Interesting News and Information." *The Witness of God* 2, no. 13 (January 1921): 7.

[Urshan, Andrew D.?] "Introduction." *The Witness of God* (September 1966): 8.

———. "Introductory Questions on the Doctrine of the New Birth." *The Witness of God* 2, no. 21 (September 1921): 1.

———. "Introductory Questions on the Doctrine of the New Birth." *The Witness of God* (March 1975): 4.

———. "Jesus the Name." *The Witness of God* (September 1966): 1.

[Urshan, Andrew D.?] "June Greetings!" *The Witness of God* (June 1966): 1.

———. "Knowing the Will of God." *Glad Tidings* 1, no. 5: 3-4.

[Urshan, Andrew D.?] "The Last Announcement and Invitation to the Chicago Spring-time Bible Conference and the Apostalic [*sic*]-Brand Revival Campaign." *The Witness of God* 3, no. 28 (April 1922): 1.

———. "The Life Story of Andrew: The Assyro-Chaldean Boy from Urmia (Reziah) Persia (Iran)." *The Witness of God* no. 2-8 (May 1946).

———. "The Life Story of Andrew Bar-David [2nd section]." *The Witness of God* (August 1946): 11-12.

[Urshan, Andrew D.?] "Lord Blessing in Montreal." *The Witness of God* 4, no. 42 (June 1923): 1.

———. "The Lord's Census and the New Birth Doctrine." *The Witness of God* 10, no. 10 (November-December 1930): 4-6.

———. "The Martyred Six of Persia." *The Latter Rain Evangel* (August 1916): 2-6.

[Urshan, Andrew D.?] "Minutes of Meeting in Chicago: October 16 and 17, 1924." *The Witness of God* 6, no. 59 (November 1924): 1, 8.

———. "My Arrival in the United States." *The Witness of God* (April 1963): 1-3.

———. "My First Six Months in America." *The Witness of God* (April 1962): 3-4.

———. "My First Six Months in America—Cont." *The Witness of God* 4, no. 37 (January 1923): 3.

———. "My Last Personal Remarks Concerning the Story of My Life." *The Witness of God* (October 1946): 3.
———. "The Mystery of God, or Who is God?" *The Witness of God* (December 1953): 8.
———. "The Necessity of Preaching Jesus Christ as God." *The Witness of God* 9 (November 1941): 6-8.
———. "The New Birth and Members of His Body." *The Witness of God* 10, no. 10 (November-December 1930): 6.
———. "The New Birth Illustrated." *The Witness of God* 10, no. 10 (November-December 1930): 28-29.
———. "The New Birth, Or the New Creation." *The Witness of God* 10, no. 10 (November-December 1930): 12-15.
———. "The New Light or the More Light." *The Witness of God* 1, no. 10 (September 1920): 1.
———. "News about the Story of My Life." *The Witness of God* 65, no. 7. (June and July 1925): 1.
———. "News of Interest." *The Witness of God* 2, no. 17 (May 1921): 8.
———. "News of Interest." *The Witness of God* 2, no. 18 (June 1921): 8.
———. "News of Interest." *The Witness of God* 2, no. 21 (September 1921): 8.
———. "News of Interest." *The Witness of God* 3, no. 25 (January 1922): 8.
———. "News of Interest." *The Witness of God* 3, no. 27 (March 1922): 8.
———. "News of Interest." *The Witness of God* 3, no. 30 (June 1922): 1.
[Urshan, Andrew D.?] "News of Interest and Current Events." *The Witness of God* 3, no. 34 (December 1922): 2.
———. "A Normal Christian Life." *The Witness of God* (March 1962): 6-7.
———. "A Normal Christian Life." *The Witness of God* (April 1962): 8.
———. "Nuggets from God's Treasury House as Given to Me." *The Witness of God* (August 1961): 3.
[Urshan, Andrew D.?] "Oakdale, Louisiana." *The Witness of God* 7, no. 62 (March 1925): 14.
———. "Old Fashioned Revival." *The Witness of God* 7, no. 66 (August 1925): 1.
———. "The One Christian Baptism." *The Witness of God* 2, no. 22 (October 1921): 7-8.
———. "The One Christian Baptism." *The Witness of God* 10, no. 10 (November-December 1930): 25.
———. "Organism and Organization." *The Witness of God* 6, no. 59 (November 1924): 1-2.
[Urshan, Andrew D.?] "Our Campaigns." *The Witness of God* 11, no. 9 (October 1930): 2.
[Urshan, Andrew D.?] "Our Campaigns." *The Witness of God* (January 1931): 2.
[Urshan, Andrew D.?] "Our Campaigns." *The Witness of God* (May 1932): 1.
———. "Our Farewell Meeting in Los Angeles." *The Witness of God* (May 1963): 7.
———. "Our Four Days Campaign in Salem, Oregon." *The Witness of God* 10, no. 96 (August 1928): 3.

[Urshan, Andrew D.?] "Our Last Campaign." *The Witness of God* (June 1933):2.
[Urshan, Andrew D.?] "Our Next Campaign." *The Witness of God* (May 1933): 2.
———. "Our Own Personal Experience with the Pentecostal Movement, and the Holy Spirit Baptism!" *The Witness of God* (September 1962): 4-6.
———. "Our Personal Testimony Concerning the New Issue People." *The Witness of God* 1, no. 10 (September 1920): 3.
[Urshan, Andrew D.?] "Our Recent Trip." *The Witness of God* (July 1958): 1.
———. "Our Recent Trip to the West Coast." *The Witness of God* 10, no. 96 (August 1928): 2.
———. "Our Responsibilities and Privileges." *The Latter Rain Evangel* (May 1913): 5.
[Urshan, Andrew D.?] "Our Shreveport Visit." *The Witness of God* 7, no. 62 (March 1925): 14.
———. "Our Visit to Seattle, Wash." *The Witness of God* 10, no. 96 (August 1928): 3.
———. "The Spring Time." *The Witness of God* 2, no. 16 (April 1921): 8.
[Urshan, Andrew D.?] "Traveling for Jesus, Our Soon Coming King!" *The Witness of God* (June 1966): 1.
———. "Overcoming Life." *The Witness of God* (May 1962): 3-5, 8.
———. "The Pentecostal People Versus Spiritualism." *The Witness of God* 1, no. 8 (July 1920): 8. Reprinted, *The Witness of God* 4, no. 46 (October 1923): 6-7.
———. "The Peril of the Lack of the Holy Oil." *Christian Unity* no. 8 (January 1924): 2.
———. "Prayers for Coming Campaigns." *The Witness of God* 1, no. 5 (April 1920): 7.
———. "The Precious Blood of Jesus." *Pentecostal Witness of the Grace and Truth* 1, no. 1 (October 1911): 2-3.
———. "A Prediction." *Historical News* 3, no. 1 (October-November-December 1983): 1-3.
———. "Questions Answered." *Pentecostal Witness of the Grace and Truth* 1, no. 1 (October 1911): 15-16.
———. "The Real and Adopted Children of God." *The Witness of God* 10, no. 10 (November-December 1930): 7-8.
———. "Receiving the Holy Spirit." *Pentecostal Witness of the Grace and Truth* 1, no. 1 (October 1911): 11-12.
———. "Republication of our First 1918 Open Letter to all Pentecostal Saints." *The Witness of God* (1941): 2-5.
———. "Revival at First Town 'Adda' in Iran Continues from Last Issue." *The Witness of God* (January 1963): 2-8.
———. "Revival of Revolution." *The Witness of God* 4, no. 41 (May 1923): 1.
———. "Rightly Spending Christmas." *The Witness of God* 7, no. 65 (June and July 1925): 3.
———. "Scriptural Facts Concerning the Godhead Question." *The Witness of God* 2, no. 19 (July 1921): 5.

[Urshan, Andrew D.?] "Season's Greetings." *The Witness of God* (October-December 1966): 1.

———. "Second Chapter—The Story of My Life." *The Witness of God* 3, no. 35 (November 1922): 2.

———. "Second Chapter—Story of My Life: The Early Life of Andrew, the Assyro-Chaldean Boy." *The Witness of God* 3, no. 34 (October 1922): 7-8.

———. "Seeing and Entering the Kingdom of God." *The Witness of God* (March 1975): 5.

———. "Seventh Chapter—The Story of My Life: My First Few Months in Chicago." *The Witness of God* 4, no. 37 (January 1923): 5-6

———. "Seventh Chapter—The Story of My Life: My First Few Months in Chicago—Cont." *The Witness of God* 4, no. 38 (February 1923): 6-8.

———. "Seventh Chapter—The Story of My Life: My First Few Months in Chicago—Cont." *The Witness of God* 4, no. 39 (March 1923): 4-5.

———. "Seventh Chapter—The Story of My Life: My First Few Months in Chicago—Cont." *The Witness of God* 4, no. 40 (April 1923): 7-8.

———. "Seventh Chapter—The Story of My Life: My First Few Months in Chicago—Cont." *The Witness of God* 4, no. 41 (May 1923): 3.

———. "The Sign of the True Christ – the Christmas Message." *The Pentecostal Outlook* (December 1935): 5.

———. "Something New Happens." *The Witness of God* (October 1962): 2-8.

———. "Some of the Lord's Work in Our Midst During the Last Fifteen Months." *Pentecostal Witness of the Grace and Truth* 1, no. 1 (October 1911): 12-14.

———. "Special Holiday Campaign." *The Witness of God* 3, no. 35 (November 1922): 1.

———. "Special Meetings at Chicago Continued." *The Witness of God* 3, no. 34 (October 1922): 6.

[Urshan, Andrew D.?] "Special Notice." *The Witness of God* 5, no. 49 (January 1924): 3.

———. "The Spirit Filled Life." *Pentecostal Witness of the Grace and Truth* 1, no. 1 (October 1911): 14-15.

[Urshan, Andrew D.?] "The St. Louis Convention." *The Witness of God* (August 1932): 1.

———. "The Story of My Life—9th Chapter—Cont." *The Witness of God* 4, no. 43 (July 1923): 5, 7.

———. "The Story of My Life—10th Chapter—Cont." *The Witness of God* 4, no. 45 (September 1923): 3-4.

———. "The Story of My Life—11th Chapter: What Happened to Me after the Baptism of the Holy Spirit." *The Witness of God* 4, no. 46 (October 1923): 2-3.

———. "The Story of My Life—13th Chapter." *The Witness of God* 4, no. 48 (December 1923): 3-4.

———. "The Story of My Life—14th Chapter." *The Witness of God* 5, no. 49 (January 1924): 4-5.

———. "The Story of My Life—15th Chapter." *The Witness of God* 5, no. 51 (March 1924): 4-5.

———. "The Story of My Life—17th Chapter." *The Witness of God* 5, no. 52 (April 1924): 2-3.

———. "The Story of My Life—21st Chapter." *The Witness of God* 6, no. 56 (August 1924): 3.

———. "The Story of My Life—24th Chapter." *The Witness of God* 6, no. 60 (December 1924): 2-3.

———. "The Story of My Life—26th Chapter: Why I Was Baptized in Jesus' Name." *The Witness of God* 7, no. 62 (March 1925): 2-5.

———. "The Story of My Life—27th Chapter." *The Witness of God* 6, no. 63 (April 1925): 2-3.

———. "The Story of My Life—28th Chapter." *The Witness of God* 6, no. 64 (May 1925): 2-4.

———. "The Story of My Life—29th Chapter." *The Witness of God* 7, no. 65 (June and July 1925): 2-3.

———. "The Story of My Life—30th Chapter, or the Last Chapter." *The Witness of God* 7, no. 65 (June and July 1925): 5.

———. "A Strange Experience in Long Beach, California." *The Witness of God* (December 1962): 2-8.

———. "Teaching on the New Birth." *The Witness of God* 11, no. 9 (October 1930): 3-15.

———. "Tenth Chapter—Story of My Life." *The Witness of God* 4, no. 44 (August 1923): 5-6.

———. "There is a Difference." *The Witness of God* 10, no. 10 (November-December 1930): 8.

———. "Third Chapter—Story of My Life: Andrew's Wonderful Conversion." *The Witness of God* 3, no. 35 (November 1922): 4.

———. "The Timely Message." *The Witness of God* (June 1962): 8.

———. "The Timely Message." *The Witness of God* (July 1962): 5-8.

———. "The Timely Message." *The Witness of God* (August 1962): 5-8.

———. "The Timely Message." *The Witness of God* (September 1962): 7-8.

———. "Trip to Western Canada." *The Witness of God* 10, nos. 99 and 100 (November and December 1928): 28.

———. "True and False Holiness." *The Witness of God* (January 1962): 6-8.

———. "The True Devotional Experience and Pious Practice is a Life of Perfect Loyalty to the Person and Name of Jesus Christ." *The Witness of God* (January-February 1976): 6-8.

———. "The True Holiness." *The Witness of God* (February 1962): 8.

———. "Twenty-Seven Questions and Answers on the New Birth." *Pentecostal Outlook* no. 12 (August 1943): 8-11, 13.

———. "Unification of the Body of Christ." *The Witness of God* 7, no. 62 (March 1925): 1.

———. "Walking in the Light." *Pentecostal Witness of the Grace and Truth* 1, no. 1 (October 1911): 7-8.

———. "Warning Against Modern Strong Delusions." *The Witness of God* (November 1931): 5-7.

———. "Watch Night." *The Witness of God* 7, no. 61 (January and February 1925): 8.

———. "We Would See Jesus." *The Latter Rain Evangel* (June 1911): 9.

———. "When Paganism Crept into Apostolic Christianity." *The Witness of God* (October 1965): 3.

———. "When We Are Ashamed of Ourselves." *The Witness of God* (April 1963): 3-5.

———. "Who is the Great I Am?" *The Witness of God* (June 1941): 1.

———. "Why I was Reimmersed Or Rebaptised in Jesus Name." *The Witness of God* no. 10 (November 1927): 20-24.

———. "The Winnipeg Revival a Successful Convention." *The Witness of God* 2, no. 13 (January 1921): 8.

———. "A Word About Our Recent Trip in Behalf of Our Dear Missionaries." *The Witness of God* 3, no. 28 (April 1922): 6.

———. "Yes, Misunderstood." *The Witness of God* 10, no. 10 (November-December 1930): 28.

Secondary Sources

Books

Augustine: Later Works. Trans. by John Burnaby. Philadelphia: Westminster Press, 1955.

A Century of Mission Work in Iran (Persia) 1834-1934. Bierut, Lebanon, Syria: The American Press, 1936.

The Chronicle. Amherst, [MA?}: The American Church in the Spirit of the Apostles, 1997.

Ecumenical Missionary Conference, New York 1900. Vol. I. New York: American Tract Society, 1900.

Evagrius of Pontus: The Greek Ascetic Corpus. Translated by Robert E. Sinkewicz. Oxford: Oxford University Press, 2003.

Historical Sketches of the Missions Under the Care of the Board of Foreign Missions of the Presbyterian Church. 3rd ed. rev. Philadelphia, PA: Woman's Foreign Missionary Society of the Presbyterian Church, 1891.

Akcam, Taner. *A Shameful Act: The Armenian Genocide and the Question of Turkish Responsibility.* New York: Metropolitan Books, 2007.

Anderson, Allan. *An Introduction to Pentecostalism: Global Charismatic Christianity.* New York, NY: Cambridge University Press, 2004.

Anderson, Robert Mapes. *Vision of the Disinherited: The Making of American Pentecostalism.* New York / Oxford: Oxford University Press, 1979.

Andrews, C. F. *Sadhu Sundar Singh.* N.p.: 1934.

Archer, Kenneth J. *A Pentecostal Hermeneutic for the Twenty-First Century: Spirit, Scripture and Community.* Journal of Pentecostal Theology Supplement Series 28. Edited by John Chrisopher Thomas, Rickie D. Moore, and Steven J. Land. London: T & T Clark International, 2004.

Baum, Wilhelm and Dietmar W. Winkler, *The Church of the East: A Concise History.* New York: Routledge Curzon, 2003.
Baumer, Christoph. *The Church of the East: An Illustrated History of Assyrian Christianity.* London: I. B. Tauris, 2006.
Beisner, E. Calvin. *"Jesus Only" Churches.* Grand Rapids, MI: Zondervan, 1998.
Bernard, David et al. *Meet the United Pentecostal Church International.* Edited by R. M. Davis. Hazelwood, MO: Pentecostal Publishing House, 1989.
Bernard, David K. *The Glory of God in the Face of Jesus Christ: Deification of Jesus in Early Christian Discourse.* Journal of Pentecostal Theology Supplement Series. Edited by John Christopher Thomas. Vol. 45. Blandford Forum, England. Deo Publishing, 2016.
_____. *A History of Christian Doctrine: The Twentieth Century A.D. 1900 – 2000.* Vol. 3. Hazelwood, MO: Word Aflame Press, 1999.
———. *Understanding the Articles of Faith.* Hazelwood, MO: Word Aflame Press, 1998.
———. *The New Birth.* Series in Pentecostal Theology. Vol. 1. Hazelwood, MO: Word Aflame Press, 1984.
———. *The Oneness of God.* Series in Pentecostal Theology, Vol. 1. Hazelwood, MO: Word Aflame Press, 1983.
Bettenson, Henry. *Documents of the Christian Church.* 2nd ed. London: Oxford University Press, 1967.
Bjornstad, James and Walter Bjorck. *Jesus Only: A Modalistic Interpretation.* Wayne, NJ: Christian Research Institute, 1970.
Blumhofer, Edith L. *Restoring the Faith: The Assemblies of God, Pentecostalism, and American Culture.* Urbana and Chicago: University of Illinois Press, 1993.
———. "William H. Durham: Years of Creativity, Years of Dissent." In James R. Goff and Grant Wacker, eds., *Portraits of a Generation: Early Pentecostal Leaders.* Fayetteville, AR: University of Arkansas Press, 2002.
Blumhofer, Edith Waldvogel. *Aimee Semple McPherson: everybody's sister.* Grand Rapids: Wm. B. Eerdmans Publishing Co., 1993.
Bobrick, Benson. *The Fated Sky: Astrology in History.* New York: Simon & Schuster, 2005.
Boyd, Gregory A. *Oneness Pentecostalism and the Trinity.* Grand Rapids, MI: Baker Book House, 1992.
Bradley, James E. and Richard A. Muller. *Church History: An Introduction to Research, Reference Works, and Methods.* Grand Rapids: Wm. B. Eerdmans, 1995.
Brock, S. "Christology of the Church of the East." In *Recent Studies in Early Christianity: A Collection of Scholarly Essays.* Edited by Everett Fergson. London: Taylor & Francis, 1999.
Brumback, Carl. *Suddenly from Heaven – A History of the Assemblies of God.* Springfield, MO: Gospel Publishing House, 1961.
———. *God in Three Persons.* Cleveland, TN: Pathway Press, 1959.
Bryce, James. *The Treatment of Armenians in the Ottoman Empire.* London: Hodder and Stoughton, 1916.

Bundy, David. "G. T. Haywood: Religion for Urban Realities." In *Portraits of a Generation: Early Pentecostal Leaders*. Edited by James R. Goff, Jr. and Grant Wacker, 237-53. Fayetteville, AR: The University of Arkansas Press, 2002.

Bunyan, John. *The Whole Works of John Bunyan*. London: Blackie and Son, 1862.

———. *The Works of that Eminent Servant of Christ, Mr. John Bunyan*. Vol. 2. Philadelphia: T. W. Lord, 1834.

Burdette, Robert Jones, and Clara Bradley Burdette, eds. *Robert J. Burdette: His Message*. Chicago: The John C. Winston Co., 1922. Reprint, Pasadena, CA: The Clara Vista Press, n.d.

Burgess, Stanley M. *The Holy Spirit: Eastern Christian Traditions*. Peabody, MA: Hendrickson Publishers, 1989.

———, ed. *The New International Dictionary of Pentecostal and Charismatic Movements*. Rev. and expanded ed. Grand Rapids: Zondervan, 2002.

Burgess Stanley M. and Gary B. McGee, eds. *Dictionary of Pentecostal and Charismatic Movements*. Grand Rapids: Zondervan Publishing House, 1988.

Butler, Daniel L. *The Last Generation of Truth*. Hazelwood, MO: Word Aflame Press, 1989.

Coan, Frederick G. *Yesterdays in Persia and Kurdistan*. Claremont, CA: Saunders Studio Press, 1939.

Clanton, Arthur L. *United We Stand: A History of Oneness Organizations*. Hazelwood, MO: Pentecostal Publishing House, 1970.

Condit, Carl W. *The Chicago School of Architecture: A History of Commercial and Public Building in the Chicago Area, 1875-1925*. Chicago: University of Chicago Press, 1998.

Cox, Harvey. *Fire from Heaven: The Rise of Pentecostal Spirituality and the Reshaping of Religion in the 21st Century*. Cambridge, MA: Da Capo Press, 2001.

Currey, Josiah Seymour. *Chicago: Its History and Its Builders*. Vol. 5. Chicago: The S. J. Clarke Publishing Co., 1912.

Dadrian, Vahakn N. *The History of the Armenian Genocide: Ethnic Conflict from the Balkans to Anatolia to the Caucasus*. Providence, RI: Berghahn Books, 1997.

Dake, Finis. *Dake's Annotated Reference Bible, NT*. Lawrenceville, GA: Dake's Bible Sales, 1963.

Davey, C. J. *Sadhu Sundar Singh*. N.p.: 1980.

———. *The Yellow Robe*. N.p.: 1950.

Davis, Leslie A., ed. *The Slaughterhouse Province: An American Diplomat's Report on the Armenian Genocide, 1915-1917*. New York: Aristide D. Caratzas, 1990.

Dayton, Donald W. *Theological Roots of Pentecostalism*. Grand Rapids, MI: Zondervan, 1987.

Dayton, Donald W., Andrew D. Urshan, Frank J. Ewart, and G. T. Haywood. *Seven "Jesus Only" Tracts*. New York: Garland Pub., 1985.

De Long, Arthur Hamilton and Allen P. De Long, comps. and eds. *Tributes of Great Men to Jesus Christ*. New York. Fleming H. Revell Company, 1918.

Dixon, A. C. *Lights and Shadows of American Life*. New York: 1898.

Dixon, A. C., ed. *The Fundamentals: A Testimony to the Truth.* Vol. 1. Grand Rapids: Baker Books, 1994.

———, ed. *The Holy Spirit in Life and Service.* New York: Fleming H. Revell Co., 1895.

———, ed. *The Person and Ministry of the Holy Spirit.* Baltimore: Wharton, Barron, & Co., 1890.

Dixon, A. D., W. H. Griffith Thomas, and James Orr, *Back to the Bible: The Triumphs of Truth.* N.p.: S. W. Partridge and Co., 1912.

Dugas, Paul D., comp. *The Life and Writings of Elder G. T. Haywood.* Stockton, CA: W.A.B.C. Press, 1968.

Dunn, James. *Jesus and the Spirit: A Study of the Religious and Charismatic Experience of Jesus and the First Christians as Reflected in the New Testament.* London: SCM Press, 1975.

Elder, John. *History of the Iran Mission.* N.p.: n.d.

Ewart, Frank J. *The Creedless Christ.* N.p.: n.d.

———. *Jesus – the Man and Mystery.* Nashville, TN: Baird-Ward, 1941.

———. *The Name and the Book.* St. Louis, MO: Pentecostal Publishing House, 1947. Reprint, Hazelwood, MO: Word Aflame Press, 1986.

———. *The Phenomenon of Pentecost.* Rev. ed. Hazelwood, MO: Word Aflame Press, 2000.

———. *The Revelation of Jesus Christ.* Hazelwood, MO: Pentecostal Publishing House, n.d.

Farrar, Frederic William. *The Life of Lives: Further Studies in the Life of Christ.* London: Cassell and Company, Ltd., 1900.

Faultless, Julian, "The Two Recensions of the Prologue to John." In *Christians at the Heart of Islamic Rule: Church Life and Scholarship in Abbasid Iraq.* Edited by David Thomas. Boston: Brill, 2003:

Faupel, D. William. *The Everlasting Gospel: The Significance of Eschatology in the Development of Pentecostal Thought.* Journal of Pentecostal Theology Supplement Series. Edited by John Christopher Thomas, Rickie D. Moore and Steven J. Land. Vol. 10. Sheffield, England: Sheffield Academic Press, 1996.

Fisher, William Bayne. *The Cambridge History of Iran: From Nadir Shah to the Islamic Republic.* Vol. 7. Edited by P. Avery, G. R. G. Hambly, and C. Melville. Cambridge: Cambridge University Press, 1991.

Fortman, Edmund J. *The Triune God: A Historical Study of the Doctrine of the Trinity.* Grand Rapids: Baker Book House, 1972.

Foster, Fred J. *Their Story: 20th Century Pentecostals.* Rev. and updated ed. Hazelwood, MO: Word Aflame Press, 2007.

French, Talmadge L. *Early Interracial Oneness Pentecostalism.* Eugene, OR: Pickwick Publications, 2014.

———. *Our God is One: The Story of the Oneness Pentecostals.* Indianapolis, IN: Voice & Vision Publications, 1999.

Frodsham, Stanley Howard. *With Signs Following: The Story of the Pentecostal Revival in the Twentieth Century.* Rev. ed. Springfield, MO: Gospel Publishing House, 1946.

Fudge, Thomas A. *Christianity without the Cross: A History of Salvation in Oneness Pentecostalism*. Boca Raton, FL: Universal-Publishers, 2003.

Gaebelein, Arno C. "Fulfilled Prophecy a Potent Argument." In *The Fundamentals,* R. A. Torrey, ed. Grand Rapids: Kregel Publications, 1990.

Geisler, Norman L. and Paul D. Feinberg. *Introduction to Philosophy: A Christian Perspective.* Grand Rapids: Baker Book House, 1980.

Gibson, John Munro. *Christianity According to Christ: A Series of Papers.* 2nd ed. London: James Nisbet and Co., 1889.

Goff, James R., Jr., and Grant Wacker, *Portraits of a Generation: Early Pentecostal Leaders.* Fayetteville, AR: University of Arkansas Press, 2002.

Golder, Morris. E. *A History of the Pentecostal Assemblies of the World.* N.p.: 1973.

Gonzalez, Justo L. *A History of Christian Thought.* Vol. 1. Rev. ed. Nashville, TN: Abingdon Press, 1970.

———. *Essential Theological Terms.* (Louisville, KY: Westminster John Knox Press, 2005.

Goss, Ethel E. *The Winds of God: The Story of the Early Pentecostal Days (1901-1914).* Reprint ed. Hazelwood, MO: Word Aflame Press, 1977.

Graves, R. Brent. *The God of Two Testaments.* Hazelwood, MO: Word Aflame Press, 2000.

Griffith, S. H. "The Thorn among the Tares." In M. F. Wiles and E. J. Yarnold, eds. *Studia Patristica.* Vol. XXXV. Leuven: Peeters, 2001.

Haldeman, I. M. "Wherein Was Jesus God's Only Begotten Son?" In Mary E. McDonough, *God's Plan of Redemption.* Anaheim CA: Living Stream Books, 1999.

Hall, J. L. *The United Pentecostal Church and the Evangelical Movement.* Hazelwood, MO: Word Aflame Press, 1990.

Hartzler, H. B. *Moody in Chicago or the World's Fair Gospel Campaign: An Account of Six Months' Evangelistic Work in the City of Chicago and Vicinity During the Time of the World's Columbian Exposition, Conducted by Dwight L. Moody and His Associates.* New York: Fleming H. Revell Company, 1894.

Harvey, Gordon Earl, Richard D. Starnes, and Glenn Feldman, eds. *History and Hope in the Heart of Dixie: Scholarship, Activism, and Wayne Flynt in the Modern South.* Tuscaloosa, AL: University of Alabama Press, 2006.

Haywood, G. T. *The Birth of the Spirit in the Days of the Apostles.* Portland, OR: Apostolic Book Publishers, n.d.

———. *Divine Names and Titles of Jehovah.* Portland, OR: Apostolic Book Publishers, n.d.

Hall, J. L. and David K. Bernard. *Doctrines of the Bible.* Hazelwood, MO: Word Aflame Press, 1993.

Hollenweger, Walter J. *Pentecostalism: Origins and Developments Worldwide.* Peabody, MA: Hendrickson Publishers, 1997.

———. *The Pentecostals* [Enthusiastisches Christentum: die Pfingstbewegung in Geschichte und Gegenwart]. Translated by R. A. Wilson. Minneapolis, MN: Augsburg Publishing House, 1972.

Holsinger, H. R. *Holsinger's History of the Tunkers and the Brethren Church Embracing the Church of the Brethren, the Tunkers, the Seventh-Day German*

Baptist Church, the German Baptist Church, the Old German Baptists, and the Brethren Church. Oakland, CA: Pacific Press Publishing, 1901.
Horton, Michael, ed. *The Agony of Deceit: What Some TV Preachers are Really Teaching.* Chicago: Moody Press, 1990.
Host, William R. and Brooke Ahne Portmann, *Early Chicago Hotels.* Postcard History Series. Chicago: Arcadia Publishing, 2006.
Hovannisian, Richard G., ed. *The Armenian Genocide in Perspective.* Oxford: Transaction Books, 1986.
Iden, Thomas M. *The Upper Room Bulletin 1920-21.* Vol. 7. Ann Arbor, MI: Ann Arbor Press, 1921.
Jacobsen, Douglas. *Thinking in the Spirit: Theologies of the Early Pentecostal Movement.* Bloomington, IN: Indiana University Press, 2003.
———. *A Reader in Pentecostal Theology: Voices from the First Generation.* Bloomington: Indiana University Press, 2006.
Jenkins, Philip. *The Lost History of Christianity: The Thousand-Year Golden Age of the Church in the Middle East, Africa, and Asia—and How It Died.* New York: HarperOne, 2008.
Joneneel, J. A. B., ed. *Pentecost, Mission and Ecumenism: Essays on Intellectual Theology: Festschrift in Honour of Professor Walter J. Hollenweger.* Studien Zur Interkulturellen Geschichte Des Christentums 75. Frankfort: Main: Peter Lang, 1992.
Lange, Christian. *The Portrayal of Christ in the Syriac Commentary on the Diatessaron.* Leuven, Belgium: Peeters Publishers, 2005.
Lawson, James Gilchrist, comp. *Greatest Thoughts About Jesus Christ.* New York: George H. Doran Co., 1919.
Longenecker, Richard. *The Christology of Early Jewish Christianity.* Studies in Biblical Theology, 2nd ser. Naperville, IL: A. R. Allenson, 1970.
Malech, George David. *History of the Syrian Nation and the Old Evangelical-Apostolic Church of the East.* Minneapolis, MN: 1910.
Marsden, George M. *Fundamentalism and American Culture: The Shaping of Twentieth Century Evangelicalism, 1870-1925.* New York: Oxford University Press, 1980.
McDonough, Mary E. *God's Plan of Redemption.* Anaheim, CA: Living Stream Books, 1999.
McGrath, Alister E. *Christian Theology: An Introduction.* Oxford: Blackwell, 1994.
Miller, Donald E. and Lorna Touryan. *Survivors: An Oral History of the Armenian Genocide.* Berkeley: University of California Press, 1993.
Moberly, F. J. *Operations in Persia, 1914-1919.* London: His Majesty's Stationery Office, 1927.
Moore, Charles E., ed. *Sadhu Sundar Singh.* N.p.: n.d.
Moseley, J. Rufus. *Manifest Victory.* Plainfield, NJ: Logos International, 1971.
Muller, Richard A. *Dictionary of Latin and Greek Theological Terms.* Grand Rapids: Baker Book House, 1985.
Norris, David S. *I Am: A Oneness Pentecostal Theology.* Hazelwood, MO: WAP Academic, 2009.

Offor, J. B. George. *The Whole Works of John Bunyan.* Vol. 1. London: Blackie and Son, 1862.
Possekel, Ute. "Ephrem's Doctrine of God." In *God in Early Christian Thought: Essays in Memory of Lloyd G. Patterson,* Supplements to Vigiliae Christianae. Edited by Andrew B. McGowan, Brian E. Daley, S.J., and Timothy J. Gaden. Leiden, The Netherlands: Brill, 2009.
Rae, Heather. *State Identities and the Homogenisation of Peoples.* New York: Cambridge University Press, 2002.
Reed, David A. *"In Jesus' Name": The History and Beliefs of Oneness Pentecostals.* Journal of Pentecostal Theology Supplement Series 31. Edited by John Christopher Thomas, Rickie Moore, and Steven J. Land. Blandford Forum, United Kingdom: Deo Publishing, 2008.
―――. "Aspects of the Origins of Oneness Pentecostalism." In *Aspects of Pentecostal-Charismatic Origins.* Edited by Vinson Synan, 143-170. Plainfield, NJ: Logos International, 1975.
Reeves, Kenneth V. *The Lost Sons of God.* Granite City, IL: Inspirational Tapes and Books, 1990.
Reynolds, Ralph V. *Cry of the Unborn: Understanding the Spirit Birth Process.* Hood River, OR: Alpha Bible Publications, 1991.
Robeck, Cecil M. *The Azusa Street Mission and Revival.* Nashville, TN: Thomas Nelson, Inc., 2006.
Seow, C. L. *A Grammar for Biblical Hebrew.* Nashville, TN: Abingdon Press, 1987.
Shaw, Stanford and Ezel Kural Shaw. *History of the Ottoman Empire and Modern Turkey.* Vol. 2. Cambridge: Cambridge University Press, 1977.
Shedd, Mary Lewis. *The Measure of a Man: The Life of William Ambrose Shedd, missionary to Persia.* New York: George H. Doran Company, 1922.
Smith, Robert Payne. *A Compendious Syriac Dictionary.* Oxford: Clarendon, 1903.
Smith, Timothy L. *Called Unto Holiness: The Story of the Nazarenes: The Formative Years.* Kansas City: Nazarene Publishing House, 1962.
Smorodin, N. P. *The Lord is Our Rock and Deliverer.* N.p.: n.d.
Spurgeon, Charles Haddon, "The Exaltation of Christ." In *Sermons of the Rev. C. H. Spurgeon.* 2nd series. New York: Sheldon and Company, Publishers, 1869.
Storrs, Richard Salter. *Memoir of the Rev. Samuel Green: late pastor of Union Church, Boston.* Boston: Perkins and Marvin, 1836.
Streeter, Burnett Hillman. *The Message of Sadhu Sundar Singh: A Study in Mysticism on Practical Religion.* New York: The Macmillan Company, 1922.
―――. *The Message of Sadhu Sundar Singh: A Biography.* N.p.: n.d.
―――. *The Message of Sadhu Sundar Singh: A Personal Memoir.* N.p.: n.d.
Symposium on Oneness Pentecostalism 1986. Hazelwood, MO: Word Aflame Press, 1986.
Synan, Vinson. *The Century of the Holy Spirit.* Nashville, TN: Thomas Nelson, 2001.
―――. *The Holiness-Pentecostal Tradition: Charismatic Movements in the Twentieth Century.* 2nd ed. Grand Rapids: Wm. B. Eerdmans Publishing Co., 1997.

Taylor, David G. K. "The Syriac Tradition." In *The First Christian Theologians: An Introduction to Theology in the Early Church*. Edited by Gillian Rosemary Evans. Hoboken, NJ: Wiley-Blackwell, 2004.

Thomas, Edmund J. and Eugene G. Miller. *Writers and Philosophers: A Sourcebook of Philosophical Influences on Literature*. New York: Greenwood Press, 1990.

Torry, R. A., ed. *The Fundamentals*. Updated by Charles L. Feinberg. Grand Rapids: Kregel Publications, 1990.

Tyson, James L. *The Early Pentecostal Revival: History of Twentieth-Century Pentecostals and the Pentecostal Assemblies of the World, 1901-30*. Hazelwood, MO: Word Aflame Press, 1992.

———. *Earnest Contenders for the Faith: A Compilation of Original Essays by Early 20th Century Pentecostal Preachers in Nine Volumes. Volume I*. Warren, OH: Pentecostal Publications, 1982.

Uras, Esat. *The Armenians in History and the Armenian Question*. Istanbul: Documentary Publications, 1988.

Wacker, Grant. *Heaven Below: Early Pentecostals and American Culture*. Cambridge, MA: Harvard University Press, 2003.

Walker, Christopher. *Armenia: The Survival of a Nation*. Rev. 2nd ed. New York: Routledge, 1990.

Wigram, W. A. *The Doctrinal Position of the Assyrian or East Syrian Church*. London: Society for Promoting Christian Knowledge, 1908.

Winfield, Aaron Burr. *Antidote to the Errors of Universalism*. Auburn, NY: Derby, Miller, and Co., 1850.

Wilson, Robert. *Revolution and Genocide*. Chicago: University of Chicago Press, 1992.

Yong, Amos. *The Spirit Poured Out on all Flesh: Pentecostalism and the Possibility of Global Theology*. Grand Rapids, MI: Baker Academic, 2005.

Journal Articles

"Andrew D. Urshan." *Gospel Tidings* (January 1968): 2-3.

"Announcement!" *The Blessed Truth* 8, no. 7 (July 1, 1923): 2.

"Baptism [Reprinted from "Eusebia" of August 1898]." *The Witness of God* 10, no. 10 (November-December 1930): 25-26.

"Baptized into What Name?" *Sunday School Times*, 58, no. 21 (20 May 1916): 322.

"Bro. Urshan Married." *The Weekly Evangel* (August 25, 1917): 13.

"The Church at Home and Abroad." Vol. 10. Philadelphia, PA: Presbyterian Board of Publication and Sabbath-School Work, 1891.

"The Coming General Assembly." *Nazarene Messenger* 12, no. 12 (September 19, 1907):1-2.

"Convention, Toronto, Canada." *The Blessed Truth* 6, no. 10 (October 1, 1921): 1.

"Have You been Baptized in the Name of Jesus Christ?" *The Victorious Gospel* (Early Spring 1915): 4-5.

"Let's Get Acquainted." *The Pentecostal Outlook* (July 1939): 4.

"Oneness Pentecostals." *Ecumenical Trends* 24 (May 1995): 73-76.

"Oneness-Trinitarian Pentecostal Final Report, 2002-2007." *Pneuma* 30 (2008): 203-224.
"A Persian Apostle: Benjamin Bodal." *The Muslim World* 21, no. 3: 223-43.
"The Present Blessed Revival in Los Angeles California." *Glad Tidings* 1, no. 5: 1-2.
"Sheep Should Be Dipped." *The Witness of God* 10, no. 92 (March 1928): 7.
"The Supreme Test." *The Witness of God* (March 1963): 123, 128-129.
"Third Annual Southern Bible Conference." *The Witness of God* 7, no. 61 (January and February 1925): 13.
"The Trinity." *Eusebius* 5, no. 6 (December 1892): 139.
"True and False Christianity." *Eusebius* 5, no. 1 (July 1892): 35, 42, 47-48.
"A Two State Camp Meeting for Arkansas and Oklahoma, North 4th and 'O' Streets, Fort Smith, Arkansas. July 20-29, 1923." *The Blessed Truth* 8, no. 7 (July 1, 1923): 2.
"The Unsectarian Old-Time Gospel World Wide Camp-Meeting at Los Angeles, Cal. Beginning June 1, 1918, and Lasting Two Months Or Longer." *Glad Tidings* 1, no. 5: 1-2.
"What the Commentators Say about Water and the Spirit in Regards of the New Birth." *The Witness of God* (January-February 1976): 4.
"Wherein Was Jesus God's Only Begotten Son?" *Upper Room Bulletin* 7 (1921): 194.
The Witness of God (October-November 1967): 1.
A. S. "The Trinity – Three in One and One in Three." *The Witness of God* (May 1935): 6-8.
Adams, John. "The Representative and Ideal Church with an Urge for Living in the Spirit." *The Witness of God* 10, no. 10 (November-December 1930): 20.
Anderson, Margaret Lavinia. "Nation-Making Amnesia." *Commonweal* 134, no. 4 (February 23, 2007): 22-25.
Argue, A. H. "Water Baptism and its Formula." *Christian Evangel* (November 30, 1918): 8.
Bartleman, Frank. "What about the Modern Flapper Evangelism?" *The Witness of God* 10, no. 101 (January 1929): 13.
Beggiani, Seely Joseph. "The Typological Approach of Syriac Sacramental Theology." *Theological Studies* 64, no. 3 (2003): 547.
Bell, E. N. "The 'Acts' on Baptism in Christ's Name Only." *Weekly Evangel* no. 94 (June 12, 1915): 1-3.
———. "Andrew Urshan's New Stand." *Christian Evangel* no. 284 and 285 (April 19, 1919): 9.
———. "Baptized Once for all." *Weekly Evangel* (March 27, 1915): 1.
———. "Bro. Bell on the Trinity." *Weekly Evangel* no. 114 (November 6, 1915): 1.
———. "David Campmeeting Report." *Weekly Evangel* (August 28, 1915): 1.
———. "Editorial." *Weekly Evangel* (April 17, 1915): 1.
———. "Explanation of the Preliminary Statement." *Word and Witness* (June 1915): 1.
———. "The Great Battle for the Truth." *Christian Evangel* no. 300 and 301 (August 9, 1919): 1-2.

———. "The Great Controversy and Confusion." *Christian Evangel* (September 6, 1919): 6-7.

———. "The Great Outlook." *Weekly Evangel* (May 29, 1915): 1.

———. "Meat in due [sic] Season Corrected." *Word and Witness* (October 1915): 4.

———. "The New Testament and Water Baptism." *Weekly Evangel* (March 9, 1918): 2-3.

———. "Personal Statement." *Weekly Evangel* (September 18, 1915): 2.

———. "Questions and Answers." *The Weekly Evangel* (August 4, 1917).

———. "Questions and Answers: Did the 'New Issue' Become an Issue Or [sic] Cause Trouble in the General Council Meeting just Past?" *Weekly Evangel* (September 29, 1917): 7.

———. "Questions and Answers: Does the Teaching that there are Three Persons in the Godhead Mean that there are Three Separate, Corporeal Or Material Bodies within the Godhead?" *Weekly Evangel* (February 17, 1917): 9.

———. "Questions and Answers: Explain John 14:9." *Christian Evangel* (February 22, 1919): 5.

———. "Questions and Answers: If Jesus is Not the Mighty God, Why does Isa. 9:6 Say so?" *Christian Evangel* (February 22, 1919): 5.

———. "Questions and Answers: In what Sense is Jesus the Mighty God as in Isa. 9:6 and what did Jesus Mean by Saying that He had Come in His Father's Name?" *Weekly Evangel* (March 24, 1917): 9.

———. "Questions and Answers: Is Jesus the Father in the Sense that Jesus Called God His Father?" *Weekly Evangel* (March 3, 1917): 9.

———. "Questions and Answers: Is there a Difference between the Spirit of Christ in Rom. 8:9 and the Holy Spirit?" *Weekly Evangel* (September 23, 1916): 8.

———. "Questions and Answers: The Eternity of the Son of God?" *Weekly Evangel* (January 6, 1917): 9.

———. "Questions and Answers: What are the Main Errors Taught by the New Issue People?" *Weekly Evangel* (March 9, 1918): 9.

———. "Questions and Answers: What do New Issue Folk Believe?" *Weekly Evangel* (July 28, 1917): 9.

———. "Questions and Answers: What does Jesus Mean in John 3:5 by 'Born of the Water and of the Spirit'?" *Weekly Evangel* (February 2, 1918): 8.

———. "Questions and Answers: What does it Mean that God Sends the Holy Ghost in the Name of Jesus?" *Weekly Evangel* (April 21, 1917): 9.

———. "Questions and Answers: What is the Correct Baptismal Formula?" *Weekly Evangel* (December 23, 1916): 9.

———. "Questions and Answers: What is Your Present Conviction as to the New Issue Doctrines?" *Weekly Evangel* (October 13, 1917): 7.

———. "The Sad New Issue." *Word and Witness* no. 12 (June 1915): 2-3.

———. "Scriptural Varieties on Baptismal Formula." *Weekly Evangel* no. 97 (July 3, 1915): 1, 3.

———. "There is Safety in Counsel." *Weekly Evangel* (September 18, 1915): 1.

———. "To Act in the Name of another." *Word and Witness* no. 11 (May 1915): 2-3.

———. "The Urshan Trouble." *Christian Evangel* no. 288 and 289 (May 17, 1919): 6-7.

———. "Who is Jesus Christ?" *Weekly Evangel* no. 103 (August 14, 1915): 1.

———. "Who is Jesus Christ?" *Word and Witness* no. 12 (September 1915): 5.

Blackstone, W. E. "The Literal Coming of the Lord from Heaven." *The Witness of God* 6, no. 64 (May 1925): 4.

Bosworth, F. F. "Triumphant Faith." *The Witness of God* 7, no. 68 (October 1925): 4-5.

Bresee, P. F. "The Doctrines of the Church." *Nazarene Messenger* 13, no. 21 (November 19, 1908.

Brock, S. P. "The 'Nestorian' Church: A Lamentable Misnomer." *Bulletin of the John Rylands University Library of Manchester* 78, no. 3: 35.

Bundy, David. "Documenting 'Oneness' Pentecostalism: A Case Study in the Ethical Dilemmas Posed by the Creation of Documentation." In *Summary of Proceedings – Fifty-Third Annual Conference of the American Theological Library Association, June 9-12, 1999*. Edited by Margaret Tacke Collins, 155-75. Evanston, IL: American Theological Library Association, 1999.

Chapell, F. L. "Names of the Deity." *The Witness of God* 4, no. 38 (February 1923): 36.

———. "Names of the Deity." *The Witness of God* 4, no. 39 (March 1923): 6-7.

———. "Names of the Deity." *The Witness of God* 4, no. 40 (April 1923): 4-6.

———. "Names of the Deity." *The Witness of God* 4, no. 41 (May 1923): 7-8.

———. "Names of the Deity." *The Witness of God* 4, no. 42 (June 1923): 6-7.

Cohan, Sara. "A Brief History of the Armenian Genocide." *Social Education* 69, no. 6 (2005): 333-337.

Collins, W. M. and A. G. Osterberg. "Committee Report of the Revival in Los Angeles." *Glad Tidings* 1, no. 5: 2-3.

Craft, Thomas L. "First Pentecostal Church." *The Witness of God* (June 1966): 8.

Davis, T. C. "Report of the Oak Hill Tabernacle, Indianapolis, Ind." *The Witness of God* 8, no. 71 (January 1926): 11.

Dayton, Donald W. "Oneness Pentecostals Meet at Harvard." *Christian Century* (October 3, 1984): 892-94.

Del Colle, Ralph. "A Catholic Response." *Pneuma* 30 (2008): 255-262.

———. "Oneness and Trinity: A Preliminary Proposal for Dialogue with Oneness Pentecostalism" *Journal of Pentecostal Theology* no. 10 (April 1997): 85-110.

Dixon, A. C. "Power from on High by Prayer." *The Witness of God* 3, no. 30 (June 1922): 7.

Durham, W. H. "Salvation in Christ for All." *The Witness of God* 8, no. 71 (January 1926): 9-10.

DuVernet, F. H. "Real Religion." *The Witness of God* (May 1928): 13.

Echols, B. E. "Some Overlooked Qualifications for the Ministry." *The Witness of God* (January 1931): 15.

Evans, Gary. "Oneness Pentecostalism." *Affirmation & Critique* 4 (October 1999): 56-61.

Ewart, Frank J. "Cyrus: A Type of the Man-Child." *End Time Witnesses* (n.d.).

———. "Defending Heresies." *The Good Report* 1, no. 3 (1912): 12.

———. "The Last Theophany." *Pentecostal Herald* 21, no. 1 (January 1946): 4.
———. "Least Yet Best Known Man." *Apostolic Herald* 17, no. 6 (June 1942): 12.
———. "Like Precious Faith." *Apostolic Herald* 17, no. 8 (August 1942).
———. "The Mystery of Jesus." *Apostolic Herald* 16, no. 3 (March 1941): 1.
———. "The Oneness of God." *Apostolic Herald* 19, no. 1 (January 1944): 3.
———. "The Significance of Water Baptism." *Apostolic Herald* 16, no. 1 (January 1941): 12.
———. "Statement of My Faith." *Apostolic Herald* 15, no. 2 (February 1940): 5.
———. "Who is the Man Child." *End Time Witnesses* (n.d.).
Farrow, Geo R. "The New Birth, what it is, what it does." *The Witness of God* 10, no. 10 (November-December 1930): 15-17.
French, Talmadge. "Andrew D. Urshan and the Impossibility of Neutrality." *Apostolic Sentinel* (January 2001): 13, 5.
Frothingham, Richard. "Symposium on Oneness Pentecostalism 1986: Sponsored by the United Pentecostal Church International." *Unitarian Universalist Christian* 44, no. 1 (Spring 1989): 74-75.
Fudge, Thomas. "Did E. N. Bell Convert to the New Issue?" *Journal of Pentecostal Theology*, no. 18 (April 2001): 122-40.
Gaebelein, A. C. "The Comfort of Christ's Presence." *The Witness of God* 1, no. 11 (October 1920): 8.
Gibson, John Monro. "The Mystery of the Father, Son, and Holy Spirit." *Pentecostal Herald* no. 28 (December 1953): 5.
———. "The Trinity in Christ." *The Witness of God* 4, no. 44 (August 1923): 6-7.
———. "Trinity in Christ." *The Witness of God* 10, no. 108 (August 1929): 16-17.
Gill, Kenneth D. "Christianity without the Cross: A History of Salvation in Oneness Pentecostalism." *Pneuma* 26, no. 1 (Spring 2004): 149-50.
Goss, Ethel E. "A Personal Viewpoint." *The Pentecostal Herald* no. 25 (March 1950): 5.
Goss, Howard A. "All About the Pentecostal Ministerial Alliance of 'The Church'." *The Witness of God* 7, no. 62 (March 1925): 13.
———. "Godhead." *The Pentecostal Herald* no. 23 (December 1949): 7.
———. "The Great Physician." *The Pentecostal Herald* no. 24 (February 1949): 3, 13.
Hall, William Phillips. "A Remarkable Biblical Discovery on the Apostolic Christian Baptism." *The Witness of God* 10, no. 108 (August 1929): 5-8.
Hammergren, D. I. "To Ministers, Assemblies and Saints of the Northwest" *The Witness of God* 2, no. 23 (November 1921): 8.
Haney, Kenneth F. "A Brief Oneness Pentecostal Response." *Pneuma* 30 (2008): 227.
Hardy, Edwin Noah. "A Remarkable Biblical Discovery." *The Witness of God* 10, no. 105 (May 1929): 6.
Harkins, Angela Kim. "Theological Attitudes toward the Scriptural Text: Lessons from the Qumran and Syriac Exegetical Traditions." *Theological Studies* 67, no. 3 (2006): 511.
Haywood, G. T. "The Mysteries of the Kingdom." *The Witness of God* 10, no. 10 (November-December 1930): 17-19.

———. "The Term 'Born again'." *The Witness of God* 10, no. 10 (November-December 1930): 11.

———. "The Witness of God Question Box." *The Witness of God* 10, no. 93 (April 1928): 11.

Hedding, Elijah. "101 Years Old Discourse on the Supreme Divinity of Christ." *The Witness of God* 5, no. 50 (February 1924): 4-8.

———. "101 Years Old Discourse on the Supreme Divinity of Christ." *The Witness of God* 5, no. 51 (March 1924): 6-7.

Higgins, Edward J. "Jesus!" *The Witness of God* 11, no. 1 (January 1930): 8-10.

Hite, B. H. "Report of a Real Revival in Saint Louis, Mo." *The Witness of God* 8, no. 71 (January 1926): 11.

Houghton, Mary L. "Satan's Strategy." *The Witness of God* 11, no. 1 (January 1930): 6-7.

Johnson, James A. "Response: A Brief Oneness Pentecostal Response." *Pneuma* 30 (2008): 225-226.

Jones, Bob. "The Modern Atheism and Our Schools." *The Witness of God* (November 1931): 3-5.

Klaus, Carl. "Lodi, California, Revival Campaign." *The Witness of God* 1, no. 2 (January 1920): 8.

Littell, Franklin H. "Halting a Succession of Evil." *Journal of Ecumenical Studies* 34, no. 2 (1997): 171.

Macchia, Frank D. "The Oneness-Trinitarian Pentecostal Doctrine: Introductory Musings of an Editor." *Pneuma* 30 (2008): 197-202.

Matthews, Mark A. "Childlessness, the Nation's Curse." *The Witness of God* 11, no. 1 (January 1930): 4-5.

McAllister, Harvey Mrs. "Bro. Urshan Married." *The Weekly Evangel* (August 25, 1917): 13.

McLain, Samuel C. "Remission of Sins in Death of our Lord Jesus Christ." *The Witness of God* 10, no. 10 (November-December 1930): 9-10.

Meehan, Brenda M. "A. C. Dixon: An Early Fundamentalist." *Foundations* 10 (January 1967): 50-63.

Menzies, William W. "A Trinitarian Pentecostal Response." *Pneuma* 30 (2008): 229-232.

Norris, David. "Christianity without the Cross: A History of Salvation in Oneness Pentecostalism." *Pneuma* 26, no. 1 (Spring 2004): 151-52.

Ooton, L. R. "Report of the Work at St. Paul, Minn." *The Witness of God* 8, no. 71 (January 1926): 11.

Opperman, Daniel C. O. "Bro. Bell Vs. Ball." *The Witness of God* (May 1935): 2-6.

———. "Camp Meeting." *The Blessed Truth* 4, no. 11 (June 1, 1919): 7.

———. "Mighty Revival in Eureka Springs, Ark. Campmeeting a Glorious Success. Evangelist Urshan Used of God." *The Blessed Truth* 4, no. 18 (October 1, 1919): 1.

———. "One Month Bible Study at Eureka Springs." *The Witness of God* 1, no. 4 (March 1920): 10.

———. "Special Bible School in Eureka Springs, Ark." *The Blessed Truth* 4, no. 22 (December 1, 1919): 2.

Patterson, John. "For the Remission of Sins." *The Witness of God* (January-February 1976): 4-5.

———. "Newspapers Preaching the Truth." *The Witness of God* 10, no. 10 (November-December 1930): 28.

Porter, Steven L. "Wesleyan Theological Methodology as a Theory of Integration." *Journal of Psychology and Theology* 32, no. 2 (2004): 190-199.

Priest, Gerald L. "A. C. Dixon, Chicago Liberals, and *The Fundamentals."* *Detroit Baptist Theological Seminary Journal* 1 (Spring 1996): 114.

Proctor, Henry. "Baptized into One Body." *The Witness of God* 10, no. 10 (November-December 1930): 30-32.

Reed, David. "An Anglican Response." *Pneuma* 30 (2008): 263-269.

———. "Origins and Development of the Theology of Oneness Pentecostalism in the United States." *Pneuma* 1, no. 1 (Spring 1979): 31-37.

———. "Oneness Pentecostalism: Problems and Possibilities for Pentecostal Theology." *Journal of Pentecostal Theology* 11, (October 1997): 73-93.

———. *The "New Issue" of 1914: New Revelation Or Historical Development?* (Paper presented at the twenty-third annual meeting of the Society for Pentecostal Studies, Wheaton, IL, November 11, 1994.)

Riley, W. B. "The Kingdom of God – it's [*sic*] Second Coming and Citizenship." *The Witness of God* 10, no. 10 (November-December 1930): 29-30.

Ramirez, Daniel. "A Historian's Response." *Pneuma* 30 (2008): 245-254.

Robins, Roger G. "Review: [Untitled]." *The Journal of Religion* 85, no. 4 (Oct., 2005): 682-683.

Rose, J. Hugh. "Farewell, Thou Man of God." *The Witness of God* (December 1967): 4.

Rowe, G. B. "The Spirit Falling at the Midway Gospel Tabernacle, Mishawaka, South Bend, Ind." *The Witness of God* 11, no. 2 (February 1930): 5.

Ryle, J. C. "Is There a Hell?" *The Witness of God* 11, no. 3 (March and April 1930): 6-7.

Saayman, J. H. "Thou Shalt Call His Name Jesus." *The Witness of God* 10, no. 10 (November-December 1930): 10-11.

Schmidt, Faith Edith. "Loving Memorial to Andrew David Urshan." *The Witness of God* (December 1967): 7.

Scism, Harry E. "A Memorial to our Beloved Andrew D. Urshan." *Pentecostal Herald* (June 1989): 5.

Scofield, C. I. "The Loveliness of Christ." *The Witness of God* 10, no. 89 (November 1927): 1, 12.

Segraves, Daniel L. "A Oneness Pentecostal Response." *Pneuma* 30 (2008): 233-239.

———. Review of *"In Jesus' Name:" The History and Beliefs of Oneness Pentecostals* by David A. Reed, *Religious Studies Review* 35, 1 (March 2009): 44.

Shaka, Richard. "A Trinitarian Pentecostal Response." *Pneuma* 30 (2008): 240-244.

Sheppard, Gerald T. "Pentecostals and the Hermeneutics of Dispensationalism: The Anatomy of an Uneasy Relationship." *Pneuma: The Journal of the Society for Pentecostal Studies,* Fall (1984): 5.

Simpson, A. B. "The Power of Stillness." *The Witness of God* 7, no. 65 (June and July 1925): 8.

———. "Thankfulness for Healing." *The Witness of God* 11, no. 8 (September 1930): 11-12.

Simpson, W. W. "The Baptismal Formula." *Latter Rain Evangel* 11, no. 8 (May 1919): 19.

Straton, John Roach. "Some Statements Concerning the Deity." *The Witness of God* 10, no. 96 (August 1928): 13.

Sturdivan, W. W. "Andrew D. Urshan." *Gospel Tidings* (January 1968): 2-3.

Urshan, Nathaniel A. "What My Father Meant to Me." *Historical News* 3, no. 1 (October-November-December 1983): 3-4.

W. B. M. "Apostolic Mode of Baptism." *The Witness of God* 10, no. 10 (November-December 1930): 26-27.

W. H. T. D. "Searching Questions for 'Born again' People." *The Witness of God* 10, no. 10 (November-December 1930): 21.

———. "Sanctification and the New Birth." *The Witness of God* 10, no. 10 (November-December 1930): 21.

———. "What Professors Say about New Birth." *The Witness of God* 10, no. 10 (November-December 1930): 21-22.

Wardin, Albert W. "Pentecostal Beginnings among the Russians in Finland and Northern Russia (1911-1921)." *Fides Et Historia* (1995): 50-61.

Warner, Wayne. "The 1913 Worldwide Camp Meeting." *Assemblies of God Heritage.* 3, no. 1 (Spring 1983): 1, 4-5.

Witherspoon, Arthur. "Andy's Obituary." *The Witness of God* (October 1951): 2.

Witherspoon, W. T. "Marriage and Divorce In and Out of the Church." *The Witness of God* (June 1948): 8.

Wood, George. "A Brief Trinitarian Pentecostal Response." *Pneuma* 30 (2008): 228.

Yong, Amos. "Oneness and Trinity: The Theological and Ecumenical Implications of Creation *Ex Nihilo* for an Intra-Pentecostal Dispute." *Pneuma* 19, no. 1 (1997): 81-107.

Dissertations and Theses

Bernard, David Kane. "Monotheistic Discourse and Deification of Jesus in Early Christianity as Exemplified in 2 Corinthians 3:16-4:6. DTh thesis, University of South Africa, 2014.

French, Talmadge. "Oneness Pentecostalism in Global Perspective: History, Theology, and Expansion of the Oneness Pentecostal Movement." MA thesis, Wheaton College, 1998.

Graham, Stephen Ray. "Conservative American Protestantism and the Origins of Pentecostalism: A Case Study of Andrew D. Urshan." MA thesis, Wheaton College, 1982.

Howell, Joseph. "The People of the Name: Oneness Pentecostalism in the United States." PhD diss., University of Florida, 1985.
Johnston, Robin M. "Howard A. Goss: A Pentecostal Life." PhD diss., Regent University, 2010.
King, Gerald Wayne. "Disfellowshiped: Pentecostal Responses to Fundamentalism in the United States, 1906-1953." PhD diss., University of Birmingham, 2009.
Reed, David A. "Origins and Development of the Theology of Oneness Pentecostalism in the United States." PhD diss., Boston University, 1978.
Rider, James Donald. "The Theology of the 'Jesus Only' Movement." ThD diss., Dallas Theological Seminary, 1956.
Segraves, Daniel Lee. "Andrew D. Urshan: A Theological Biography." PhD diss. Regent University, 2011.

Dictionary and Encyclopedia Articles

The Columbia Encyclopedia. 6th ed. New York: Columbia University Press, 2009.
Alexander, P. H., "Finis Jennings Dake." In *The New International Dictionary of Pentecostal and Charismatic Movements.* Edited by Stanley M. Burgess and Eduard M. van der Maas. Rev. and exp. ed. Grand Rapids, MI: Zondervan, 2002.
Arrington, F. L. "Dispensationalism." In *The New International Dictionary of Pentecostal and Charismatic Movements.* Edited by Stanley M. Burgess and Eduard M. van der Maas. Rev. and exp. ed. Grand Rapids, MI: Zondervan, 2002.
Balmer, Randall. *The Encyclopedia of Evangelicalism.* Waco, TX: Baylor University Press, 2004.
Blaising, C. A. "Monarchianism." *Evangelical Dictionary of Theology.* Edited by Walter A. Elwell. Grand Rapids: Baker Book House, 1984.
Blumhofer, E. L. "Daniel Charles Owen Opperman." In *The New International Dictionary of Pentecostal and Charismatic Movements.* Edited by Stanley M. Burgess and Eduard M. van der Maas. Rev. and exp. ed. Grand Rapids, MI: Zondervan, 2002.
———. "Glad Tidings Tabernacle." In *The New International Dictionary of Pentecostal and Charismatic Movements.* Edited by Stanley M. Burgess and Eduard M. van der Maas. Rev. and exp. ed. Grand Rapids, MI: Zondervan, 2002.
Blumhofer, E. L. and C. R. Armstrong. "Assemblies of God." In *The New International Dictionary of Pentecostal and Charismatic Movements.* Edited by Stanley M. Burgess and Eduard M. van der Maas. Rev. and exp. ed. Grand Rapids, MI: Zondervan, 2002.
Dieter, M. E. "Methodist Churches." In *Dictionary of Christianity in America.* Edited by Daniel G. Reid et al. Downers Grove, IL: InterVarsity Press, 1990.
Gohr, G. W. "Franklin Small." In *The New International Dictionary of Pentecostal and Charismatic Movements.* Edited by Stanley M. Burgess and Eduard M. van der Maas. Rev. and exp. ed. Grand Rapids, MI: Zondervan, 2002.
Hall, J. L. "Andrew David Urshan." In *The New International Dictionary of Pentecostal and Charismatic Movements.* Edited by Stanley M. Burgess and Eduard M. van der Maas. Rev. and exp. ed. Grand Rapids, MI: Zondervan, 2002.

———. "Frank J. Ewart." In *The New International Dictionary of Pentecostal and Charismatic Movements*. Edited by Stanley M. Burgess and Eduard M. van der Maas. Rev. and exp. ed. Grand Rapids, MI: Zondervan, 2002.

———. "United Pentecostal Church, International." In *The New International Dictionary of Pentecostal and Charismatic Movements*. Edited by Stanley M. Burgess and Eduard M. van der Maas. Rev. and exp. ed. Grand Rapids, MI: Zondervan, 2002.

Jackson, Samuel Macauley, ed. *The New Schaff-Herzog Encyclopedia of Religious Knowledge*. Vol. 4. New York: Funk and Wagnalls Company, 1909.

Lacoste, Jean-Yves, ed. *Encyclopedia of Christian Theology*. New York: Routledge, 2005.

McIntire, C. T. "Fundamentalism." In *Evangelical Dictionary of Theology*. Edited by Walter A. Elwell. Grand Rapids: Baker Book House, 1984.

Reed, David A. "Oneness Pentecostalism." In *The New International Dictionary of Pentecostal and Charismatic Movements*. Edited by Stanley M. Burgess and Eduard M. van der Maas. Rev. and exp. ed. Grand Rapids, MI: Zondervan, 2002.

———. "Pentecostal Assembles of the World." In *The New International Dictionary of Pentecostal and Charismatic Movements*. Edited by Stanley M. Burgess and Eduard M. van der Maas. Rev. and exp. ed. Grand Rapids, MI: Zondervan, 2002.

Riss, R. M. "Fred Francis Bosworth." In *The New International Dictionary of Pentecostal and Charismatic Movements*. Edited by Stanley M. Burgess and Eduard M. van der Maas. Rev. and exp. ed. Grand Rapids, MI: Zondervan, 2002.

Robeck, C. M., Jr. "Aimee Semple McPherson." In *The New International Dictionary of Pentecostal and Charismatic Movements*. Edited by Stanley M. Burgess and Eduard M. van der Maas. Rev. and exp. ed. Grand Rapids, MI: Zondervan, 2002.

———. "Garfield Thomas Haywood." In *The New International Dictionary of Pentecostal and Charismatic Movements*. Edited by Stanley M. Burgess and Eduard M. van der Maas. Rev. and exp. ed. Grand Rapids, MI: Zondervan, 2002.

Segraves, Daniel L. "Oneness Theology." In *Encyclopedia of Pentecostal and Charismatic Christianity*. Edited by Stanley M. Burgess. New York: Routledge, 2006.

Tittle, R. G., Jr. "The Wesleyan Tradition." In *Evangelical Dictionary of Theology*, edited by Walter A. Elwell. Grand Rapids: Baker Book House, 1984.

Wilson, E. A. Hall, "Andrew Harvey Argue" In *The New International Dictionary of Pentecostal and Charismatic Movements*. Edited by Stanley M. Burgess and Eduard M. van der Maas. Rev. and exp. ed. Grand Rapids, MI: Zondervan, 2002.

Magazine and Newspaper Articles

"Andrew D. Urshan Died on July 28, 1951 (b. April 26, 1929)." *Long Beach (CA) Press Telegram,* July 30, 1951.

"Assyrian Pastor Goes 'Home'." *Assyrian Star,* May-June 1961.

"'Sin of Pride' Hit by Urshan." *The Shreveport Journal,* January 24, 1925.

Lang, J. Stephen. "'Jesus Only' Isn't enough." *Christianity Today* (April 1, 2002): 60.

Pryce-Jones, David. "Remembering Genocide." *National Review,* December 8, 2003.

Web Sites

"1915: Urmia: Statement by the Rev. William A. Shedd, D.D., of The American (Presbyterian) Mission Station at Urmia; Communicated by The Board of Foreign Missions of The Presbyterian Church in The U.S.A." http://www.atour.com/~history/1900/20000718a.html (accessed March 8, 2010).

ANI. "Frequently Asked Questions about the Armenian Genocide." http://www.armenian-genocide.org/genocidefaq.html (accessed March 3, 2010).

The Armenian Genocide. History does not fade away. http://www.theforgotten.org (accessed November 23, 2010).

Armenian Genocide. Resource Library for Teachers. http://www.teachgenocide.org (accessed November 23, 2010).

Armenian National Institute. http://www.armenian-genocide.org/1915-1.html (accessed March 1, 2010).

Assyrian International News Agency. Assyrian Maps. "115 Assyrian Villages in Urmia, Iran." http://www.aina.org/maps/urmiamap50p.htm (accessed March 2, 2010).

Bloxham, Donald, "Rethinking the Armenian Genocide: Ninety Years Ago This Summer Saw the Start of the Armenian Genocide in Turkey. In His Account of the Complex Historical Background to These Events Donald Bloxham Focuses on the Issue of Great Power Involvement," *History Today,* June 2005. http://www.questia.com/PM.qst?a=o&d=5009587189; Internet; accessed 30 November 2010.

Christian Resources & Links. Doctrinal & Practical Writings. *Supreme Divinity of Our Lord and Saviour Jesus Christ.* http://www.wholesomewords.org/resources/deityofchrist.html (accessed April 16, 2010).

The Choices Program. History and Current Issues for the Classroom. http://www.choices.edu (accessed November 23, 2010).

Chronology of the Armenian Genocide—1915 (January-March). http://www.armenian-genocide.org/1915-1.html (accessed November 22, 2010).

Chronology of the Armenian Genocide—1915 (April-June). http://www.armenian-genocide.org/1915-2.html (accessed November 22, 2010).

Chronology of the Armenian Genocide—1915 (July-September). http://www.armenian-genocide.org/1915-3.html (accessed November 22, 2010).

Chronology of the Armenian Genocide—1915 (October-December). http://www.armenian-genocide.org/1915-4.html (accessed November 22, 2010).

"Church History, Christ Temple Apostolic Faith Assembly." http://www.christtempleac.org/history.php (accessed February 11, 2009).

Cinema Treasures. "Clunes Auditorium." http://cinematreasures.org/theater/13960/ (accessed March 15, 2010).

The Concert Hall at Victoria Hall. http://www.concerthallatvictoriahall.com/index_1.htm (accessed April 5, 2010).

De Imperatoribus Romanis. *An Online Encyclopedia of Roman Emperors.* "Eusebia Augusta (353-360 A.D.) and Faustina (360-361 A.D.). Michael DiMaio, Jr. http://www.roman-emperors.org/eusebia.htm (accessed April 19, 2010).

Facing History and Ourselves. Helping classrooms and communities worldwide link the past to moral choices today. http://www.facinghistory.org (accessed November 23, 2010).

The First Baptist Church in the City of New York. "Haldeman." http://firstbaptist-nyc.org/litesite.cfm?id=316 (accessed April 26, 2010).

Flower Pentecostal Heritage Center. http://ifphc.org/index.cfm?fuseaction=products.agpublications (accessed April 21, 2010).

Fr. Andrew Younan, lecture: "Christology in the Patristic Period," Part III—Christ in the East. http://www.kaldu.org/ Theology_Course_2007/ 06_B_ PChristology_03_Video.html (accessed May 10, 2010).

Frank Bartleman, "The Deity of Christ." http://frankbartleman-deity. blogspot.com/2010/01/chapter-vi.html (accessed April 21, 2010).

Frank Bartleman, "The Deity of Christ – Chapter II." http://frankbartleman-deity.blogspot.com/2010/01/chapter-ii_01.html (accessed May 2, 2010).

"From Adams Street, Looking South." http://tigger.uic.edu/depts/ahaa/ imagebase/intranet/chiviews/page157.html (accessed, April 13, 2009).

The Genocide Education Project. http://genocideeducation.org (accessed November 23, 2010).

Glad Tidings Tabernacle. http://gladtidingsnyc.com/ (accessed March 12, 2010).

"Great Northern Hotel." http://www.patsabin.com/illinois/GreeatNorthern.htm (accessed April 13, 2009).

GTSF History. http://gtsf.org/history-of-glad-tidings-church-san-francisco/ (accessed March 13, 2010).

Hpathy, Homeopathic Treatment, Cure, & Medicines. "Locomoter Ataxia." http://health.hpathy.com/locomotor-ataxia-symptoms-treatment-cure.asp (accessed April 5, 2010).

I. N. H. Beahm and S. N. McCann, *Two Centuries of the Church of the Brethren* (Elgin, IL: Brethren Publishing House, 1908). http://www.archive.org/ stream/cu31924006259257/cu31924--6259257_djvu.txt (accessed March 27, 2010).

Iran Chamber Society, History of Iran, "Qajar Dynasty." http://www.irancham ber.com/history/qajar/qajar.php (accessed June 12, 2009).

Ishaya, Arianne, "From Contributions to Diaspora: Assyrians in the History of Urmia, Iran." *Journal of Assyrian Academic Studies* 16, no. 1 (2002). http://www.jaas.org/toc/v16012002toc.htm (accessed December 1, 2010).

———. "A Commentary on Professor Zirinsky's Article." *Journal of Assyrian Academic Studies* 12, no. 1 (1998): 30-31. http://www.jaas.org/toc/v12011 998toc.htm (accessed December 1, 2010).

"Joint Communiqué of the Second Non-Official Consultation on Dialogue within the Syriac Tradition, Vienna February 1996." http://www.pro-oriente.at/dokumente/2SyrCons1996.doc (accessed June 27, 2009).

The Legacy Project. http://www.legacy-project.org (accessed November 23, 2010).

Leon Bible, "Theological Summary of the Writings of 'Finis Jennings Dake,'" 1998. http://www.dakebible.com/WebPages/dake-theology.htm(accessed November 20, 2010).

Letter from W. A. Shedd to The Honorable J. L. Caldwell, American Minister, Teheran. June 23, 1915. Gomidas Institute Armenian Genocide Documentation Project. http://www.gomidas.org/gida/index_and_%20documents/ 867.4016_indexand_documents/docs/4016.270.pdf (accessed March 6, 2010).

Majidi Ann Warda, TAAS—Chairperson of the Publication Committee. Symposium Syriacum VIII & The Assyrian Genocide Seminar, Posted: Wednesday, July 19, 2000 10:07 am CST. http://www.atour.com/education/ 20000719a.html (accessed March 6, 2010).

Manchester College. Archives and Brethren Historical Collection. "Mount Morris College." http://www.manchester.edu/OAA/library/archives/ mountmorris.htm (accessed March 27, 2010).

Manchester College. "Manchester College History." http://www.manchester.edu/Common/AboutManchester/History.htm (accessed March 27, 2010).

Mar Babai the Great, *Libere de Unione,* I.17, quoted by Fr. Andrew Younan. http://www.kaldu.org/Theology_Course_2007/06_B_PChristology_03_Video.html (accessed May 10, 2010).

"The Moody Church, Information. The History of the Moody Church." http://www.moodychurch.org/information/history.html (accessed January 23, 2010).

The New York Times Sunday Book Review. "The Heretic Jew," by Harold Bloom. June 18, 2006. http://www.nytimes.com/2006/06/18/books/review/ 18 bloom.html (accessed May 22, 2010).

Official site of the international Church of the Nazarene. "Preserving a legacy. Historical Statement. From the 2001 Manual of the Church of the Nazarene." http://www.nazarene.org/ministries/administration/archives/history/statement/display.aspx (accessed February 10, 2010).

"Our History." http://www.apostolicfaith-gr.org/History.htm (accessed September 15, 2008).

Paul Halsall Mar, *Medieval Sourcebook: Pliny on the Christians* (1996). http://fordham.edu/halsall/source/pliny1.html (accessed April 19, 2010).

Paul Shimmon, "The Plight of Assyria," a letter to the editor of *The New York Times* (September 18, 1916). http://www.atour.com/~history/ny-times/ 20001-126g.html (accessed March 2, 2010).

Pentecostal Pioneers. Heaven Sent Revival. "Robert A. Brown." http://www.pentecostalpioneers.org/RobertABrown.html (accessed March 12, 2010).

Pleasant Places Press. "A. T. Pierson.http://pleasantplaces.biz/authors/ pierson_a.php (accessed November 22, 2010).

Redford, M. E. *The Rise of the Church of the Nazarene* (Digital edition 04/12/95, Holiness Data Ministry; Kansas City, MO: Beacon Hill Press of Kansas City, 1948). http://wesley.nnu.edu/wesleyctr/books/0101-0299/HDM0145.PDF(accessed February 10, 2010.

Roman Lunkin, "Traditional Pentecostals in Russia," *East-West Church and Ministry Report* 12, no. 3 (Summer 2004). http://www.eastwestreport.org/ articles/ew12302.html (accessed March 10, 2010).

Sidney Griffith, "A Spiritual Father for the Whole Church: the Universal Appeal of Saint Ephraem the Syrian." *Hugoye: Journal of Syriac Studies* 1, no. 2 (July

1998). http://syrcom.cua.edu/Hugoye/vol1No2/ HV1N2Griffith.html #FN46 (accessed May 23, 2010).

Smith, Timothy L. *Called Unto Holiness: The Story of the Nazarenes: The Formative Years* (Digital edition 08/14/06, Holiness Data Ministry; Kansas City, MO: Nazarene Publishing House, 1962). http://wesley.nnu.edu/wesleyctr/books/2501-2600/ HDM2593.PDF (accessed February 10, 2010).

The Spurgeon Archive. *The New Park Street Pulpit.* "The Eternal Name." http://www.spurgeon.org/sermons/0027.htm (accessed April 20, 2010).

Stanford Encyclopedia of Philosophy. "Baruch Spinoza." http://plato.stanford.edu/entries/spinoza/#Oth (accessed May 22, 2010).

University of Toronto Monthly. http://www.archive.org/stream/ universityoftoro22univuoft/_universityoftoro22univoft_djvu.txt (accessed April 21, 2010).

Zion Apostolic Church. Who We Are. http://www.shadesofgraydesign.net/zion-apostolic/about/ (accessed November 22, 2010).

Letters

Bell, E. N. Letter to J. C. Brickey. Springfield, MO: August 20, 1920.

Urshan, Andrew D. Letter to Nathaniel A. Urshan. November 9, 1964.

General Index

Abajalu, 11, 14, 16, 54–55, 57–61, 63–64, 73, 83, 131, 150, 229, 239
Aberdeen, Washington, 119
Abrahamic Covenant, 226
Absolute deity, 9, 49, 109, 140, 142, 161, 164, 168, 173, 189–192, 199, 206, 239–240,
   See Pentecostalism: Oneness
Ada, 57–61, 63, 73, 74
Adonai, 199
Afghanistan, 68
Akron, Ohio, 118
Albany, Oregon, 131
Alexandria, Louisiana, 132
Allah, 68, 75, 76
America, 7, 14, 16–17, 19, 21–22, 25, 26–27, 34, 35, 43, 52, 55, 58, 63, 64, 68, 77–82, 85, 91, 123, 125, 139, 150, 154, 171, 203, 229, 238–39, 242–43, 259, 269, 272, 275, 295
American Board of Commissioners for Foreign Missions, 8, 10
American Board of Foreign Missions, 7, 11–12
American Presbyterian College, 139, 149
American Presbyterian Mission Compound, 71–72
American Presbyterian Training College, 13, 16–17, 35, 55
Amsterdam, Holland, 55
Andrew D. Urshan, vi
Andrew David Urshan
   Urshan, Andrew, vi
Ante-Nicene Fathers, 170
Antichrist, 181
Antiochene theology, 144
Apostolic, 142
Apostolic Church of Jesus Christ, 121, 135

Apostolic Church of Pentecost of Canada, 2
Apostolic Church of the East, 141
Apostolic Churches of Jesus Christ, 116
Apostolic Faith Christians, 140, 141
Arabia, 68
Arianism, 167–68, 174, 178, 212
Aristotelian, 144, 206
Ark of the Covenant, 192
Armavir, 57, 78
Armenian Genocide, 57, 65–68, 70, 77–78, 238, 240, 280, 282, 285, 290, 297, 299
Armenians, 13–14, 57, 61, 64–67, 69, 77–78, 281, 287
Arrested, 44
Arroyo Seco, 52, 56, 246–47
   Apostolic Faith World-Wide Camp Meeting, 51
Asia, 9–10, 181, 285
Assemblies of God, xii, 2, 50, 52, 85, 88–90, 93–94, 97, 100–103, 106–107, 109, 112, 116, 121, 130, 134, 154, 158–59, 162, 176, 180, 182, 185, 189, 204, 225, 229–32, 234, 237, 240, 246, 250, 254, 261, 268, 281, 294, 295
   General Council 2016, 100
Assyria, 140–41
Assyrian, 2, 7, 9, 11, 12–14, 21, 59, 61, 63, 67–68, 130, 132, 140–42, 146, 148, –50, 154–155, 205, 246, 251, 269, 281, 287, 296–99
Assyrian Presbyterian Church, 132
Assyrian Protestant Church, 12–13
Assyrian-Chaldean, 2, 14, 67, 140, 246, 269
Assyrians, 11, 14, 22, 61, 67, 70, 78, 246, 298

Astrology, 245, 255
Atheism, 152
Augustine, 194, 209
Auroraville, Wisconsin, 121
Azerbaijan, 8–10, 14
Azusa, 257

Babai, 145, 148
Balkan states, 67
Baltimore, Maryland, 122
Baptism in Jesus' name, 1
Baptism, Holy Spirit, 2–3, 37, 40, 41, 44–45, 48, 50, 53, 55, 59, 61–65, 76, 78, 82, 91, 94–95, 99–100, 108–110, 116, 139, 151, 153–154, 156, 158, 180, 220–23, 226–29, 235, 239, 251–52, 254, 256
  tongues, 35–36, 38–40
  Tongues, 3
Baptism, of fire, 250
Baptism, water, 218, 220–21, 226, 242
  believers, 27, 150
  birth of water, 121
  formula, 79, 83, 85, 92, 100, 182
    in the name of the Lord Jesus, 79, 80, 159, 225
  in Jesus' name, 108, 110, 120, 227, 235
  in the name of Jesus, 162, 229
  in the name of Jesus Christ, 2, 107, 158, 197
    in the name of the Father, Son, and Holy Ghost
    in the name of the Lord Jesus Christ, 1
  in the name of Jesus Christ, the Lord, 180
  in the name of Jesus, our Lord, 225
  in the name of the Lord Jesus Christ, 3, 127, 139, 159, 227, 234, 240, 248

  mode, 16, 19, 26–27, 33, 55, 150–51, 157, 159, 176–77, 181, 238–39, 242
  neutrality, 82, 87
  rebaptism, 57, 79–81
Baptist, 53–54, 78
Baton Rouge, Louisiana, 133
Bay City, Texas, 124, 133
Beaumont, Texas, 118, 133
Being, 204, 232
Bell, Louisiana, 117
Bend, Oregon, 118
Berlin, Germany, 20
Birmingham, Alabama, 132
Birth, Spirit, 49
Boise, Idaho, 127
Bossier City, Louisiana, 133
Brethren, American, 19, 25–27, 55, 81, 109, 140, 150–51, 158, 238–239, 269, 284–85, 298–99
Brethren, Plymouth, 58
Buchara, 68

Canada, 51, 53, 123, 156
Caucasia, 55
Center for the Study of Oneness Pentecostalism, xii
Central Bible Institute, 204
Chalcedon, 143, 145, 148, 202
Chaldeans, 14, 66, 255
Chicago, Illinois, xi, 23, 26–28, 33, 39, 42, 48, 54, 56, 87, 90, 113–125, 130, 153, 238
Christ
  deity, 49
Christ Temple Apostolic Faith Assembly, 2, 297
Christian Science, 28, 30, 56, 152, 173–74, 181
Christology, 3, 137, 143, 144–48, 168, 202–210, 216, 218, 241, 260, 265, 269, 281, 285, 298
  Alexandrine, 144, 146
  charts, 144
  Antiochene, 144, *See*

Antiochene theology charts, 144
Church of the East, 7, 9–10, 12, 17, 19, 140–49, 158–59, 193, 202–210, 216, 226, 241, 245, 247, 250, 261, 280–81, 285
Cincinnati, Ohio, 120
Circumincession, 164, 172, 186, 232
Clement of Alexandria, 170
Cleveland, Ohio, 54
Cochrane, Wisconsin, 87, 114–15, 126
Columbus, Ohio, 118, 122, 129
Confession of Faith, 97, 134, 230, 233
Conversion, 3, 12, 15, 17, 33, 35, 55, 139, 149–50, 154, 156–57, 214, 219, 223, 225, 238–39, 245–47, 251, 254, 257, 259, 260, 266, 269
Council of Chalcedon, 143, 148, 204
Cyril, 144, 206

Dallas, Texas, 133
Darwinism, 152
Dayton, Ohio, 113
Deification
  theosis, 226
DeQuincy, Louisiana, 118, 133
Deridder, Louisiana, 133
Detroit, Michigan, 54
Dispensation of Grace, 98
Dispensationalism, 181, 217
Divine healing, 45, 48, 82, 107, 116, 134, 257
Divorce, 85, 90, 124, 126–127, 240, 249
Dreams, 52, 74, 124, 180
Dresden, Ontario, Canada, 113
Duluth, Minnesota, 122, 130

Ebionites, 170
El Elyon, 199
El Olam, 199

El Shaddai, 199
Ellis Island, 21, 54–55, 57
Elohim, 197, 199, 201, 241
Embodiment, 188, 193–94, 199
England, 28, 40, 50–52, 55, 57, 68, 77–78, 82, 153, 176, 283
Enlightenment, 157, 211, 215
Ephrem, 140, 210, 212–14, 216, 239, 286
Epiphanius, 170
Episcopal, 19, 22, 26–27, 50, 122
Epworth League, 27, 30
Eschatology, 49, 56, 113, 180–81, 262
Eternal Son, 190, 192, 194
Eunice, Louisiana, 118
Eureka Springs, Arkansas, 109, 111
Europe, 8, 10, 68, 85, 90
Evagrius, 245, 252
Evangelical, 9, 19, 25–26, 83, 152, 159, 196, 284–285, 295–296
Evidence, 257
Experience, 159

False reports, 57, 65, 78, 182
Farrow, George R., 221
Father, 165
Filioque, 147
Finished Work, 1, 3, 50, 157, 235, 274
Fleece, 89, 159
Flint, Michigan, 120
Flower Pentecostal Heritage Center, xii, 176, 298
Fort Smith, Arkansas, 115
France, 68
Frazier Park, California, 130
Free Protestant Mission, 78
Fundamentalism, 19, 28, 49–50, 80, 152, 162, 169, 181, 262, 269
  five essential doctrines, 152
Fundamentals, The, 152

Genocide, 82
Geogtapa, 57, 64–65, 69–72, 75
Germany, 20, 55, 68

Glad Tidings Mission, 86, 106–107
God the Father, 200
God the Son, 169, 193
Godhead, 49, 85, 92, 142–43, 147–48, 159, 161, 171, 182, 189–190, 193, 197, 206, 211, 215, 218–19, 241, 249, 257
God-man, 168, 173
Grand Cane, Louisiana, 117
Grand Rapids, Michigan, 133
Great Britain, 8, 82, 243
Great Tribulation, 181
Great Tribulation, The, 225
Greek, 142–43, 148
Greek Catholic Church, 63, 73
Greencastle, Indiana, 2

Hamburg, Germany, 20
Hamilton, Ontario, Canada, 113
Hammond, Indiana, 133
Haynesville, Louisiana, 120
Haywood, G. T., 221
Healing, divine, 20, 49
Hebrews, book of, 168
Heresy, 148, 263
Heterodoxy, 263–64
Higher Criticism, 28, 30, 56, 102, 152–53, 174, 181–82, 189, 257
Hodge, Louisiana, 122
Holiness, 2, 27, 32–36, 48–49, 142, 153–54, 251–52, 260–61, 269
Holy Spirit baptism, 3
Holy Spirit Research Center, xii
Homoousios, 143
House of Light, 108, 111, 232, 274
Houston, Texas, 115, 117, 133
Hypostasis, 142–46, 148, 202–203, 205–206, 208–10

Incarnate, 164, 171, 199–200
Incarnation, 96, 161, 184, 188, 194, 197, 199–200, 206, 211, 215, 241, 250
India, 8, 146
Indianapolis, Indiana, 2, 112, 116, 117–22, 127–30
Indonesia, 9
Interpenetration, 232
Iran, 132
Iraq, 9, 209, 259, 283
Irenaeus, 170
Israel, 132

Jackson, Mississippi, 133
Jackson, Tennessee, 117
Jacobite Christianity, 9
Jacobites, 66
Japan, 9, 96
Jehovah, 171–75, 179, 197, 199
Jesus Christ, 142
Jesus Only, 101, 118, 121, 140, 191–92, 240, 258, 263
Jews, 67, 98, 119, 158, 218, 231, 255, 258
Jihad, 68–69, 70, 74
Jim Crow, 122
John Wesley, 142
Justification, 254
Justification by faith, 142
Justin Martyr, 170

Karajalu, 57, 62–63
Kenooma, 141
Kiev, 20
kingdom of God, 219
Kingdom of God. *See* Soteriological language
Kingdom of heaven, 259
Kirbyville, Texas, 120
Kurdistan, 9, 13, 17, 282
Kurds, 12
Kurds, 10–11, 20, 61, 64, 67–69, 70–77
Kyana, 142–43, 144, 148

Kyane, 146, 148

Lake Michigan, 39–40, 42, 57
Lake Urmia, 10
Lansdowne, Ontario, Canada, 112
Latin, 142–43
Laurel, Mississippi, 120
League of Nations, 181
Legalism, 101, 182, 234
Leningrad, 57, 78–79, 82
Little Rock, Arkansas, 112, 114
Liverpool, 57
Liverpool, England, 54, 82
Lodi, California, 111
Logos, 96, 146, 148, 201, 241
London, England, 55, 82
Long Beach, California, 53, 127–29
Los Angeles, 33, 36, 45, 51–52, 85, 89, 91–97, 100–101, 108–110, 123, 130, 155, 157, 162, 230–31, 233, 239–40, 253
Los Angeles meeting, 91, 107
  World-Wide Camp Meeting, 93
Los Angeles, California, 1, 51–54, 56, 85, 91–95, 97–100, 102, 107–108, 110, 122, 129, 154, 157, 162, 230–31, 233, 239–240, 253
Los Angeles, California, 251
Louann, Arkansas, 120
Louisiana, 111, 116–22

Madison, Wisconsin, 133
Manifest, 164, 168, 173, 199
Manifestation, 164, 169, 188, 196
Manifestations, 201
Mansfield, Louisiana, 117
Mar Akakios, Synod of, 145
Mar Odisho, 147, 204
Markham, Ontario, Canada, 113
Marriage, 85–88, 134, 240, 245, 246, 248
Martin Luther, 142
Martyrs, 57, 61, 64, 69, 71, 73–74, 76, 82, 141, 252

Massacres, 61, 64–65, 72, 74–76
McCleary, Washington, 119
Meat in Due Season, 1, 109
Melbourne, Florida, 122
Merryville, Louisiana, 118
Mesopotamia, 9, 68, 141, 250
Methodist, 48
Methodist Episcopal, 19, 26–27
Miami, Florida, 122
Middle East, 9, 85, 132, 285
Milwaukee, Wisconsin, 130
Minaki, Ontario, Canada, 90
Minden, Louisiana, 120, 133
Minneapolis, Minnesota, 129
Mississippi, 133
Modalism, 196
Mohammedanism, 142
Mohammedism, 9, 11, 13, 63, 67–72, 74–75, 288
Mohmmedism, 8, 30, 74, 209, 250, 283
Montesano, Washington, 119
Montreal, Quebec, Canada, 90, 112, 115
Moody Bible Church, 140, 152, 158
Moody Bible Institute, 153, 159
Moody Church, 19, 28, 38, 40–41, 44–45, 49, 55, 152–53, 162, 169, 238–39, 299
Moody Rescue Mission, 40
Morgantown, West Virginia, 120
Mormonism, 152
Mount Ararat, 20
Mount Seir, 10
Murphysboro, Illlinois, 131
Muslims, 9, 61, 63, 68, 71–72, 74, 77
Mystery, 140, 161–64, 169, 170, 171, 183, 189, 190, 193, 197–198, 200–201, 204, 210–16, 230, 238, 241, 245, 248, 250, 257

Name, 165, 168
  I Am that I Am, 166

306 General Index

Immanuel, 166
Jehovah, 166
Yahweh, 166
Name of God
  dispensational, 197
  personification, 197
Name theology, 239
Names of God, 49, 213, 232, 265
  dispensational, 202
  Divine Name, 51
  I AM, 200
  I AM THAT I AM, 200
  Jesus, 81
  Lord Jesus Christ, 49, 97, 104
Nampa, Idaho, 121
Napa, California, 133
Nature, 34, 85, 139–40, 142–46, 148, 153, 167, 190–91, 201–202, 205–12, 226, 235, 241, 250, 252
Nature, divine, 207–209, 241
Nature, human, 207–209, 226, 235, 250
Natures
  individualized, 206
Nazarene, 19, 33, 55, 139, 150, 153–54, 156, 158–59, 238–39, 286–290, 299, 300
Nazlu River, 12
Neo-Platonism, 144
Nestorian Christianity, xii, 7, 9–11, 12, 14, 67, 142–43, 145, 205, 209, 246, 255, 261, 265, 290
Nestorianism, 140
Nestorians, 7, 9, 10–14, 66, 140, 141, 246, 250, 261
Nestorius, 141, 144–45, 206, 216, 245, 249
Neutrality, 97, 159, 232
New Birth, 48, 60, 155, 157, 174, 218–26, 248, 259–60, 271, 273–76, 279, 281, 288, 291, 294
New Issue, 82, 85, 87, 91–92, 94, 97, 100, 102–103, 106–107, 131, 140, 157–59, 173, 178, 185, 204, 229, 230, 231, 235, 240, 263, 277, 289, 291, 293
New Salem, Ohio, 120
New York City, 19–21, 23, 54–55, 57, 82, 85–86, 100, 103, 106, 112, 121, 125–26, 131, 172, 183–84, 225, 240, 259
Newark, Ohio, 119–21, 123
Newcastle, England, 82
Nicaea, 164, 167, 191, 209
Nicene Creed, 146–47
Noah's ark, 192
Norphlet, Arkansas, 120
North Avenue Mission, 154–55
Norway, 57, 82, 243

Oak Park, Michigan, 130
Oakdale, Louisiaia, 117
Oakdale, Louisiana, 133
Oakland, California, 54, 91, 110
Old Issue, 91, 229–30, 235
Old Testament saints, 220, 222, 227–28, 260, 267
Oneness, 147, 148
Oneness Pentecostalism, 85
  Oneness, 1–3, 19, 85, 99, 101, 114, 142, 157, 210–11, 222, 229, 240, 242, 263, 266–67, 269, 285, 291–94
Oneness Pentecostals
  Oneness, 214
Ordained, 240
Ordination, 52, 88, 154, 229, 239
Oriental Catholic Churches, 146
Oriental Orthodox Churches, 146
Ottoman Empire, 61, 64–69, 77, 281, 286
Ousia, 143–45, 207

PAJC. *See* Pentecostal Assemblies of Jesus Christ
Parsopa, 144–46, 207
PAW, 121, *See* Pentecostal Assemblies of the World

Pentecostal Assemblies of Canada PAOC, 2, 87, 90
Pentecostal Assemblies of Jesus Christ, 121–22, 127, 242
Pentecostal Assemblies of the World, 2, 112, 115, 120–121, 130, 189, 268, 284, 287
Pentecostal Assembly Tabernacle, 108
Pentecostal Bible Institute, 133
Pentecostal Church of the Nazarene, xi, 33, 55, 139, 153–154, 158–59, 238
Pentecostal Church, Inc., 242
Pentecostal Ministerial Alliance, 117, 120
Pentecostal Outlook, The, 121
Pentecostalism, xii, 1–3, 19, 27, 36–38, 45, 49, 51–52, 54–55, 57, 61, 78–79, 83, 86, 101, 115, 122, 131, 134, 139, 142, 150–151, 154–58, 169, 180–82, 191, 211, 223, 229–30, 235, 237–38, 242, 256–57, 262–69, 280–84, 286–87, 290–96
  Oneness, 86, 88, 97, 107, 114, 131, 135, 139, 158–59, 161–62, 173, 188, 197, 211, 236–38, 240, 264, 266–69
  Trinitarian, 97, 135, 158, 173, 236
Pentecostalism, Oneness, 142, 223, 230, 264, 265
Pentecostalism, Trinitarian, 230
Perichoresis, 195, 200, 232
Persecution, 44, 48, 61–62, 73, 77, 82, 102, 140
Persia, 2, 7–19, 25–26, 35, 44, 52–109, 130, 139–141, 145, 148, 150, 156, 205, 216, 219, 229, 237, 239–40, 243, 246–47, 250, 259, 269, 272, 275, 280, 282, 285–86
Persian Pentecostal Mission, 40, 43–46, 49, 51, 56, 239

Person, 141, 143–49, 164, 169, 194, 199, 203, 204, 209, 210, 232
Persona, 210
Persons, 144, 194, 206
Persons as beings, 194
Petra, 141
Philadelphia, Mississippi, 118
Philadelphia, Pennsylvania, 54, 115
Philosophy, 152
Physis, 142, 144
Picton, Ontario, Canada, 112
Pliny the Younger, 170
PMA, 117, 120, *See* Pentecostal Ministerial Alliance
Poland, 67
Port Arthur, Texas, 118, 133
Portland, Oregon, 54, 90, 111, 131
Portsmouth, Ohio, 120
Preexistence, 201–202
Presbyterianism, 2, 7–23, 27, 35, 49–51, 55, 64, 68, 71–72, 76, 81, 132, 139–40, 145–53, 156, 159, 176, 219, 238, 247, 269, 280, 287, 297
Prineville, Oregon, 127
Printing, 53, 87, 93, 109–110, 162, 198, 246
Prophecy, 71
Prosopon, 144–45, 148, 206, 210
Protestantism, 12, 13, 63, 78–79, 162, 210, 253
Puyallup, Washington, 131

Qajar Dynasty, 8, 298
Qnoma, 142–49, 202, 204–10, 216, 246, 261
Qnome, 145–46, 148
Qnuma, 146
Qnume, 146

Rapture, 181, 224
Rationalism, 212
Reason, 159
Regent University, xii, 27, 242, 295

Regina, Saskatchewan, Canada, 119
Repentance, 48, 60, 75, 80
Restorationism, 142
Rewey, Wisconsin, 121
River Falls, Wisconsin, 122
Roman Catholic Church, 9, 45, 141, 147, 152, 204
Rush Medical College, 23
Russellism, 28, 30, 56, 101, 120, 174, 182
Russia, 8, 10, 16, 20, 52, 55–57, 64–65, 67–69, 70, 74, 77–79, 81–83, 85, 87–90, 100–101, 103, 106–107, 115, 131, 139, 159, 229, 240, 243, 248–49, 259, 271–72, 294, 299

Salem, Oregon, 119, 131
Salvation, 3, 28–30, 34, 37, 44, 55, 60, 92, 143, 147, 154, 160, 164, 219, 221, 225, 227, 249, 257, 260, 267, 269
Salvation Army, 51, 82
San Antonio, Texas, 125
San Diego, California, 130, 133
San Francisco, California, 54, 90, 128
Sanctification, xi, 3, 19, 27, 32–38, 55, 139, 142, 150, 153–59, 238–239, 254, 269
Scofield Reference Bible, The, 211
Scripture, 43–44
    authority, 2, 10, 19, 28–29, 44, 55, 105, 150, 152, 154, 157, 158–59, 161, 163, 164, 169, 173–75, 178, 180, 190, 193, 220, 223, 251–52, 265, 280
Scriptures, 10, 29, 34, 44, 104–105, 159, 161, 163, 165, 167, 173, 179–81, 183, 187, 188, 194, 195, 202, 253–54
Seattle, Washington, 119
Second Work, 235
Seleucia-Ctesiphon, 9

Separate and distinct, 187, 203–204, 208, 210, 234, 241, 245–46
Shah, 8, 24, 283
Shaking, 257
Shelby, Michigan, 46
Shirabad, 57, 63
Shreveport, Louisiana, 116, 120, 122
Sign, 257
Sin, 15, 19, 21, 28, 30, 32, 34, 39, 43, 60, 96, 143, 147, 149, 177, 192, 227, 247, 260
Socialism, 152
Soteriological language
    begotten, 217, 219, 227
    born, 217, 219
    born again, 217, 219
    conception, 219, 227
    conversion, 223
    kingdom of God, 217–18, 221–24, 226–27
    Kingdom of God, 221
    kingdom of heaven, 217, 221, 223–26, 228
    saved, 217
    tribulation saints, 224
    walking in the light, 219
Soteriology, 3, 217–19, 221, 225, 226–27, 241–42, 260, 263
South Bend Mishawaka, Indiana, 120
South Wales, 55
Spiritualism, 28, 30, 56, 152, 181, 277
Springfield, Oregon, 131
St. James, Minnesota, 122
St. Louis, Missouri, 88, 106, 110, 117, 120, 122, 234
St. Paul, Minnesota, 54, 85, 87, 89, 90, 110–12, 115, 117–21, 128, 129, 195, 292
Stockton, California, xi, 132–33
Stone Church, 45, 54, 78, 176
Subsistentia, 210

Swedenborg, 172
Swedenborg, Emanuel, 171
Symbolism, 140, 210, 212, 216, 238–39
  Typology, 212
Syriac, 162
  Ancient, 10, 38, 216
  Modern, 10, 216
Syriac language, 7, 10, 14, 17, 22–23, 26–27, 30, 32, 40, 68, 132, 140, 142–46, 148, 150, 151, 158–59, 202, 204–207, 212, –14, 246, 251, 255, 259, 285, 286–88, 291, 298–99
Syrian Catholics, 66
Syrian Christianity, 2, 7, 9–10, 140, 148–49, 159, 174, 210, 214, 246, 251, 253, 258, 262, 269, 287
Syrian Orthodox Church, 144, 147, 204
Syrians, 9, 14, 67, 145

Tabernacle, 192, 224
Tabriz, 12, 61, 64, 77
Teheran, Iran, 132
Terre Haute, Indiana, 133
Texas, 111, 133
The Pentecostal Outlook, 121
Theological liberalism, 181
Theology, 1–3, 16–17, 19, 26, 34–35, 49, 56, 99, 105–106, 139–42, 146–47, 148–53, 157–59, 161, 166, 168, 174, 180, 182, 188, 191–94, 198–99, 201–206, 209–211, 214, 216, 220, 238–239, 241–42, 245, 247, 253, 260–61, 263, 265–67, 298
  Church of the East, 140
  divine names, 216
  liberal, 152
  monastic, 245, 252
  of divine names, 210

Oneness, 201, 203, 211, 215, 261
Oneness, 242
  Trinitarian, 203
Theology, New, 174
Theology, Oneness, 195, 199
Theophilus, 170
Theotokos, 143
Three-One, 141, 202
Three-One God, 98, 166, 179, 183, 188, 195–96, 199, 231, 253, 262
Tiflis, 57, 77–78
Tiflis, Georgia, 20
Tongues, 40–41, 44, 46–47, 54–55, 59–61, 73, 95, 124, 140, 152–153, 155, 159, 180, 217–19, 222, 226–28, 235, 246, 251, 252, 256–57, 259, 260, *See* Baptism, Holy Spirit: tongues
Topeka, Kansas, 257
Toronto, Ontario, Canada, 112, 115, 117–18
Tradition, 159
Trinitarian Pentecostalism, 19
Trinitarian Pentecostals
  Trinitarianism, 3, 87, 107, 134, 204, 214, 230, 233, 240, 266
Trinitarian Theology, 146
Trinitarianism, 164, 169, 172, 184–86, 194, 203, 209–10, 214, 216, 232
Trinitarians, 82
Trinity, 28, 30, 49–50, 86, 140–49, 163–64, 167–69, 172–73, 175, 185–99, 204, 208, 209, 213-15, 232, 242, 245, 247, 249, 257-58, 261–262, 265, 271, 273, 281, 283, 288, 290, 291, 294
  in Christ, 199
  redefinition, 192
Tri-One, 193, 245, 258
Tritheism, 210, 216
Triune 192, 197, 251

Triunity, 22, 49, 99, 105, 141, 172, 177–78, 180, 183, 190, 192, 199, 203–204, 209, 213, 245, 246–47, 248, 250, 253, 258, 262
Tupelo, Mississippi, 133
Turkestan, 68
Turkey, 9, 65–66, 68–69, 286, 297
Turks, 17, 61, 64–77, 280
Twin Falls, Idaho, 121, 127, 129

UGST, xii
Unitarianism, 172–74, 182
United Pentecostal Church International, 130, 242
  UPCI, xii, 52, 130, 267–68, 281, 291
  Western District, 131
United Pentecostal Church International Illinois District, 131
United States, 1, 7, 16, 19, 21, 26, 44–45, 51, 53, 57–59, 61, 64, 74, 78–79, 85–87, 117, 123, 129, 131, 159, 176, 178, 203, 206, 224, 229, 238, 240, 249, 263, 275, 293, 295
UPCI, 130, 131, 134, *See* United Pentecostal Church International
Urmia, 8–12, 15–16, 23, 26, 54–55, 61, 63–65, 68–69, 71–72, 74, 76–77, 82, 131, 139, 145, 149, 219, 275, 297–98
Urshan, Andrew D., vi
Urshan, Ethel, vi
Urshan Graduate School of
  Theology, vi, xii, 89
Urshan, Abraham, vi
Urumia, 8, 12–13, 14, 69

Visions, 39, 73, 195

Wales, 257
Warsaw, Poland, 20
Welsh evival, 254
Welsh Revival, 257
Wesleyan Quadrilateral, 159
Western Apostolic Bible College, xi, 132–133
Wewoka, Oklahoma, 121
Winnipeg Revival, 2, 111, 280
Winnipeg, Manitoba, Canada, 2, 54, 87, 90, 110, 111, 120
Witness of God, The, xi, xii, 2, 11, 22–63, 71, 76, 80, 87, 90–92, 93, 97, 99–101, 104, 107–135, 149–152, 155, 157–59, 162, – 64, 168, 174, 183, 188–89, 193, 198–99, 201–202, 209, 214– 215, 217–25, 230–35, 238, 241, 245–50, 254, 256, 258, 260, 262, 271–80, 287–88, 290–94
Word, 164
World War I, 13, 66–68, 180, 240
Worldliness, 102, 182
Worldwide Camp Meeting, 1–2, 107, 108, 239, 294
WWI, 68

Yahweh, 166, 199–200
Yakima, Washington, *118*
Yonkers, New York, 21, 131

Scripture Index

OLD TESTAMENT

Genesis 1:1, 190–191
Genesis 1:26–27, 193
Genesis 3:22–24, 193
Genesis 11:5–8, 193

Numbers 13:16, 167

Psalm 45:16, 165
Psalm 51, 60
Psalm 114:2, 222

Isaiah 6:8, 193
Isaiah 9:6, 80, 165
Isaiah 66:5, 189, 233

NEW TESTAMENT

Matthew 1:22–23, 177
Matthew 10:22, 230
Matthew 11:27, 98, 168, 201, 231, 241
Matthew 13, 223
Matthew 28:17–19, 178
Matthew 28:19, 49, 80, 98, 102, 104, 106, 163, 176, 178–179, 183, 198, 230, 248

Mark 16:14-19, 178, 179, 224

Luke 24:44–48, 104
Luke 24:45–49, 178–179, 219

John 1:1, 198
John 1:10-13, 218
John 1:14, 218
John 1:18, 98, 231
John 14:19, 185

John 14:9, 105, 177
John 15:5, 44
John 14:26, 219
John 14:7-11, 98, 231
John 17:11, 21–23, 26, 196
John 3, 60, 217, 218, 235, 242
John 3:1–5, 120
John 3:1-6, 49, 199
John 3:3–5, 221, 224
John 3:5, 218, 242

Acts 10:48, 106
Acts 19:13, 177
Acts 19:1-7, 219
Acts 19:5, 106
Acts 2:38, 80, 101, 104, 106, 176, 179, 217, 219–20, 222, 224, 229, 242, 266, 267
Acts 8:12, 106
Acts 8:16, 79

Acts 8:36–37, 219
Acts 10:48, 105
Acts 19:1-7, 219
Acts 19:5, 106
Acts 19:13, 177

Romans 1:20, 215
Romans 10:17, 98

1 Corinthians 2:7-8, 215
1 Corinthians 4:7, 89
1 Corinthians 4:20, 218
1 Corinthians 7, 89
1 Corinthians 11:3, 196
1 Corinthians 11:4-6, 104, 183
1 Corinthians 11:12, 104, 183
1 Corinthians 11:13, 98, 231
1 Corinthians 12:3, 37
1 Corinthians 12:4–6, 105, 183
1 Corinthians 12:13, 98, 231

2 Corinthians 4:13, 98
2 Corinthians 13:14, 98, 231

Galatians 4:6, 227

Ephesians 4:4-6, 105, 183

Ephesians 4:5-6, 98, 231

Colossians 1:15-19, 98, 231
Colossians 2:1-9, 168
Colossians 2:2, 215
Colossians 2:9, 98, 162, 168, 177, 231
Colossians 3:17, 98, 179, 231

1 Timothy 3:16, 168
1 Timothy 6:16, 98, 231

2 Timothy 3:6, 16, 98, 231
2 Timothy 3:14, 98
2 Timothy 4:7-8, 134

Hebrews 1:3, 98, 231

1 John 2:23, 185, 187
1 John 5:7, 105, 163, 178, 183, 231
1 John 5:20, 231

2 John 5:5, 98

Revelation 1:8, 191
Revelation 21:2, 165
Revelation 22:4, 177

www.ingramcontent.com/pod-product-compliance
Lightning Source LLC
Chambersburg PA
CBHW050335230426
43663CB00010B/1865